GOING WEST

Program in Judaic Studies
Brown University
Box 1826
Providence, RI 02912

BROWN JUDAIC STUDIES

Edited by

David C. Jacobson
Saul M. Olyan
Rachel Rojanski
Michael L. Satlow
Adam Teller

Number 369
GOING WEST

by
Reuven Kiperwasser

GOING WEST

MIGRATING PERSONAE AND CONSTRUCTION OF THE SELF IN RABBINIC CULTURE

by

Reuven Kiperwasser

Brown Judaic Studies
Providence, Rhode Island

© 2021 Brown University. All rights reserved.

No part of this work may be reproduced or transmitted in any form or by any means, electronic or mechanical, including photocopying and recording, or by means of any information storage or retrieval system, except as may be expressly permitted by the 1976 Copyright Act or in writing from the publisher. Requests for permission should be addressed in writing to the Rights and Permissions Office, Program in Judaic Studies, Brown University, Box 1826, Providence, RI 02912, USA.

Library of Congress Control Number: 2021947246

Contents

Preface vii

Abbreviations xiii

Introduction 1

1. Symbolic Violence 23

2. Mocking Babylonians 39

3. Going West 53

4. Hosting Babylonians 79

5. The Appointment of Babylonians 101

6. "He is one of them!": Showing the Other His Place 121

7. Going West but Remaining at Home 143

8. Going East 169

Epilogue: Going Back and Forth 201

Bibliography 207

Passage Index 231

General Index 235

Preface

The title of this book, *Going West*, was inspired by the Aramaic term used by Babylonian sages for the Land of Israel, *ma'arava* (west). From the perspective of Babylonia, the Land of Israel is in the West. The title also recalls the bracing nineteenth-century American exhortation: "Go West, young man, and grow up with the country." This coincidence may be a fortuitous one. American "westerns" often feature a young man who heads westward and receives a rough reception, forging a new identity in the process. Palestinian rabbinic literature preserves numerous stories in which young Babylonians go west, confront the Land of Israel's unwelcoming inhabitants, and recreate themselves, so to speak. In both contexts, a new persona is forged in the crucible of masculine combat.

This is a book about migrating rabbinic personae on the way between Babylonia and the Land of Israel. In the first centuries of the Common Era, Jews lived in many lands. We know about their lives from writings of their gentile contemporaries, as well as from inscriptions and archaeological artifacts. Only two of the many Jewish communities of late antiquity, those of Sasanian Babylonia and Roman Palestine, left us written texts. Eventually, these texts would become one corpus, perceived by future generations as "rabbinic literature."

Babylonia, located in Central-Southern Mesopotamia, was a fabulously wealthy country, a province in the mighty Persian Empire whose ruling Sasanid dynasty was established in 224 CE. Eastern Aramaic was the language of communication and literature. Under the Sasanids, followers of the religion of Iranian Mazdaism or Zoroastrianism, Jews, and Christians experienced a certain degree of coexistence and were thus free to develop their literacy. Jewish academies in Babylonia flourished, apparently under the auspices of the Exilarch, who was the head of Jewish autonomy. Although the Sasanian Empire waged several wars with the Roman Empire, these conflicts did not interfere overall with the mobility of Jews between the territories of the two empires.

Roman Palestine was the one of the eastern provinces of the Roman Empire. Its economic condition was inferior to that of Sasanid Babylonia, partly due to lesser richness of natural resources, partly due to the province's management. The echo of suppressed rebellions still impeded relations between Jews and the Roman Empire. Here too, however, the Jews had relative autonomy, headed by the Patriarch. Babylonian Jews were respectful of the land of their ancestors; the Palestinian Jews sought ties with the Babylonian community. The head of the Palestinian Jews was interested in presenting his family tree as related to the exilarchal house in Babylonia.

The Roman rulers of Palestine followed a typical Roman urban religion, flooding public spaces with images of their deities. The province was home to Jews, Christians, Samaritans, and many other groups. These different religious communities coexisted in a sort of tense status quo. In 312 CE, Christianity began to receive the support of the empire and lay claim to hegemony in the Holy Land, which consequently disturbed the balance.

The Babylonian Jews created the Babylonian Talmud, and the Palestinian Jews the Palestinian (or Yerushalmi/Jerusalem) Talmud as well as the anthologies of Midrash. The textual communities of Roman Palestine and Sasanian Babylonia, consisting of masters, students, and affiliated laypeople, were characterized by their devotion to the Written Torah, canonized several centuries earlier, and the Oral Torah, created by the rabbinic sages. These two communities developed a network of educational institutions in which students studied the Mishnah from their mentors. The communities also saw themselves as linked from ancient times, and the route from Babylonia to Palestine had always been filled with mythological content. The path, initially laid by their progenitor Abraham, was followed in the opposite direction by the exiles of the Babylonian captivity and reversed once again in Ezra's and Nehemiah's time. That return to Zion breathed a new spirit into the Judaism of the Land of Israel, imported from Babylonia. In the first centuries of the Common Era, and especially in the fourth century, this route became the axis of the unfolding dialogue between the two intellectual Jewish cultures, organized around rabbinic academies. It was through this dialogue that a cultural exchange was carried out between the two textual communities. As it turns out, however, the exchange was a fraught one, marked by struggle for hegemony. Scholarship has often presented the center in the Land of Israel as primary and the one in Babylonia as a dependent periphery. This study takes a different tack, suggesting that the dialogue between the Land of Israel and Babylonia was conducted by rivals of equal intellectual strength and comparable cultural baggage. Complicating the picture, however, the former suffered from a kind of inferiority complex and therefore exerted a significant effort to prove its worth. The latter, quite self-confident, viewed the rabbis of the Land of Israel as respectable partners in learning but tainted by a blemished lineage.

Such a constellation of passions inevitably ignited conflict, particularly when one of the parties became the host and the other a guest. This book analyzes the literary representations of such confrontations, preserved in works created in Babylonia and Palestine. In so doing, it aims to shed light on the cultural exchanges of the time.

I am fascinated by rabbinic narratives about Babylonians and their encounters in the Land of Israel, one that extends beyond purely academic inquiry. This is especially true regarding a series of accounts found in the Yerushalmi (Berakhot 2:8, 5c), which form the basis for much of the discussion. These narratives deal with guests' reception and are sensitive to travelers' troubles along the way. Such accounts perhaps resonate well with the personal experience of a modern twentieth-/twenty-first-century stranger trying to settle in a promised land that turns out to be a land with little promise.

Stories are cultural products. Not only do they convey the fears and tensions of a particular culture, but they also offer comfort to the contemporary reader. The typological power of these stories charmed the famous talmudist Saul Lieberman, whose personal story of (non-)acceptance in the Land of Israel brought him to relate what he had himself endured with the help of these stories in a celebrated article, entitled "As It Was, So It Will Be."[1] However, despite his strong identification with the Babylonian protagonists of the stories, Lieberman's apologetic interpretation of these figures is, in some ways, flawed; this is on account of the positivistic scholarly approach to such literature common at the time he wrote. In my own way, I identify with the ancient protagonists and apply here my understanding of rabbinic culture. The result is less positivistic and sheds light on previously unexplored aspects of this theme.

This book, which deals with rabbinic hosts' changing roles and their guests' migrations between East and West in late antiquity, was itself conceived and delivered on the road. The idea for the book was born of two different proposals. The first examined rabbis who wandered between the two great empires of late antiquity—Rome and Sasanian Persia—for the research group "Jews and Empires" in the Jean and Samuel Frankel Center for Judaic Studies (Ann Arbor, Michigan) in 2014–2015. The second proposal was for a much bigger project, "Migrating Tradition and Migrating Persona," for the Alexander von Humboldt Fellowship.

Consequently, I wrote the first part of the book in Ann Arbor in 2014–2015. The group was chaired by Mikhail Krutikov, who was a wonderful and generous host. The book's idea was conceived in snow-covered but warm and welcoming Ann Arbor, and first drafts of two chapters of the book were written and discussed with the group members, the guests of the institute. My experience as a migrating persona in the United States,

---

1. See further Saul Lieberman, "As It Was, So It Will Be" [Hebrew], in *Studies in Palestinian Talmudic Literature*, ed. D. Rosenthal (Jerusalem: Magnes, 1991), 331–38.

where I had never spent any substantial period previously, provided inspiration for the conception of this book.

I continued working on this book as an Alexander von Humboldt fellow at the Freie Universität Berlin (2015–2017), where Prof. Tal Ilan hosted me. During my stay at Hamburg University Maimonides Center for Advanced Studies (April–September 2016), while I was in Germany as a guest of Giuseppe Veltri, I continued to work on it. I thank my hosts sincerely.

The book's main body was written in Berlin, the ultimate metropolis of migrating people who set out to find themselves and receive shelter in a city that is no less diligently looking to find itself. I finished the first draft of the book shortly before returning to my home in Jerusalem, the city of dreamers and strangers. Thus, the route of the author has come full circle. The book, however, continued its journey overseas, experiencing adventures typical of the migration of texts and encountering locals (see ch. 4) before finally arriving at BJS's welcoming port. Thus, the route of the book ended where it was conceived, in the United States. I am exceptionally thankful to Michael Satlow for the readiness to consider my book and to the anonymous readers who helped bring the book to its present shape.[2]

---

2. Some of the drafts of chapters of this book have been presented at conferences, seminars and invited lectures: (1) "The Guests Are from Babylonia, the Hosts Are from the Land of Israel" and (2) "Going West" were read at the conference "Jews and the Roman Empire: Beyond the Resistance/Accommodation Paradigm," and at a workshop, both held in the Frankel Center for Judaic Studies Symposium, Ann Arbor, Michigan, and afterwards they were used in the third and fourth chapters of this book. (3) "Going West: Palestinian Hosts and Babylonian Guests" was presented at the Judaic Studies Lecture Series, Department of Judaic Studies, Yale University, and was also used in the third chapter of the book. (4) "Wives of Commoners and the Masculinity of the Rabbis: Jokes and Serious Matters" was delivered in the Department of Near Eastern Languages and Civilizations and the Center for Jewish Studies at Harvard University and was partially used in chapter 7. (5) 'Face Value: Facing the Other in the Stories of Palestinian Talmud" was read at the "Jewish Studies and Sociology of Knowledge: Discourse, Lifeworld and the Transformation of Traditions" International Conference at Hochschule für Jüdische Studien Heidelberg (HfJS) and lies in chapter 4. (6) A presentation titled "Mother Tongue/Mother Land in Rabbinic Rhetoric" was given at the conference "Untying the Mother Tongue on Language, Affect, and the Unconscious" at ICI Berlin Institute for Cultural Inquiry and is now included in chapter 1. Two subsequent presentations, (7) "A Question of Identity: Formation, Transition, Negotiation" at the International Conference, Mandel Scolion Interdisciplinary Center, and the Israel Science Foundation, Jerusalem, and (8) "What Have the Romans Ever Done for Us? Creating Identity in Rabbinic Literature, Constructions of the Self in Ancient Mediterranean Cultures" at the Institute of Advanced Studies, Hebrew University of Jerusalem, Research Group Conference, 27–31 May 2018 were used for chapter 3. (9) "Narrating the Self: Stories about Rabbi Zeira's Encounters in the Land of Israel" Seminar of the Research Group "The Subject of Antiquity: Contours and Expressions of the Self in Ancient Mediterranean Cultures" at the Institute of Advanced Studies, the Hebrew University of Jerusalem, on 15 February 2018 was used for chapters 3, 6, and 7.

My peers and friends have read numerous drafts (full or partial) of the book, and their remarks and advice have greatly influenced my writing, though the responsibility for the errors is entirely mine.

Many thanks go to the readers of different drafts and parts of the book, mentioned in alphabetical order: Tali Artman, Daniel Boyarin, Geoffrey Herman, Tal Ilan, Joshua Levinson, Maren Niehoff, Yohanan Petrovsky-Stern, James Redfield, Serge Ruzer, Amram Tropper, Shani Tzoref.

This manuscript's English was corrected first by Sarah Garibova in the initial stages of my work, by Johanna Hoornweg later, and received its final shape in the caring hands of Sara Tropper. I am most grateful for their careful work. The responsibility for errors left in the manuscript is, of course, mine alone.

I thank the hosts of these conferences for inviting me, and I am grateful to them and the participating guests for their incisive comments, which enriched my book.

Two of these presentations were subsequently published: (1) "Going West: Migrating Babylonians and the Question of Identity," in *A Question of Identity: Social, Political, and Historical Aspects of the Formation, Transition, and Negotiation of Identity in Jewish and Related Contexts*, ed. Dikla Rivlin Katz et al. (Oldenbourg: de Gruyter, 2019), 111–30; (2) "Narrating the Self: Stories about Rabbi Zeira's Encounters in Land of Israel," in *Self, Self-Fashioning, and Individuality in Late Antiquity*, ed. Maren R. Niehoff and Joshua Levinson, Culture, Religion, and Politics in the Greco-Roman World 4 (Tübingen: Mohr Siebeck, 2019), 353–72. I benefited from the helpful comments of the editors of these volumes.

Abbreviations

Academia ed.	*Talmud Yerushalmi according to Ms. Or. 4720* (Jerusalem: Academy of the Hebrew Language, 2001).
AGJU	Arbeiten zur Geschichte des Spätjudentums und Urchristentums
ANRW	Hildegard Temporini and Wolfgang Haase, eds., *Aufstieg und Niedergang der römischen Welt: Geschichte und Kultur Roms im Spiegel der neueren Forschung: part 2, Principat* (Berlin: de Gruyter, 1972–).
AOAT	Alter Orient und Altes Testament
ArOr	*Archív Orientální*
BJS	Brown Judaic Studies
CCSL	Corpus Christianorum: Series Latina
CRINT	Compendia Rerum Iudaicarum ad Novum Testamentum
Danby	Herbert Danby, *The Mishnah: Translated from the Hebrew with Introduction and Brief Explanatory Notes* (Oxford: Oxford University Press, 1933).
HdO	Handbuch der Orientalistik
HTR	*Harvard Theological Review*
HTS	Harvard Theological Studies
HUCA	*Hebrew Union College Annual*
JAOS	*Journal of the American Oriental Society*
JBL	*Journal of Biblical Literature*
JJS	*Journal of Jewish Studies*
JQR	*Jewish Quarterly Review*
JSJ	*Journal for the Study of Judaism in the Persian, Hellenistic, and Roman Period*
JSJSup	Supplements to the Journal for the Study in the Persian, Hellenistic, and *Roman Period*
JSPSup	Journal for the Study of the Pseudepigrapha: Supplements
JSQ	*Jewish Studies Quarterly*
LCL	Loeb Classical Library

Margulies ed.	Mordecai Margulies, ed., *Midrash Wayyikra Rabbah: A Critical Edition based on Manuscripts and Genizah Fragments with Variants and Notes*, 5 vols. (New York: JTS Press, 1972).
MGWJ	*Monatsschrift für Geschichte und Wissenschaft des Judenthums*
NovT	*Novum Testamentum*
PL	J.-P. Migne, ed., *Patrologiae Cursus Completus: Series Latina*, 217 vols. (Paris: J.-P. Migne, 1844–1864).
REJ	*Revue des études Juives*
StPB	Studia Post-biblica
SymS	Symposium Series
Theodor-Albeck	Julius Theodor and Chanoch Albeck, *Midrash Bereshit Rabbah: Critical Edition with Notes and Commentary* (Jerusalem: Wahrmann Books, 1965).
TSAJ	Texte und Studien zum antiken Judentum
WUNT	Wissenschaftliche Untersuchungen zum Neuen Testament
ZNW	*Zeitschrift für die neutestamentliche Wissenschaft*

Introduction

1. Migrating Traditions and Migrating Personae

This book examines rabbinic narratives in which rabbinic figures travel or emigrate either westward from Babylonia to Palestine or eastward from Palestine to Babylonia and, in these new settings, encounter local rabbis and the local lay people and their practices and customs. The sources are drawn primarily from the rabbinic literature of late Roman Palestine (third to sixth centuries), although consideration is also given to related material found in the Babylonian Talmud.

The universe of rabbinic literature emerged in both the East and the West. The Western realm of classical rabbinic literature is Roman Palestine, and the Eastern domain is Sasanian Babylonia.[1] In late antiquity, Jewish communities were to be found not only in Palestine and Babylonia, but also in much of the Roman and Sasanian Empires, and in particular within the Greco-Roman diaspora. Rabbinic culture, however, developed almost entirely in Roman Palestine and Sasanian Babylonia. Rabbinic literature highlights the relations between these two communities and the interaction between them in the realms of halakha, aggada, and almost every aspect of knowledge. The rabbis perceived the Jewish universe as a hierarchically well-organized structure with two *loci* of significance: Sasanian Babylonia and Roman Palestine.[2]

During the first centuries of the Common Era, literary traditions migrated from West to East and, simultaneously, from East to West. While crossing the political border between the Roman and Sasanian Empires, rabbinic literary traditions also traversed the cultural barriers between

---

1. I use the term *Palestinian* in this book to refer to Jews living in the Land of Israel during the talmudic era. Babylonians are the Jewish inhabitants of Mesopotamia (under Persian rule), which is now southern Iraq. Persia (or Iran) in the Arsacid and Sasanian periods was a region lying to the west and the east of the Tigris River, including modern Iraq, Azerbaijan, and Afghanistan. However, Babylonia was the name for the lower region of Mesopotamia dominated by the Tigris and Euphrates, where once ancient Babel was located.

2. See Geoffrey Herman, "Babylonia: A Diaspora Center," in *Oxford Handbook of the Jewish Diaspora*, ed.Hasia R. Diner (Oxford: Oxford University Press, forthcoming).

these two realms, as is evidenced by the travel of rabbinic masters and students between Babylonia and Roman Palestine at that time.[3] In the following pages, readers will become acquainted with stories about rabbinic *migrating personae* on the move between two major academic centers, as well as a larger underlying narrative of the enduring coexistence of two academic communities.

To set the stage, I will provide an overview of these narratives' background, namely, the historical relations between the Babylonian and Palestinian rabbinic communities. The history of rabbinic communities has been derived mainly from rabbinic stories and from a single early medieval source, the Epistle of Rab Sherira Gaon (986/987 CE).[4] Historians of the talmudic period have tended to embrace Sherira's narrative, which constructs the unfolding dialogue between two communities by compromising and harmonizing it with the talmudic sources.[5] Some scholars have criticized the details of Sherira's account while keeping the narrative structure more or less intact.[6] In the Epistle, the mutual history of the two communities begins with the personal story of a Babylonian who traveled west, then returned to Babylonia after some period of study. The western sojourn of this student, nicknamed simply Rab, is said to have inspired the

---

3. Catherine Hezser, *Jewish Travel in Antiquity*, TSAJ 144 (Tübingen: Mohr Siebeck, 2011), 311-64.

4. See Robert Brody, "The Epistle of Sherira Gaon," in *Rabbinic Texts and the History of Late-Roman Palestine*, ed. Martin Goodman and Philip Alexander, Proceedings of the British Academy 165 (Oxford: Oxford University Press, 2010), 253-64, Margarete Schlüter, *Auf welche Weise wurde die Mischna geschrieben? Das Antwortschreiben des Rav Sherira Gaon, mit einem Faksimile der Handschrift Berlin Qu. 685 (Or. 160) und des Erstdrucks Konstantinopel 1566*, Texts and Studies in Medieval and Early Modern Judaism 9 (Tübingen: Mohr Siebeck, 1993); Amram Tropper, "From Tatlafush to Sura" [Hebrew], *ʾOqimta* 2 (2014): 1–16; Geoffrey Herman, *A Prince without a Kingdom: The Exilarch in the Sasanian Era*, TSAJ 150 (Tübingen: Mohr Siebeck, 2012), 300–336; Simcha Gross, "When the Jews Greeted ʿAlī: Sherira Gaon's Epistle in Light of Arabic and Syriac Historiography," *JSQ* 24 (2017): 122–44.

5. See Aharon Oppenheimer, *Between Rome and Babylon: Studies in Jewish Leadership and Society*, ed. Nili Oppenheimer, TSAJ 108 (Tübingen: Mohr Siebeck, 2005).

6. Jacob Neusner, *A History of the Jews in Babylonia*, vol. 3, *From Shapur I to Shapur II*, StPB 12 (Leiden: Brill, 1968), 217–20; Moshe Be'er, "Nehutei," *Encylopaedia Judaica*, 2nd ed., ed. Fred Skolnik and Michael Berenbaum, 22 vols. (Detroit: Macmillan Reference, 2007), 15:65; Ezra Z. Melamed, *An Introduction to Talmudic Literature* [Hebrew] (Jerusalem: Galor, 1972/1973), 442–47; Baruch Bokser, "An Annotated Bibliographical Guide to the Study of the Palestinian Talmud" ANRW 2.19.2:139–256, here 187; Isaiah M. Gafni, *Land, Center and Diaspora: Jewish Constructs in Late Antiquity*, JSPSup 21 (Sheffield: Sheffield Academic, 1997), 103; Alyssa M. Gray, *A Talmud in Exile: The Influence of Yerushalmi Avodah Zarah on the Formation of Bavli Avodah Zarah*, BJS 342 (Providence, RI: Program in Judaic Studies, Brown University, 2005), 5–9; Richard Kalmin, *Migrating Tales: The Talmud's Narratives and Their Historical Context* (Berkeley: University of California Press, 2014), 6 n. 8; Catherine Hezser, "Crossing Enemy Lines: Network Connections between Palestinian and Babylonian Sages in Late Antiquity," *JSJ* 46 (2015): 224–50, here 233–36.

foundation of the Babylonian academy in Sura (see b. Shabb. 29a). In both Talmudim, Rab was a companion of the famous Palestinian Rabbi Levi bar Sisi (b. Meg. 29a; y. Ketub. 2:6, 26a). The latter was a close disciple of Rabbi Yehuda the Patriarch ("Rabbi"). The Babylonian Talmud presents Rab and Levi bar Sisi as equals but expresses an explicit preference for the former (b. Betzah 24b). For reasons unknown to us, probably after his teacher's death, Rab decided to emigrate to Babylonia, apparently settling in Nehardea (b. Ketub. 103b). Rab Sherira Gaon[7] dates the first rabbinic academies in Babylonia to Rab's return to Babylonia in 218 CE.[9] According to Sherira, Babylonia already had an academic infrastructure, as evidenced by the fact that the new repatriate immediately found his place in the study house of Rab Sheila, the local sage, in Nehardea; Rab Sheila's study house already engaged in analysis of the Mishnah and the Tannaitic traditions.[8] There, Rab studied with another sage, Shmuel—a Babylonian who never went to the Land of Israel. The father of this sage, called by later rabbis simply Abūha-de-Shmuel (the father of Shmuel), was a rabbinic scholar in his own right.[9] Thus, even though it is customary to say that talmudic scholarship in Babylonia begins with Rab, rabbinic literature attests that it appeared earlier. The story of migration from the East to the West and the West to the East was a foundational narrative of the relationship between these two locations.

After the death of the head of the study house, Rab found himself competing for the chair of the academy with Shmuel. Rab is praised by the transmitters of the story for deciding to quit the competition and leave Nehardea, Shmuel's city of residence. Subsequently, he founded an alternative academy in Sura. As scholars have noted, however, this foundation story is based on another one from b. Hul. 110b, with one small difference: Rab did not go to Sura but to Tatlafush, a small city presumably in the vicinity of Sura.[10] The narrators of the Bavli thus emplace an encounter between Babylonian and Palestinian learning—Rab and Shmuel's overlapping sojourn in the same study house—at the very birth of the two leading academic centers in Babylonia (Nehardea and Sura), probably in order to claim that Babylonian learning is nourished by Palestinian knowledge.

This story roughly reflects the main structure of Sherira's narrative, itself based on the Babylonian Talmud. The foundation narrative begins the story with the figure of Rab; however, the real beginning of rabbinic presence in Babylonia is much more ancient. From the earliest times of the two centers' existence, Babylonian students went to Palestine to learn

---

7. See above n. 4.
8. Abraham Goldberg, "The Babylonian Talmud," in *The Literature of the Sages*, ed. Shmuel Safrai, 2 vols., CRINT 2.3 (Philadelphia: Fortress, 1987–2006), 1:325–33.
9. Ibid.
10. Tropper, "From Tatlafush," 1–16.

from the local sages. Rabbinic literature from both Palestine and Babylonia mentions several scholars who traveled from Babylonia to Palestine. One of them, Hillel, was the prototypical figure of the rabbinic sage. Tannaitic sources present him as a renowned sage who came from Babylonia to disseminate his wisdom in specific learning disciplines.[11] Other Babylonian scholars of the Tannaitic period, such as Rabbi Nathan the Babylonian and Rab Issi the Babylonian, lived in and constituted part of the rabbis' community in Palestine (see t. Shabb. 15:8; t. B. Qam. 2:11). The most central figure of the rabbinic community in Palestine, whose period of activity is customarily used to date the end of the Tannaitic period, is Rabbi Yehuda ha-Nasi ("Rabbi"). Rabbi is frequently portrayed together with Babylonian expatriates and is described in Palestinian sources as sitting in the shade of the so-called Babylonian Synagogue.[12] The number of Babylonian visitors in this early literature, however, is still small. The picture changes radically at the beginning of the fourth century, when mentions of Babylonian rabbis journeying to Palestine multiply. These figures frequently appear as students of Palestinian teachers.[13] At the same time, Babylonian rabbinic traditions begin to be cited in Palestinian rabbinic compositions.[14] This change seems to have occurred soon after the Mishnah was accepted as the main subject of academic study.[15] Due to the complete absence of literary sources of Babylonian origin until the first generations of the Amoraim, only from the third century onward, is it possible to trace the contours of Babylonian Jewry, including its attitude to the Land of Israel in rabbinic literature.[16] Narratives of a vivid exchange between the Land of Israel and Babylonia, in both Babylonian and Pales-

---

11. Sipra Tazria 5:9; t. Neg. 1:16; t. Pesah. 4:14 (for an analysis of this text, see further 104). For a recent discussion of these texts see Cana Werman, "Was Hillel a Pharisee?" in *Sources and Interpretation in Ancient Judaism: Studies for Tal Ilan at Sixty*, ed. Meron M. Piotrkowski, Geoffrey Herman, and Saskia Dönitz, Ancient Judaism and Early Christianity 104 (Leiden: Brill, 2018), 66–104.

12. See Gen. Rab. 33:3; Julius Theodor and Chanoch Albeck, *Midrash Bereshit Rabbah: Critical Edition with Notes and Commentary* (Jerusalem: Wahrmann Books, 1965), 1:304 (hereafter Theodor-Albeck).

13. See Hezser, *Jewish Travel*, 344–49, esp. the list on 344.

14. See Jacob N. Epstein, *Prolegomena ad Litteras Amoraiticas, Talmud Babylonicum et Hierosolymitanum* [Hebrew], ed. Ezra Z. Melamed (Jerusalem: Magnes, 1962), 314–22.

15. About the Mishnah and its role in the development of rabbinic literacy, see Catherine Hezser, "The Mishnah and Ancient Book Production," in *The Mishnah in Contemporary Perspective*, vol. 1, ed. Jacob Neusner, and Alan J. Avery-Peck, HdO 1.65 (Leiden: Brill, 2002), 167–92; Yaacov Sussman, "Torah Shebe'alpeh' Peshutah Kemashma'ah: Kokho shel Kotzo shel Yud" ['Oral Torah' Literally—The Power of the Tip of Yod], in *Mehqerei Talmud III: Talmudic Studies Dedicated to the Memory of Professor Ephraim E. Urbach*, ed. Y. Sussman and D. Rosenthal, 2 vols. (Jerusalem: Magnes, 2005), 1:209–384.; Elizabeth Shanks Alexander, *Transmitting Mishnah: The Shaping Influence of Oral Tradition* (Cambridge: Cambridge University Press, 2006).

16. See Hezser, "Crossing Enemy Lines," 225.

tinian sources, are chronologically framed within the second half of the third century and the fourth century. Catherine Hezser explains that contacts between Palestinian and Babylonian sages and the transmission of halakhic knowledge from one place to the other declined from the end of the fourth century onward because, as the Babylonian academies gained power and knowledge, they freed themselves from the hegemony of the center in Roman Palestine. Although first- and second-generation Babylonian sages (210–250 CE), such as Rab and Rab's successor Rab Huna (or other Babylonians named Huna), are mentioned hundreds of times in the Yerushalmi, prominent fourth-generation (320–350 CE) Babylonian sages such as Abayye (d. 339) and Raba (d. 352) are rarely, if ever, mentioned; this is evidence of a parting of the ways.[17] Concentrating on the narrative traditions about third- to fourth-century sages, I wish to assess the cultural Palestinian rabbinic milieu of these centuries, which considered the traditions about migrants from Babylonia important enough to merit recording in their literature.

It has been customary to say that both academic Mishnah-oriented textual communities were involved in a prolonged exchange. It was accepted practice for sages from Palestine to disseminate their learning in Babylonia and for Babylonians to study and teach in Palestine.[18] A careful reading of the rabbinic literature, however, reveals that the praise of Babylonians who achieved academic success in Palestine is largely found in the Babylonian Talmud.[19] In literature from both places, during the formative period of both centers' early history, the status and lineage of the two academic communities' leaders were compared.[20] However, while the Pal-

---

17. See Yaacov Sussman, "We-shuv le-Yerushalmi Neziqin," in *Mehqerei Talmud I: Talmudic Studies*, ed. Y. Sussmann and D. Rosenthal, 2 vols. (Jerusalem: Magnes, 1989–1990), 55–133.

18. See the brief portrait of the relationships between Babylonia and the Land of Israel in Aharon Oppenheimer, *By the Rivers of Babylon: Perspectives on the History of Talmudic Babylonia* [Hebrew] (Jerusalem: Zalman Shazar Center, 2017), 111–21.

19. For example, only in b. B. Qam. 117a is Kahana compared to the "lion ascending from Babylonia," though he was not greatly appreciated in the Yerushalmi; see 34 and 55 below. Eleazar bar Pedat, who immigrated to Palestine in the fourth century, is described in the Babylonian Talmud as "master of the Land of Israel" (b. Nid. 20b) and is glorified extensively by the Babylonian rabbis (see b. Hul. 110a–111b, b. Ketub. 77a), but he never receives such praises in Palestinian texts. Rabbi Ami and Rabbi Asi, titled as "the significant priests of the Land of Israel" (b. Git. 59b) could be mentioned here as well, and the list is not complete.

20. For studies comparing the Babylonian Exilarchate to the Palestinian Patriarchate, see, for instance, Isaiah Gafni, "'Scepter and Staff': Concerning New Forms of Leadership in the Period of the Talmud in the Land of Israel and Babylonia," in *Priesthood and Monarchy: Studies in the Historical Relationships of Religion and State* [Hebrew], ed. I. Gafni and G. Motzkin (Jerusalem: Zalman Shazar Center, 1986–1987), 84–91; Gafni, *The Jews of Babylonia in the Talmudic Era* [Hebrew] (Jerusalem: Zalman Shazar Center, 1990), 98–104; David M. Goodblatt, *The Monarchic Principle: Studies in Jewish Self-Government in Antiquity*, TSAJ 38 (Tübingen: Mohr Siebeck, 1994), 279–80, Herman, *Prince without a Kingdom*, 210–14.

estinian rabbinic sources hint at rivalry between Babylonia and Palestine, the Babylonian Talmud, already in the last generations of Tannaim,[21] represents the relationship between the heads of the centers in terms of reciprocal respect, with the Palestinians showing humility toward the greatest of the Babylonian scholars (see b. Hul. 95b, 137b).

The editors of the Babylonian Talmud indeed attributed many of the traditions they transmitted to the so-called *naḥotei*, those who went down to Babylonia from Palestine and shared their knowledge with the locals. Since the time of Sherira Gaon, a specific group of sages has been considered responsible for the transmission of rabbinic traditions from Palestine to Babylonia from the late third to fourth centuries CE. According to Sherira, this group escaped Christian persecutions (*shmada*)[22] and left their country when the talmudic learning there began to decay. This is a highly tendentious etiological narrative, according to which the rabbinic learning from the West was rescued from Christian persecution[23] and brought to the bosom of the East, where it would not suffer the West's decline of "instruction" (a technical term for practical rabbinic legislation) but, on the contrary, entered the golden age of Abaye and Raba.[24] Following Sherira, historians have identified this particular type of sage as transmitters of knowledge. While the early scholars were eager to assume that the *naḥotei* were responsible for transmitting Palestinian teachings to Babylonia on a large scale, modern scholars are more skeptical, viewing the contribution as more modest.[25] The *naḥotei* traditions in the Babylonian Talmud are numerous;[26] some have no parallels at all in the Yerushalmi, while the ones

---

21. See further below, 112.

22. Although he does not explicitly say Christian, in view of the time period and historical background, it is quite obvious.

23. Simcha Gross demonstrates that "persecutions" were part of a historiographic tradition invoked to ingratiate the minority community with the incoming regime by denigrating the outgoing regime as cruel and persecutory.

24. See James Adam Redfield, "Traveling Rabbis and the Talmud as History" (unpublished lecture).

25. See the survey of scholarship in Mordecai Schwartz, "As They Journeyed from the East: The Nahotei of the Fourth Century and the Construction of the Rabbinic Diaspora," *HUCA* 86 (2015): 63–99, here 65–69. His own study accepts the assumption that they did indeed import some small number of Palestinian rabbinic materials to Babylonia in the fourth century. However, he claims that, at least as depicted in b. Seder Mo'ed, they did little more than clarify, modify, or reassign the authorship of traditions already known in Babylonia before their reports. See ibid., 80–93. Redfield debated some of these theses, esp. how Schwartz labels this evidence as either "new" or "already known" in Babylonia; thus, seemingly, this is still an open question.

26. See the extensive list of *naḥotei* traditions compiled by Melamed, *Introduction to Talmudic Literature*, 442–45. See also Wilhelm Bacher, *Tradition und Tradenten in den Schulen Palästinas und Babyloniens: Studien und Materialien zur Entstehungsgeschichte des Talmuds,*

who do have parallels often differ from them significantly.[27] Scholars have discussed the relationships between the *naḥotei* traditions and the entire corpus of parallel traditions between the Palestinian and the Babylonian Talmud regarding particular topics in the rabbinic curriculum.[28] According to Marcus Mordecai Schwartz, the *naḥotei* did import some Palestinian rabbinic material to Babylonia;[29] however, the bulk of this material was already familiar in Babylonia before their arrival. This thesis raises some doubts about the authenticity of the traditions attributed to Palestinians in the Babylonian Talmud.[30] Recently, James Adam Redfield has explained some scenes of the arrival of *naḥotei* in the Bavli as an editorial device "to support and/or critique the circulation of culture across institutional, chronological, and geographical lines" and to serve as "an oblique mirror of the redactors' authority."[31] This productive approach resonates with my own readings below.

Babylonian Amoraic traditions arrived in the Land of Israel quite early. That the Yerushalmi and related literature incorporated a significant number of Babylonian traditions, especially those attributed to Rab and Shmuel, means that the debates between these two Babylonian opponents were reverberating in the air of Palestinian academia.[32] The story of the founding of the two rabbinic study centers in Babylonia is a story of a long coexistence between the rabbinic community in Galilee and these two centers in Babylonia, one of them founded by the disciple of Rabbi Yoḥanan of Tiberias. It is also a story, however, of a significant clash between Palestinians and Babylonians. In the words of Rab Huna (late third century), "We made ourselves in Babylonia the equivalent of Eretz Israel from the day Rab came to Babylonia" (b. Git. 6a, b. B. Qam. 80a).[33] Although the remark

---

Schriften herausgegeben von der Gesellschaft zur Förderung der Wissenschaft des Judentums (Leipzig: Gusav Fock, 1914), 524–33.

27. For attempts to resolve this problem harmonistically, see Chanoch Albeck, "Studies in Babylonian Talmud" [Hebrew], *Tarbiz* 9 (1938): 163–78; and Zwi Moshe Dor, *The Teaching of Eretz Israel in Babylon* [Hebrew] (Tel Aviv: Dvir, 1971), 116–202. See recently Redfield's online essay "When X Arrived, He Said …" for a detailed assessment of Dor's interpretation, https://www.academia.edu/29627483/_When_X_Arrived_he_said_The_Historical_Career_of_a_Talmudic_Formula_appendix_to_Redacting_Culture_.

28. See Gray, *Talmud in Exile*, 5–7.

29. Schwartz, "As They Journeyed," 63–93.

30. I found only one systematic comparison of the traditions of *naḥotei* in the Babylonian Talmud with their Palestinian parallels, in Oded Rosenblum, "The Activities of the Nehutei, Ulla and Rav Dimi, According to Sugiot in the Babylonian Talmud" (PhD diss., Haifa University, 2007), 242–43, and I doubt that most of these traditions were of Palestinian origin.

31. See James Adam Redfield, "Redacting Culture: Ethnographic Authority in the Talmudic Arrival Scene," *Jewish Social Studies* 22 (2016): 29–80, here 43.

32. See Epstein, *Prolegomena ad Litteras Amoraiaticas*, 312–14.

33. According to Gafni's translation in *Land, Center and Diaspora* 116.

pertains solely to the Babylonian sages' expertise in divorce law, Isaiah Gafni elucidates the conceptual process behind it and concludes,

> There emerges over the years a Babylonia enjoying all the attributes of the historically central Land of Israel: Davidic leadership, remnants of the Jerusalem Temple, links with the Patriarchs, and even hallowed earth and sacred boundaries.[34]

This Babylonian declaration of independence prompted a mirror response in Palestine, which reached a climax in the fourth century. Presumably, Babylonian learning became prominent and independent, and Palestinians, whose identity was based on their hegemony in learning, began questioning their identity and shaping it after the Jewish-Babylonian culture.[35]

Rabbinic storytelling of the third and fourth centuries paid significant attention to the cultural clash between Palestinian and Babylonian scholars, clearly preferring to focus on these two Jewish communities to the exclusion of others, such as the Roman, Alexandrian, or Greek Jews. The latter groups are only mentioned in passing in this literature and are treated as insignificant Others. Since this book has a narratological bent, in these introductory remarks I would like to offer a delightful example of talmudic rhetoric, in which the positions of the Palestinian literati and their Others are well expressed. As a scholar of texts, I wish to allow Palestinian rabbinic writers to introduce their perception of the model of relationships between Palestinians, or more precisely Galileans, and their Others:

---

34. Ibid.; see also Moulie Vidas, "The Bavli's Discussion of Genealogy in Qiddushin IV," in *Antiquity in Antiquity: Jewish and Christian Pasts in the Greco-Roman World*, ed. Gregg Gardner and Kevin L. Osterloh, TSAJ 123 (Tübingen: Mohr Siebeck, 2008), 285–326; and Daniel Boyarin, *A Traveling Homeland: The Babylonian Talmud as Diaspora*, Divinations (Philadelphia: University of Pennsylvania Press, 2015), 33–36.

35. Here and further on, I use the term *culture* in its broad sense, influenced by Yuri Lotman, who defined culture as the whole of uninherited information and the ways of its organization and storage. For analyses of his approach, see Boguslaw Zylko, "Culture and Semiotics: Notes on Lotman's Conception of Culture," in "Reexamining Critical Processing," special issue *New Literary History* 32.2 (2001): 391–408. See also Terry Eagleton's seminal work about culture, which begins with an attempt to define culture, which does not start optimistically. "Culture is an exceptionally complex word," the book commences, "but four major senses of it stand out. It can mean (1) a body of artistic and intellectual work; (2) a process of spiritual and intellectual development; (3) the values, customs, beliefs, and symbolic practices by which men and women live; or (4) a whole way of life" (*Culture* [New Haven: Yale University Press, 2016]). My use of this term is closest to the last meaning.

Genesis Rabbah 11:4[36]	
Rabbi Ishmael ben Rabbi Yose asked Rabbi: On account of what virtue do the Babylonians live? By virtue of the Torah. And in Eretz Israel? By virtue of the tithes. And the people from abroad? Because they honor the Shabbat and festivals.	ר' ישמעאל בר' יוסי שאל לר'. אמר לו: בני בבל בזכות מה חיים? אמר לו: בזכות תורה. ובארץ ישראל? בזכות מעשרות. ואנשי חוץ לארץ? בזכות שהן מכבדים השבתות וימים טובים.

This short dialogue between Rabbi and an ancient *tanna*, Rabbi Ishmael ben Rabbi Yose, encapsulates schematically but precisely the cultural universe of the rabbis. This pericope mentions three cultural values that a rabbinic Jew would happily embrace: the separation of tithes, Torah, and the celebration of Shabbat and the holidays. The text aims to equate the three communities, who all merit the same reward but by excelling in different spheres. The text explicitly declares that all three merit life, but the merit accrues to them as a reward for different things. Babylonians merit life by virtue of their excellence in Torah study, Greek diaspora Jews by virtue of their excellence in observing God's appointed seasons, and Palestinian Jews by virtue of their diligence in separating agricultural tithes. Even as it recognizes difference, the text equates all of them—all merit life, but they do so by different, almost equally valuable pathways. It seems that the entire Jewish universe of our sage, outside of Palestine, is divided into two: Babylonians and others. The thing of high importance that Babylonians share with Palestinians, which other Jews do not, is Torah study. The Others share with them the celebration of Shabbat and holidays. He benevolently praises in this way "the people from abroad," that is, the people of the Greek-speaking diaspora,[37] about whom nothing more significant can be uttered. This passage intends to state that the Jews of Palestine are manifestly superior to other Jews because they can perform all three groups of commandments. It is quite possible that this tradition, which marks the Babylonians as superior in Torah learning to all other diaspora Jews, is based on the growing reputation of Babylonian academic centers.

Moreover, the passage indicates that their Palestinian brethren are already crediting the Babylonians with great prowess and devotion to learning. The text refers to three groups, thus seemingly attesting to a tripartite division. However, only two locales are named—the Land of Israel and Babylonia. Thus, this short passage allows us to see the structure

---

36. Theodor-Albeck, 1:91.
37. This is evident from the subsequent Genesis Rabbah text (Theodor-Albeck, 1:91), which speaks about the people of Laodicea, an ancient city built on the river Lycus, located in Lydia in Asia Minor, which later became the Roman province of Phrygia.

of the rabbinic universe constructed around these two meaningful loci: Roman Palestine and Sasanian Babylonia. Moreover, it informs us that the division of the commandments, between those that can be performed only in the Land of Israel and all others, is a Palestinian corollary to the rise of Torah study as a paramount "virtue" and skill-set in Babylonia.[38] This is a microcosm of the long-lasting story of the coexistence and collision of these two communities.

2. Methodological Remarks

In the following subsection of the introduction, I introduce my key terms and explanatory models (lifeworld, self/Other; textual community; xenophobia/philoxenia; narrative as self-fashioning; host/guest) and explain how they operate in my analyses of the selected narratives.[39] By combining these terms, I aim to offer a new angle from which to read the travel stories about migrating Babylonians versus migrating Palestinians, seeking to understand the relationships between the two main rabbinic communities of late antiquity. These relationships have often been represented in the literature as relationships between the center and the margins. Approaching this topic from a broad history-of-culture perspective, I hope to show that they were much more complex and fluid.

The book builds on a set of interlocking themes within the study of rabbinic literature and Jewish culture in late antiquity. There is much work to be done on the plain textual study of rabbinic literature, since so many rabbinic texts have yet to be adequately analyzed. Jonah Fraenkel and Jeffrey Rubenstein stand at the forefront of the significant development in the critical literary reading of the rabbinic story in recent decades.[40]

---

38. Complementary evidence for Palestinian alternatives to Babylonian virtues and Babylonian alternatives to Palestinian ones would follow. Palestinians will represent Babylonians as more exact literati but less capable in creative interpretation. Babylonians will accept this characterization, but they will color this difference differently. Palestinians will present Babylonians as more eager to be buried in the Holy Land than to live there. They will also express their disdain regarding Babylonians' preoccupation with their lineage, and Babylonians as well will express some self-irony on this score.

39. In this work about the acceptance of the Other in the rabbinic culture, I am using the common neologism *xenophobia*, the unwillingness to accept the foreigner. As the antonym to it, I use the word *philoxenia*, an ancient Greek word for hospitality. I noticed that recently in academic debates, people sometimes coin the term *xenophilia*, which sounds like a modern construct for the xenophobia's contrary. I prefer to use philoxenia as the already-existing literary word, albeit in a slightly new sense, as the antonym to the already well-rooted neologism: xenophobia.

40. See Yonah Fraenkel, *The Aggadic Narrative: Harmony of Form and Content* [Hebrew] (Tel Aviv: Hakibbutz Hameuḥad, 2001). See also his *Studies in the Spiritual World of the Aggadic Narrative* [Hebrew] (Tel Aviv: Hakibbutz Hameuḥad, 1981); *Darkhei ha-Agadah ve-Hamidrash*

Fraenkel introduced a critical paradigm shift, revolutionizing rabbinic stories' interpretation by defining the rabbinic story genre as fiction or, more precisely, as dramatic narrative, and proposing the use of New Criticism methods. Rubenstein brought new methodological theories to the critical study of the rabbinic narrative, advocating for reading the rabbinic story in its cultural and literary contexts. Thus, these scholars would agree that a typical rabbinic story is seldom a depiction of a real event.[41] Seth Schwartz, doubting whether these stories provide us with specific historical information, further insists that "what they primarily tell us is what the rabbis thought worth committing to writing (or at any rate to a fixed oral form)."[42] Accordingly, it is crucial to understand why a particular story was so meaningful to its narrators and what may have inspired its telling. The editors of Palestinian rabbinic literature carefully selected and preserved numerous stories about the Babylonians in the Land of Israel, precisely because the stories in question were significant to those sages. They attest to what could be called the narrators' lifeworld.

The term *lifeworld* is rooted in Edmund Husserl's phenomenological thought. It denotes the world of lived experience inhabited by people as conscious beings, incorporating how phenomena (events, objects, emotions) appear to them in their conscious experience or everyday life.[43] According to a currently popular view, discussed below, selfhood or identity is constituted by the narratives that narrators tell about themselves.

Moreover, narrators impose a narrative structure upon the world, such that this narrative is the "lens" through which their lives are experienced. Experience, in other words, is essentially narrative in form.[44] Throughout this book, I read rabbinic stories as seriously as possible in order to explore how the narrators shaped their experiences.

In the following chapters of this book, I examine several early talmudic stories depicting students' arrival from Babylonia to the new and unfa-

---

(Givatayim: Dvir, 1991), esp. 235–85; *Midrash ha-Agadah* (Tel Aviv: Dvir 1996), esp. 329–97; Jeffrey L. Rubenstein, *Talmudic Stories: Narrative Art, Composition, and Culture* (Baltimore: Johns Hopkins University Press, 1999). Rubenstein (8–12) provides an insightful assessment of Fraenkel's method against the backdrop of various schools of twentieth-century literary theory. See also Hillel I. Newman, "Closing the Circle: Yonah Fraenkel, the Talmudic Story, and Rabbinic History," in *How Should Rabbinic Literature Be Read in the Modern World?*, ed. Matthew Kraus, Judaism in Context 4 (Piscataway, NJ: Gorgias Press, 2006), 105–35.

41. See Rubenstein, *Talmudic Stories*, 8–12; and Amram Tropper, *Like Clay in the Hands of the Potter: Sage Stories in Rabbinic Literature* [Hebrew] (Jerusalem: Zalman Shazar Center, 2011).

42. See Seth Schwartz, *Were the Jews a Mediterranean Society? Reciprocity and Solidarity in Ancient Judaism* (Princeton: Princeton University Press, 2009), 118.

43. See Jonathan A. Smith, Paul Flowers, and Michael Larkin, *Interpretative Phenomenological Analysis: Theory, Method and Research* (London: Sage, 2009), 15.

44. See Samantha Vice, "Literature and the Narrative Self," *Philosophy* 78 (2003): 93–108.

miliar environment of the Galilee.⁴⁵ I then discuss the opposite process, namely, the arrival and the acceptance of a Palestinian in Babylonia. These stories raise vital questions about ethnicity and identity, migration, and mobility. In doing so, they reflect their narrators' attitudes and the attitude of the visitor from abroad toward the diaspora itself. Joshua Levinson has insightfully observed

> ... when cultures feel threatened, they begin to tell tales. Sometimes these are retellings that strengthen the dominant fictions, and sometimes they are new or revised narratives. Through these narratives, the imagined community guards its borders and defines for itself who is inside, who is outside, and why.⁴⁶

Why did this particular culture produce these specific stories? This question calls to mind the eminent twentieth-century cultural theorist Yuri Lotman, who characterized culture as a machine whose purpose is to produce meanings. Under normal circumstances, a machine will produce the same products all the time, provided that its operators supply it with the same materials. However, the machine of culture is a bit erratic and unable to produce identical products consistently. It perpetually produces something new, owing to the glitches in its working mechanism.⁴⁷

This modern paradigm informs my thinking about Palestinian and Babylonian rabbinic cultures and their relationship to their ancestors.⁴⁸

---

45. See the series of articles by Joshua Schwartz: "The Patriotic Rabbi: Babylonian Scholars in Roman Period Palestine," in *Jewish Local Patriotism and Self-Identification in the Graeco-Roman Period*, ed. Sián Jones and Sarah Pearce, JSPSup 31 (Sheffield: Sheffield Academic, 1998), 118–31; "Tension between Palestinian Scholars and Babylonian Olim in Amoraic Palestine," *JSJ* 11 (1980): 78–94; "Babylonian Commoners in Amoraic Palestine," *JAOS* 101 (1981): 317–22; "*Aliya* from Babylonia during the Amoraic period (200–500 C.E.)" [Hebrew], *Jerusalem Cathedra* 3 (1983): 58–69; "Southern Judaea and Babylonia," *JQR* 7 (1982): 188–97. See also the numerous studies collected in Oppenheimer, *Between Rome and Babylon*, 374–93, 409–31.

46. See Joshua Levinson, "Bodies and Bo(a)rders: Emerging Fictions of Identity in Late Antiquity," *HTR* 93 (2000): 343–72, here 344. Levinson used the term *imagined community* coined by Benedict Anderson in his book *Imagined Communities: Reflections on the Origin and Spread of Nationalism* (London: Verso, 1983). Even though the term aims to describe nationalism specifically, now it is used more broadly, almost blending with "community of interest," or, as in our case, with "community dedicated to the sacred text or a complex of text-oriented customs." For our case, the term *textual communities* is more suitable, following Brian Stock, *The Implications of Literacy: Written Language and Models of Interpretation in the Eleventh and Twelfth Centuries* (Princeton: Princeton University Press, 1983).

47. For one of the oral transmissions of this saying, see Michail Gasparov, *Zapiski I Vipiski* [Notes and Quotes] (Moskow: Novoe Lit. Obozrenie, 2001), 215: (Записки и выписки): Лотмановское представление «культура есть машина, рассчитанная на сохранение старых смыслов, но из-за своей плодотворной разлаженности порождающая новые смыслы» лучше всего иллюстрируется у Рабле диспутом между Панургом и Таумастом.

48. See 8 n. 35 above.

Both cultures appear to draw on the cultural legacy of the biblical and the early postbiblical period. However, they utilize different elements of this cultural heritage in dissimilar ways. These rabbinic cultures produced extensive stories and narratives that sometimes paralleled each other. Yet in these parallels, the meaning of the stories almost always differs in the two locations.[49] This fact attests to the differences between the two cultures, which produced varying cultural products from almost identical raw materials. The question arises: what caused these two virtually identical machines of rabbinic culture to produce divergent meanings from the available narrative bricolage?

In exploring the content and meaning of the narratives on encounters with Babylonians, I analyze rabbinic literary traditions as evidence for the acceptance/rejection of the Other by rabbinic culture and how border-crossers were seen as exporting features of the previous environment to the new realm. At the core of these stories lies a conflict between the alien and one's new surroundings. The newcomer from Babylonia is simultaneously portrayed as a prestigious figure whom the Palestinian Jewish community hopes to retain for itself and as a stranger struggling for acceptance. Elements of xenophobia and philoxenia in Palestinian rabbinic culture are reflected in these stories; by analyzing them, we can understand how Palestinian rabbis viewed themselves. Behind the construction of the image of a Babylonian as the crucial internal Other, we find a whole complex of historical and cultural circumstances that I hope to clarify.

3. Textual Communities and Their Others

Larger developments notwithstanding, inner rabbinic processes are perhaps more significant for explaining our narratives. The reason for the intense existential anxiety reflected in the figure of the Babylonian Other in Palestinian rabbinic narratives lies in a theme that I will focus on in this book. In her article "The Other in Rabbinic Literature," Christine Hayes states,

> Dramatic changes in the political and cultural conditions of Jewish life in Antiquity led inevitably to [the] revision and renegotiation of the self.... Identity construction is thus a complex task, as a group defines itself not only in contrast to other groups ("external others") but also in contrast to

---

49. See Kalmin, *Migrating Tales*; and Ronit Nikolsky and Tal Ilan, eds., *Rabbinic Traditions between Palestine and Babylonia*, Ancient Judaism and Early Christianity 89 (Leiden: Brill, 2014).

members of its group that would contest the group's identity or construct it in a different way ("internal others").⁵⁰

Who are these external and internal Others? According to Hayes, external Others included gentiles, converts, and Godfearers (Judaizers), while internal Others included Christians, holy men (*hasidim*), and the *am ha-aretz* (i.e., uneducated Jewish neighbors).⁵¹ She extrapolated these categories from rabbinic literature itself without differentiating between the two rabbinic cultures of Babylonia and Palestine, which I would contend had distinct types of Others. For example, I would argue that, in fact, Christians were not a significant Other for the creators of the Yerushalmi, whose primary Others tended instead to be women, Babylonian Jews, and students who were unruly or simply disobeyed their teachers. Nevertheless, I concur with Hayes's proposed criteria for distinguishing between the internal and external Other:

> At the heart of the rabbinic self-understanding lies a text. A rabbi devotes himself to this text and associated traditions of learning and practice as developed by the sages' class. Rabbinic literature imagines the alterity of persons who are not committed to this text and its rabbinic elaboration. Some of these "others"—gentiles—are, by birth and culture, entirely far removed from the text. Interaction with these persons must be negotiated and controlled. The rabbis resist simple dichotomies and locate many gentiles along a spectrum of proximity, as seen in rabbinic discussions of the righteous gentile, the venerator of heaven, and the convert.⁵² Some others—non-rabbinic Jews of various types—are, by birth and culture,

---

50. Christine Hayes, "The "Other" in Rabbinic Literature" in *The Cambridge Companion to the Talmud and Rabbinic Literature*, ed. Charlotte Elisheva Fonrobert and Martin S. Jaffee, Cambridge Companions to Religion (Cambridge: Cambridge University Press, 2007), 243–69, here 243.

51. Here I wish to mention the work by Cynthia Baker, "Bodies, Boundaries, and Domestic Politics in a Late Ancient Marketplace," *Journal of Medieval and Early Modern Studies* 26 (1996): 391–418. Baker argues that, for the rabbis, the *bet ha-midrash*—the study house—functioned as a private space in another sense, internal to Jews, not only in the conflict between Jews and Romans. The study house was the ideal place for the formation of rabbinic identity as distinct from and even antagonistic to other Jews, the so-called ignorant ones, the *am ha-aretz*. We will see below that, even in the narratives under consideration here, the figure of the illiterate Jew appears instrumental in shaping a rabbi's identity, enabling the acceptance of Babylonians with some empathy despite their foreignness.

52. After I wrote this introduction, the work of Ishay Rosen-Zvi and Adi Ophir, *Goy: Israel's Others and the Birth of the Gentile*, Oxford Studies in the Abrahamic Religions (Oxford: Oxford University Press, 2020) was published. Apparently, this statement is not uncontroversial in light of these authors' recent depiction of rabbinic attitudes to gentile others as strictly dichotomous and undifferentiated. The latter approach has been critiqued for its lack of nuance and its repudiation of a "spectrum" of identities; see Christine Hayes, "The Complicated Goy in Classical Rabbinic Sources," in *Perceiving the Other in Ancient Judaism and Early Christianity*, ed. Michal Bar-Asher Siegal, Wolfgang

heirs to the text but have neglected, distorted, or abandoned it in some way. Because they embody a genuine alternative—alterity within— the *min*, the holy man, and the *'am ha'aretz* pose a unique threat to and resource for the rabbinic attempt to construct a stable self.[53]

From this point of view, the rabbinic community is a typical textual community. In this regard, Brian Stock has discussed the process by which—in the face of growing levels of literacy and the rise of heretical movements in eleventh- and twelfth-century France—religious communities came to understand their identities through the mediation of written texts, which often were interpreted for them by key individuals. The text, the written word, became central to communal identity, affecting even the nonliterate through its dissemination and acceptance by community members. He argues that text-centered communities are groups of people whose social activities are centered around texts, or, more precisely, around a literate interpreter of texts.

The text in question need not be written down, nor do the majority of auditors need to be literate. The texts' interpreters may relate it verbally, and the group's members must associate voluntarily; their interaction must take place around an agreed meaning for the text. Above all, they must make the hermeneutic leap from what the text says to what they think it means; this common understanding then provides the foundation for changes in thought and behavior.[54]

Stock proposed that communities such as monasteries may center their social activities on the shared interpretation of a text or a corpus of texts. The community either agrees on a specific interpretation of these texts or follows a rabbinic authority, an interpreter, whose teachings are then accepted. According to Stock, the sharing of such interpretations in communities leads to the emergence of shared communal goals. This emphasis on communality leaves little room for dissent between community members. Thus, it is much easier to integrate an illiterate, so-called *am ha-aretz* into a textual community when he or she is devoted to the interpreter or interpreters of the texts.[55] A problem may arise when the textual community needs to absorb a member devoted to the same texts

---

Grünstäudl, and Matthew Thiessen, WUNT 394 (Tübingen: Mohr Siebeck, 2017), 147–67. Hayes's approach is consonant with my view here.

53. Hayes, "'Other,' in Rabbinic Literature," 262–63.

54. See Stock, *Implications of Literacy*. Stock emphasizes that the community could also base itself on texts in the plural, as long as they shared one interpretation of those texts.

55. On the evolution of the term *am ha-aretz* recently, see Yair Furstenberg, "Am Ha-Aretz in Tannaitic Literature and Its Social Contexts" [Hebrew], *Zion* 78 (2013): 287–319, and the literature cited there. On the specific approach of the Babylonian Talmud to this subject, see Jeffrey L. Rubenstein, *The Culture of the Babylonian Talmud* (Baltimore: Johns Hopkins University Press, 2003), 123–42.

but to different modes of interpretation or the ideas of different interpreters. I suggest that Palestinian rabbis' acceptance of Babylonian migrant scholars was even more crucial for the construction of the rabbinic self than the approval of nonrabbinic Jews and others into the Jewish community: these migrant scholars had a relationship to the text and, therefore, at least according to their self-perception, belonged to the same textual community.

In principle, the rabbis of Palestine had no reason not to accept this challenge, although, as we will see, it was often fraught with difficulty. Sometimes they redrew the borders of rabbinic culture to include Babylonian migrant scholars as insiders. In other cases, the migrant scholars were only partially accepted, becoming liminal groups that would forever wander on the rabbinic community's margins.

4. Narratives of Xenophobia and Philoxenia

Many stories in Palestinian rabbinic literature feature a Palestinian narrator who attempts to cope with the figure of a Babylonian Other, a fact that reflects the Palestinian rabbis' anxiety in the face of these formidable strangers.[56] These stories indicate that the formation of Palestinian rabbinic identity was a central concern, and that the presence of competing Babylonian scholars was perceived as a threat to the stories' narrators. The Babylonian Talmud includes a relatively small number of similar stories narrated by Babylonian figures hosting their Palestinian brethren, perhaps demonstrating that they were less preoccupied with identifying themselves relative to Palestinian Jewry. The focus on the Babylonian Other by Palestinian rabbinic narrators exposes the xenophobic elements in Palestinian rabbinic culture—a feature it shares with all the cultures of late antiquity. In fact, a fully phyloxenic culture never existed. In our context, it is worthwhile to mention that xenophobia serves as vital fuel for cultural evolution, facilitating the construction of the self via a whole range of fear of the Other, from concern about physical or spiritual harm to less well-defined anxieties.

To define the Other's alterity in order to declare superiority or to construct a contrasting identity is a crucial need of both ancient and con-

---

56. Mira Wasserman, analyzing a selection of texts from b. Avodah Zarah, discussed the threat posed by the internal Other and the resulting insecurity (*Jews, Gentile, and Other Animals: The Talmud after the Humanities*, Divinations [Philadelphia: University of Pennsylvania Press, 2019]). She noticed that rabbis' anxiety flows from the realization that hierarchical differences are not essential but are established only by Torah learning/observance, which, because others can achieve it, pose a threat to rabbinic identity. Some of my decisions below are consonant with this observation.

temporary cultures. Analysis of such self-fashioning through the disparagement of alien societies has long been a staple of academic discourse.[57] As Erich Gruen points out:

> Denigration of the "Other" seems essential to shaping the inner portrait, the marginalization that defines the center, the reverse mirror that distorts the reflection of the opposite, and enhances that of the beholder.[58]

Similarly, Benjamin Isaac has described widespread negative Greek and Roman attitudes toward an array of foreigners across the Mediterranean, concluding that these amounted to either ethnic prejudice or proto-racism.[59] However, the construction of the Other in ancient cultures still enabled the expression of more nuanced and complex opinions about the Other.[60] Sometimes the shaping of identity involved both distancing oneself from the Other and appropriating the Other.[61] I explore a similar tendency in rabbinic culture, namely, how the rabbinic community of Palestine encountered and even embraced the tradition of one particular Other, the Babylonian—and introduced him into their self-consciousness.[62] This embracing of the Babylonian's tradition is combined with rabbinic rhetoric that humiliates the Other, along with the rationalization behind these sentiments. My goal is to place this rhetoric in its historical context in order to understand how rabbinic culture thrived within its historical surroundings. Central to my concern is the struggle between xenophobic and phyloxenic tendencies and how the balance between these two shaped rabbinic identities or the rabbinic self.

5. Hosts, Guests, and Selves: Explanatory Models

In this book, I use the term *self* mostly as a hermeneutic category, applying personal characteristics to culture types or models of self-reflexivity produced by culture. While I deal here with the self of the rabbinic narrator, I am interested not only in the selves of persons or agents but also in the self

---

57. See the analysis of scholarship on this topic in Erich S. Gruen, *Rethinking the Other in Antiquity*, Martin Classical Lectures, New Series (Princeton: Princeton University Press 2011), 1–5.
58. Ibid., 1
59. See Benjamin Isaac, *The Invention of Racism in Classical Antiquity* (Princeton: Princeton University Press, 2004).
60. Arnaldo Momigliano, *Alien Wisdom: The Limits of Hellenization* (Cambridge: Cambridge University Press, 1975).
61. As was convincingly shown by Gruen, *Rethinking the Other*, 4.
62. On self-reflexivity in rabbinic texts, see Dina Stein, *Textual Mirrors: Reflexivity, Midrash, and the Rabbinic Self*, Divinations (Philadelphia: University of Pennsylvania Press, 2012).

as a product of the narrator's culture. Across cultures, we find narrative used as a tool for making sense of experience. When a narrative is simultaneously born of and gives shape to experience, self and narrative become inseparably entwined.[63] The narrative activity allows narrators to impose order on otherwise disconnected events and create continuity between past, present, and future. Moreover, narrative interfaces self and society, constituting a crucial resource for socializing identities, developing interpersonal relationships, and establishing membership in a community. In this way, narratives bring multiple, partial selves to life.[64]

Studying the Christian subculture of the Roman Empire, Guy Stroumsa, among others, has emphasized the crucial importance of the emergence of a "newly reflexive self" in early Christianity. Tracing its Judaic and Hellenic roots, he has shown how this new thought crystallized in the period from the second to the fourth centuries of the Common Era.[65] This period coincides with the initial formation of classical rabbinic culture and, therefore, Jewish expressions of self-reflectivity are similar. Rabbinic literature, with its unique medley of imaginative discourses, provides us with an opportunity to follow this question across various registers.[66] The newly reflective self emerges from the stories told about migrants going East and West and finding themselves at the mercy of their hosts. Thus, the encounter between the guest and the host is a powerful narrative situation that allows the self to emerge. This encounter is usually dramatic, not without comic overtones, and far from peaceful. Analyzing the encounter between the host and the guest, I borrow Jacques Derrida's terminology about hospitality as a test of ethics and the interrupted self of the Palestinian rabbinic narrator.[67] In his writings, Derrida, following

---

63. See Elinor Ochs and Lisa Capps, "Narrating the Self," *Annual Review of Anthropology* 25 (1996): 25–43.

64. See Joshua Levinson, "Post-Classical Narratology and the Rabbinic Subject," in *Narratology, Hermeneutics, and Midrash: Jewish, Christian, and Muslim from Late Antiquity through to Modern Times*, ed. Gerhard Langer and Constanza Cordoni, Poetik, Exegese und Narrative (Vienna: Vienna University Press 2014), 81–107.

65. Guy Stroumsa, "'Caro salutis cardo': Shaping the Person in Early Christian Thought," *History of Religions* 30 (1990): 25–50; Stroumsa, "Interiorization and Intolerance in Early Christianity," in *Die Erfindung des inneren Menschen: Studien zur religiosen Anthropologie*, ed. Jan Assmann, Studien zum Verstehen fremder Religionen 6 (Gütersloh: Mohn, 1993), 168–82. This intellectual and religious transformation reached a certain maturity in the writings of Augustine, who gave unprecedented prominence to the place of free will in moral and religious life, declaring that "in the inward man dwells truth" (*De vera religione* 39.72; Augustine of Hippo, *De vera religione*, ed. Josef Martin, CCSL 32 [Turnhout: Brepols, 1962], 234), quoted in Charles Taylor, *Sources of the Self: The Making of the Modern Identity* (Cambridge: Harvard University Press, 1989), 129.

66. Levinson, "Post-Classical Narratology," 81-107.

67. See the discussion of this term in the work of Derrida in Mark W. Westmoreland, "Interruptions: Derrida and Hospitality," *Kritike* 2.1 (2008): 1–10.

Emmanuel Levinas, suggests that in some ways, ethics and hospitality are isomorphic concepts. In hospitality, opposition exists between fundamental law and social or juridical laws. Derrida presents two concepts of hospitality—unconditional and conditional. For him, conditional hospitality operates within an economy of exchange and reciprocity, whereas unconditional hospitality is given beyond norms and laws, without expecting reciprocity. He states:

> [A]bsolute hospitality requires that I open up my home and that I give not only to the foreigner, but to the absolute, unknown, anonymous other, and that I *give place* to them, that I let them come, that I let them arrive, and take place in the place I offer them, without asking of them either reciprocity (entering into a pact) or even their names.⁶⁸

Unconditional hospitality is thus an ideal rather than a feature of everyday life. It is a test of the irresolvable tensions built into the concept of hospitality. Or in the words of Derrida, "[W]e will have to negotiate constantly between these two extensions of the concept of hospitality."⁶⁹ Since unconditional hospitality sets the measure for all acts of hospitality (or inhospitality), the ideal Derrida sets is almost messianic; hospitality is still "to come"; it has not yet arrived, elusive and beyond our grasp. Perhaps it functions only as a call, but a demanding one.

Absolute hospitality, then, destabilizes existing laws and structures and compels us to challenge our ready-made judgments and our sense of self-mastery. The ideal host questions him/herself and obtains, as Derrida suggests, the interrupted self. In explaining the interrupted self, Derrida argues that by accepting the host's role one takes upon oneself the admission of guests without conditions or boundaries. Yet no one ever manages to be the perfect host.

Derrida situates his discussion of the relationship between the host and the guest (or the foreigner) in the home.⁷⁰ Absolute hospitality is an impossible form of hospitality. If the host allows his guest to do anything he wishes, the host becomes a hostage in his own home. Consequently, one cannot be hospitable unless one demotes self to Other. This is the

---

68. Jacques Derrida, *Acts of Religion*, trans. Gil Anidjar (New York: Routledge, 2002), 25.

69. See Jacques Derrida, *Of Hospitality*, trans. Rachel Bowlby, Cultural Memory in the Present (Stanford, CA: Stanford University Press, 2000).

70. To illustrate this relationship, he cites examples such as Oedipus, Abraham, Lot, Socrates, and foreigners who enter cities of refuge, mentioning fictional characters and contemporary political figures, ancient Greece and the Middle East, monotheistic worldviews, and immigration policies. In all his examples, the relationship between host and guest is reciprocal, while hospitality and welcome are deemed synonymous. See Jacques Derrida, *Adieu: To Emmanuel Levinas*, trans. Pascale-Anne Brault and Michael Naas, Meridian (Stanford, CA: Stanford University Press, 1999), 83–85; Derrida, *Of Hospitality*, 147.

interrupted self of the host who is willing to accept the guest. An "interrupted self" is a condition of alternating attraction and aversion within the same host. Derrida thus claims that hospitality cannot exist without the sovereignty of oneself over one's home, but since there is also no hospitality without finitude, sovereignty can be exercised only by filtering . . . and doing violence.[71]

For Derrida, limits and conditions are set in place to secure the host as master of the house. Guests cannot do whatever they want; wherever they go, they have to learn the local social or cultural norms in order to make their behavior acceptable to the hosts. These meditations are echoed in a rather humorous form in b. Pesah. 86b: כל מה שיאמר לך בעל הבית עשה חוץ מצא ("All that your host instructs obey; except 'be on your way!'"). However, even this playful rhetoric hints that the host, who has limited his hospitality's unconditionality, de facto loses his honorary status.

I borrow from Derrida a hermeneutic model for explaining specific cultural behavior. This model provides a useful framework for understanding the expression of cultural values in the rabbinic stories I discuss. Derrida's terminology about guests and hosts fits the contents of the stories to be analyzed below and is fruitful in shaping the discussion about the acceptance of the Other in rabbinic culture.

Now to our stories and their host/guest typology. A new arrival, or guest, stands at the door, on the border, and is welcomed inside without preconditions. This welcoming stance makes the host vulnerable to violence, which is liable to turn the home inside out, transforming the host into a guest and the guest into the master of the house. In the following pages, we will read stories about Babylonian rabbinic foreigners who enter Galilean cities. Following convention, their hosts have to accept them, accord them equal rights, and refrain from treating them as strangers. If the guests share membership in the textual community, they are also the heirs of the promised land.

The demand that the host's hospitality be unconditional leads to violence and the construction of the interrupted self. As we will see, however, this painful interruption of the self is a way of obtaining a new self.[72]

---

71. Derrida, *Acts of Religion*, 55.
72. On self-reflexivity in rabbinic texts, see Stein, *Textual Mirrors*. See also Christine Hayes "Displaced Self Perceptions: The Deployment of Minim and Romans in Bavli Sanhedrin 90b–91a," in *Religious and Ethnic Communities in Later Roman Palestine*, ed. Hayim Lapin, Studies and Texts in Jewish History and Culture 5 (Lanham, MD: University Press of Maryland, 1998), 249–89. On the interrupted self, see Westmoreland mentioned above.

6. The Structure of the Book

This book is divided into two parts. The first is based on readings from the Yerushalmi and related literature and anthologies of Amoraic Midrash (chs. 1–6), and the second on passages from the Babylonian Talmud (chs. 7–8).

Chapter 1 is dedicated to the relations between the Land of Israel and Babylonia, spatial and symbolic, as these are expressed in rabbinic literature. It analyzes meaningful metaphors shared by both cultures, as well as the Palestinian rabbis' tendency to add some dystopic nuances to the portrait of Babylonia. This brings us to an ongoing discourse on two essential loci in the Palestinian narrator's symbolic geography. Chapters 2 and 3 are concerned with the reception of Babylonian immigrants in the Palestinian rabbis' domain. Here, I discuss the Palestinian rabbis' use of the figure of the Babylonian Other in shaping their collective self. These chapters deal with mocking Babylonian newcomers. However, while the objects of mockery in chapter 2 are Babylonian simpletons and unlearned outcasts, in chapter 3, the object is the Babylonian literati, mocked by Galilean commoners. Under consideration are the Palestinian narrator's strategies as he meditates on how to be a host for a Babylonian.

Chapter 4 centers on a story about the life and death of a particular Babylonian sage and explores the appropriation of the Other's cultural values within the framework of local rabbinic culture or, in other words, how the Other becomes a part of a self.

Chapter 5 deals with a Babylonian student's rabbinic appointment in Palestine and the Palestinian rabbinic culture's search for alternative leadership. We will see that the Babylonian Other image helps clarify leadership and the structure of the rabbinic hierarchy. My readings will explore how the narrator's benevolent self tries to decide whether he must embrace the Other or erect a fence between them.

The tendency to shape Palestinian identity by distancing from the figure of the Other is discussed in chapter 6. Unlike the previous empathetic treatments of the Other, in the stories analyzed in this chapter, the narrator's antipathy toward the Other leads him to marginalize the Other eternally for his ancestors' "historical crime." The figure of one particular and very influential anti-Babylonian appears here, and his image is discussed. Chapter 7 relates to Palestinians who migrate to Babylonia. Naturally, the focus is on the ensuing conflicts, through which we will see how Babylonians reshaped their own identity. In both of these chapters, I compare the process of self-definition in these two cultures. Chapter 8 draws on texts from the Babylonian Talmud about Babylonians who migrated to the Land of Israel. Here I show how the Other–self conflict of Galilean origin was mirrored by much later Babylonian literary tradition and how the echoes of Palestinian traditions still reverberate under the new narrative tissue.

In the epilogue, a summary of previous chapters leads us to the analysis of a final rabbinic narrative. I aim to show how the split parts of the Palestinian narrator's self finally come together. The epilogue closes with a list of different rabbinic selves reflected in the analyzed literary traditions.

1

Symbolic Violence

The language of talmudic narrators reflects both the spatial and the symbolic relations between the Land of Israel and Babylonia. These relations continue to resonate in Jewish culture to this day. When a Jew immigrates to the Land of Israel, this process is (still) referred to in Hebrew as *aliyah*, literally, "ascent." If the immigrant experience is not successful and the individual returns to his land of origin, he is referred to as a *yored*, one who "descends." This metaphorical depiction of migration was common in medieval and modern times and is evident in the well-known Jewish Americanism "making *aliyah*." The notion of "ascending" to the Land of Israel from Babylonia first appears in the book of Ezra (7:6). It occurs repeatedly in rabbinic literature, usually in verb form—*'ala* in Hebrew, *salaq* in Aramaic: "Someone went up to the Land of Israel." One can easily account for this usage by observing topographical realities.

Southern Mesopotamia, where most Jews lived during the talmudic period, is located in the plains, but Palestine lies mainly in the highlands. This linguistic construction contributed to the perception that migration to the Holy Land was superior to remaining in the diaspora. Palestinian narrators clearly perceived the Land of Israel as a locus of higher status than any other foreign land, including Babylonia. However, in the case of Babylonia, it is difficult to declare it unambiguously inferior and utterly identical to the lands inhabited by the peoples of the world, because Abraham, the progenitor of the Jews, came to Canaan from Mesopotamia, that is, from Babylonia to the Land of Israel. Babylonia had always been accepted by Palestinians as the mythological birthplace of their ethnos, as evident from the statement attributed to Rabban Yoḥanan b. Zakai in t. B. Qam. 7:3, who remarks, "For what reason were the people of Israel exiled [only] to Babylonia [rather than to all] other countries? Because the house of Abraham, our father, is from there."[1] Thus, for contemporary émigrés, as for the Babylonians referred to by the Palestinian narrators,

---

1. See Yaron Z. Eliav, "The Material World of Babylonia as Seen from Roman Palestine: Some Preliminary Observations," in *The Archaeology and Material Culture of the Babylonian Talmud*, ed. Markham J. Geller, IJS Studies in Judaica 16 (Leiden: Brill, 2015), 153-85.

going West to Roman Palestine is a re-creation of the mythological route taken by the progenitor of the nation. Perhaps this analogy is an expression of the Palestinian rabbis' displeasure with the Babylonian students' desire to return to their homeland after their sojourn in the Holy Land. Here, the custom spread among the students of Palestinian rabbis of asking permission from their masters to leave the Promised Land comes to the aid of the Palestinian sages. Let us analyze this custom with the help of Pierre Bourdieu's concepts of symbolic violence and symbolic capital.

Bourdieu sees symbolic capital (e.g., prestige, honor, attention) as a crucial source of power. When holders of symbolic capital use it against agents who hold less power of this sort and seek to alter their actions, they exercise symbolic violence. Symbolic violence fundamentally imposes categories of thought upon dominated social agents who eventually accept the social order as just. It is the incorporation of unconscious structures that tend to perpetuate the structures of action of the dominant agent. In some senses, symbolic violence is much more powerful than physical violence, in that it is embedded in individuals' very modes of action and structures of cognition.[2] Symbolic power is the power to impose the principles of the cognitive construction of reality.[3] The efficacy of symbolic power, according to Bourdieu, reflects the tendency of particular modes of vision to be so deeply rooted within both the individual habitus and surrounding social fields that they are no longer understood as patterns of domination. Instead, these models of domination are rarely formally articulated but come to reflect a "preverbal," taken-for-granted understanding of the world that "flows from practical sense."[4]

Bourdieu is quite skeptical about the politically progressive nature of marginalized social groups,[5] and there is, in his analysis, a consistent tendency to examine how relations of domination are naturalized. I also seek to show, further on, how the employer of symbolic violence can end up marginalizing himself, and how that marginalization can then be used to gain power.[6]

In the following discussion, I will analyze several stories, trying to answer the question, for what purpose do the rabbis use their political

---

2. Bourdieu contends that the relations of "domination" are rarely solely secured and legitimated through overt physical violence, and he uses the concept of "symbolic power" to refer to the capacity of individuals, groups, and institutions to shape social life ("Social Space and Symbolic Power," *Sociological Theory* 7 (1989): 14–25, esp. 18–19.

3. See Pierre Bourdieu, *Outline of a Theory of Practice*, trans. Richard Nice, Cambridge Studies in Social Anthropology 16 (New York: Cambridge University Press, 1977), 165.

4. Pierre Bourdieu, *The Logic of Practice*, trans. Richard Nice (Stanford, CA: Stanford University Press, 1990), 68.

5. See James Bohman, "Reflexivity, Agency and Constraint: The Paradoxes of Bourdieu's Sociology of Knowledge," *Social Epistemology* 11 (1997): 171–86.

6. See 106 below.

influence, and what do they seek to achieve by doing so? I hope to show how Palestinian sages used symbolic violence toward their Babylonian rivals in two directions: (1) Babylonia, the land of the ancestor of Abraham, acquired the characteristics of a dystopia. (2) The arbitrary decision of their teachers limited Babylonian students' freedom of movement from the Land of Israel outward.

1.1 Dys-toping Babylonia

Distant Babylonia was imagined by the Palestinian rabbis as a dystopic place, inferior to their own land. Palestinian narrators knew about the wealth and power of the Sasanian Empire, and they were acquainted with some former Babylonian residents. It is likely, however, that the primary source of their information about the Land of Israel was the Bible. The reconstruction of this vital locus in their day was performed as a bricolage from pieces of contemporary information combined with some biblical notions, adding a dystopic intent. This is evident from the following texts, in which the dwelling place of the Babylonians is given a symbolic evaluation:

Genesis Rabbah 38:11[7]

| "Therefore, is the name of it called Babel" (Gen 11:9). A disciple of Rabbi Yoḥanan was sitting before him and could not grasp his teaching. He asked him: What is the cause of this? He answered: It is because I am exiled from my home. He asked: Whence do you come? He answered: From Borsif. He said: That is not its name, but rather Bolsif, in accordance with the verse, "Because there the Lord did confound [*balal*] the Language [*sefat*] of all the Earth" (Gen 11:9). | ["על כן קרא שמה בבל" (בראשית יא ט)] חד תלמיד מדר' יוחנן הוה יתיב קומיה. [הוה] מסבר ליה ולא סבר. אמר ליה: מא יהאי? אמר ליה: דאנא גלי מאתרי. אמר ליה: מן הידן אתר את? [אמר ליה:] מן בורסיף. אמר ליה: לא כן, אלא בולסיף, "כי שם בלל יי"י שפת כל הארץ" (בראשית יא ט). |

The student, a Babylonian immigrant, is unable to understand the lessons of his teacher, the famous Rabbi Yoḥanan. His lack of success, the student explains, is due to homesickness and feelings of dislocation. The teacher does not even consider his excuse.[8] He claims to have a better

---

7. See Theodor-Albeck, 1:360.
8. One could suggest that perhaps Rabbi Yoḥanan has nothing to say about the student's difficulties and merely comments on the name of his hometown; however, such an interpretation makes the dialogue meaningless.

explanation, based on a phonetic interpretation of a biblical verse. The city of Borsip(pa) is located close to ancient Babel (Babylon). This city's name is pronounced "Bolsippa" by Aramaic-speaking persons (due to the well-known phonetic difficulty of pronouncing the letter *r* and its subsequent exchange with *l*).⁹ The sage now explains this pronunciation as deriving from the fact that in this place, in times of old, the languages were confounded (*Bol* from *balal* means "to confound" and *sip*, from *saf*, means "language"). The Palestinian sage is knowledgeable about Babylonian topography; he is aware that Borsippa, which is not mentioned in the Bible, and ancient Babylon are quite close. Therefore, the verse could be interpreted as referring to the contemporary city as well as the ancient one. The city's name is represented as reminiscent of the ancient Tower of Babel event, which had left traces of its inhabitants' particular mental sluggishness. God had confounded the languages spoken by the builders of the Babylonian tower. From that point in history, in the view of the midrashist, the Babylonians have difficulties understanding others, and their own language is not identifiable.

An even bolder Palestinian dystopic interpretation of Babylonia appears in y. Ber. 4:1, 7a, apropos a discussion of the times of prayer.

y. Berakhot 4:1, 7b¹⁰

Rav Ada's mother's brother used to hold the cloak of Rab on the great fast. [Rab] said to him, "When you see the sun reach the tops of the palm trees, give me my cloak so that I may recite the Afternoon Prayer."	אחוי דאימיה דרב אדא הוה מצייץ גולתיה דרב בצומא רבא אמר ליה כד תיחמי שימשא בריש דיקלי תיהב לי גולתי דנצלי דמנחתא

---

9. This phonetic phenomenon is sometimes mocked in Palestinian rabbinic literature, for example, in the humoristic dialogue between Elisha ben Abuya and a lad; in its Palestinian version, see Ecclesiastes Zuta 7, 7 (Buber ed. 135) and the parallel in Ecclesiastes Rabbah (which is unfortunately omitted in the standard printed edition; see Reuven Kiperwasser, *Midrash Kohelet Rabbah 7–12: Critical Edition and Commentary* [Jerusalem: Schechter Institute Press, 2021], 56). For the time being, the reader can see a quotation of the Ecclesiastes Rabbah story in Moses Gaster, *The Exempla of the Rabbis: Being a Collection of Exempla, Apologues, and Tales Culled from Hebrew Manuscripts and Rare Hebrew Books* (London: Asia Publishing Company, 1924), 102. To explain the phenomenon mentioned above, see Menachem Kister, "Addenda to the Talmudic Lexicon" [Hebrew], in *Mehqerei Talmud II: Talmudic Studies Dedicated to the Memory of Professor Eliezer Sh. Rosenthal*, ed. M. Bar-Asher and D. Rosenthal (Jerusalem: Magnes, 1993), 431–47; and Reuven Kiperwasser, "Early and Late in Kohelet Rabbah: A Study in Redaction-criticism" [Hebrew], in *Bible and Its World, Rabbinic Literature and Jewish Law and Jewish Thought*, ed. Baruch J. Schwartz, Abraham Melamed, and Aharon Shemesh, Iggud: Selected Essays in Jewish Studies 1 (Jerusalem: Magnes, 2008), 291–312.

10. *Talmud Yerushalmi According to Ms. Or. 4720 (Scal. 3) of the Leiden University Library* (Jerusalem: Academy of the Hebrew Language, 2001), 33 (hereafter Academia ed.).

[At the time of day] when the sun is yet at the tops of the palm trees there [in Babylonia,] it is still daytime here [in the Land of Israel].	ושמשא ביר' בריש דיקלי תמן איממא הוא הכא

This halakhic case of Babylonian origin relates how, during the Yom Kippur fast, Rab requested that his disciple bring him a certain garment when the sun reached the tops of the date palms. In this manner, the teacher indicated to the student at what time he wished to recite the *minḥah* prayer. The story implies that Rab asked for his garment early, before sunset, something that seemed strange to the Palestinian editor. According to his Palestinian perception of time, the sun appeared over the date palms quite early in the day, but the Yom Kippur *minḥah* took place only late after midday. The explanation the Talmud gives is that in Babylonia, where the terrain of settlement is level, by the time the sun sank down to the treetops, it would have been close to nightfall. The answer is supported by a midrash attributed to Rabbi Yoḥanan based on Isa 44:27:

y. Berakhot 4:1, 7b[11]

As Rabbi Yoḥanan said, "Who says to the deep, 'be dry' (Isa 44:27), this is Babylon, for it is in the lowest part of the world. Said Rabbi Yoḥanan, why is it çalled "The deep"? Because there, the dead of the Deluge were submerged. [This verse supports this teaching:] "Babylon must fall for the slain of Israel, as in Babylon have fallen the slain of all the earth" (Jer. 51:49).	דמר רבי יוחנן: "האומר לצולה חרבי" (ישעיהו מד כז), זו בבל שהיא זוטו של עולם. אמר רבי יוחנן: למה נקרא שמה "צולה"? ששם צללו מיתי דור המבול. גם "בבבל לנפול חללי ישר' גם בבבל נפלו חללי כל הארץ" (ירמיה נא מט).

This interpretation is far from a dry topographical description of the inhabited world. It gives a specific symbolic evaluation of Babylonia: it is the lowest place in the world. All the dead bodies, which are a source of impurity, pass through this geographical location, as though it were the drainage system. As in a city, its lowest part is not a particularly respected area. The lowest part is the last part where you are likely to meet live people; beneath it, you will find only the dead and garbage.[12] The description of Babylonian geography as inferior continues in the following midrashic composition, dealing with the Tower of Babel:

---

11. Academia ed., 33. See Herman, "Babylonia: A Diaspora Center."
12. This geographic location in the Babylonian Talmud (b. Pesah. 87b), on the other hand, is interpreted as one of the most significant in their land for the eschatological future; see 36 below.

y. Berakhot 4:1, 7b[13]

"They found a valley in the land of Shinar and settled there" (Gen 11:2). Said Resh Laqish, why did they call it "Shinar"? Because all the corpses of the generation of the flood were dumped [*nin'aru*] there.	"וימצאו בקעה בארץ שנער וישבו שם" (בראשית יא ב). אמר ריש לקיש: למה נקרא שמה שנער? ששם ננערו מיתי דור המבול.

Here Resh Laqish, expounding on the nature of Babylonia, cites the next verse, Gen 11:12, mentioning Shinar, which, strictly speaking, is not a synonym for Babylon. On a poetic level of interpretation, however, it is perceived as a substitute for the events related to the story of the Tower of Babel. His interpretation is again based on wordplay—the toponym is phonetically close to the word that can be translated as "poured out." Once again, it turns out that this land of biblical prehistory constitutes the last resting place for all dead bodies.[14] The midrash continues with other negative remarks about Babylonia:

y. Berakhot 4:1, 7b[15]

Another explanation: "Shinar" Because they are dying in torment, they are without oil lamps [*nr*], because they are without a bathhouse.	דבר אח': "שנער" שהם מתים בתשנוק, בלא נר, בלא מרחץ.

The anonymous interpreter seem to be speaking here not about the biblical Babel but about the Babylonia of his own time. It is difficult to say why he describes the Babylonians as dying in torment. The details here are obscure, but it is clear that the exegete perceives the Babylonians' land as a sick place, damaging to one's health. Samuel Krauss, who first argued for this explanation, supported his claims with other Palestinian traditions, which maintain that there is a sickness in Babylonia stemming from the inferior quality of its water and its inhabitants' bad drinking habits.[16] Possibly, as also suggested by Krauss,[17] the sickness is related to their deprivation of the light from oil lamps, having no olive oil in Babylonia for this purpose. Babylonians used sesame oil, which does not adhere well to

---

13. Academia ed., 33. See Herman, "Babylonia: A Diaspora Center."
14. An abbreviated parallel to this tradition appears in Gen. Rab. 37:4 (Theodor-Albeck, 1:346); see further 29.
15. Academia ed., 33. See Herman, "Babylonia: A Diaspora Center."
16. See Samuel Krauss, *Kadmoniot Ha-Talmud* [Hebrew], 4 vols. (Berlin and Vienna: Benjamin Herz Krauss 1896–1948), 1:18.
17. Ibid., 1:17.

wicks and is not customarily used in baths. Moreover, in Babylonia, they did not have the public baths that had been brought to Palestine by the Romans, because these were considered sacrilegious by the Zoroastrian Sasanians.[18]

y. Berakhot 4:1, 7b[19]	Genesis Rabbah 37:4[20]
דבר אחר: "שנער" שהן מנוערין מן המצות. בלא תרומ' ובלא מעשר.	"שנער" שמנוערת ממצוות. לא תרומה, ולא מעשרות, לא שביעית.
Another explanation: "Shinar," because they are stripped [mnw'ryn] of the commandments without heave offerings [terumah] or tithes.	"Shinar" means that it is emptied [shemenu 'eret] of commandments, of terumah, tithes, and the Sabbatical year.

Additionally, the Babylonians were not obligated in the important religious duties of *terumah* and tithes, because these obligations devolved only upon those who were located in the Land of Israel.[21]

y. Berakhot 4:1, 7b[22]	Genesis Rabbah 37:4[23]
..'דבר אחר: "שנע", ששריה מתי' נערי	["שנער"] ששריה מתים נערים. "שנער" ששריה מביטים בתורה עד שהם נערים.
Another explanation: "Shinar," because its officials die as lads [ne'arim].	"Shinar" means that its princes [sareah] die young [ne'arim]. "Shinar" because its princes consult the Torah only as long as they are youths.

To this rather extensive list of differences between Babylonia and Palestine, the narrator adds the early deaths of certain high Babylonian officials (perhaps referring to the Resh Galuta family?).[24] A parallel version of this

---

18. I explain this difference in the urban culture of Roman Palestine and Sasanian Babylonia farther on; see 67–68.
19. Academia ed., 33. See Herman, "Babylonia: A Diaspora Center,"
20. Theodor-Albeck, 1:346
21. This motif appeared previously, see 9 above.
22. Academia ed., 33.
23. Theodor-Albeck, 1:346
24. The Exilarch is commonly perceived in the Bavli as a prince (שר). An example appears in the homily from b. Hul. 92a: "'For you have striven [with God and people]'" (Gen 32:21). Rabbah said: This alludes to two princes who shall come forth from him, the Exilarch in Babylonia, and the Patriarch in Palestine." See the analyses of this text in Herman, *Prince without a Kingdom*, 211, 274–75. As he explains, the word שר did not always refer to this noble family. Because of our text's brevity and puzzling ambiguity, it is unclear that it refers to the family of the Resh Galuta. If it does refer to them, however, we see here a harsh critique of this leadership.

tradition in Gen. Rab. 37:4 offers similar explanations for the word *Shinar*, but instead of referring to the early death, it adds a detail: a land whose Jewish leaders study Torah only as youths, but do not continue studying as adults. The text continues:

y. Berakhot 4:1, 7b[25]

Another explanation: "Shinar," because it produced an enemy and hater [*sone' we'er*] of the Holy One, blessed be He. And who was that? The evil Nebuchadnezzar.	דבר אחר: "שנער" שהעמידה שונא וער להקב״ה. ואי זה? זה נבוכר נצר הרשע.

The pericope ends by referring to another biblical episode—Nebuchadnezzar, the destroyer of the Temple.

It appears, however, that this passage mainly expresses the idea that the distant and obscure Babylonia, despite being the mythological birthplace of the Jewish people, has become a nightmarish place with appalling living conditions, deprivation, oppression, and terror; almost everything there is undesirable or frightening.[26] The Palestinian Talmud creates a monstrous myth of Babylonia and surrounds this remarkable locus with pejorative connotations.

Nevertheless, from a Palestinian perspective, Babylonia, despite these dystopic features, bears a strong significance and a connection to Palestine. After all, the Palestinians share with the Babylonians a language, a culture, and a relationship to the Land of Israel, as evident in the following pericope.

y. Ma'aser Sheni 5:2, 56a[27]

One man was plowing when his cow ran away, and he ran after it; it ran further, and he pursued it. He ended up in Babylonia. They asked him: When did you leave? He said to them: Earlier today. They said to him: What route	חד בר נש הוה קאים רדי. פסקת תורתי׳ קומוי. הוות פריא והוא פרי. פריא והוא פרי. עד דאשתכח יהיב בבבל. אמרו ליה: אימת נפקת? אמר לון: יומא דין. אמרין: בהיידא אתיתא? אמ׳ לון: בדא. אמר לון: אית אחמי לן. נפק בעי מיחמיי אלון ולא חכים בהיידא

---

25. Academia ed., 33.

26. See, e.g., Erika Gottlieb, *Dystopian Fiction East and West: Universe of Terror and Trial* (Montreal: McGill-Queen's University Press, 2001).

27. Academia ed., 305. See Fraenkel, *Studies in the Spiritual World*, 156–59; and recently Dina Stein, "The Wild Goat Chase Models of Diaspora and Salvation" [Hebrew], *Jewish Studies* 51 (2016): 93–130, esp. 101–2; and even more recently the English version of this paper, "Following Goats: Text, Place and Diasporas," in *Talmudic Transgressions: Engaging the Work of Daniel Boyarin*, ed. Charlotte Elisheva Fonrobert et al., JSJSup 181 (Leiden: Brill, 2017), 523–37.

did you take? He said to them: This one. They said to him: Show it to us. He tried to show the road but didn't know which one he took.

An unnamed simple plowman is working his field, that is, performing an everyday, routine chore. But something extraordinary, if not wondrous, occurs during this ordinary day: a cow breaks free of its yoke.[28] Wishing to escape the hated furrow, the cow chooses to escape on a path unknown to the plowman, despite his repeatedly passing over it. The cow is bent on changing its lot in life, and the owner, running to catch his animal, suddenly finds himself in a place where he had never been before, in a foreign land named Babylonia.[29] There, local people immediately identify him as a stranger, probably because of his accent or dress. When they learn that he has arrived from the Land of Israel, having left it on that very same day, they ask him to show them this excellent shortcut leading to the Land of Israel. However, the plowman has gone this way not by choice but by accident, and now he is no longer able to find the path he took in pursuing his cow. The short trail that leads to the Holy Land is now hidden, not only from the unlucky plowman but also from the Babylonian Jews.

Palestinian narrators, like other residents of the Roman Empire, had no doubt heard about the wealth of the Sasanian Empire and the natural splendor of Mesopotamia. From their sacred texts, they were aware of Babylonia's status as the Jewish people's cradle, the homeland of Abraham. At the same time, wanting to emphasize the authority of the Land of Israel to the proud Babylonian emigrants, they added many dystopic elements to the symbolic geography of Babylonia, derived from both biblical history and contemporary geography. Babylonia has become a land of obscure language and verbal misunderstandings, a land of darkness, bad hygiene, and early mortality. One who comes from there to the Land of Israel ascends from a low place to a high one. He will accept the gift of the Promised Land with gratitude, having forgotten the way back. The secret passage through which the Babylonians will cross easily into the Land of Israel in the future is ready—but none of them knows it.

---

28. This plot's possible intention is that the animal, not having human intelligence and being much closer to nature, could sense something inaccessible to its owner. Regarding a similar motif in rabbinic literature, see Lam. Rab. 1 (Buber ed., 89–90) and y. Ber. 2:4, 5a; and Fraenkel, *Studies in the Spiritual World*, 159.

29. Not infrequently, humans act as automatons, performing habitual actions and moving in familiar circles. Like a prisoner in Plato's Cave, he sees only the limited view that is before his eyes. About the theme of routine living in antithesis to the life of full awareness in the context of this story, see Fraenkel, *Studies in the Spiritual World*, 157.

1.2 Seeking Permission

The Palestinian sages, distributing their knowledge and their symbolic capital among their students, aimed to control them, employing their symbolic power, and not neglecting symbolic violence. This is evident, for example, in a custom that they established according to which a student who wishes to leave the Land of Israel must first ask permission to do so from his master. The following story is a representative example of the custom, widespread among Rabbi Yoḥanan's disciples, both Palestinian and Babylonian.[30]

y. Berakhot 3:1, 6a–b[31]

Rabbi Yasa heard that his mother had come to Bosra.[32] He went to ask Rabbi Yoḥanan whether he may go out [of the country] to meet her.[33] He said to him: If you wish to go [to protect her] because of the road's dangers, then go. If you want to go to honor your mother, then I do not know whether to allow you to go or not.	ר׳ יסא שמע דאתת אימיה לבוצרה. אתא שאל לר׳ יוחנן, מהו לצאת? א״ל: אי מפני סכנת דרכי׳, צא. אי משו׳ כבוד אביו ואמו, איני יודע.
Said Rabbi Shmuel bar Rab Itzhak: Rabbi Yoḥanan is still in doubt concerning this issue. Because [Yasa] pressured Rabbi Yoḥanan, he said: If you have decided to go, then may you return in peace. Rabbi Eleazar heard this and said: There is no greater permission than this.	א״ר שמואל בר רב יצחק: עוד היא צריכה. אטרח ר׳ יוחנן עלוי ומר: אם גמרת לצאת תבא בשלום. שמע ר׳ אלעזר ומר: אין רשו׳ גדולה מזו.

Rabbi Yasa is a Babylonian who is probably looking to leave the Land of Israel.[34] When he hears that his mother is changing her place of resi-

---

30. The parallels, y. Naz. 7:1, 56a, y. Shev. 6:2, 36c, are simple doublets of the tradition. A very distant parallel of the tradition appears in b. Qidd. 31b; see Admiel Kosman, *Gender and Dialogue in the Rabbinic Prism*, Studia Judaica 50 (Berlin: de Gruyter, 2012), 108–26.

31. Academia ed., 26. The story was analyzed by Louis Ginzberg, *A Commentary on the Palestinian Talmud* [Hebrew], 4 vols., Texts and Studies of the Jewish Theological Seminary of America 10–12, 21 (New York: Jewish Theological Seminary, 1941–1961), 2:99–100; Shulamit Valler, *Women and Womanhood in the Talmud*, trans. Betty Sigler Rozen, BJS 321 (Atlanta: Scholars Press, 1999), 114; and Kosman, *Gender and Dialogue*, 127–28.

32. See 137 n. 43 below.

33. He does not explain why. One can hypothesize, but I think that he intends to leave the Land of Israel and join his mother, never to return.

34. About his uneasy absorption in the Land of Israel, see 66 below. According to the Babylonian version of the story, he used this opportunity and went to Bosra to meet his

dence, he sees an opportunity. R. Yasa requests permission to leave the Land in order to greet his mother in the Syrian city of Bosra. From his master's answer, we learn the two possible reasons for exiting the Land of Israel: first, to protect women from potential dangers on the road, and, second, to honor a parent, namely, to fulfill a religious commandment. For Rabbi Yoḥanan, the sojourn of a Jew in the Land of his ancestors is more important than the sacred obligation to honor one's parents. Nonetheless, the case does involve a woman on the road, and, following the student's insistence, the master blesses Rabbi Yasa's travel with the phrase, "Return in peace." Thus, even this permission is granted on the condition of the student's return to the Land.

In the next example, the commandment to honor a biological mother is not discussed, but the Land as a metaphorical mother appears.

y. Mo'ed Qatan 3:1, 71c[35]

A priest came to Rabbi Ḥanina. He said to him: What is the law about going to Tyre to perform a religious duty [mitsvah], to deliver the rite of halitsah, or to enter into levirate marriage? He said to him: Your brother went abroad. Blessed is the Omnipresent, who has smitten him. And now you want to do the same thing?	חד כהן אתא לגבי ר׳ חנינה. אמ׳ ליה: מהו לצאת לצור לעשות דבר מצוה, לחלוץ או לייבם? אמ׳ ליה: אחיו של אותו האיש יצא. ברוך המקום שנגפו. ואת מבקש לעשות כיוצא בו?
Some wish to say that this is what he said to him: Your brother left the bosom of his mother, and embraced the bosom of a foreign woman, and blessed be He who smote him! And now you wish to do the same thing?	אית דבעי מימר, הכין אמר ליה: אחיו של אותו האיש הניח חיק אמו וחיבק חיק נכריה, וברוך שנגפו, ואת מבקש לעשות כיוצא בו?
Shimeon bar Ba came to Rabbi Ḥanina. He said to him: Write me a letter of recommendation since I am going abroad to make a living. He said to him: Tomorrow I go to your ancestors, and they will say to me: That single precious sapling that we had in the Land of Israel have you permitted to go forth from the Land?	שמעון בר בא אתא לגבי רבי חנינה. אמר ליה: כתוב לי חדא איגרא דאיקר. ניפוק לפרנסתי לארעא ברייתא. אמר לו: למחר אני הולך אצל אבותיך, יהו אומרים לי: נטיעה אחת של חמדה שהיתה לנו בארץ ישר׳ התרתה לה לצאת לחוץ לארץ?

---

mother, but she passed away before his arrival. It seems that he never returned to the Land of Israel.

35. Academia ed., 809.

These stories occur in the context of a discussion about Israelites and priests cutting their hair during a festival; they pertain to priests leaving the Land of Israel for a given period. Two cases are discussed, one of which has two different versions of its finale.[36] In both, Rabbi Ḥanina, a former Babylonian who, not without drama, became an exemplary Palestinian sage,[37] warns one priest and one rabbi, questioning their motivation for leaving the Holy Land. In the second variant of the rabbi's warning to the priest, the "mother/stepmother" metaphor reappears. The priest is represented as a stupid child who does not want to be nursed by his own mother, looking instead for nourishment in the bosom of a "strange woman." To leave the mother for a strange woman is evil, according to R. Ḥanina. The Land of Israel symbolizes the real mother, and any other land is always "the other woman."[38] Therefore, a son of the promised land must always obey his natural mother, whatever the quality of her caretaking may be, and no matter how attractive he finds his stepmother.[39]

Although the second case does not feature the mother/stepmother metaphor, it bears relevance to our discussion. Shimon bar Va is a Babylonian immigrant who has not managed to become acculturated in the Land of Israel.[40] Now he seeks the help of his Palestinian master to assist him in making a new life abroad. Presumably, he wants to go back to Babylonia with a letter of recommendation from this teacher. The master's answer is a politely formulated refusal. The narrator has his honored hero (i.e., the master) articulate the ideal behavior of the Babylonian Other: he should embrace his birth mother's bosom, even if he suffers in her house.

I offer now one Palestinian story about a Babylonian who seeks permission to leave the Land, which I will later analyze in depth:

y. Berakhot 2:8, 5c[41]

| [Kahana] said: ... I shall go and descend from here. [Before] he left, he came to Rabbi Yoḥanan and asked him: If a person's mother despises him, but the wife of his father respects him, where should he go? [Rabbi Yoḥanan] said to him: He | אמר: ... ניזול וניחות לי מן הן דסליקית. אתא לגבי רבי יוחנן. א"ל: בר נש דאימיה מבסרא ליה, ואיתתיה דאבוהי מוקרא ליה, להן ייזיל ליה? א"ל: ייזיל להן דמוקרין ליה. נחת ליה כהנא מן הן. דסלק, אתון אמרין ליה לר' יוחנן: הא נחית כהנא לבבל. אמר: |

---

36. See 33 above.
37. See further chapter 6 below.
38. See further 35–37, 55–60, 174–76 for other usages of the same metaphor.
39. Therefore, it is typical of the "folkloristic" approach that the real mother is always better than the stepmother, see n. 43 below.
40. Chanoch Albeck, *Introduction to the Talmud Bavli and Yerushalmi* [Hebrew] (Tel Aviv: Dvir, 1969), 268.
41. Academia ed., 22–23.

should go to where he is honored. Kahana descended from here. After he left, they came and said to Rabbi Yoḥanan: Kahana has descended to Babylonia. He asked: Would he leave without asking permission? They said to him: That which he asked you was (from his point of view) asking permission.

מה הוה מיזל ליה דלא מיסב רשותא? אמרין ליה: ההיא מילתא דאמר לך היא הוה נטילת רשות דידיה.

Kahana has decided to leave the Land of Israel, and he expresses this desire explicitly. When it comes to securing his master's permission for this move, however, the situation changes. He dare not broach the subject directly. Instead, he presents a hypothetical halakhic case: a man seeks his mother's love, but she shows him no sign of affection. There is a stepmother, however, in the picture, who loves the young man and takes care of him.[42] To whom should he turn? Rabbi Yoḥanan, not expecting to be manipulated by a student, takes the bait. The boy should of course go to where he is loved. In this manner, the clever student manages to secure permission to return to his homeland.

These stories belong to a familiar genre in which students seek their masters' permission to leave the Land of Israel and are usually refused; almost no reason is considered good enough to justify such departure. Indeed, not to leave the Land of Israel is a rabbinic norm with a clear political message. The Palestinian rabbis want people of their own kind in the Land of their ancestors, and they are willing to employ their power to keep their people there. Naturally, this power could be used only with the consent of both parties. Students were obedient to their teachers due to the structures of power in the academy. From this point of view, the second (p. 33) of the above stories has particular bearing on our inquiry. In it, the person obedient to rabbinic instruction is named *kohen*, a priest—that is, a member of the ancient Jewish religious elite, a genealogy that imparts power to its holder. The rabbis thus wielded the power of religious instruction, a form of symbolic violence, to ensure that the Land of Israel would be populated by people of desirable origin and appropriate status.

---

42. The opposition of mother/stepmother also appears in b. Ta'an 20a: "People say: Better are the lashes of a mother than the kisses of the father's wife." The saying appears in only one of the manuscripts; see Henry Malter, *The Treatise Ta'anit of the Babylonian Talmud* [Hebrew] (New York: American Academy for Jewish Research, 1930), 79 n. 20. It introduces the concept of the wicked stepmother, a well-known folkloristic motif; see Tal Ilan, *Feminist Commentary on the Babylonian Talmud*, vol. 2.9, *Massekhet Ta'anit* (Tübingen Mohr Siebeck, 2008), 194–95. Kahana's parable disproves the traditional folkloristic motif that the biological mother is always good for the child, while the stepmother is always bad.

A textual counterpart of this model, found in the Babylonian Talmud, presents a different picture:[43]

b. Pesahim 87b

Rabbi Ḥiyya taught: What is meant by the verse: "God understands the way thereof, and He knows the place thereof" (Job 28:23)? The Holy One, blessed be He, knew that Israel was unable to endure the decrees of Rome; therefore, He exiled them to Babylonia.	רבי חייא: מאי דכתיב: "אלהים הבין דרכה והוא ידע את מקומה" (איוב כח כג)? יודע הקדוש ברוך הוא את ישראל שאינן יכולין לקבל גזרות של רומיים, לפיכך הגלה אותם לבבל.
Rabbi Eleazar said: The Holy One, blessed be He, exiled Israel to Babylonia only because it is as deep as the netherworld, for it is said: "I shall ransom them from the power of Sheol; I shall redeem them from death." (Hos 13:14).	ואמר רבי אלעזר: לא הגלה הקדוש ברוך הוא את ישראל לבבל אלא מפני שעעמוקה כשאול, שנאמר: "מיד שאול אפדם ממות אגאלם" (הושע יג יד).
Rabbi Ḥanina said: Because their language is akin to the language of the Torah.	רבי חנינא אמר: מפני שקרוב לשונם ללשון תורה.
Rabbi Yoḥanan said: Because He sent them back to their mother's house. It may be compared to a man who becomes angry with his wife: Whither does he send her? To her mother's house.	רבי יוחנן אמר: מפני ששיגרן לבית אמן. משל לאדם שכעס על אשתו, להיכן משגרה? לבית אמה.

We are presented here with four reasons why Babylonia, as a country of exile, is better than other possible locations: (1) Divine plan—knowing that Rome would eventually rule over the Land of Israel, God had prepared a place for Jews in Babylonia, whose laws would always be more lenient than the Roman ones. (2) Geographical position: Babylonia is located "very low" and thus close to the underworld. It would not be difficult for its inhabitants to join the freshly resurrected crowd in the eschatological era.[44] (3) In Babylonia, people speak in the language of the Torah.[45] And

---

43. I will continue to show how the Bavli will mirror Palestinian traditions, inverting them according to its own cultural values; see below.

44. Interestingly, the same geographical location in a Palestinian midrash is interpreted as having a dystopic nature; see 27 above.

45. In Babylonia, the spoken language was Aramaic. Moreover, according to this criterion, some other countries also fit this requirement.

(4) Babylonia is the place from which the Jewish people emerged. Curiously, Babylonia is represented here as the Jews' motherland on the symbolic level of a birth mother who gave birth to a child, namely, a daughter. The Land of Israel is the family of this daughter's husband, her "new parents"—meaning, the spouse's parents, who are not the girl's biological parents but who are called parents after her nuptials.

This perception of Babylonia as "mother" and the Land of Israel as the "new home" of the "spouse's family" may be a Babylonian concept developed in a much later period and pseudepigraphically attributed to Rabbi Yoḥanan.[46] However, it could be contemporaneous with our story. Therefore, the narrator ascribes to his Babylonian hero the familiar motif of this Palestinian rhetoric: the Land of Israel is the mother of all the Jews but is cruel to the Babylonians, poor sons of a good-natured biological mother.

It is the Palestinian sages, then, as the prominent participants in the scholarly hierarchical structure, who possess symbolic capital—prestige and honor. From this capital, they draw their strength. Babylonian emigrants also possess a share of symbolic wealth and strength, but to a much lesser extent. The primary holders of symbolic capital use it against agents who hold less power of this sort, exercising symbolic violence to keep the Babylonians subdued to the values of the rabbinic hierarchical framework. Palestinian rabbinic leaders impose their categories of thought and perception on all Palestinian textual community members, who take the social order to be just. Babylonian rabbis, possessing their own symbolic capital, and perhaps even holding a monopoly on all the available symbolic wealth, rewrote the dystopic depiction of their land and recast metaphors according to their own categories of thought, imposing their social order on the members of their textual community.

---

46. It is not entirely surprising that the diasporic rabbinic community in Babylonia neutralizes the component of place in its corporate identity. Perhaps only in this exilic community, which famously vied with Palestine for hegemony, was it possible to replace a physical homeland with a textual one, as recently proposed by Boyarin, *Traveling Homeland*, 44: "the concepts of homeland and Holy Land are thus, at least for these Rabbis not coterminous." The narrative discussed here seems a possible illustration of his idea that the Babylonian project envisions a "deterritorialized diaspora" (20) wherein "the Babylonian Talmud replaces Babylon, which has replaced Palestine as the homeland" (18). The variations introduced in the Babylonian version exemplify his point that "what renders Jewry diasporic are the connections with other Jews in other places all over the world, owing to common discourses and practices, primarily the study of Talmud" (21).

2

Mocking Babylonians

Palestinian rabbinic literature often poked fun at devout Babylonians, sometimes with a tinge of benevolence, sometimes with menacing severity.[1] And yet, in distancing themselves and mocking the internal Other, its authors were shaping their own identity, cultivating their distinctiveness.[2] The following analyses of Palestinian stories illustrate Palestinian stereotypes about Babylonians.

Stereotypes about minorities among a majority are quite common. The characteristic chosen for that purpose is usually something that the mocker sees as significant for himself. According to Alan Dundes, however, an ethnic slur, often has its origin in the mocked society, and only then becomes common property.[3] In this manner, an invented ethnic slur becomes part of a constructed identity. When dealing with minorities of late antique Jewish communities, it is difficult to know if these mocked identity markers came from within or from without. As we will see, however, the self-mockery of Babylonians is only partially in agreement with Palestinian anti-Babylonian slurs. Below, I present a list of Palestinian identity-shaping stereotypes about the Babylonians, illustrated by examples in the following sections of this chapter.

1. Babylonians are preoccupied with the idea of the resurrection of the dead. The Babylonian, who shares the Palestinian belief that the Land of Israel is the only platform for the resurrection of the dead in the eschatological era, is ready to commit senseless acts in order to be buried in the Land of Israel.

2. Babylonians are preoccupied with the superiority of their origins and the purity of their lineage. Yet, in the Palestinians' perspective, they often commit impure actions despite their pure origins. As a result, they

---

1. See Samuel Krauss, *Persia and Rome in Talmud and Midrash* [Hebrew] (Jerusalem: Mossad ha-Rav Kook, 1948); see also Catherine Hezser, "Samuel Krauss' Contribution to the Study of Judaism, Christianity, and Graeco-Roman Culture within the Context of *Wissenschaft* Scholarship," *Modern Judaism* 33 (2013): 1–31.

2. See recently Boyarin, *Traveling Homeland*, 46–53. See further 42–51.

3. See Alan Dundes, "A Study of Ethnic Slurs: The Jew and the Polack in the United States," *Journal of American Folklore* 84, 332 (1971): 186–203.

give birth to *mamzerim* [sing: *mamzer*, one who cannot join the congregation of Israel for reasons of impaired parentage, e.g., if born from a man's illicit union with a married woman], who often emigrate to the Holy Land.[4] In other words, these people of pure lineage bring Babylonians their sons whom we cannot marry, some of them because they are too pure, others because they are outcasts.[5]

3. Babylonians are proud of their land of Babylonia, the homeland of Abraham, but in fact it is a dark land in which there are less remarkable fruits than in Palestine, there is no good olive oil, and hygienic practices leave much to be desired.[6]

All this may or may not reflect how the Babylonians viewed their own identity, but it does show the main outline of the Babylonian identity according to the most basic, stereotyped Palestinian approach.

At this point, I wish to make some preliminary remarks regarding humor in rabbinic stories, a topic upon which I will later elaborate in greater depth.[7]

In her seminal study "Laughter in Ancient Rome," Mary Beard asks, "How comprehensible, in any terms, can Roman laughter now be? How can we understand what made the Romans laugh, without falling into the trap of turning them into a version of ourselves?"[8] These questions are highly relevant to the present topic. In this regard, as the reader may question my designation of specific texts as humorous, I offer a brief survey of humor theories.[9] I begin with Alexandre G. Mitchell, who notes:

---

4. This term will be explained further, 47 n. 28.

5. Babylonians themselves mocked their own obsession with purity of lineage, see further 163.

6. See 29 above.

7. The definitive work about rabbinic humor is still unwritten, but I shall here list a few studies on the subject: Rella Kushelevsky, "The Function of Humor in Three Versions of the Theme 'Rabbi Joshua Ben Levi and the Angel of Death'" [Hebrew], *Jerusalem Studies in Jewish Folklore* 19–20 (1998): 329–44; Eliezer Diamond, "But Is It Funny? Identifying Humor, Satire, and Parody in Rabbinic Literature," in *Jews and Humor*, ed. Leonard J. Greenspoon, Studies in Jewish Civilization 22, Proceedings of the Twenty-Second Annual Symposium of the Klutznick Chair in Jewish Civilization Harris Center for Judaic Studies, (West Lafayette, IN: Purdue: University Press, 2011), 33–53; Arkady B. Kovelman, *Between Alexandria and Jerusalem: The Dynamic of Jewish and Hellenistic Culture*, Brill Reference Library of Judaism 21 (Leiden: Brill, 2005), 82–83; Daniel Boyarin, *Socrates and the Fat Rabbis* (Chicago: University of Chicago Press, 2009), esp. 191–92; Tal Ilan, "The Joke in Rabbinic Literature: Home-born or Diaspora Humor?" in *Humor in Arabic Culture*, ed Georges Tamer (Berlin: de Gruyter, 2009), 57–75; Carol Bakhos, "Reading against the Grain: Humor and Subversion in Midrashic Literature," in *Narratology, Hermeneutics, and Midrash: Jewish, Christian, and Muslim from Late Antiquity through to Modern Times*, ed. Gerhard Langer and Constanza Cordoni, Poetik, Exegese und Narrative (Vienna: Vienna University Press, 2014), 71–80.

8. Mary Beard, *Laughter in Ancient Rome: On Joking, Tickling, and Cracking Up*, Sather Classical Lectures 71 (Berkeley: University of California Press, 2015), 18, 27.

9. Thus, a major part of Erich Gruen's book (*Diaspora: Jews amidst Greeks and Romans*

> Comic genres and mechanisms are similar in all cultures, but reference points and taboos differ, sometimes dramatically, in time and place. Humor keeps shifting from category to category and cannot be fitted neatly into clean-cut theories.[10]

Thus, the fact that a modern reader does not find an example of ancient humor funny does not mean that the example was not, in fact, humorous at some time in history. Of course, scholars of humor are not immune to overinterpretation.[11] When studying humor in rabbinic stories, one needs to observe how different a potentially comical image is from its "serious" model or "usual" situation. It is hard to know if a freestanding image was intended to be comical. For instance, the arrival of a foreigner to the Holy Land is not an inherently comic situation. However, it is normally framed by the citation of biblical verses and the performance of significant deeds in a serious setting. To make this situation a comic one, the narrator must add a deliberate dose of incongruity, as will be shown below.

With respect to humor theories, I aim to balance two approaches. The first is "Superiority Theory," which assumes that laughter is generated by a feeling of *Schadenfreude*, that is, pleasure at another's misfortunes or inferiority. The second approach is "Incongruity Theory," which proposes that laughter is generated by realizing the ridiculousness or absurdity of a situation or object. Additionally, I aim to show that laughter opens a moment of potential rupture in the continuity of interactions. In other words, laughter catalyzes some reorganization, which redirects the interaction toward continuity and away from chaos. For Simon Critchley, jokes and humor operate partially as distancing devices, inviting us to view the world awry.[12] In the process of laughing, we are not only freed from common sense; we also recognize the misrepresentations, shortcuts,

---

[Cambridge: Harvard University Press, 2002], 135–212) seeks to show that popular literature of the Jewish diaspora (whether written there or read there) is marked by humor, comic intent, and playfulness. Gruen then uses the comic features of this literature as further support for his positive reconstruction of the situation of Jews in the diaspora. This approach has received critique; see Tom Robinson, review of *Diaspora: Jews amidst Greeks and Romans*, by Erich S. Gruen, *Bryn Mawr Classical Review* 2002.10.33, https://bmcr.brynmawr.edu/2002/2002.10.33/.

10. Alexandre G. Mitchell, review of *Looking at Laughter: Humor, Power, and Transgression in Roman Visual Culture, 100 B.C.–A.D. 250*, by John R. Clarke, *Bryn Mawr Classical Review* 2008.09.55, http://bmcr.brynmawr.edu/2008/2008-09-55.html.

11. See, e.g., John R. Clarke, *Looking at Laughter: Humor, Power, and Transgression in Roman Visual Culture, 100 B.C.–A.D. 250* (Berkeley: University of California Press, 2007), 9. For a fascinating chapter on the history of humor criticism, see Paul Lewis, *Comic Effects: Interdisciplinary Approaches to Humor in Literature* (Albany: State University of New York Press, 1989), 1–30.

12. See Simon Critchley, *On Humour*, Thinking in Action (London: Routledge, 2011), 14; Beard, *Laughter in Ancient Rome*, 197 n. 54.

and occlusions on which common sense rests. Analyzing appearances of mockery below, I will show that ridicule in our context does not make the Other inferior or minimize his importance, nor is it intended to alienate him. Intentionally, trying to subject the system of coexistence with an Other to a shock through the use of laughter, the narrator nevertheless seeks to return afterwards to the previously inhabited borders and ensure the continuity of order (albeit an updated one).

2.1 A Babylonian Fool

In the following story, the protagonist is not a rabbi but rather a man-on-the-street, a Babylonian stranger who finds himself in a position that does not befit his status.

Leviticus Rabbah 22:4:[13]

| A tale of a certain man who was ascending from Babylonia. He sat down to rest on the road. He saw two birds fighting with each other, and one of them killed the other. The surviving bird went to fetch some herbs and, by placing them on the other bird, revived her. He said: It would be a good deed, if I take some of these herbs and revive in addition to that the dead of the Land of Israel. As he was running and going up, he saw a dead fox decaying on the road. He said: It would be a good thing, if I try the same on this fox. He placed [the herbs] on him and revived him. He continued going up until he reached [the] Ladder of Tyre.[14] When he arrived at [the] Ladder of Tyre, he saw a lion, slain and decaying on the | עובדא הוה בחד גבר דהוה סלק מן בבל. יתיב למקרטא באורחא וחמא תרתין ציפריא מתכתשין באורחא חדא עם חדא וקטלת חדא מנהון חברתא. אזלת ההיא אחריתי ואיתיית עשב ויהבית עלה ואחיית יתה. אמ': טב לי נסב מן הדין עישבא מסיק מחיי מיתיא דארע דישראל. מיפרי וסליק חמה תעל מית מקלק באורחא, אמ' טב לי מנסייא בהדין תעלה. ויהב עילוי וייחי. והלך וסליק עד שהגיע לסולמי דצור. כיון שהגיע לסולמי צור חמא חד ארי קטיל מקליק באורחא. אמ': טב לי מנסייא בהדין אריא. יהב עילוי מן ההוא עישבא וחיה. קם ואכלתיה. הוא דברייתא אמרין טב לביש תעביד, טב לביש לא תעביד וביש לא מטי לך. |

---

13. Mordecai Margulies, *Midrash Wayyikra Rabbah: A Critical Edition Based on Manuscripts and Genizah Fragments with Variants and Notes*, 5 vols. (New York: JTS Press, 1972), 3:508. Some parallels in rabbinic literature are mentioned there.

14. This toponym is frequently mentioned in rabbinic literature as the gate to the Land of Israel (see y. Nez. BQ 4:3 4a; Gen. Rab. 39:1). Already Josephus mentions a mountain located nineteen miles from Acco, named by locals the Ladder of Tyre (*War* 2.188). In rabbinic literature, this toponym was used to mark the road that passed near the city of Tyre, along the seashore near the mountain.

road. He said: It would be a good thing if I try the same on this lion. He placed some of the herbs on [the lion], and it came back to life and devoured [the man]. This bears out what people say: Do no good to the bad, and no harm will befall you."

The stranger in this story is portrayed as well meaning but impractical.[15] On his way from Babylonia to Palestine, after witnessing a bird perform a miraculous healing with herbs on his murdered fellow, he is seized by an absurd desire: to revive the dead of the Land of Israel. At first, he is quite successful in reviving harmless animals. Despite this stroke of luck, however, he remains a fool who is oblivious to the simple common sense imparted by a popular local proverb. While traveling across the countryside, he revives a dead lion, who promptly devours him. A Babylonian in Palestine is no less comical than an American in nineteenth-century Europe or a shtetl Jew in St. Petersburg. This story is a typical fool's tale of the kind found in all popular storytelling traditions. We recall that the idea of reviving the dead appealed to Babylonians, and, thus, this story mocks them. Resurrecting the dead is a common trope in Christian *mirabilia* of late antiquity as well. Still, when it appears in this Palestinian rabbinic narrative, the wonderworker is the object of ridicule, perhaps because the story also fulfills the function of mocking Christian beliefs. By contrast, in the Babylonian Talmud, the notion of reviving the dead through the use of a magical object is taken as entirely plausible, and the narrator is neither skeptical nor ironically scornful of the protagonists in these narratives.[16] In order to understand why the narrator decided to send the gullible Babylonian to revive the deceased people of the Land of Israel, we must bear in mind that Babylonians, like other diaspora Jews, believed that it was important for Jews to be buried in the Land of Israel.[17] It was thought that

---

15. The plot of this story refers to a common archetypal folklore type that appears in many cultures; see, e.g., the Indian anthology of tales from approximately 3–6 BCE, *The Panchatantra*, translated from Sanskrit by Arthur W. Ryder (Bombay: Jaico, 1949), 380–81.

16. See b. B. Bat. 74b. About the different approaches of Babylonians and Palestinians to the theme of death and eternal life, see Reuven Kiperwasser, "Elihoref and Ahiah – The Metamorphosis of the Narrative Tradition from the Land of Israel to the Sassanian Babylonia," in *Rabbinic Traditions between Palestine and Babylonia*, ed. Ronit Nikolsky and Tal Ilan, Ancient Judaism and Early Christianity 89 (Leiden: Brill, 2014), 255–73.

17. The theology of the resurrection of the dead in eschatological times is to be dated to the Second Temple period; that is, it was inherited by rabbis from their predecessors. See George W. E. Nickelsburg, *Resurrection, Immortality, and Eternal Life in Intertestamental Judaism*, HTS 26 (Cambridge: Harvard University Press, 1972); Harry Sysling, *Tehiyyat Ha-Metim: The Resurrection of the Dead in the Palestinian Targums of the Pentateuch and Parallel Traditions*

burial in the Holy Land could help the deceased in the afterlife and that resurrection of the dead would occur first there.[18] It seems, however, that even for Palestinian narrators, the Holy Land is the only appropriate place for the future resurrection (y. Ketub. 12:2, 35b):[19]

Rabbi Shimeon ben Laqish said: "I shall walk before the Lord in the lands of the living" (Ps 116:9) and is it not a fact that the "lands of the living" are only Tyre and Caesarea and their surroundings? There is everything in abundance. R. Shimeon b. Laqish in the name of Bar Qappara [said]: It is the land where the dead will be the first to return to life in the time of the Messiah. What is the scriptural support for that view? "… who gives breath to the people upon it" (Isa 42:5). If that is the case, then do our masters who are in Babylonia lose out? Said R. Simai: The Holy One, blessed be He, goes in front of them toward the Land, and they roll to the Land like leather bottles, and once they get there, their soul comes back to them. What is the scriptural basis for that view? "And I will place you in the Land of Israel and I will put my spirit within you, and you shall live" (Ezek 37:14).	ר' שמעון בן לקיש אמר: "אתהלך לפני יי' בארצות החיים" (תהלים קטז ט). והלא אין ארצות החיים אלא צור וקיסרין וחברותיה. תמן כולה תמן שבע. רשב"ל בשם בר קפרא: ארץ שמתיה חיים תחילה לימות המשיח. מה טעמא? "נותן נשמה לעם עליה" (ישעיהו מד ה). מעתה, רבותינו שבבבל הפסידו. אמר ר' סימאי: הקדוש ברוך הוא מהלך לפניהן אל הארץ והן מתגלגלין כנודות. וכיון שמגיעין לארץ ישראל נפשותיהן עמהן. מה טעמא? "והבאתי אתכם אל אדמתכם ונתתי רוחי בכם וחייתם" (יחזקאל לז יד).

---

in *Classical Rabbinic Literature*, TSAJ 57 (Tübingen: Mohr Siebeck, 1996); Alan F. Segal, *Life after Death: A History of the Afterlife in the Religions of the West* (New York: Doubleday, 2004); Claudia Setzer, *Resurrection of the Body in Early Judaism and Early Christianity: Doctrine, Community, and Self-Definition* (Leiden: Brill, 2004); Géza Vermès, *The Resurrection* (New York: Doubleday, 2008). For a survey of methodologies in researching the resurrection, see Casey D. Elledge, "Future Resurrection of the Dead in Early Judaism: Social Dynamics, Contested Evidence," *Currents in Biblical Research* 9 (2011): 394–421.

18. See Shmuel Safrai, *In the Days of the Temple and in the Days of the Mishnah: Studies in the History of Israel* [Hebrew], 2 vols. (Jerusalem: Magnes, 1994), 1:182–93 (esp. 191–93), 307–10; Isaiah Gafni, "Reinterment in the Land of Israel: Notes on the Origin and Development of the Custom," *Jews and Judaism in the Rabbinic Era: Image and Reality – History and Historiography*, TSAJ 173. (Tübingen: Mohr Siebeck, 2019), 305–14.

19. Academia ed., 1010.

Here we have two exegetical traditions interpreting Ps 116:9, specifically the words "the lands of the living." According to the first tradition, "the lands of the living" are Tyre and Caesarea; neither place is far from the Galilee and both cities were known for their fertility. According to the second tradition, these are all the lands included in the term "Land of Israel," where in the eschatological era the process of resurrection will begin and the dead will be revived. This assumption leaves one with a problem—what should be done with important deceased people from abroad? Notably, this dilemma does not arise concerning Cappadocians or Alexandrians, but only concerning "our masters in Babylonia."[20] It turns out that these distant internal Others will "lose out," and their remains will be delivered to the Holy Land in small packages by rolling transportation dispatched by God himself.[21] There is something rather amusing, albeit macabre, in the picture of the remains of prominent Babylonians being delivered in such a way to the Land of Israel and then being resurrected together with not-so-important Palestinians who were lucky enough to die in the right place.[22] The idea that burial in the Land of Israel facilitated the dead's future resurrection was entirely accepted by the early Babylonian rabbis (b. Ketub. 111a), though the idea declined in popularity over time. Indeed, the last generations of Babylonian rabbis proposed precisely the opposite—that burial in Babylonia would not decrease anyone's chances of being resurrected, thereby placing burial in the Babylonian diaspora on the same footing as burial in the Land of Israel.[23] However, when the Yerushalmi was composed, the idea of diaspora Jews wishing to be buried in the Land of Israel[24] was quite familiar—and quite laughable—to Palestinian Jews.[25]

---

20. See 44 above.

21. Of course, the argument of Rabbi Simai is the answer to why they will not lose out. Still, I note the incongruity between the ease of resurrection for inhabitants of the Land of Israel and the difficult achievement of the same result on the Babylonian side.

22. Obviously, this strange kind of transport of human remains is part of the divine plan, which seems to indicate that, according to the Palestinian scenario, the mockery on the clumsiness of the Babylonians is sanctioned from above.

23. See Jeffrey L. Rubenstein, "Coping with the Virtues of the Land of Israel: An Analysis of 110b–112a" [Hebrew], in *Israel–Diaspora Relations in the Second Temple and Talmudic Periods*, ed. Isaiah M. Gafni (Jerusalem: Shazar Institute, 2004), 159–88. See as well recently Yoav Rosenthal, "Transportations: Text and Reality," *AJS Review* 41.2 (2017): 333–73. See Boyarin, *Traveling Homeland*, 42-45.

24. The burial of important Babylonians in the Land of Israel, mentioned in rabbinic literature, occurred in the time of Rabbi Yehuda ha-Nasi (Patriarch, second century CE; see further ch. 5 below). In no ancient sources was burial in the Land of Israel praised; see Safrai, *In the Days of the Temple*, 1:191–92; *Jews and Judaism in the Rabbinic Era*, 307. The Babylonians' high valuation of burial in the Land of Israel seems to have appeared in the second half of the third century and declined after the fourth century.

25. See Gen. Rab. 96:30, 1240, and see further 118, 198, 204.

y. Kil'ayim 9:4, 32c[26]

Rabbi bar Qiriya and Rabbi Eleazar were strolling down the road and saw biers that were being brought from abroad to the Land [of Israel]. Rabbi bar Qiriya said to Rabbi Eleazar: What have these profited? I recite [the verse] concerning them: "you defiled my land" (Jer 2:7). This you did while you were alive and in death "and made my heritage an abomination" (ibid.). [Rabbi Eleazar] said to him: Once they reach the Land, they take a clump of earth and place it on their bier, in accordance with that which is written, "and he makes atonement with the land for his people" (Deut 32:43).	ר' בר קיריא ורבי לעזר הוון מטיילין באיסטרין. ראו ארונות שהיו באין מחוצה לארץ לארץ. אמ' ר' ברקיריא לרבי לעזר: מה הועילו אילו? אני קורא עליהם "ונחלתי שמתם לתועיבה" (ירמיה ב ז). בחייכם, "ותבואו ותטמאו את ארצי" (שם) במיתתכם. אמר ליה. כיון שהן מגיעין לארץ ישראל הן נוטלין גוש עפר ומניחין על ארונן. דכתיב: "וכפר אדמתו עמו" (דברים לב מג).

The Palestinian rabbi comments to his colleague that these poor foreigners think that they are striking a good deal by bringing their dead to the Land of Israel. Halakhically speaking, however, all they accomplish is to bring more ritual impurity there, since corpses are nothing more than a source of ritual impurity. The alternative opinion voiced in the above Palestinian source interprets Babylonians' burial in the Land of Israel in terms of purifying the deceased because the Land of Israel is purer than other lands. Is he unaware of the Babylonian belief that a person buried in the Land of Israel will be resurrected first, or does he not share this belief? Also notable is that Rabbi bar Qiriya relates his point of view to none other than Rabbi Eleazar (Lazar), whose full name was Lazar/Eleazar ben Pedat, a Babylonian immigrant in Tiberias.[27] Referring to Babylonians, the local figure implies that he distinguishes this particular newcomer from his brethren because he had come to the Land while still alive. Yet he also wishes to humiliate the ethnic group to which the immigrant belongs. Thus, Rabbi Eleazar's interpretation of an obscure verse, Deut 32:43, is somewhat controversial, implying that the dead bodies of diaspora Jews are purified by the land instead of defiling the earth.

---

26. Academia ed., 176.

27. Rabbi Eleazar (ben Pedat), a Babylonian who studied with Rabbi Yoḥanan (y. Sanh. 1:2, 18c). Another story of Rabbi Eleazar as poor and suffering appears in b. Ber. 5b; see Kiperwasser, "Narrative Bricolage and Cultural Hybrids in Rabbinic Babylonia: On the Narratives of Seduction and the Topos of Light," in *The Aggada of the Babylonian Talmud and Its Cultural World*, ed. Jeffrey L. Rubenstein and Geoffrey Herman, BJS 362 (Providence, RI: Brown Judaic Studies, 2018), 23–45.

Thus, we can say that, in matters of death and resurrection, some Palestinians liked to belittle their Babylonian brethren—this is a moment of self-aggrandizement, showing a self-serving sense of superiority.

2.2 A Babylonian *Mamzer*

Another story about the painfully comic arrival of a Babylonian is told in the Palestinian midrash Leviticus Rabbah and the Yerushalmi Tractate Qiddushin; it also contains elements of mockery. The story appears in a pericope on the problems of a *mamzer*.[28] The paragraph in Leviticus Rabbah also mentions the motif of the Babylonian newcomer exploring the promised land's customs. In y. Qiddushin this pericope appears after a *mamzer* tale; I provide both in the synopsis.

Leviticus Rabbah 32:7[29]	y. Qiddushin 3:12, 84c[30]
ר' זעורה, כד סלק להכא, שמע קלהון קריין: ממזירה וממזירתה. אמ': הא אזלה ההיא דאמ' רב הונא: אין הממזר חיי יתיר משלשים יום.	ר' זעירא, כד סליק להכא, שמע קלין קריי: ממזרה וממזרתא. אמר לון: מהו כן? הא אזלה ההיא דרב הונא. דרב הונא אמ': אין ממזר חיי יותר משלשים יום.
אמ' ליה ר' יעקב בר אחא: עמד היית כדאמ' ר' בא ורב הונא בשם רב: אין הממזר חיי יתיר מל' יום. אימתי? בזמן שאינו מפורסם. אבל אם נתפרסם, חיי הוא.	אמר רבי עוקבא בר אחא: עמו הייתי כדאמ' רבי בא רב הונא בשם רב: אין ממזר חיי יותר משלשים יום. אימתי? בזמן שאינו מפורסם. אבל אם היה מפורסם חיה הוא.
Rabbi Zeira, when he came up here, heard voices calling: Male-*mamzer*, female-*mamzer*! He said: So, goes the saying of R. Huna: A *mamzer* does not live more than thirty days!	Rabbi Zeira, when he came up here, heard voices calling: Male-*mamzer*, female-*mamzer*! He told them: Why is this? So goes the saying of Rab Huna, for Rab Huna said: A *mamzer* does not live more than thirty days.

---

28. The first reference to the illegitimate child or bastard (*mamzer*) is found in Deut 23:2: "No *mamzer* shall be admitted into the congregation (assembly or community) of the Lord; even to the tenth generation none of the descendants shall enter the congregation of the Lord." No definition is given for such a person. It seems that here Leviticus Rabbah relies on m. Yevam. 4:13. On the *mamzer* theme in early rabbinic literature, see Joseph Levitsky, "The Illegitimate Child (Mamzer) in Jewish Law," *Jewish Bible Quarterly* 18 (1989): 6–12; Meir Bar Ilan "The Attitude Toward Mamzerim in Jewish Society in Late Antiquity," *Jewish History* 14 (2000): 125-17; Simcha Fishbane, *Deviancy in Early Rabbinic Literature: A Collection of Socio-Anthropological Essays*, Brill Reference Library of Judaism 27 (Leiden: Brill, 2007), 1–10.

29. Margulies ed., 3:552–53.

30. Academia ed., 1176.

Rabbi Jacob bar Aḥa said to him: I was with you when Raba and Rab Huna told it in the name of Rab. Namely, that a *mamzer* does not live longer than thirty days only. When? When he is unknown, but when he is known, he lives on.	Said Rabbi Uqba bar Aḥa: I was with him when Rabbi Ba, Rab Huna in the name of Rab, stated: A *mamzer* does not live more than thirty days. When? When it is unknown, but when it is known, he lives on.

Rabbi Zeira, whom we will meet later,[31] and whose arrival inspired a variety of stories,[32] discovers that the Galilee's inhabitants are accustomed to calling some of their brethren "bastards," namely, male and female *mamzer*.[33] This practice surprises him, as *mamzer* is not a particularly respectable attribute, and it contradicts his Babylonian learning that a real bastard would die by the hand of heaven by the age of thirty days. Such a benevolent assumption was probably meant to allay suspicions that certain living children were *mamzerim*. Another Palestinian scholar, Rabbi Uqba bar Aḥa,[34] explains to the novice the background of this saying by bringing a Babylonian halakhic tradition attributed to the famous Rab: a *mamzer* can survive if the community knows for a fact that he is one. This prologue is now appended with an exemplum:

y. Qiddushin 3:12, 84c[35]

Rav Huna said: A *mamzer* does not live more than thirty days.	רב הונא אמר אין ממזר חייה יותר משלשים יום.
In the time of Rabbi Berekhiah [there] came up here a certain Babylonian, whom he knew to be a *mamzer*. He said to him: Acquire merit in me! He said to him: Tomorrow, you will appear in the congregation, and I shall provide you	ביומוי דר' ברכיה סלק חד בבלאי להכא, והוה ידע ביה דהוא ממזר. אמ' ליה: ר', זכה עימי. אמ' ליה: למחר את קאים בציבורא ואנא עביד לך פסיקא. אתא. יתיב דריש. מן דחסיל מידרש אמ' לון: אחונן זכון עם הדין דהוא ממזר. מן דאזל ליה קהלא אמ' ליה: ר' חיי שעה בעית

---

31. See 61, 80, 88, 122, and 144 below.

32. See Reuven Kiperwasser, "Narrating the Self: Stories about Rabbi Zeira's Encounters in Land of Israel," in *Self, Self-Fashioning and Individuality in Late Antiquity: New Perspectives*, ed. Maren R. Niehoff and Joshua Levinson, Culture, Religion, and Politics in the Greco-Roman World 4 (Tübingen: Mohr Siebeck, 2019), 353–72.

33. Another possible interpretation of the event described here is to assume that an actual *mamzer* and *mamzerta* are being referred to. However, I assume that, as in our society, these words were employed as curse words, not describing real-life situations.

34. See about him Albeck, *Introduction*, 247–48.

35. Academia ed., 1176. A remarkably close parallel appears in Lev. Rab. 32:7, Margulies ed., 3:552–53.

a donation. He came. He sat and expounded. When he had finished expounding, he said to them: Brethren, provide for this one, for he is a *mamzer*. When the congregation had gone, he said to him: Rabbi, I asked you for temporal life, and you have cut my life short! He said to him: By your life! I have given you life! For Rabbi Ba, in the name of Rab Huna in the name of Rab stated: A *mamzer* lives only thirty days. When? When the matter is not known. But if the matter is public, he lives.

גבך, ואובדתא חיין דההוא גברא. [אמר ליה:] חייך. (ההין) [חיין] יהבית לך, דאמ׳ רבי בא רב הונא בשם רב: אין ממזר חיה אלא שלשים יום. אימתי? בזמן שאינו מפורסם. אבל אם היה מפורסם חיי הוא.

In the Bavli and in Palestinian rabbinic literature, Babylonians are known to be preoccupied with lineage.[36] Our narrator suggests that among those immigrating to the Land of Israel are those who lack a pure lineage, including some who are illegitimate. One such person emigrated from Babylonia in the days of Rabbi Berekhiah. His lineage problem was known to R. Berekhiah (despite the story's vagueness on this point). This figure, who probably left his country to begin a new life in a new place, where the ghosts of his birth story would not chase him, was also not wealthy—as is often the case with new immigrants—nor did he have friends and relations in the new place from whom he could ask assistance.[37] Therefore he went to the rabbi to ask him for help, using the typical formula for charity: Acquire merit in me. He probably meant to say that he was not expecting the rabbi to give him money outright, but that he wanted to enlist his aid in receiving alms from the community.[38] The rabbi promised help at a particular time in the presence of the community. At the appointed time, the Babylonian found the rabbi sitting before the community and delivering his sermon. The newcomer politely waited until the end of the talk and then found himself at the center of public attention.[39]

The rabbi then appealed to the community for charity: the man merited help simply for being a *mamzer*, without a proper family, socially deprived, and therefore needy. He called the congregation "our brethren," clearly demarcating this group from the Otherness of the Babylonian, who

---

36. See Rubenstein, *Culture of the Babylonian Talmud*, 80–101.

37. See Yael Wilfand, *Poverty, Charity, and the Image of the Poor in Rabbinic Texts from the Land of Israel*, Social World of Biblical Antiquity 9 (Sheffield: Sheffield Phoenix, 2014), 171.

38. See and compare the story in Gen. Rab. 33:3, Theodor-Albeck, 1:304–5.

39. It is difficult to know whether the stranger approached the rabbi or whether the rabbi went up to the stranger to focus the audience's attention on him.

was not only a foreigner but forbidden to enter the congregation of Jewish men. After donations had been collected, the Babylonian expressed his feelings to the rabbi in a well-formulated way. His response is constructed on the contradiction, well-known in rabbinic rhetoric, between what is called *ḥaye shaa*—temporary life, literally [a] life of the hour—and eternal life.[40] Here, however, the usage diverges from the usual one concerning toiling for a living as opposed to a life dedicated to Torah study. The *mamzer* speaks not only about the "short" life with which he has now been provided by the generous donation of the congregation (in contrast to the rest of his life, when the money will be gone), but also about the shame of his miserable lineage, previously a secret, which will haunt him until his death, even in his new homeland. We can understand his immigration to the Land of Israel as an attempt to begin a new life, leaving behind his ignominious birth. These rather delicate feelings of the stranger were entirely misunderstood by Rabbi Berekhiah, who now placates him with argumentation borrowed from the teachings of the Babylonian sages, hoping that it will impress him. But here these arguments, already known to us from the beginning of the paragraph, are weak. According to the teachings mentioned above, making his problematic lineage known to all is a good thing because it enables the newborn *mamzer* to survive longer than thirty days. However, this Babylonian's illegitimacy was known from birth onward, which is what, in our rabbi's eyes, helped him to survive. As he arrived in the Land of Israel as an adult, the issue of his surviving thirty days is irrelevant. Perhaps the rabbi wants to propose that, now in the Land of Israel, the newcomer is like a newborn baby. Once again, the publicity about his unfortunate lineage will prevent his death in the initial thirty-day period. At this point, however, it would be inappropriate for R. Berekhiah to try to conciliate the upset Babylonian and make excuses for his own lack of sensitivity.[41] This is a story of a painful misunderstanding between an insider and an outsider. As in the tale of the Babylonian fool eaten by a lion, in this story the Other was brought to the gate of the host.

---

40. See, e.g., b. Ta'an. 21a. Fraenkel, *Studies in the Spiritual World*, 89–91; David Levine, "Holy Men and Rabbis in Talmudic Antiquity," in *Saints and Role Models in Judaism and Christianity*, ed. Marcel Poorthuis and Joshua Schwartz, Jewish and Christian Perspectives 7 (Leiden: Brill, 2004), 45–57; Chaim Licht, *Ten Legends of the Sages: The Image of the Sage in Rabbinic Literature* (Hoboken NJ: Ktav, 1991), 181–206. Jeffrey L. Rubenstein, *Stories of the Babylonian Talmud* (Baltimore: Johns Hopkins University Press, 2010), 41–42.

41. Another explanation would be that that Rabbi Berekhiah set up the Babylonian, asking him to return so that he could make his problematic lineage public knowledge. But in such a case, the story would not be about a comic misunderstanding but, rather, would be a tale of cold cruelty, in which the poor Other—both a Babylonian and a *mamzer*—suffers at the hands of an inconsiderate Palestinian rabbi. This reading seems to me far-fetched. Regarding the problems of defining a comic situation in ancient texts, see 53–54 below.

After a humorous situation, not without humiliation, he remained there, but no attempt was made to truly welcome him.

For whom, we ought to ask, would this story be funny? The answer is clear: to Palestinian commoners who are annoyed by naïve Babylonian simpletons, so enamored of their lineage. How do these jokes embody or reinforce a value system? The narrator is trying to protect a host from a frightening guest. One who is mocked is defanged. In ridiculing the Other, he keeps him at bay and maintains intact his own role as host. The outline of the Babylonian's identity is tested, and the local identity is found to be stable, unlike the Babylonian one. It is worth mentioning, however, that in the second story, there is some doubt about the justifiability of a host feeling superior.

3

Going West

The Yerushalmi, in y. Ber. 2:8, 5c, relates a series of anecdotes about the arrival of Babylonian Jews in the Land of Israel and their awkward encounter with their new country of residence. The heroes of these stories are talmudic sages raised in talmudic academies and whose relationship to the promised land was shaped by religious reverence. In each of these narratives, a Babylonian is ridiculed by a Palestinian commoner. I propose that the humor in these stories emerges from the following scenario: a rabbinic protagonist appears in public; his words are calmly expounded; the audience accepts him eagerly; and the dialogue between him and his listeners, which consists of rabbinic students or respectful laymen, does not involve any form of inappropriate physical contact.[1] This respectable, "serious" body is covered and protected. The mocked body, by contrast, is exposed and vulnerable. The comic effect appears when the response to the above-mentioned incongruity in the rabbinic body's treatment is playful and amusing.[2] In this context, I argue that the conventional question of whether particular stories are funny or not is irrelevant. In my view, the real question is: funny to whom? How do these jokes embody or reinforce a value system? How do they serve psychic, social, cultural, or political objectives?[3]

Poking fun at Babylonians is a familiar trope in Palestinian rabbinic literature, sometimes with benevolence, sometimes with malice. But the three stories I consider next differ from the aforementioned in significant

---

1. See Lewis, *Comic Effects*, 11: "Noting that to be amused a person must feel safe and not too bewildered"; Lewis notes that Mary K. Rothbart ("Incongruity, Problem-Solving and Laughter," in *Humor and Laughter: Theory, Research, and Applications*, ed. A. J. Chapman and H. C. Foot [New York: Routledge, 1976], 37–54) has described a "continuum of response" to incongruity, a continuum that includes humor, fear, problem solving and fight.

2. As concluded by Lewis, *Comic Effects*, 13: "In every situation … the force of humor is underpinned by the implied assertion that a particular combination of ideas is incongruous and that it would be correct, appropriate and ethical to find this incongruity amusing." When a rabbi is spat on, slapped in the face, exposed in an inappropriate position or fed inappropriate food, I define the situation as far from being serious. Some humoristic tropes are discussed in Reuven Kiperwasser, "Wives of Commoners and the Masculinity of the Rabbis: Jokes, Serious Matters and Migrating Traditions," *JSJ* 48 (2017): 418–45.

3. See Lewis, *Comic Effects*, 13.

ways. They are not merely amusing folkloristic tales, mobilized for the needs of mockery, like the one about the Babylonian devoured by a lion we met above. Far from being harmless simpletons, their protagonists are much more prominent than the Babylonian *mamzer* from the previous chapter. Moreover, the rabbis define themselves within the Jewish populace not as commoners but as a particular kind of man whose masculinity differs from that of the unlearned man. My assumption is that the humor in the stories examined here can serve as a lens through which to understand rabbinic social politics.

This chain of stories was analyzed by the renowned talmudic scholar Saul Lieberman in one of his final works, titled "As It Was, So It Will Be."[4] There, he offered a trenchant historical and social reading of these narratives. He also applied to them a far-reaching model of relations between Babylonians and Palestinians in the Holy Land of late antiquity in terms of xenophobia and philoxenia.[5]

Lieberman argued that, despite the appearance of expressions in the Palestinian rabbinic canon that may seem xenophobic and unsympathetic toward Babylonian immigrants, the rabbis were in fact not xenophobic. Rather, they saw themselves as the intellectual elite of society, distinct from uneducated Palestinian commoners, who were contemptuous of the Babylonian newcomers. Finding themselves caught between the two groups (i.e., the Babylonians and the lower-class Palestinians), the Palestinian sages wisely balanced between them yet pragmatically maintained their loyalty to their local constituency. At the same time, in their stories they tried to present the Babylonian expatriates in a favorable light, asking that they be treated with compassion and respect.

It seems worth mentioning that, in the title of Lieberman's aforementioned article, we catch a glimpse of the scholar's view of this model of relationship (that it was a valid one), and that of Lieberman's own, difficult relationship with the Land of Israel—the nascent State of Israel. For Lieberman, Israel's "Babylonians" were former European Jews, urban literati who found themselves surrounded by their more rural Israeli brethren ("Palestinians"), whose role models were far removed from the images of typical European intellectuals.[6]

---

4. See Saul Lieberman, "As It Was, So It Will Be" [Hebrew], in *Studies in Palestinian Talmudic Literature*, ed. D. Rosenthal (Jerusalem: Magnes, 1991), 331–38. See also Saul Lieberman, "Palestine in the Third and Fourth Centuries," in *Texts and Studies* (New York: Ktav, 1974), 112–79, here 159–60.

5. See Lieberman, "Palestine in the Third and Fourth Centuries," 159–60.

6. For a sociological analysis of the situation, see Luis Roniger and Michael Feige, "From Pioneer to Freier: The Changing Models of Generalized Exchange in Israel," *European Journal of Sociology* 33.2 (1992): 280–307, esp. 285–86. See also Anita Shapira, *Visions in Conflict* [Hebrew] (Tel Aviv: Am Oved, 1989), 325–54; Tom Segev, *The Seventh Million: The Israelis and the Holocaust*, trans. Haim Watzman (New York: Straus & Giroux, 1993), 35–64. Though

3.1 Sons of a Stepmother versus a Mother's Children

This is the first of the three stories mentioned above, and perhaps the most illustrative of the "going west" stories. A typical talmudic tale, it is short and dramatic, and, moreover, it contains the elements of specific Palestinian inventions already discussed earlier, such as the metaphor of the Land of Israel as a mother and the custom of asking permission to leave the promised land.[7] Returning to Bourdieu's terminology, it expresses a clash between the owners of symbolic capital and the applicants for their share in it.[8]

y. Berakhot 2:8, 5c[9]

Kahana was a very young man when he ascended here [to the Land of Israel]. He met a certain empty man [lit., son of emptiness], who said to him: What is being said in heaven? [Kahana] said to him: The verdict for that man [i.e., you] has been sealed. And so, it was.	כהנא הוה עולם סגין כד סליק להכא. חמתיה חד בר פחין. אמר ליה: מה קלא בשמיא? אמר ליה: גזר דיניה דההוא גברא מיחתם. וכן הוות ליה.
Another man saw [Kahana] and said to him: What is being said in heaven? [Kahana] said to him: The verdict for that man [i.e., you] has been sealed. And so, it was.	חמתיה חד חרן. אמ' ליה: מה קלא בשמיא? אמר ליה: גזר דיניה דההוא גברא מיחתם. וכן הוות ליה.
[Kahana] said: Have I come to do good, and I have caused sin? Have I come to kill the sons of the Land of Israel? I shall go and descend from here. [Before] he left, he came to Rabbi Yoḥanan and asked him: If a person's mother despises him, but the wife of his father respects him, where should he go? [Rabbi Yoḥanan] said to him: He should go to where he is honored. Kahana descended from here. After he left, they came and said to Rabbi Yoḥanan:	אמר: מה סליקית מזכי ואנא איחטי? מה סליקית למיקטלה בני ארעא דיש'? ניזול וניחות לי מן הן דסליקית. אתא לגבי רבי יוחנן. א"ל: בר נש דאימיה מבסרא ליה, ואיתתיה דאבוהי מוקרא ליה, להן ייזל ליה? א"ל: ייזל להן דמוקרין ליה. נחת ליה כהנא מן הן. דסלק, אתון אמרין ליה לר' יוחנן: הא נחית כהנא לבבל. אמר: מה הוה מיזל ליה דלא מיסב רשותא? אמרין ליה: ההיא מילתא דאמר לך היא הוה נטילת רשות דידיה.

Segev deals with the immigration to Palestine of German Jews in Nazi times, the book is still evidence regarding the common mindset.

7. See 33 above.
8. See 32–37 above.
9. The text according to the Academia ed., 22–23.

Kahana descended to Babylonia. He
asked: Would he leave without asking
permission? They said to him: That
thing that he asked you was (from his
point of view) asking permission.

The main protagonist of this story is Kahana—one of the prominent figures in the second generation of the Babylonian Amoraim (end of the third century).[10] He was also a favorite disciple of the great figure, Rab. It appears that the narrator is unfamiliar with Kahana's origins and does not assign him any academic title. In the Babylonian Talmud, he is always presented as distinguished and honorable, whereas in the Yerushalmi, at least at the beginning of this narrative, he appears as an unremarkable young man. The Yerushalmi does not supply information about why this scholar left his native Babylonia and traveled to the Land of Israel.[11] From his exclamation: "Have I not come to do good, and I have caused sin?" (the verb מזכי is used to mean "doing good"), it seems that his relocation to the Land of Israel was motivated by purely religious reasons.[12] For the Palestinian narrator, it is self-evident that this young Babylonian, like every Babylonian youth, wished to reside in the Land of Israel, near the sources of holiness and learning. However, the Babylonian Talmud (b. B. Qam. 117a) tells us the details of an intrigue that caused the young Kahana to conflict with government spies. Consequently, his teacher, Rab, insisted on his "exile" to Palestine; had the circumstances been different, he would not have left his homeland.[13]

Kahana immigrated to the Land of Israel, where he studied under Rabbi Yoḥanan. His study and rivalry with Rabbi Yoḥanan are related in the Babylonian Talmud in an unusual story (b. B. Qam. 117a–b) that serves as a panegyric to the Babylonian academy.[14] Both Talmudim tell stories

---

10. There were a few holders of this name among the Babylonian Amoraim, and two of them quite close to each other. This one is probably the later and the younger sage, who was a student of Rab and Samuel (see about him in b. Yev. 102b, b. Ket. 101a and y. Ter. 4:7, 43c, See Albeck, *Introduction*, 203). The older Kahana was a contemporary of Rab and Samuel, probably even older than them and no less honored (see b. Sanh. 36b; b. Shabb. 146b; b. B. Qam. 80b). Both Babylonians named Kahana had sojourned for a while in the Land of Israel. See Albeck, *Introduction*, 174, 203; and Shamma Friedman, "The Further Adventures of Rav Kahana: Between Babylonia and Palestine," in *The Talmud Yerushalmi and Graeco-Roman Culture*, ed. Peter Schäfer, 3 vols., TSAJ 71, 79, 93 (Tübingen: Mohr Siebeck, 1998–2002), 3:247–71, here 267.

11. All this appears in the Babylonian story about the arrival of Kahana to the Land of Israel, which had attracted much attention of scholars. See further 146 and 202

12. I owe this observation to Geoffrey Herman.

13. See Friedman, "Further Adventures," 252–53.

14. See further 146.

about Kahana's arrival in the Holy Land, expressing their ideology rather than a historical reality.

The Palestinian narrator does not introduce his hero to the reader or share any background story on his life in Babylonia. After his arrival, Kahana encounters two natives of the Land of Israel, who are not rabbis but street bullies. The local men are referred to by the common expression—*bar paḥin* (lit., "son of emptiness," but figuratively, "son of fools"). The narrator suggests that these locals are uncultured and brutish.[15]

If the commoner is marked by his emptiness, the stranger is marked by his youth, and Kahana's youthfulness certainly plays a role in the story. The narrator even uses the strange phrase *olam sagin* (too young) to describe Kahana. According to Shlomo Na'eh, this may be an indication of the excessive force our hero uses, or of his height, or of his proclivity to be bullied.[16] As these interpretations are not based on textual evidence, I prefer to understand this literary phrase as merely a reference to Kahana's youth. The word עולם is an adjective in Aramaic meaning "young," and the word סגין is used adverbially to mean "much" or "greatly."

The story depicts a standard role alignment in male social groups. A foreign boy in an unfamiliar city becomes an object of ridicule by two common men who are loitering in the streets. Perhaps they are criminal "apprentices" in a tough neighborhood or in an army unit, but soon they make the young stranger the victim of their macho jokes.[17]

Like the young hero of Apuleius's *Golden Ass*, who becomes the victim of a cruel ritual immediately after arriving in the strange city, young Kahana comes from distant Mesopotamia to Galilee and becomes the

---

15. See Aharon Amit, "The Epithets ברפחין, בן פיחה and ברפחתי and Their Development in Talmudic Sources" [Hebrew], *Tarbiz* 72 (2003): 489–504.

16. Michael Sokoloff translates as "strong" (he sees a similarity between this expression and another one in Eccl. Rab. 3:2) (*A Dictionary of Jewish Palestinian Aramaic of the Byzantine Period*, 3rd rev. ed. [Ramat Gan: Bar-Ilan University Press, 2017], 449). However, regarding this expression, see my explanation in Reuven Kiperwasser, "The Visit of the Rural Sage: Text, Context and Intertext in a Rabbinic Narrative" [Hebrew], *Jerusalem Studies in Jewish Folklore* 26 (2009): 3–24. For another explanation, proposed by Shlomo Na'eh, see "From the Bible to Talmud (and Back): Lexical Studies in Hebrew and Aramaic" [Hebrew], in *Hebrew through the Ages: In Memory of Shoshanna Bahat*, ed. Mosheh Bar-Asher (Jerusalem: Academy of the Hebrew Language, 1997), 133–50. According to Na'eh, סגין here acts like שגיא in Biblical Aramaic (see Dan 2:31), stating that Kahana was very big and tall, and therefore attracted the bully's attention. His height indeed could explain why they ask him what is going on in heaven. But, as mentioned by Na'eh, no such meaning for this word in the Yerushalmi is evidenced. I agree with him that this must be an idiomatic expression, but it probably means, as I have suggested, that he was very young in the social context.

17. See Alan Dundes, *From Game to War and Other Psychoanalytic Essays on Folklore* (Lexington: University Press of Kentucky), 27–39; and Kiperwasser, "Visit of the Rural Sage," 9–10.

object of scorn.[18] The story resembles another one of Palestinian origin (Eccl. Rab. 3:2): a particular village rabbi arrives in the city of Sepphoris, where he is accosted by a band of youths who try to force him to dance for them.[19] The young men demand that he dance because he is "so handsome and young," but the rabbi energetically protests against dancing in public by claiming: "I am an old man!" The rabbi's real age is unclear, but it is evident that someone who is accepted by the community as an intellectual "elder" cannot dance with street boys, even if he is "young and handsome."[20] Moreover, labeling someone a "youngster" imputes a low social status, which would make him more vulnerable to violent urban "rituals."[21]

The question addressed by the bully to the stranger in the story under discussion here initially seems enigmatic: How could a foreign youngster know what is happening in the higher realms, or what the heavenly voice decrees? I would argue that his question reflects aggressive masculine provocations. The tough guy asks the perceived weakling: "Are they calling for you in heaven?" The latter replies meekly: "How would I know?" The bully now shoves his victim in the direction of heaven, demanding, "Now, do you hear?" However, our Babylonian is not prepared to accept the traditional victim script and responds boldly and courageously that he has indeed been up to heaven and heard the decrees issued against the bully. Kahana's remark turns out to be prophetic; at the end of the encounter, the health of the aggressor is damaged, and he dies soon after. One mishap is not enough, and a second bully soon attacks Kahana, resorting to the same provocative come-on of male combat.[22] Again, the young

---

18. Apuleius, *Metam.* 3:1–11; in Stephen Gaselee, *The Golden Ass: Being the Metamorphoses of Lucius Apuleius*, LCL (London: William Heinemann; New York: Macmillan, 1915).

19. See on this Kiperwasser, "Visit of the Rural Sage," 7–10. The perception of youth here could be compared to Luke 7:32.

20. See n. 21 below.

21. The same topos of "youngster in the city" can be seen in the Life of Bar Sauma; see Reuven Kiperwasser and Serge Ruzer, "The Holy Land and Its Inhabitants in the Pilgrimage Narrative of the Persian Monk Bar-Sauma" [Hebrew], *Cathedra* 148 (2013): 41–70 (for the updated English version, see Kiperwasser and Ruzer, "Competition for the Sacred Space: Barsauma's Vita and Rabbinic Traditions," in Aryeh Kofsky and Serge Ruzer, in collaboration with Reuven Kiperwasser, *Reshaping Identities in Late Antique Syria-Mesopotamia: Christian and Jewish Hermeneutics and Narrative Strategies,* Judaism in Context 19 (Piscataway, NJ: Gorgias, 2016), 181–216, esp. 187.

22. When I presented these thoughts before my audience at Yale University (winter 2015), I received a remark whose charm I found irresistible, even though I was unable to find convincing proof of its proposition. As is known, the word בבל ("Babel") appears in the biblical story of the Tower of Babel. There it is stated: Then they said, "Come, let's build ourselves a city and a tower with its top in the heavens so that we may make a name for ourselves. Otherwise, we will be scattered across the face of the entire earth" (Gen 11:4). However, the ironic ending of the story is: "That is why its name was called Babel—because there the Lord confused the language of the entire world, and from there the Lord scattered

stranger proves his mettle, and again the local fellow dies. Note that even though the narrator respectfully acknowledges the strange power of Kahana's utterance, the deaths of these two men serve to tarnish his image slightly. He is no longer merely a weakling; instead, he is a sorcerer of sorts, a danger to the narrator's Palestinian compatriots. Paradoxically, the Other in this story is both an actual victim and a perceived threat.

After the offending bullies are removed from the scene by the hand of Heaven, what can Kahana do? He states that he needs to return home, to "descend" from the Land of Israel, because his presence is both dangerous for the local inhabitants and sinful. From what follows, though, it seems that the real reason for his decision to return home is his disappointment with his Palestinian brethren. He inquires whether he should remain a stranger in the promised land, where a veritable aura of fear surrounds him, or return to the shores of the Euphrates. Young Kahana, now identified as a disciple of Rabbi Yoḥanan, can leave only with his teacher's permission.

As we already know, the custom whereby Rabbi Yoḥanan's disciples, Palestinian and Babylonian, ask permission from the master to leave the Holy Land is well attested in rabbinic literature.[23]

I now return to the story with which I began. Following the tradition to ask permission from the master, Kahana appears before the doyen of the Galilean sages, whose negative attitude to this sort of license, as

---

them across the face of the entire earth" (Gen 11:9). It has been widely recognized by scholars that the explanation of Babel is the climax of the account, a parody on the hubris of Babylon. In Babylonian literature, the name *bab-ili* meant "the gate of God." An audience member suggested that the question posed by the Galilean street bully is an ironic paraphrase of the biblical interpretation of the word Babel as the gate of heaven. The ruffian says, "If you, O young Babylonian, arrived from the place which is named 'the Gate of Heaven,' did you hear something behind the gate?" However, despite the appeal of this proposition, which perfectly fits the meaning of the story, I was unable to find any proof that rabbis were aware of the Old Babylonian meaning of "Babel" as a place connected to the heavenly realm. It is more likely that they took the ironic interpretation of the biblical narrator seriously. More typically, they described Babylonia as the lowest place in the world; see 27 above. Even Philo, a much earlier author than the rabbis, was apparently not aware of the meaning of Babel and named the Tower of Babel "Phanuel," based on Judg 8:8–9 (compare LXX Judg 8:8–9) in Philo, *Conf.* 26. Though, from another point of view, Babylonian rabbis knew the word *bab/bava* = gate, and widely used this word; see further 161. Apparently, they know that *-el* is a divine designation. Thus, perhaps the audience member's suggestion, that the Palestinian mocker is asking a person from Bab-el, the gate of heaven, what is going on in the heavenly realms, is a probable one.

Another ingenious, harmonistic explanation for what was heard in heaven was suggested by Mordechai Margaliot, *Encyclopedia of the Sages of the Talmud and the Geonim* [Hebrew] (Tel Aviv: Chechik, 1969), 2:245: the story told in the Yerushalmi occurred after the story told in the Babylonian Talmud b. B. Qam. 117a–b (see further 146), during which Kahana died and was revived by his master. The mocker, knowing about the temporary death of the Babylonian, asks him what it was like in the heavenly realm.

23. See 32 above.

we have just seen, was famous. Perhaps Kahana hopes that the rabbi can resolve his uncomfortable situation. Thus, we find ourselves in the second act of our drama, when Kahana is no longer juxtaposed with a common man of the Land of Israel but interacts with a person of his intellectual class—the famous and much-loved Rabbi Yoḥanan. Given the older sage's opposition to leaving the promised land, Kahana does not dare to speak directly about his decision to leave. Instead, he brings before his teacher a hypothetical halakhic case. Here, a man seeks his mother's love, but his mother shows him no sign of affection out of cruelty or ignorance. However, his stepmother loves the young man and takes care of him.[24] To whom should he turn? Rabbi Yoḥanan's answer is predictable: concerned about the boy's welfare, he sends him to the place where he is loved.

However, let us ponder the hidden meaning of the Kahana parable. The land of his birth is foreign to him. Babylonia is only his stepmother, but there he found love and respect. The Land of Israel, which he considers his true homeland for religious and cultural reasons, is unwelcoming and full of idle idiots. And he finds no love there at all. What is he to do?

It turns out that the mother/stepmother metaphor is significant for self-reflection for both Palestinian and Babylonian narrators concerning their relationship to their lands and serves both of them in their rhetoric.[25]

One question now becomes particularly important: What is the role of the father in this story? With which of the women does he reside, the mother or the stepmother? Or has he abandoned his family, leaving the son to fend for himself? The father in the parable probably represents not God but Abraham, the progenitor of the Jews. Abraham came to Canaan from Mesopotamia—the same region from which young Kahana emigrated to the Land of Israel. Rabban Yoḥanan b. Zakai in t. B. Qam. 7:3 explains, "For what reason were the people of Israel exiled [only] to Babylonia [rather than to all] other countries? Because the house of Abraham, our father, is from there."[26] Returning to his stepmother's country means that Kahana would journey in the opposite direction to the one taken by Abraham, but if he remained in the land of his mother, he would die of abuse and neglect.[27] Kahana presents this dilemma to his teacher in the form of a parable, hoping that the wise man will provide him with a solu-

---

24. See 35 n. 42 above.

25. As I showed regarding other usages of the same metaphor, see 34–37 above and further 198–99.

26. See Eliav, "Material World of Babylonia," 153–85.

27. Albeck assumed that Kahana peacefully returned and continued to be a sage among his Babylonian brethren (b. Hul. 19b, 111b; b. Yevam. 17a, 101b; b. Shebu. 36a) (*Introduction*, 203). According to the above-mentioned story from b. B. Qam. 117 a–b, Kahana died in Palestine. See further chapter 7 and the Epilogue, 202.

tion to the problem.[28] Rabbi Yoḥanan apprehends only the parable's external outline, not its underlying meaning. Nonetheless, Kahana receives the answer he is looking for—he is free to go.

With Rabbi Yoḥanan, the misunderstandings between Kahana and the natives of the Land of Israel are replicated at the highest social level. When Kahana decides to "descend" from the Holy Land to his homeland, he realizes that even his teacher has failed to understand him.[29]

Rabbi Yoḥanan is dismayed when he learns of Kahana's return to Babylonia, and the passage leaves the reader with a parable about the complicated relationship between individuals, homelands, and the countries to which they immigrate. But something significant took place in the failed dialogue between Kahana and Rabbi Yoḥanan. By proposing a riddle that the master was unable to solve, the student demonstrated his intellectual superiority, inadvertently staking a claim for the master's position; nonetheless, he departed without tasting victory. To borrow Derrida's terminology, the stranger left his position at the gate, entered the house (of study), and assumed the host's place. Following a moment in command, he departed, leaving the original host perplexed, nursing his interrupted self.[30]

3.2 The Price of a Pound of Flesh

I now move on to another anecdote from the same story collection in the Yerushalmi, which features Rabbi Zeira.[31]

y. Berakhot 2:8, 5c[32]

Rabbi Zeira, when he ascended here, went to let blood. [Then] he wished to buy a pound of beef from the butcher. [Zeira] asked him: How much does a pound cost? [The butcher] answered: Fifty *mana* and a slap on the face. [Zeira] said to him: I will give you	רבי זעירא כד סלק להכא, אזל אקיז דם. אזל בעי מיזבון חדא ליט' דקופד מן טבחא. א"ל: בכמה [הדין] ליטרתא? אמ' ליה: בחמשין מניי וחד קורסם. א"ל: סב לך שיתין. ולא קביל עילוי. סב לך ע', ולא קביל עילוי. סב לך פ', סב לך צ', עד דמטא מאה, ולא קביל עילוי. א"ל: עביד כמנהגך. ברומשא נחית לבית וועדא. אמר לון: רבנן, מה

---

28. In a manner of speaking, he hopes to trick Rabbi Yoḥanan into giving him the permission he desires.
29. Which means, of course, as I noted above, that he tricked his teacher intentionally.
30. My thanks to Joshua Cole for his thoughtful notes.
31. I believe that this is the first and not the second Zeira; see L. Bank, "Rabbi Zeira et Rab Zeira," *REJ* 38 (1899): 47–63. See as well Kiperwasser, "Narrating the Self," 353–72.
32. The text according to the Academia ed., 22–23.

sixty, but he refused. I will give you seventy, but he refused. I will give you eighty; I will give you ninety, until [Zeira] offered one hundred, but he [still] refused. Zeira said to him: Do as your custom requires. In the evening, he went to the study house. He said: Masters! How bad is the local custom whereby one may not eat a pound of beef before he is slapped on the face?! They asked him: Who [said] this? He said: A butcher. They sent for [the butcher] and found his coffin being taken out. They said to [Zeira]: To such a degree? He answered: I swear I was not furious with him because I thought it was [your] custom?

ביש מנהגא דהכא, דלא אכיל בר נש ליטרא דקופד עד דמחו ליה חד קורסם? אמרין ליה: ומה הוא דין? אמ' לון: פלן טבחא. שלחון בעיי מייתיתיה ואשכחון ארוניה נפקא. אמרין ליה: ר'" כל הכין? אמר ליה: וייתי עליי דלא כעסית עילוי, מי סברת דמנהגא כן.

This young Babylonian scholar managed to carry out his wish of ascending to the promised land.[33] The path from his native Babylonia to Palestine was long and arduous and, upon reaching his destination, he sought to restore his depleted energy.[34] Bloodletting was a standard medical procedure in antiquity for the prevention and treatment of various diseases.[35] In terms of the current context, it was thought to help one recuperate one's strength after a long journey; supposedly, it released bad humors that could accumulate en route. After bloodletting, the patient generally dined on red meat to compensate for the loss of nutrients from the bleeding. This explains Zeira's eagerness to buy meat at any cost. Thus, the protagonist finds himself at the marketplace, specifically the meat market, a promi-

---

33. On Zeira's arrival in the Holy Land as a popular topic for Palestinian narrators and even for their Babylonian colleagues, see Lieberman, "As It Was, So It Will Be," 336; and Meir Ben Shahar, "The Restoration in Rabbinic Literature: Palestine and Babylonia from Past to Present" (Hebrew), *Zion* 59 (2014): 19–52; and below.

34. I think that for the sake of the dramatic effect of the story, it should be read as though the events are happening immediately upon arrival.

35. About bloodletting, see Julius Preuss, *Biblical and Talmudic Medicine*, trans. Fred Rosner (New York: Ktav, 1971; German original, 1911), 248–57. The popularity of bloodletting in the Mediterranean world was reinforced by the ideas of Galen, according to whom humoral balance was the basis for illness or health, the four humors being blood, phlegm, black bile, and yellow bile, relating to the four Greek basic elements of air, water, earth, and fire, respectively. Galen believed that blood was the dominant humor and the one in most need of control. To balance the humors, a physician would remove "excessive" blood (plethora) from the patient. For "Bloodletting," see Markham J Geller., "Bloodletting in Babylonia," in *Magic and Rationality in Ancient Near Eastern and Graeco-Roman Medicine*, ed. Herman Frederik J. Horstmanshoff and Marten Stol, Studies in Ancient Medicine 27 (Leiden: Brill, 2004), 305–24.

nent site in the city's structure, and the scene of many dramatic narratives in Palestinian rabbinic literature.[36]

He buys a *litra* [a Roman unit of weight, close to a pound/*libra*] of meat. This was a significant amount of meat, perhaps excessive for a physically weak man like Rabbi Zeira,[37] even though he came from a country where a high-protein diet was the norm.[38] In describing the purchase of meat, the narrator uses an Aramaic term borrowed from the Greek. However, our Babylonian uses a strange word, *litreta*, the same Aramaism but feminized. The narrator thereby indicates that Zeira's manner of speaking differed from that of the native inhabitants of the Land of Israel, revealing his Babylonian origins.[39] Thus, the meeting of two different Jews, one from Mesopotamia and the other from the Land of Israel, is presented as a meeting of two Aramaic idiolects, expressing grotesque forms of speech, which is a typical feature of narratives in rabbinic literature.[40]

Scholars have attempted to date the story based on the financial details of the transaction.[41] When talmudic sources refer to exorbitant sums paid

---

36. See, e.g., y. Sheqal. 7:2, 50c. For a brief discussion of this account, see Stuart S. Miller, *Sages and Commoners in Late Antique 'Ereẓ Israel: A Philological Inquiry into Local Traditions in Talmud Yerushalmi*, TSAJ 111 (Tübingen: Mohr Siebeck, 2006), 290–91.

37. As is probably evident from his name, which actually means small. Lieberman assumed that Rabbi Zeira was of poor health, referring to the notion about his ascetic deeds and numerous fasts ("As It Was, So It Will Be," 336); see y. Ta'an. 2:13, 76a; b. B. Metz. 85a and further 81–82.

38. See Saul Lieberman, *Tosefta ki-fshuta: A Comprehensive Commentary on the Tosefta*, 10 vols. in 9 (New York: Jewish Theological Seminary, 1955–1988), 1:186; Lieberman, "As It Was, So It Will Be," 336; and Moshe Beer, *The Babylonian Amoraim: Aspects of Economic Life* [Hebrew] (Ramat Gan: Bar Ilan University Press, 1982), 116–55 (on growing cattle in rabbinic Babylonia and about meat consumption, see 289–326).

39. I know only one source where this word appears in this form; however, I doubt that there it is a Babylonian tradition. I am referring to the remnants of a lost midrash on the Ten Commandments included in Pesiqta Rabbati 23; see Meir (Ish-Shalom) Friedmann, *Pesikta Rabbati* (Vienna, 1880), 119a–b. See Rivka Ulmer, *Pesiqta Rabbati: A Synoptic Edition of Pesiqta Rabbati Based upon all Extant Manuscripts and the Editio Princeps*, 3 vols., South Florida Studies in the History of Judaism 155, 200 (vols. 1 and 2), Studies in Judaism (vol. 3) (Atlanta: Scholars Press, 1997), 574–75. On the identification of the lost late ancient midrash on the Ten Commandments and midrash fragments in Pesiqta Rabbati, see Binyamin Elizur, "Pesikta Rabbati – perek mavo" [Hebrew] (PhD diss., Hebrew University, Jerusalem, 2000), 45. For the text under discussion, see Shlomi Efrati, "Pesiqata of Ten Commandments and Pesiqta of Matan Torah: Text, Redaction and Tradition Analysis" (PhD diss., Hebrew University, Jerusalem, 2019), 1:48—I am grateful to the author for sharing with me a draft of his dissertation. See also the English translation of William G. Braude, *Pesikta Rabbati: Discourses for Feasts, Fasts, and Special Sabbaths*, 2 vols., Yale Judaica Series 18 (New Haven: Yale University Press, 1968), 484–85. There "fish at a denar a pound" ליטרתא דינר is mentioned three times. Perhaps this can be explained by the fact that the incident occurs in Rome and the narrator imagined that this was an expression used there. In a parallel story in Gen. Rab. 11:4 (Theodor-Albeck, 1:91–92), this expression does not appear.

40. See further 157.

41. See Daniel Sperber, *Roman Palestine, 200–400: Money and Prices*, Bar-Ilan Studies

for everyday goods, scholars tend to hypothesize that these stories date from a period of inflation, 274–284 CE. The original amount quoted by the butcher is 50 *min*, the equivalent of 5000 silver *denarii*, or 1.38 grams of gold—quite a high price for a pound of meat.[42] In his analysis of the economic situation in Roman Galilee, Daniel Sperber reservedly drew certain conclusions despite the unreliability of his source of information here— the Yerushalmi.[43] However, the exaggerated price may be a literary device, unconnected to any reality. The meat mentioned in the story is beef, which has always been expensive in the Mediterranean region and was usually reserved for festive family meals. Only the wealthy could afford to eat meat on weekdays. Those who were poor dined on poultry or fish, or just bread.[44] Thus, the culinary culture of the Land of Israel was markedly different from what Rabbi Zeira was accustomed to in wealthy Mesopotamia. According to Tannaitic regulations, a man with an income of 50 *maneh* could consume a *litra* of meat from Friday to Friday, a man with an income of 100 *maneh* a *litra* of meat every day (t. Arak. 4:26–27).[45] However, the Babylonian Talmud does not mention income associated with meat consumption; it merely states that meat consumption is inappropriate for an *am ha-aretz* but beneficial for scholars (b. Shabb. 140b).[46]

A frail Babylonian stranger appears before our butcher, that is, a man

---

in Near Eastern Languages and Culture (Ramat Gan: Bar-Ilan University Press, 1974), 35, 196 n. 8.

42. This led Louis Ginzburg to propose an emendation here and to read מעי (obols) for מני (*manehs*), but, as he noted, even then the price would still be too high. This emendation was rejected by Sperber; see below.

43. Sperber, *Roman Palestine*, 104, 152; his detailed reflections on our story appear in his articles "Inflation in Fourth Century Palestine," *ArOr* 34 (1966): 54–66, and "The Value of '*manah*'" [Hebrew], *Talpioth* 9 (1970), 591–611. Sperber refused to emend the version of the Yerushalmi and suggested that the price demanded by the butcher was reasonable on the basis of a notation in a certain papyrus from the J. Rylands collection that listed the price of meat in Byzantine Egypt (namely, in Oxyrhynchus) at 50 denari (= 50 *maneh*); the document is dated 317–325 CE. Therefore, he thinks, Zeira's migration occurred in that period (325 CE) and our hero is the second Zeira. Actually, there is no hint that the first price was reasonable, and so the suggestion that we are dealing here with the second Zeira is not persuasive. I think that all three Babylonians were from the same generation, contemporaries of Rabbi Yohanan. This is likely playful hyperbole of the narrator.

44. See Samuel Krauss, *Griechische und Lateinische Lehnwörter im Talmud, Midrasch und Targum* (Berlin: S. Calvary, 1898–1899), 548–49. Most of the sources for evidence about poor meat consumption are in fact Palestinian.

45. See also Jacob Neusner, *The Tosefta: Kodoshim* (New York: Ktav, 1979), 204. There are four categories of income, according to Tannaitic tradition: 10 *mane*, 20 *mane*, 50 *mane* and 100 *mane*. People in the first two categories are deprived of meat. Thus, the third category is middle-class, while the fourth is a rich class. It turns out that our Babylonian is about to consume in one evening alone the weekly portion of an average person, or the daily portion of a rich man. There is a reason enough for the butcher to be angry.

46. Yet not every ordinary Babylonian Jew was able to consume meat every day; see Beer, *Babylonian Amoraim*, 306 and n. 62.

whose profession requires a robust emotional constitution. The stranger's Babylonian origin becomes apparent not only from his accent or attire but also when he requests an extravagant portion of meat on a weekday, annoyingly calling it *"litreta."* The butcher feels that he should teach this stranger a lesson. He names an outrageous price for a pound of beef and adds that a slap in the face will accompany the meat purchase.[47] In the eyes of the butcher, the stranger has earned this harsh treatment by virtue of requesting such an extravagant amount of meat. In overcharging for the beef and threatening the stranger with physical abuse, the butcher taunts the naïve Babylonian. Everyone except the Babylonian would have realized the abnormality of such behavior. He, however, innocently attempts to negotiate his new circumstances. Embarrassed by the Land of Israel's seemingly cruel customs, Zeira proposes to resolve the problem through negotiation. The butcher, however, remains obstinate and, with mock seriousness, insists on the value of his invented custom, arguing that cash cannot substitute for a slap in the face (even if its value is as high as the pound of meat). Apparently, the butcher's urge to slap the face of the Babylonian intellectual was more potent than his desire to earn more money. Given the butcher's unwavering stance, the visitor ultimately accepts the terms of the purchase.

Rabbi Zeira appears ridiculously gullible, but we must consider his newcomer's reverence for the traditions of the Land of Israel. In his view, its people are as filled with *mitsvot* (religious, virtuous deeds) as a pomegranate is filled with seeds, and their commitment to local traditions, even if they seem silly, is a result of their observance. Zeira's pious tolerance, though quite ludicrous and completely overblown, is typical of the depictions of Babylonians in Palestinian literature.[48]

Having acquainted himself with the "traditions" of the Galilean people, Rabbi Zeira visits his peers at the Academy, where he freely relates what happened to him, inquiring about the cruel customs that he believes are prevalent among the commoners of the Land of Israel. Only now does the vicious nature of the butcher's deed become clear to him. The enraged sages send a messenger to the butcher either to scold him or to demand an apology. However, the case has already been settled by the heavenly court, as the butcher's remains are on their way to be buried. Like his protagonists, the narrator clearly does not see this turn of events as a meaningless coincidence. The Palestinian narrator views the stranger as a formidable figure, worthy of both fear and respect. The puzzling question of the anonymous heroes of the story, "To such a degree!?" indicates their

---

47. Usually, a butcher—or any tradesman—would be happy when someone asks to buy a significant quantity of a product. Therefore, the trigger for the abuse is Kahana's foreignness.

48. See 39–40 above.

possibly ambiguous reaction, asking if the butcher's "punishment" is not too severe. If such is the fate of a person who slaps a stranger for fun, how much more serious will be the punishment for someone who dares to truly harm him? How can they ever integrate such a hopelessly naïve and laughable foreigner after one scoffer has already taken his place in the cemetery for mocking him? Here the author seems to identify more with Rabbi Zeira than with the butcher, though he keeps a distance between himself and the Babylonian. Zeira laments the unhappy fate of the butcher, confessing that he did not intend such consequences. Despite his anger at the butcher, he was under the genuine impression that the man was behaving according to local custom and, therefore, meekly accepted the mistreatment as necessary for gaining acceptance in the Land of Israel. At the end of the tale, the rabbinic students, bewildered by what they perceive to be the stranger's magical abilities, express their doubt to him, while he himself is still stunned by the course of events.

As in the previous and the following stories, this story recounts a conflict between local and foreign men. The insider dies, and the Other accepts the locals' admiration; does this necessarily mean that the narrator is on the side of the Other? Rabbi Zeira undergoes a metamorphosis from gullible to fearsome but remains the Other. The Palestinian narrator challenges Palestinian stereotypes about Babylonians by rethinking the values of his own native, "authentic" culture via-à-vis the diasporic one. Of note is that for the construction of local identity via-à-vis that of the foreigner, the narrator needs to involve Roman urban culture elements and local Roman terms. This strategy will be reinforced in the following example.

3.3 Crucifixion? This Way, Please!

Now let us turn to the final anecdote in the tragicomic trilogy of encounters between Babylonian immigrants and the Galilee's inhabitants. The protagonist is Rabbi Yasa/Isi bar Hiney, a contemporary of Rab, who turned up in Tiberias around the same time as Rab Kahana. Apparently, he did not put down roots in the Land of Israel. [49]

y. Berakhot 2:8, 5c

| When Rabbi Yasa ascended here, he went to the barber and wished to wash in the public baths of Tiberias. He met | ר' יסא, כד סליק להכא, אזל ספר. בעי מסחי באהן דימוסן דטיבריא. פגע ביה חד ליצן ויהב ליה פורקדל חד. א"ל: עד כדון עונקתיה דההוא |

---

[49]. See 32 above. We find him in Babylonia engaged in academic activities (b. Eruv. 39b) and serving as host to Palestinian immigrants (b. Shabb. 147a). Both events probably occurred many years after the narrative in the Yerushalmi that we will examine here.

a jester who gave him a punch on the nape of his neck. [The jester] said to him: The noose, on which I will hang is not yet tightened! There was an archon [there] who was judging a robber. He [the jester] went to stand there and grinned at them. The archon said [to the robber]: Who was with you? [The robber] raised his eyes and saw [the jester] grinning. He said: The one who grins was with me. They took him and judged him and sentenced him to death. When both were taken, they were loaded with two beams while Rabbi Yasa was done with bathing. [The jester] said to him: The noose that was loose is now tight. [Yasa] said to him: Bad luck to that man [= you]. Is it not written: "And now do not mock for your yoke will be tightened" (Isa 28:22)?

גברא רפיא. והוא ארכונא קאים דאין אחד ליסטיס. ואזל קם ליה גחיך כל קבליה.[50] אמ' ליה [ארכונא]: מאן הוא עמדך? תלה עינוי וחמא דהוא גחיך. אמ' ליה: אהן דגחיך הוא עמי. נסבי הודני הוא ודיליה על חד קטיל. מי נפקין תרויהון, טעינין תרתי שרין. דעבד רבי יסא מסחי, אמ' ליה: עונקתא דהות רפיא כבר שנצת. אמ' ליה: ביש גדא דההוא גברא. ולא כתיב. "ועתה אל תתלוצצו פן יחזקו מוסריכם" (ישעיהו כח כב)?

The first meeting of this Babylonian immigrant with a native of the Land of Israel is painful. The young rabbi is preparing to celebrate his arrival in the Land as one might prepare to meet with one's bride.[51] Wishing to appear well-groomed before his new compatriots, he plans to visit the barber and then the public baths. Is it purely coincidental that he begins his exploration of the new city in the public bath?[52] The other two protagonists in the trilogy of which this is a part also start to explore the city from its central public loci. Where Kahana, the protagonist of the first story,

---

50. I prefer here the version of Leiden Ms. and not the version of Ms. Rome (מן הוה ליה חורי עמודא), according to which the text was corrected in the edition of the Academy of the Hebrew Language; see Shlomo Na'eh, "Talmud Yerushalmi of the Academy of the Hebrew Language," *Tarbiz* 71 (2002): 569–603, here 580.

51. Here and above, I follow Lieberman ("As It Was, So It Will Be," 335) in assuming that these activities are performed at the rabbi's very arrival. This is the literal meaning of כד סליק להכא. However, it also could mean sometime shortly after he ascended here; see above n. 34.

52. See Hezser's description of the Roman bath as a travel destination for rabbis, in *Jewish Travel*, 234–37. I disagree with the critique of Yaron Z. Eliav, "Catherine Hezser, Jewish Travel in Antiquity," *JAOS* 133 (2013): 382–84. The bath as a cultural institution and a place from which the newcomer explores the city appears not only in rabbinic stories but in Roman novels as well. See Petronius, *Satyricon*, LXXII, trans. Sarah Ruden (Indianapolis, IN: Hackett, 2000), 19.

met his commoner is not disclosed. Still, presumably, it was in a public place such as a street or in the marketplace where one might likely meet a "son of emptiness." Zeira, the protagonist of the second story, clearly met his militant Palestinian in the market at the butcher's stall. Now, our final story involves an equally crucial urban institution—the public bath. By placing the last, culminating story in the bathhouse, the editor follows a certain narrative logic. The bathhouse is a purely Roman institution, a marker of imperial culture that was extremely popular and widely accepted throughout the Roman Empire by both Jews and gentiles.[53]

In Babylonia, where Zoroastrian priests influenced the population, there were no public baths, because of a reluctance to defile the sacred element of water.[54] Even King Khosrow traveled all the way to Antioch to experience the joys of the Roman bath and was condemned for his actions by his priests. The archaeological remains of the most ancient baths in Iran date to the Islamic period, when the Zoroastrian priesthood could no longer prevent their construction. Even these later baths contain nei-

---

53. See Martin Jacobs, "Römische Thermenkultur im Spiegel des Talmud Yerushalmi," in *The Talmud Yerushalmi and Graeco-Roman Culture*, ed. Peter Schäfer, 3 vols., TSAJ 71, 79, 92 (Tübingen: Mohr Siebeck, 1998–2002), 1:219–311. Yaron Z. Eliav writes: ". . . in a range of issues, the baths operating among the Jews transcended the conventional practice in the Roman Empire. On one level, Jews neutralized factors that did not conform to their standards of conduct. On another level, some of their unique practices, manners and customs became correlated with the baths. Thus, the bath was remodeled" ("The Roman Bath as a Jewish Institution: Another Look at the Encounter between Judaism and the Greco-Roman Culture," *JSJ* 31 [2000]: 416–54, here 430). See also the following works by Eliav: "Did the Jews at First Abstain from Using the Roman Bath-House?" [Hebrew], *Cathedra* 75 (1995): 3–35; "Pylè – Puma – Sfat Medinah and a Halakha Concerning Bath-houses" [Hebrew], *Sidra* 11 (1995): 5–19; "A Scary Place: Jewish Magic in the Roman Bathhouse" [Hebrew], in *Man near a Roman Arch: Studies Presented to Prof. Yoram Tsafrir*, ed. Leah Di Segni et al. (Jerusalem: Israel Exploration Society, 2009), 88–97; "Bathhouses as Places of Social and Cultural Interactions," in *The Oxford Handbook of Jewish Daily Life in Roman Palestine*, ed. Catherine Hezser, Oxford Handbooks in Classics and Ancient History (Oxford: Oxford University Press, 2010), 605–22; "Baths," in *The Eerdmans Dictionary of Early Judaism*, ed. John J. Collins and D. C. Harlow (Grand Rapids: Eerdmans, 2010), 432–34.

54. According to Willem M. Floor, some sort of bathhouses, different from the Roman bathhouses, existed prior to the Islamic period in the Iranian cultural sphere ("Bathhouses," *Encyclopædia Iranica*, ed. Ehsan Yarshater, 16 vols. [London: Routledge & Kegan Paul; Leiden: Brill, 1982–2019] 3:863–69, http://www.iranicaonline.org/articles/bathhouses). However, their number seems to have been limited. Archeological finds in Kārazm, for example, have uncovered the existence of cellars under houses that were cooled by water basins in which the inhabitants may have bathed, though these cellars could have been used for other purposes. Other sources confirm the rarity if not the absence of baths in pre-Islamic Iran. For example, King Vologeses (484–488) incurred the wrath of the Zoroastrian priests by building public baths in which people could pollute the holy element, water. Kavād (488–531), having enjoyed a bath in Amida after his conquest of that city, ordered the construction of such baths throughout his empire, see A. Mez, *Die Renaissance des Islams* (Heidelberg: C. Winter, 1922), 365.

ther encaustic heating nor a caldarium [hot room] and, at least according to Persian miniatures, visitors did not appear in them completely naked. Thus, even if public or semipublic baths existed in some form in Sasanian Babylonia, they did not feature the Roman innovations just mentioned. We may assume that Babylonians who found themselves in a Roman-style bath did not know how to conduct themselves there.[55]

Our Babylonian, unaccustomed to Roman bathhouse etiquette, comes to the bath and is easily recognized as an outsider. As with our previous protagonists, his behavior invites ridicule. The narrator does not explain precisely how the foreigner was identified as such, apparently relying on the reader's understanding that a stranger is recognizable even when naked.[56] Because his home country had no Roman baths, our hero simply did not know how to behave in his new surroundings and became the object of mockery. Finding himself surrounded by a crowd of naked people,[57] our shy Babylonian felt uncomfortable; perhaps he was still covering his nudity, as was customary in his homeland.[58]

Carlin Barton, citing ancient textual evidence, lists the places and points of passage where a person was especially vulnerable: "corners, bridges, baths, doorways." Such liminal areas were positively charged and dangerous.[59] Indeed, for our protagonist, passing through the bath serves

---

55. Bathhouses in the Persian realm are documented also in the Babylonian Talmud; see, e.g., b. Shabb. 41a, but it is doubtful that they resembled Roman bathhouses.

56. Lieberman proposed an amusing explanation for these circumstances: The young Babylonian arrived in the Holy Land on the eve of Sukkot (see y. Sukkah 3:4, 63d, but there is no hint that our episode happened on such a day), and that is why he went to the bath, for at that time all "Israelites" were wearing sandals, whereas the Babylonian wore shoes because there were no sandals in Babylonia. Lieberman quotes y. Yevam. 12:2, 12c here, but nothing is said about the absence of sandals in Babylonia. Only *taman amrin* is recorded, indicating that there (i.e., in Babylonia), people speak of a specific term, *qansuras*, which is like a sandal with a heel mentioned in the Mishnah. Thus, perhaps this means that the sandal style was different in Babylonia, not necessarily that the sandal was unknown. I suspect that here, given the fact that Lieberman's paper had initially been a public lecture published more or less intact, the great master was allowing himself a joke. Of course, sandals are mentioned in literary traditions by non-Jewish authors of Babylonian provenance, roughly from the talmudic period onward.

57. On nudity in public bathhouses in the Roman Empire, see Fikret Yegül, *Bathing in the Roman World* (Cambridge: Cambridge University Press, 2010), 27–33. The Roman bath was a tripartite place. In certain areas people were nude, but in other areas they wore some clothing; see, e.g., the evidence from t. Ber. 2:20. Regarding nudity in the bath of Roman Palestine, see Eliav, "Baths," 605–22, esp. 610.

58. Regarding differences in cultural norms in public behavior in general and regarding nudity specifically, see Yael Wilfand, "Did the Rabbis Reject the Roman Public Latrine?," *Bulletin Antieke Beschaving: Annual Papers on Mediterranean Archaeology* 84 (2009): 183–96.

59. See Carlin A. Barton, *The Sorrows of the Ancient Romans: The Gladiator and the Monster* (Princeton: Princeton University Press, 1993), 168–72. Liminal space, the liminal state, derives from the Latin word *limen*. "Boundary, threshold" refers to the situation when a person "passes through a cultural realm that has few or none of the attributes of the past or

as a rite of passage; he encounters something clearly different from everything he knew before, after which his perception of the world changes.

In the misty, liminal space of a public bath, a typical aggressive male episode occurs. Hidden in darkness, an assailant attacks his victim with a skillful blow, referred to by a term that appears nowhere else in talmudic literature: *purqadal*. This word is a haplographic construction of פורקדל= פרקא קדלא, literally, destroying or dislocating the nape of the neck.[60] Thus, *purqadal* represents a very violent form of attack, and its usage shows that this is a collision between the insider and the outsider, inevitably in the form of masculine combat. Confident of impunity, the scoffing joker utters a metaphorical maxim, which should be interpreted as: "the noose of the rope with which I will be hanged for this has not yet been knotted."[61]

Having had his fun, the aggressor goes in search of further adventures in the bath, grinning contentedly. He then peers around, probably at some other curious event in the bathhouse, some distance away. It is there that he becomes not only a witness to another man's game but himself an object of amusement.

On the other side of the bathhouse, a dramatic scene is under way. An *archon*, that is, an important official, is absorbed in the work that he has brought with him to the bathhouse. Perhaps he is trying to resolve an unfinished court case with the robber, his defendant, or maybe the culprit in this case was apprehended in the bathhouse and faced an immediate arraignment before the magistrate, who simply happened to be on the scene.[62] As part of the legal proceedings, the accused is asked a standard question about his accomplices. At that very moment, he glances up and sees the scoffer standing behind the pillar, still grinning from his previous antics. The defendant probably interpreted his smile as the malicious mockery of a free man among thieves.[63] Out of spite, the robber proclaims that the scoffer is his accomplice. Without further ado, the judges of the Roman justice system condemn the robber and the jester to be crucified.

---

coming state." See Victor Turner, *Ritual Process: Structure and Anti-Structure*, Lewis Henry Morgan Lectures 1966 (Chicago: Aldine, 1969), 94.

60. A remarkably similar expression does appear in Syriac: *purqe burqe*, meaning the dislocation of the knee, which is the Syrian translation of פיק ברכיים from Nah 2:11. See Michael Sokoloff, *A Syriac Lexicon: A Translation from the Latin; Correction, Expansion, and Update of C. Brockelmann's Lexicon Syriacum* (Winona Lake, IN: Eisenbrauns, 2009), 1172. I thank Gerold Necker for wisely proposing the idea of some sort of haplogram here, although he offered another explanation for the expression.

61. Following the convention of rabbinic literature, the narrator does not specify who utters this phrase, but, according to the plot's logic, it must be the joker. Some of my students, with whom I read this text, insisted on putting this phrase into the mouth of the rabbi, but I remain unconvinced.

62. From the end of the story, it is obvious that the court case was tried on the spot.

63. This misunderstood smile is reminiscent of Kahana's misunderstood smile in a Babylonian story to be discussed below, 149, 151.

This plot might strike the modern reader as rather artificial. The court's occurrence in the bathhouse, the comic haste of the decision, the execution as an immediate consequence of the random coincidence of events—everything seems strange, almost staged. But this motif appears elsewhere in late antiquity. In a work dedicated to the life of the Coptic saint Shenoute, the author relates a story about a former robber from the district of Pshoi who became repentant and decided that he nevertheless deserved to die for his deeds. However, his crime, killing and robbery, went unnoticed at the time; now it was outdated, and nobody wished to judge him for these past misdeeds. Shenoute sends him to a distant city where the local judge would sit on the riverbank and interrogate robbers.

> Do not stay here, but get up quickly and go to Smin, where you will find the duke. He has come south down the river and is being greeted by his people. Some thieves who robbed an eminent man of the city of Shmin will be handed over to him, and he will be incensed with them. You too must go and join the thieves, and they will say to the duke: He is here with us. The duke will ask you: Is it true? Say to him: It is accurate, and he will, therefore, kill you with the others.[64]

The protagonist is advised to be in the vicinity of robbers during their interrogation, and in this way attain his long-awaited opportunity to be executed. As in our case, the Roman judge is holding court in the public sphere, and the interrogation is a public affair. I am not proposing that the Coptic narrator knew our story or vice versa. Rather, I am suggesting that behind both stories lies a common topos, possibly based on the assumption that a condemned criminal will willingly incriminate any person unfortunate enough to be nearby at the sentencing.[65]

Returning to the condemned Galileans, who are already equipped with beams for crucifixion, it is difficult to ascertain how the logs necessary for this form of execution appeared out of thin air in the public baths of Tiberias.[66] But we may assume that the narrator's need to engineer an encounter between the crucified robber or the aggressive jokester and Rabbi Yasa allowed him to step beyond the bounds of reason. The tendency to joke can be dangerous. In a joke, the storyteller takes an everyday situation and injects an element from a completely different context; this

---

64. See Besa, *The Life of Shenoute*, ed. David N. Bell, Cistercian Studies Series 73 (Kalamazoo, MI: Cistercian Publications, 1983), 46–47.
65. One big difference between the stories is worth mentioning: the condemned in the Jewish story thinks he is being mocked, so he does not take down just anyone, but someone whom he sees as mocking him.
66. The bathhouse is the site of several rabbinic stories; see Yaron Z. Eliav, "What Happened to Rabbi Abbahu at the Tiberian Bath-House? The Place of Realia and Daily Life in the Talmudic Aggada" [Hebrew], *Jerusalem Studies in Jewish Folklore* 17 (1995): 7–20.

is what makes it funny. The joke-teller is simultaneously the master of the situation and its victim. While he draws laughter, his ploy backfires, and he becomes the target of those he sought to ridicule.[67]

A few words about crucifixion.[68] Like the Roman bath, crucifixion was another marker of the Roman imperial presence in Palestine. It was the most brutal and shameful form of capital punishment, reserved for slaves, brigands, and rivals to imperial rule.[69] Death on a cross was designed to be as painful as possible. The victim was humiliated and shamed, symbolic of the destruction of the physical body and the person's identity.

In most cases, the corpse was left to rot or be eaten by birds, and the victim's remains were left unburied. In Roman culture, crucifixion was the opposite of a "noble Roman death."[70] It was so offensive that civilized people preferred not to talk about it, and few Roman writers dwelt on the details.[71]

Crucifixion was a public act. Crosses were meant to be seen, not only to act as a deterrent but also to provide an entertaining spectacle for onlookers. Martin Hengel has remarked that "crucifixion was a punishment in which the caprice and sadism of the executioners were given free rein."[72] Historical sources confirm this notion. Josephus mentions soldiers

---

67. About the ambiguity of laughter, see Catherine Hezser, *Rabbinic Body Language: Non-verbal Communication in Palestinian Rabbinic Literature of Late Antiquity*, JSJSup 179 (Leiden: Brill, 2017), 229–42.

68. See Helen Bond, "You'll Probably Get Away with Crucifixion: How Brian (and Jesus) Ended Up on a Roman Cross," in *Jesus and Brian: Exploring the Historical Jesus and His Times via Monty Python's Life of Brian*, ed. Joan E. Taylor (London: Bloomsbury T&T Clark, 2015), 113–26. I am thankful to the author for sharing with me her paper before publication.

69. See Peter Garnsey, *Social Status and Legal Privilege in the Roman Empire* (Oxford: Clarendon, 1970), 126–29; Martin Hengel, *Crucifixion in the Ancient World and the Folly of the Message of the Cross* (London: SCM, 1977); Kathleen M. Coleman, "Fatal Charades: Roman Executions Staged as Mythological Enactments," *Journal of Roman Studies* 80 (1990): 44–73; Gunnar Samuelsson, *Crucifixion in Antiquity: An Inquiry into the Background and Significance of the New Testament Terminology of Crucifixion*, WUNT 2/310 (Tübingen: Mohr Siebeck, 2011). For a survey of crucifixions in this period, see John Granger Cook, "Roman Crucifixions: From the Second Punic War to Constantine," ZNW 104 (2013): 1–32; Cook, "Crucifixion as Spectacle in Roman Campania," *NovT* 54 (2012): 68–100; Cook, "Envisioning Crucifixion: Light from Several Inscriptions and the Palatine Graffito," *NovT* 50 (2008): 262–85; Bond, "You'll Probably Get Away with Crucifixion," 115.

70. On the "noble Roman death" tradition, see Valerie M. Hope, *Death in Ancient Rome: A Sourcebook* (London: Routledge, 2007), 39–45. Because it was such a humiliating form of execution, Jesus's death on the cross urgently needed to be transfigured and reinterpreted, a challenge to which the evangelists rose admirably. The shameful, desolate end, still vivid in Mark's account, was transformed by the later gospels into a noble Roman death. Jesus dies as he has lived, with courage, mastery of his emotions, and concern for those he leaves behind. See Bond, "You'll Probably Get Away with Crucifixion," 115–17.

71. So Cicero, *Pro Rabirio* 16; more generally, Hengel *Crucifixion*, 37–38, Bond, "You'll Probably Get Away with Crucifixion," 115.

72. Hengel, *Crucifixion*, 25.

who, after the fall of Jerusalem, nailed their prisoners to crosses in various postures. Tacitus notes the derision that accompanied Christians' crucifixion as punishment for the Great Fire of Rome in 64 CE. Other writers comment on victims nailed through their genitalia, hung on ridiculously high crosses to deride their self-styled "high status," or crucified amid theatrical spectacles.[73] Of course, the mockery made the victim an object of ridicule and exacerbated his humiliation.[74] Culturally speaking, crucifixion seems to have functioned similarly for the Roman arena, where pain and bloodshed served as entertainment.[75] As a degrading and public form of execution, crucifixion also served an essential function by encouraging onlookers to identify with the upholders of justice.[76] As Helen Bond explains:

> The humiliation of the offender served to distance him from the onlookers: the more the crowd laughed and jeered, the greater their own sense of moral superiority, and the more they felt that justice had been seen to be done. The last thing Roman executioners wanted was to encourage a spirit of sympathy amongst the crowd—horror, ridicule, and rejection were much more useful emotions—but of course, the theatre didn't always work. Sometimes people retained their sympathy for the victim to the end.[77]

The centrality of mockery is clear from the gospels, particularly in Mark, the earliest account. Jesus is ridiculed as a false prophet immediately after his trial before the Sanhedrin (Mark 14:65), mocked by Roman soldiers as a false emperor, the "King of the Jews," after the trial before Pilate (15:16–20), and lampooned on the cross by onlookers, the chief priests, and even those crucified alongside him (15:29–32).[78]

No such violent strategies appear in the talmudic story. The narra-

---

73. Bond, "You'll Probably Get Away with Crucifixion," 116.

74. If the crucified was a brigand or a rebel leader, the mockery would be extreme, as the soldiers poked fun at his pretensions in a particularly grotesque way; see Joel Marcus, "Crucifixion as Parodic Exaltation," *JBL* 125 (2006): 73–87.

75. See Coleman, "Fatal Charades," 54–58; Hope, *Death in Ancient Rome*, 28–31, Chris Epplett, "Spectacular Executions in the Roman World," in *A Companion to Sport and Spectacle in Greek and Roman Antiquity*, ed. Paul Christesen and Donald G. Kyle, Blackwell Companions to the Ancient World: Literature and Culture (Malden, MA: Wiley-Blackwell, 2013), 520–32; Bond, "You'll Probably Get Away with Crucifixion," 116; and Joshua Levinson, "Athlete of Faith and Fatal Fictions" [Hebrew], *Tarbiz* 68 (1998): 61–86.

76. See Bond, "You'll Probably Get Away with Crucifixion," 116; and my discussion on death by fire in Reuven Kiperwasser, "Body of the Whore, Body of the Story and Metaphor of the Body," in *Introduction to Seder Qodashim*, ed. Tal Ilan, Monika Brockhaus, and Tanja Hidde, Feminist Commentary on the Babylonian Talmud 5 (Tübingen: Mohr Siebeck, 2012), 305–19.

77. See Bond, "You'll Probably Get Away with Crucifixion," 117.

78. See ibid.

tor does not identify with the imperial Roman culture, nor does he show any appreciation for the idea of Roman justice. Yet he does seem to share the Roman notion of a "noble death" and is thus aware of crucifixion's degrading nature; he does not look to shame the two villains as they die on the cross. Instead, he seems to be laughing at the absurdity of the entire situation: a real rebel and a bath jester, both evildoers from the narrator's point of view, although only one is a criminal according to Roman law, while the other is actually innocent (albeit with an innocence that cannot be proven). Both seem resigned to their fate, carrying their crosses to their death.[79]

Our nameless mocker, who has tasted the destructive power of laughter, is nonetheless able to crack another joke when faced a second time with the Babylonian. This joke is based on the previous one, drawing on the same idiomatic formula: "The noose of the rope on which I will be hanged is now fully stretched." Thus, he seems to be saying to the Babylonian: You are avenged! Yet the Babylonian does not even think of gloating. On the contrary, he laments the Palestinian's unenviable fate and indicates that the opposite of mockery can be found by interpreting Isa 28:22. Although this verse might not seem relevant to our plot, I endorse Lieberman's explanation[80] of the phrase, "Your yoke will be tightened." Here the word "tightened" is a derivative of חזק, which can mean "to be bound." Therefore, the jester's declaration "The noose on which I will hang is not yet tightened" is seen as a reference to this verse. By citing it, the narrator seems to say, "Your noose was already waiting to be bound." Thus, a witty banter, a form of talmudic "gallows humor," is woven throughout this comic yet violent story.

Ancient Roman literature includes instances of victims joking about their imminent execution. Josephus relates the story of a prisoner from Jotapata who "had held out under every variety of torture, and, without betraying to the enemy a word about the state of the town, even under the ordeal of fire, was finally crucified, meeting death with a smile" (*War* 3.321). Jewish valor, even humor, in the face of death is a theme Josephus uses elsewhere, and it is difficult not to see this trope as a subtle hint at Jewish superiority.[81] Strabo relates a story about Spanish prisoners after the Cantabrian wars who continued to sing victory songs even when nailed to their crosses (*Geogr.* 3.4.18). For Strabo, this was a sign of madness, but from the prisoners' point of view, their songs were a final act of heroic, mocking defiance in the face of Roman oppression.

---

79. To any Monty Python viewer, this inevitably recalls the impressive end of *Life of Brian*.

80. See Saul Lieberman, *Ha-Yerushalmi Kipshuto: A Commentary* (Jerusalem: JTS, 1935), 153.

81. See also *War* 2.153 (on the Essenes) and 7.418 (on the Sicarii).

Of course, there is nothing heroic about the two talmudic characters condemned to death. The narrator does not paint them as models of masculine behavior even though they are much closer to him than the oppressive Romans. As Mark Masterson puts it, in keeping with his analysis of Greco-Roman masculinity:

> If we generally think of ancient manhood, we will note that it was a structure elaborated in a dichotomous relationship with femininity. As it was regarded as an attribute of elites, it was also in dichotomous relationships with servility and foreignness.[82]

The humiliated rabbi, whose neck was probably still aching from the jester's blow, offered an appropriate evaluation of subsequent events by interpreting a prophetic verse, as was customary for rabbinic intellectuals. Here, we see that rabbinic masculinity was quite different from the Roman *vir* and from the common Galilean *bar paḥin*.[83]

The logic of power and its depiction, entangled with fundamental notions of maleness, suggests that hierarchies are constructed according to the principle of male superiority within any specific context. For a male, there is always someone who can be defined as lower than himself.[84] Violence plays an ambivalent and disputed role in the behavior and expectations of masculinity across the social spectrum. For diverse male groups, power was integrated into the definition of manhood, however problematically, in part because it was never seen as a feminine characteristic.

The three stories examined in this chapter present situations in which a commoner, a jokester, mocks a stranger. The surrounding society generally reinforces a jokester's social advantage. Humans enjoy laughter, and a jokester provides them with the opportunity to indulge in mirth. Most human societies find a place for laughter within their social practices. Is there any social scenario behind these rabbinic stories? Although slightly outdated in its intent to find what he calls the "structural settings of society," William Martineau's model for the social function of humor has particular relevance for the study of ancient rabbinic humor.

Martineau's model distinguishes three kinds of humor in terms of their relation to groups.[85] The first is humor that is internal to a group.

---

82. See Mark Masterson, "Studies of Ancient Masculinity," in *A Companion to Greek and Roman Sexualities* ed. Thomas K. Hubbard, Blackwell Companions to the Ancient World 100 (Chichester, UK: Wiley, 2014), 28.

83. Regarding some aspects of rabbinic masculinity, see Kiperwasser, "Wives of Commoners."

84. Lin Foxhall, "Introduction," in *When Men Were Men: Masculinity, Power and Identity in Classical Antiquity*, ed. Lin Foxhall and John B. Salmon, Leicester-Nottingham Studies in Ancient Society 8 (London: Routledge 1998), 1–15, here 4.

85. William H. Martineau, "A Model of the Social Functions of Humor," in *The Psychol-*

The second is humor that ridicules the Other but focuses on the internal structure of the in-group. The third also looks at an inter-group setting but focuses on the interaction between that group and a second external group. Martineau sets four variables into three structural settings: actor (the person initiating the humor), audience, subject (i.e., the topic of the humor), and judgment (the audience's reception of the humor).[86] In our stories, we have an actor (i.e., a Palestinian commoner) and a subject (i.e., a Babylonian other), but what is the judgment?[87] Can we know what the implications of these humorous plots were for the intra- and intergroup dynamics? Depending on how the audiences received these plots, the humor could control group behavior, intensify group identity, or control conflict within the group. The intergroup situation describes the effects of humor initiated by an "out-group" on the in-group. Depending on how the in-group evaluates the humor provoked by the out-group, that humor can either boost the in-group's morale or create hostility toward the out-group. We do not know how ancient audiences received these stories, but we can try to reconstruct the narrator's intent behind them. Through the humorous collision between in-group and out-group, when an outsider is ridiculed but an insider is hardly glorified (and is even gently ridiculed), I believe the narrator sought to boost the political status of his particular group. The narrator is clearly distancing himself from the brutish commoners and sympathizing with the alien. The ties within the rabbinic community seem to be stronger than the ties to the problematic butcher, jester, or commoner in these stories.

The work of two pioneers in laughter theory, Henri Bergson (1889–1941) and Mikhail Bakhtin (1895–1975) are particularly relevant to this discussion. Bergson demonstrates how laughter can shake us out of our own conformity, often by showing the absurdity of routine behavior.[88] Yet, while Bergson identifies humor as a tool for freeing the individual from society's strictures, it is Bakhtin who shows how one socially created institution—carnival—simultaneously reverses and reinforces social differences. According to Bakhtin, carnival is a cultural phenomenon in which the "bottom" and the "top" strata change places, reversing the hierarchies of everyday life:

> We find here a characteristic logic, the peculiar logic of the "inside out" (a l'envers), of the "turnabout," of a continual shifting from top to bottom,

---

ogy of Humor: Theoretical Perspectives and Empirical Issues, ed. Jeffrey H. Goldstein and Paul E. McGhee (New York: Academic Press, 1972), 101–25.

86. Ibid., 115.

87. The text, of course, has an audience, but we know little about them and their reception of the text.

88. See Henri Bergson, *Laughter: An Essay on the Meaning of the Comic*, trans. Cloudesley Brereton and Fred Rothwell (London: Macmillan, 1900).

from front to rear, of numerous parodies and travesties, humiliations, profanations, comic crowning and uncrowning. A second life, the second world of folk culture, is thus constructed; it is, to a certain extent, a parody of the extra-carnival life, a "world inside out." However, we must stress that the carnival is a far cry from the negative and formal parody of modern times. Folk humor denies, but it revives and renews at the same time. Bare negation is utterly alien to folk culture.[89]

Bakhtin called the carnival primarily an attempt to explain the breakthrough of radical and violent forces, countering cultural imposition more than piety. A carnival element in a literary work, according to Bakhtin, is mainly a remnant of former pagan revelry being transformed into a protest against present cultural convention. A feature of historical poetics, "carnival" was useful for Bakhtin in explaining the radical tendencies in the culture he witnessed during his lifetime (radical totalitarianism).

As in Bakhtin's carnival model, in our stories, too, the social differences that existed at the outset remain intact in the end. In the story itself, however, the distribution of roles is reflected upon and revised for a while.

Let us now return to our stories from the Yerushalmi. All three revolve around a Babylonian newcomer to the promised land, welcomed by a Palestinian commoner in an unexpected manner. All the stories contain elements of physical violence toward the newcomer, and death overtakes each aggressor in the end. All three cases concern a conflict between local and foreign men. In rabbinic literature, sages sometimes kill their enemies by their words or even by their gaze.[90] The victim in such instances is always a heretic or an enemy who, according to the narrative logic, has to die as soon as possible. But this may not be the case in our three stories. Here, the insider dies and the Other triumphs. Does this indicate that the narrator is rooting for the Other? More likely, these stories express a fear of the internal Other. The Otherness of the Babylonian is due to his cultural background. Behind the clash between our Babylonians and Palestinians, I believe, lies the more significant encounter between two dominant cultures of that period—namely, the Roman Empire and Sasanian Mesopotamia, that is, between West and East. Although the heroes are minorities in their respective imperial contexts, it is in these contexts that their customs and behavioral norms originate. The Palestinian narrator depicts his Babylonian Jewish characters following a commonly

---

89. Mikhail Bakhtin, *Rabelais and His World*, trans. Helene Iswolsky (Cambridge: MIT Press, 1968), 11.
90. See Tamás Turán, "'Wherever the Sages Set Their Eyes, There Is either Death or Poverty': On the History, Terminology and Imagery of the Talmudic Traditions about the Devastating Gaze of the Sages," *Sidra* 23 (2008): 137–205; and Rachel Neis, *The Sense of Sight in Rabbinic Culture: Jewish Ways of Seeing in Late Antiquity,* Greek Culture in the Roman World (New York: Cambridge University Press, 2013), 64–65.

accepted image of Persians in Western literature: their bravery in combat, their carnivorous eating customs, and their ignorance of bath etiquette. Of course, the Palestinian Jewish narrator had many other Jewish Others to choose from—Alexandrian Jews, other Greek-speaking Jews, Roman Jews, and Jews from other Eastern diasporas. Yet, despite the presence of these groups in Palestinian society at the time, the existing literature is almost silent about them. Evidently, none of these potential Others bore the ultimate Otherness of the Babylonian Jew.

The appeal of the Babylonian Otherness to Palestinians stems from the fact that it is only Babylonians who share with Palestinians the value of traditional biblical literacy. Nonetheless, the estrangement of the Babylonians from the Land of Israel makes them into outsiders. The relationship between the diaspora Jew and the Land of Israel is expressed in this conflicted image of the Babylonians constructed by a Palestinian: "a man whose mother despises him and whose stepmother honors him." Conflicts are resolved in various ways in these stories. Still, the Palestinian narrator repeatedly challenges Palestinian stereotypes about people in the diaspora by rethinking his own native land's values and "authentic" culture via-à-vis the diasporic culture. The Palestinian narrator seems to acknowledge that Babylonia is not just a distant country with a sizable Jewish diaspora but also, to some extent, the birthplace of the mythological ancestors of the Jewish people and the land where the tribes of Israel found shelter in exile.

The narrator of the Yerushalmi is a Palestinian insider who tells stories about the attempts of Babylonian guests in the Land of Israel to blend in. The Palestinian narrator is prepared to extend absolute hospitality. A newly arrived Babylonian guest stands at the door, at the border, and is welcomed inside unconditionally. This very welcome can provoke violence.[91] The ensuing violence turns the home inside out, making the host in part a guest, and the guest a host, at least temporarily—recalling Derrida's formulation, "the master of the house is at home, but nonetheless, he comes to enter his home through the guest—who comes from outside."[92] In welcoming the guest, the self is interrupted. In this chapter, we have followed the attempts of a Palestinian narrator to construct his own interrupted self as the host of a guest who takes over his home.[93]

---

91. See Derrida, *Acts*, 77.
92. Ibid., 125.
93. Here and above, I am not talking about the host portrayed in the story. This one is a rather poor host who seeks to take advantage of his guest. Unbeknownst to the host, the guest is a powerful rabbi, and mocking him comes with a steep price. I am talking about the host represented in the mind of the Yerushalmi, in the mind of the narrator. This one has an interrupted self.

4

Hosting Babylonians

Three encounters between Galileans and Babylonians from the Yerushalmi made up our case study for examining the dynamics of accepting/rejecting the Other in Palestinian rabbinic culture.[1] There we observed Derrida's interrupted self in the Yerushalmi, manifested in Palestinian attempts to accept the figure of the Babylonian "Other." Even though rabbinic education encouraged the virtue of hospitality, the appearance of the Other caused the rabbis to be instinctively mindful of the borders of their own realm and, therefore, to draw a line between themselves and the Other. The host's self is interrupted, but the forms in which the interruption is expressed can differ—from a benevolent sorting of their own kind and Others into different but equal groups to the creation of some kind of hierarchy, whether hidden or manifest. Earlier, I followed the narrator's attempts to construct his own interrupted self as a host of the guest who takes over his house. Now we will see one of the methods adopted by Palestinian and Babylonian rabbinic cultures to incorporate the cultural values of the Other while at the same time preserving their borders.

4.1 The Dancing Rabbi

In the charming and rarely discussed story below, the narrator consistently shows how the cultural baggage of the Other is rejected and his personality questioned. However, when he is no longer among the living, his cultural values become the property of the community that formerly rejected him. This story is preserved in two different versions. It appears in both the Yerushalmi and Genesis Rabbah.

Genesis Rabbah 59:4[2]	y. Pe'ah 1:1, 15d[3]
ר׳ שמואל בר רב יצחק פתח: "רודף צדקה וחסד וגו'"(משלי כא כא). כד דמך ר׳ שמואל	דכתיב: "רודף צדקה וחסד ימצא חיים צדקה וכבוד" (משלי כא כא). כבוד בעולם הזה וחיים

---

1. See 53–78 above.
2. Theodor Albeck, 2:632–33.
3. Academia ed., 88.

בר רב יצחק (הוה מרקד אתלת) נפקין רוחין
ועלעולין ועקרין כל אילני טביא דארעא
דישראל. למה כן? דהוה לקיט מינהון שיבשבן
ומהלך קודם כליא, והוו רבנין אמרין: למה הוא
עבד כדין ומבזה אוריתא? אמר ר' זעירא: שבקו
יתיה, דהוא ידע מה עבד. כד דמך, נפקון למגמל
חסד ונחתת שגבשבה דנור ואיתעבידת כמין
שבשבה דהדס ואפסיקת בין ערסה לציבורא.
אמרין: חזווהי דהדין סבא דקמת ליה מתלי
שבשבתיה.
ד"א "רודף צדקה וחסד" (שם), זה אבינו
אברהם שנ': "ושמרו דרך י"י" (בראשית יח
יט). "וחסד" שגמל חסד לשרה. "ימצא חיים"
שנ': "ואלה ימי שני חיי אברהם אשר חי מאת
שנה וגו' (בראשית כה ז). "צדקה וכבוד", אמר
ר' שמואל בר רב יצחק: אמר לו הקדוש ברוך
הוא: אני אומנותי גומל חסדים. תפשת אומנותי,
בוא לבוש לבושי.

לעולם הבא. רבי שמואל בר רב יצחק הוה נסיב
שיבשתיה והוה מקלס קומי כליא והוה רבי
זעירא חמי ליה וטימטמר מן קומוי. אמר: חמי
להדין סבא, איך הוא מבהית לן. וכיון דדמך
הוה תלת שעין קלין וברקין בעלמא. נפקת ברת
קלא ואמרה: דמך רבי שמואל בר רב יצחק,
גמיל חסדיא. נפקון למיגמול ליה חסד. נחתת
אישתא מן שמיא ואיתעבידת כמין שבשא דנור
בין ערסא לציבורא, והוון ברייתא אמרין: חייו
דדין סבא דקמת ליה שבישתיה.

Rabbi Shmuel bar Rabbi Itzhak, interpreted with the help of the verse: "He who strives to do good and kind deeds attains life, success, and honor" (Prov 21:21). When Rabbi Shmuel bar Rab Itzhak died [he used to dance with three branches], winds and eddies arrived and uprooted all the good trees of the Land of Israel. Why did they do it? He had collected branches from them and had marched with these [branches] before the brides. The rabbis used to say: Why was he doing this and degrading the Torah? Said Rabbi Zeira: Leave him because he knows what he is doing. And when he died, they came to pay their respects; suddenly, a branch of fire that appeared like a branch of myrtle came down and intervened between his bier and the congregation. Then they said: The elder showed us that his branch has stood up.
Another teaching: "He who strives to do good and kind deeds attains life, success and honor" (Prov. 21:21).

For it is written, "He who strives to do good and kind deeds attains life, success and honor" (Prov 21:21). He receives honor in this world and life in the world to come. Rabbi Shmuel bar Rabbi Itzhak would take a branch and praise a bride. And Rabbi Zeira, when he saw him, he hid himself. He said: Look at this elder, how he is shaming us. When he died, for three hours there were thunder and lighning in the world. [Then] a *bat-qol* (heavenly voice) emerged and declared: Rabbi Shmuel bar Rabbi Itzhak, the doer of merciful deeds, has died. They went out to pay their respects. A flame came forth from heaven and formed a branch that intervened between his bier and the congregation. And all the people of the community exclaimed: Come and see the elder whose branch has stood up.

"He who strives to do good" refers to Abraham, as it is said: "That they keep the way of the Lord, to do righteousness and justice" (Gen 18:19). "kind deeds"—for he dealt kindly with Sarah (in burying her); "attains life,"—"And these are the days of the years of Abraham's life which he lived, a hundred and seventy-five years" (Gen 25:7). "success and honor"—said Rabbi Shmuel bar Itzhak: Said the Holy One, blessed be He to him: My art is to practice acts of Love. Since you have taken over my art, put on my cloak as well.

In both of these versions, this story expounds a verse from Prov 21:21: רֹדֵף צְדָקָה וָחָסֶד יִמְצָא חַיִּים צְדָקָה וְכָבוֹד, "He who strives to do good and kind deeds attains life, success, and honor." The story's lesson is strongly connected to the conventional and nonconventional meaning of the values mentioned in it: What does it mean to do virtuous deeds, and what exactly is honor?

Let us begin with the story from the Yerushalmi, an anecdote typical of this composition: it has a brief but dramatic plot with an unexpected ending, and, like all good talmudic tales, it has several versions.[4]

Both protagonists are Amoraim of the third generation (the beginning of the fourth century), and both are Babylonians now living in the Galilee. In their youth, they fell in love with the distant Land of Israel and left the fertile, wealthy west of the Sasanian Empire to live and die in the Land of Israel, where both, in time, won the respect of their colleagues, yet always remained strangers. It is not clear whether they traveled from Babylonia together or how close they were in everyday life, but they certainly shared the same destiny. Shmuel bar Rabbi Itzhak was a connoisseur of aggada and famous for doing honorable deeds in the public sphere. Rabbi Zeira, whom we encountered in the previous chapter, was an expert in halakhah and an ascetic.[5]

B. B. Metzi'a 85a relates how Rabbi Zeira fasted a hundred days to forget the learning of Babylonia.[6] Readers have wondered what was so unpal-

---

4. In addition to the two versions given above, the story appears in y. Avod. Zar. 42c 3:1 and b. Ketub. 17a. For a comparative reading of these stories, see Valler, *Women and Womanhood*, 21–27.

5. See 47, 61 above and further 122, 143, and Admiel Kosman, *Men's World: Reading Masculinity in Jewish Stories in a Spiritual Context*, trans. Edward Levin (Würzburg: Ergon, 2009), 87–92.

6. The story has a parallel in the Yerushalmi, see y. Ta'an. 2:13, 76a. There he fasts three

atable to Rabbi Zeira about the Babylonian academies once he acquired a taste for Palestinian learning. Some assumed that he was dissatisfied with the style of Babylonian learning or with Babylonian talmudic discussions. However, in a close study of R. Zeira's teachings and habits, Abraham Goldberg argues that the sage was troubled by the conflict between Palestinian learning and his Babylonian tradition.[7] Goldberg discusses a series of texts in which Zeira appears to recommend Babylonian customs to the head of the Palestinian leadership and other Babylonians living in the Land of Israel. Goldberg concludes that Rabbi Zeira fasted not to forget Babylonian learning as such but to succeed in his purpose of making his Babylonian tradition seem "authentic," that is, Palestinian, so that its former Babylonian character could be "forgotten." I agree with Goldberg that there is indeed a contradiction between the story of Rabbi Zeira's fasts and his Babylonian teachings dispersed throughout the rabbinic corpora. But I am not sure that Goldberg's harmonistic attempt to accommodate the two is necessary. The story of Rabbi Zeira fasting to forget his Babylonian learning can, in my opinion, be seen as a polite expression of his inability to give up his old Babylonian ways (which he never did) and adjust to Palestinian practices. He was typical of many of his contemporaries, as well as later Babylonians, who felt that their own tradition was superior and, therefore, should prevail.

Nevertheless, in Palestinian narratives, Rabbi Zeira appears as someone who sought to immerse himself fully in the teachings of the Land of Israel, to merge with his new chosen culture, even though things did not always go smoothly.[8] About Rabbi Shmuel bar Rabbi Itzhak, whose aggadic interpretations are scattered throughout rabbinic literature, we know very little, except that the story of his death is recorded in four different versions. Although the Palestinian narrator (in the Yerushalmi as in Genesis Rabbah) does not openly declare that both sages are of Babylonian origin, I think this point is crucial for understanding the whole story.

According to the version in the Yerushalmi, Rabbi Shmuel was zealous in the performance of the commandment to honor brides. Such a demon-

---

hundred days, but the reason given for this action—his wish to forget his Babylonian learning—is not stated. Regarding the practice of fasting in rabbinic culture, see Eliezer Diamond, *Holy Men and Hunger Artists: Fasting and Asceticism in Rabbinic Culture* (Oxford: Oxford University Press, 2004). However, he does not discuss this tradition.

7. See Abraham Goldberg, "Rabbi Zeira and Babylonian Custom in Palestine" [Hebrew], *Tarbiz* 36 (1964): 319–41.

8. On Rabbi Zeira's assimilation difficulties in the promised land, there are stories of both Palestinian and Babylonian origin, and I refer to them elsewhere; see 122 and 143 below.

stration of honor is marked in rabbinic literature by the word *kilus* (from Greek καλός, "beautiful"), and rabbis assign considerable importance to it.⁹ Accompanying the bride to her future husband's home, the wedding guests were expected to praise her and dance or walk before her to please her and make the whole event more festive. What kind of dance was it? Two Hebrew roots describe the action of dancing—רקד and חול. A close reading of biblical and talmudic texts reveals a starkly gendered differentiation in using these two roots.¹⁰ All the examples of women dancing in the Hebrew Bible use the root חול.¹¹ The root רקד appears less frequently in the Bible and is usually gender neutral.¹² In rabbinic literature, this strict gender division is maintained.

Here we see another marker of the body language of our protagonist. Presumably, the sages were not dancing the dance usually indicated by the verb *raqad*, meaning jumping and skipping, which is inappropriate for distinguished elders. And, indeed, they were not dancing the dance usually expressed by the root מחל—a circular-movement dance performed by women.¹³ The dance of the sages was neither masculine nor feminine. The use of the words *halakh* and *kalas* probably hints at the movement toward or around the bride.¹⁴ We find another example of dancing before the bride with the verb *raqad* in the Babylonian Talmud, which presents this custom as quite popular. Even the sages paid attention to it.

---

9. Krauss, *Griechische und Lateinische Lehnwörter*, 547; Sokoloff, *Jewish Palestinian Aramaic of the Byzantine Period*, 565.

10. See Tal Ilan, "Dance and Gender in Massekhet Ta'anit," in *A Feminist Commentary to the Babylonian Talmud: Introduction and Studies*, ed. Tal Ilan et al. (Tübingen: Mohr Siebeck, 2007), 217–25.

11. See ibid., 222. See Exod 15:20; Judg 11:34; 21:20; 1 Sam 18:6; Song 7:1; Jer 31:12.

12. Ilan, "Dance and Gender," 217–24; see Ps 114:4.

13. One example of the root מחל (*mahol*) is found in y. Meg. 2:4, 63b with a very vivid scene from the eschatological era, when God becomes ראש חולה: He stands at the head of the circle (חולה) of pious dancing men, who are requested to put their hearts in that dance, while pointing toward the divine presence with their fingers and exclaiming certain biblical verses. As explained by Ilan ("Dance and Gender,"), this form of dance is usually strictly female. Why would pious dancing men at an eschatological celebration accept certain feminine characteristics is an interesting topic for speculation, for which I have no room here.

14. These circumstances were correctly noted by Valler, *Women and Womanhood*, 20: "this story is cited in three Eretz Israel sources, and in none does the protagonist actually dance." She goes on to state, however, that "the original story does not appear to have been related to dancing but rather to the cutting branches of trees in Eretz Israel, in order to beautify and honor the wedding ceremony." Yet cutting the trees could not have embarrassed the sage. It seems more likely that his activities at the wedding ceremonies included some elements of the performing arts and therefore were unacceptable to his colleagues. The Babylonian Talmud got the point of the story right—it is about dancing.

b. Ketubbot 16b–17a

Our Rabbis taught: How does one dance before the bride? Beth Shammai says: The bride as she is. And Beth Hillel says: Beautiful and graceful bride.	תנו רבנן: כיצד מרקדין לפני הכלה? בית שמאי אומרים: כלה כמות שהיא. ובית הלל אומרים: כלה נאה וחסודה.

The Babylonian Talmud in b. Ketub. 16b–17a claims that the schools of Shammai and Hillel had already argued about how to praise the bride, namely, how one dances before the bride and which *kilus*, or panegyric, should be delivered to her. Therefore, it is strange that our hero's attempt to perform a dance or ritual with branches before the bride was regarded as inappropriate for a sage. Does it mean that only the sages in Babylonia used to entertain brides by dancing, and that in Palestine, such activities were left to the common people but considered shameful for the sages? It is hard to say how or why this distinction emerged among the many differences between the cultures of the Babylonian and the Palestinian Amoraim. Perhaps we should accept the evidence of the Babylonian Talmud at face value—that in the tannaitic period, all the sages, along with the common people, danced in front of the bride. This would mean, however, that in the Amoraic period in Roman Palestine, an elitist view prevailed: sages did not dance before uneducated, ordinary people. The Babylonians, however, remained faithful to the custom of dancing before the bride—if we will assume that the custom is pre-Amoraic. Yet, because the baraita about the dancing rite of the *Tannaim* appears only in late Babylonian sources such as the Babylonian Talmud and Massekhet Kallah Rabbati 9:1,[15] it is possible that these dancing customs were observed only in Babylonia and, to justify them, the Babylonian rabbis attributed them to the ancient *Tannaim* of the Land of Israel, thus creating a pseudo-baraita.[16] Such an act of transmission by the Babylonian editors—namely, creating a link to much earlier Jewish authoritative figures—is typical of their redactional approach.[17]

This, at least, is my approach to the encounter at the outset of our story. I suggest that it was a clash of cultures, between two contradictory images of the sage: should a representative of the rabbinic class dance before the bride, as King David had danced before the ark, or should he distance himself from dancing boys and look at them indulgently? Should an elder dance with the youths, or should he take his place among his

---

15. See about this text further 95.

16. As stated by Valler, *Women and Womanhood*, 99: "The Babylonian Talmud is the only source that introduces and develops the theme of dancing," but she does not doubt the Tannaitic attribution of this debate.

17. A similar phenomenon is described by Moshe Benovitz, *Talmud Ha-Igud: BT Berakhot, Chapter 1, With Comprehensive Commentary* (Jerusalem: Union for Interpretation of the Talmud, 2006), 441; and see also Kiperwasser and Ruzer, "To Convert a Persian," 100.

dignified colleagues? The Babylonian immigrant Rabbi Shmuel bar Itzhak behaves like the Babylonian sage that he is—tirelessly dancing in front of the brides, whirling around and waving branches. Presumably, this pleases the bride and guests. But the second Babylonian immigrant, Rabbi Zeira, when confronted with the behavior of his colleague and compatriot, is embarrassed, tries to hide, and even reprimands Rabbi Shmuel, stating that his behavior disgraces the entire rabbinic class, as though saying, Well, I am no longer a Babylonian, and their customs are now alien to me.[18]

This goes on until the inevitable happens: the dancing rabbi dies. His death occurs against a dramatic setting—prolonged thunder and lightning from heaven. To avert any explanation of these pyrotechnics as a chance natural disaster, a *bat qol,* the feminine personification of the divine voice, which in rabbinic works replaces the heavenly voice of the biblical prophets, explains the nature of all these happenings.[19] She proclaims that the dancing elder whose extravagant actions have shamed his associates is, like Rabbi Zeira, a man of virtue; in the terminology of the Talmud, he is a *gomel hisdaia,* a doer of good only for the sake of doing good, who expects no reward or gratitude.

Now the people listening to the divine voice eagerly go out to honor the deceased because they demonstrate their religious devotion by doing so. They view attendance at a funeral a highly virtuous act, because the dead are unable to express gratitude. Following a bride is apparently not as highly valued by this audience. As proof of the esteemed virtues of the deceased, a branch of fire descends from heaven. It resembles the branches with which the sage had danced at weddings. However, the celestial branch is not as harmless as the sage's actions had been—it blocks the way to the coffin, a sight that makes the sages aware of the distance between them and the deceased, whom they had not revered in his lifetime. In this scene, the branch that comes down from heaven, separating mainstream society and the outsider, represents a mute reproach of the dead to the living.

Now let us turn to the Genesis Rabbah version of the story. Here, our hero amuses the bride by dancing before her with branches of "good trees," apparently alluding to her fertility. After the sage's death, winds and storms break the good (fruit) trees as a sign of mourning, since their branches have no other use than to entertain the bride, and now there is no

---

18. At a conference in Ann Arbor, Ellen Muellenberg suggested to me that Rabbi Zeira is worried that Rabbi Shmuel's actions reflect on him; she claims that he is not really the Other, because the behavior of the Other would not bring shame. People tend to disparage Others or ridicule them but save their corrections for those who could be seen to be "ours" in some fashion. It is difficult for me to accept this. Otherness is not something that can be measured. The Otherness of Shmuel here is obvious—he is an Other by reason of his motherland and his customs, but of course since he belongs to the community of rabbis, he is an internal Other whose acceptance is even more challenging than that of a distant Other.

19. See Ilan, *Massekhet Ta'anit,* 259–64.

one to use them for this purpose. The conspicuous coming of "winds and eddies" lends a distinctive character to this event.

The expression "winds and eddies" paraphrases the Aramaic targumic tradition of 2 Kgs 2:11: "... and Elijah ascended in a whirlwind," which is retold in the Aramaic targum with the words, "Elijah was taken away by winds and eddies into heaven." Thus, there is something prophetic in depicting the sage's death and the heavenly realm's concern about his reputation.[20] In this version, the rejection of the Babylonian sage by his Palestinian colleagues finds more explicit expression: they complain about his behavior, and Rabbi Zeira, not so timid as in the previous version, is trying to rehabilitate his friend.

However, Rabbi Shmuel, recognized or rejected, remains an outsider in any case, a stranger, and his Palestinian brethren regard their colleague with some detachment. Thus here, without the intervention of the *bat qol*, the fiery branch descends from heaven, striking fear into the funeral guests. Closer to the ground, however, it becomes a normal myrtle branch, like the one waved at wedding rituals by the now-deceased sage, and blocks the path from the living Galileans to the deathbed of the Babylonian. Unlike the fiery branch, one can cross or step over a myrtle branch. Yet it retains its divine nature, maintaining the same distance that the Palestinian colleagues kept from the Babylonian in his lifetime. In this version, the last words express remorse and a willingness to accept the deceased, for whom the heavens have produced the myrtle branch, and to follow his example.

The editor of Genesis Rabbah tells this story in the context of interpreting Gen 25:7, which describes Abraham's old age. The interpretation of a verse from the Psalms, "He who strives to do good and kind deeds attains life, success, and honor" (21:21), is used here to illustrate the honored patriarch's old age. Surprisingly, this verse is put into the mouth of Rabbi Shmuel ben Itzhak, the main character of our story, thereby raising the question about a possible connection between this verse and the story. It is not difficult to note a slight discrepancy. Rabbi Shmuel, of course, meted out justice and mercy—as he understood them—and eventually gained honor, but only after his death. Is the editor of Genesis Rabbah ironic? Perhaps he wishes to say that to "attain life" is to find life after death? The myrtle branch that appears after the sage's death symbolizes the honor finally accorded to him, the honor of which he had been deprived in his lifetime.

This is a case of a not-so-easy integration of a Babylonian sage into the intellectual culture of the Land of Israel. Some rabbis want to erase their

---

20. The targum uses the same rare world עלעול that is used in our story and appears also in another story in which a no less significant encounter between this world and the heavenly realm take place. See Jonah Fraenkel, *Studies in the Spiritual World*, 163 n. 9; and Galit Hasan-Rokem, *Web of Life: Folklore and Midrash in Rabbinic Literature*, Contraversions (Stanford, CA: Stanford University Press, 2000), 158–59.

former self, memory, and loyalties in order to become integrated into their new environment. Others dare to be true to themselves, and their cultural baggage over time becomes part of their adopted culture, albeit only after eddies and winds have borne the baggage carriers to other worlds. It is probably not very comforting, but it is the way the world moves on.

The dancing customs of the deceased rabbi were frowned upon by the Palestinian sages, possibly because, according to their cultural mindset, dancing in public was inappropriate for sages or older men. Curiously, we discover in Roman culture, on the margins of which the Palestinian rabbinic culture thrived, the same disapproval of dancing. Romans enjoyed watching female and male dancers and praised their art,[21] but considered the act of dancing improper for respectable citizens. Cicero, for example, remarked:

> For no man, one may almost say, ever dances when sober, unless perhaps he be a madman; nor in solitude, nor in the moderate and sober party, dancing is a last companion of prolonged feasting, of luxurious situation, and of many refinements. (*Mur.* 6:13)[22]

Plutarch expressed similar disdain (*Mor.* 9:15). These Roman authors articulated a cultural attitude to dance that parallels that which we saw in our Palestinian texts.[23] By contrast, ancient Greek culture was quite positive about dancing. Like the Greeks, our Babylonian protagonists and the narrators of the Babylonian Talmud stemmed from a culture in which dance was part of their world, including their religious celebrations. Thus, criticisms about dance were difficult for them to grasp.

Let us return to the interrupted self of the Yerushalmi. Whereas in the previous chapter, we followed the attempts of the narrator of the Yerushalmi to construct his own, interrupted self as host of the guest who takes over his house, here the author of the narrative tradition common to Yerushalmi and Genesis Rabbah attempts to reunite the interrupted self, to incorporate the values of the Other into his heritage.

At some point this narrative tradition left its Galilean homeland, made its way back to our Babylonian immigrants' homeland in Mesopotamia, and was retold there in Bavli. It appears in a series of stories where different rabbis compete to best praise the bride, and their dancing customs are explored in great detail.

---

21. See Lucian of Samosata, *De saltatione* (trans. A. M. Harmon, LCL); Antonis K. Petrides, "Lucian's 'On Dance' and the Poetics of the Pantomime Mask," in *Performance in Greek and Roman Theatre*, ed. George W. M. Harrison and Vayos Liapis, Mnemosyne Supplements 353 (Leiden: Brill, 2013), 433–50.

22. See http://www.perseus.tufts.edu/hopper/text?doc=Perseus:abo:phi,0474,014:6:13.

23. For a concise description of the place of dance in ancient cultures, see Keith N. Schoville, "Dance," in *Dictionary of Daily Life in Biblical and Post-Biblical Antiquity*, ed. Edwin M. Yamauchi and Marvin R. Wilson, 3 vols. (Peabody, MA: Hendrickson, 2014), 1:374–86.

b. Ketubbot 17a

Rav Shmuel bar Rabbi Itzhak danced three [times].[24] Rabbi Zeira said: The old man is putting us to shame. When he died, a pillar of fire came between him and the whole [of the rest of the] world. And there is a tradition that a pillar of fire has made such a separation only for one in a generation or only for two in a generation. Rabbi Zeira said: His sticks [befitted] the elder, and some say: His folly [befitted] the elder, and some say: his habit [befitted] the elder.	רב שמואל בר רב יצחק מרקד אתלת. א"ר זירא: קא מכסיף לן סבא. כי נח נפשיה, איפסיק עמודא דנורא בין דידיה לכולי עלמא; וגמירי, דלא אפסיק עמודא דנורא אלא אי לחד בדרא אי לתרי בדרא. א"ר זירא: אהנייה ליה שוטיתיה לסבא, ואמרי לה: שטותיה לסבא, ואמרי לה: שיטתיה לסבא.

The narrator here does not seem to understand why the sage's behavior posed a problem and why Rabbi Zeira derided the customs of his compatriot. He is sure that the story was a panegyric to the Babylonian and proposes three different readings of R. Zeira's statement with the problematic word *shtut*: It refers to (1) his whip (*shot*), (2) his folly (*shtut*), and (3) his rabbinical method (*shita*). I would suggest that, in the original Palestinian tradition, we find only "folly," which the Babylonian Talmud apologetically balances with the other two.[25]

During the centuries in which the basic narrative traditions of the

---

24. The expression מרקד אתלת is elliptical and, because in the previous anecdote in the sequence in the Bavli the other sage is dancing with a branch of myrtle, commentators assumed that "the three" in our story are three branches of myrtle. Therefore they assumed that the old rabbi was dancing with three twigs. However, see Mira Balberg and Haim Weiss, "'That Old Man Shames Us': Aging, Liminality, and Antinomy in Rabbinic Literature," *JSQ* 25 (2018): 17–41. Balberg and Weiss argue against the accepted reading of this sentence. They claim that the preposition used in this term "makes this an unlikely interpretation: assuming that one holds myrtle branches in one's hands, why would one be dancing 'on' the branches? Rather we find it more likely that the three on which Shmuel is said to dance are three legs—that is, his own two legs and a cane" (39). However, I find their interpretation highly unlikely, taking into account the fact that the above-mentioned preposition, which they, probably influenced by their mother tongue, simply understand as "on" (which is in Modern Hebrew), actually means something like "near, upon, close to, according to" (see Sokoloff, *Jewish Palestinian Aramaic of the Byzantine Period*, 1–2). It is true, though, that branches of myrtle are not mentioned here, and therefore the word *three* could be interpreted differently. However, the second part of their interpretation, regarding "three legs" is even more problematic, in light of the fact that the verb *rqd* means bouncing on the spot, which is apparently not so easy to do for a limping old man with a staff in his hands. In sum, if one wishes to reject the traditional reading "to dance with three myrtle branches," the appropriate understanding would be, to the best of my knowledge, that he bounced a three-cubit distance; that is, he made a dancing leap that covered a distance of three cubits, which is no small thing for an old man. For a similar word usage see b. Eruv. 52b: "one who left the second (cubit) and was within the third (קם אתלת)."

25. Unless שוטיתיה means his sticks/twigs here also, and then the meaning is again ambiguous.

Yerushalmi and Genesis Rabbah evolved, the Galilee was rife with tensions between competing identity narratives. When scholars talk about the shaping of Jewish identities, they generally do so within the framework of a region's various cultures. Naturally, they speak in our context about hellenization and the growth and expansion of Christianity and other Jewish and gentile heresies. These exerted considerable pressures on rabbinic culture formation and acted as catalysts for redefining the parameters of an imagined rabbinic community. Here I have shown how the identity of this community was shaped through its encounter with the internal Other, a related but independent rabbinic culture.[26]

Palestinian rabbinic literature is filled with stories in which the Palestinian narrator attempts to cope with the figure of the Babylonian Other. The sheer volume of these stories indicates that the shaping of Palestinian rabbinic identity was crucial at that time and that our storyteller felt threatened by the presence of a Babylonian scholar in his vicinity. The relatively small number of stories by Babylonians about hosting their Palestinian brethren may also be taken as evidence for specific patterns; I will examine these stories later.[27] The Babylonian Other's significance for the Palestinian rabbinic narrators does not mean that Palestinian rabbinic culture was less xenophobic than other cultures of late antiquity, but instead attests that the presence of this particular Other was necessary for their identity formation. Rabbinic narrative tradition opens a window into the process of identity building and allows us to hypothesize about power relationships in Palestinian society concerning commoners and outsiders.

Concluding this chapter with the help of Derrida's explanatory model, we can see the life story of this Babylonian as the story about the guest at the gate of the house he felt that he had the right to enter. As a result of this feeling of entitlement, his manners were repulsive and unacceptable to the hosts; the assigned place for him became the threshold outside the host's dwelling. Surprisingly, he was eventually welcomed inside, but only posthumously, thus establishing a tradition of a postmortem acceptance, when one's pranks become a text to interpret. Here we can see at work a new, more radical model of the guest being appropriated. The guest is welcomed, and his cultural values are accepted; eventually, they are even adopted by the host himself.

4.2. The Silent Student

Analyzing the narrative tradition below, I make use of the above mentioned term *life-world*.[28] Here I will also introduce the term *life conditions*,

---

26. See quotation from Joshua Levinson above, 12.
27. See chapter 8
28. About the term see 89 above.

which Bjorn Kraus has derived from Edmund Husserl's phenomenological ideas (German *Lebenslage*), juxtaposing the two terms.[29] Further, I incorporate this opposition into the analyzed tradition, or, more precisely, into the culture that produced the rabbinic narrative. Now, life-world refers to an individual's subjectively experienced world, and life conditions to the individual's actual circumstances in life. Thus, it could be said that a person's life-world depends on his or her particular life conditions. These, in turn, include the material and immaterial circumstances of life, such as the social environment. The life-world, as noted, describes the subjective perception of these conditions.

In the second half of the fourth century, Palestinian rabbis lived in a social environment inhabited by Others, some of them internal and some of them external. It is quite possible that the rabbinic community played a relatively modest social role in contrast to the other elites.[30] In their own life-world, however, the rabbis perceived their role as significant. I propose here a case study, showing how Palestinian rabbis created their life-world.

y. Mo'ed Qatan 3:7, 83c[31]

[Sufficient time for] one person to greet another. Abbah bar bar Ḥanna in the name of Rabbi Yoḥanan: Sufficient time for a master to be greeted by a disciple, saying to him: Peace be with you, my master.	שאילת שלום בין אדם לחבירו, אבא בר בר חנה בשם רבי יוחנן: כדי שאילת שלום בין הרב לתלמיד, ויאמר לו: שלום עליך רבי.

---

29. Björn Kraus, *Erkennen und Entscheiden: Grundlagen und Konsequenzen eines erkenntnistheoretischen Konstruktivismus für die Soziale Arbeit* (Weinheim: Beltz Juventa, 2013), 66, 145.

30. See Seth Schwartz, *Imperialism and Jewish Society, 200 B.C.E. to 640 C.E.*, Jews, Christians, and Muslims from the Ancient to the Modern World 32 (Princeton: Princeton University Press, 2002).

31. Academia ed., 820. Partial parallels to this more extended tradition are found in y. Ber. 2:1, 4b; y. Sheqal. 2:6, 47a; and b. Yevam. 96b–97a. Apparently, however, they are all secondary. In y. Sheqalim the pericope is used to illustrate the idea that citation in the name of the master is obligatory, as is related in a baraita: "Rabbi Shimeon ben Gamliel says: They do not make funerary monuments [*nefashot*] for righteous men, for their words are their memorial." It seems, however, that the tradition is not original to the context in y. Sheqalim: it appears neither in the Leiden manuscript nor in the Genizah fragments of the same pericope. Furthermore, the y. Sheqalim text has been revised to bring it in line with b. Yevamot. To be sure, Ginzberg appears to have argued that all versions of the pericope were influenced by, or "taken from," the Babylonian Talmud, at least in part, but this is not true regarding the version provided in y. Mo'ed Qatan cited here. On the problems created by this passage, see Epstein, *Prolegomena ad Litteras Amoraiticas*, 536; Ginzberg, *Commentary on the Palestinian Talmud*, 1:235 and n. 7; Yaakov Sussman, "Masoret Limmud u-Mesoret Nusah shel ha-Talmud ha-Yerushalmi: Le-Verur Nusha'otehav shel Yerushalmi Masekhet Sheqalim," in *Researches in Talmudic Literature: A Study Conference* in Honour of the Eightieth Birthday of Sha'ul Lieberman [Hebrew] (Jerusalem: Israel Academy of Sciences and Humanities, 1983), 12–76, here 48.

Rabbi Yoḥanan was leaning on Rabbi Jacob bar Idi, and Rabbi Lazar saw Rabbi Yoḥanan and hid. Rabbi Yoḥanan said: This Babylonian committed two wrongs against me, one that he did not greet me, and another that he did not recite a teaching in my name. Rabbi Jacob bar Idi said to him: This is the custom among them [i.e., the Babylonians], that a lesser man does not greet a greater man, since they are accustomed to observing the verse: "Youths saw me and hid, elders arose and stood" (Job 29:8).

As they were walking, they saw a study house. Rabbi Jacob bar Idi said to Rabbi Yoḥanan: Here Rabbi Meir would sit and expound, and recite teachings in the name of Rabbi Ishmael, but not in the name of Rabbi Aqiva. He responded, everyone knows that Rabbi Meir is the student of Rabbi Aqiva [and so it would have been superfluous to cite him by name]. Rabbi Jacob responded: And everyone knows that Rabbi Lazar is the student of Rabbi Yoḥanan.

Rabbi Jacob said to Rabbi Yoḥanan: Is it permitted to pass before the image of Adori? He responded: Do you show honor to him? Pass before him and ignore him. He responded: Then Rabbi Lazar acted properly when he did not pass before you.
He said to him: Rabbi Jacob bar Idi, you truly know how to pacify.

רבי יוחנן הוה מיסתמיך על רבי יעקב בר אידי והוה רבי לעזר חמי ליה ומיטמר מן קומוי. אמר: הא תרתין מילין הדין בבלייא עבד לי: חדא, דלא שאל בשלמי, וחדא דלא אמר שמועתא מן שמי. אמר ליה: כן אינון נהגין גבון זעירא לא שאיל בשלמיה דרבה דאינון מקיימין "ראוני נערים ונחבאו וישישים קמו עמדו" (איוב כט ח).

מי מהלכין, חמי ליה חד בית מדרש. אמר ליה: הכין הוה רבי מאיר יתיב ודרש ואמר שמועתא מן שמיה דרבי ישמעאל, ולא אמר שמועתא מן שמיה דרבי עקיבה. אמר ליה: כל עמא ידעין דרבי מאיר תלמידיה דרבי עקיבה. אמר ליה: וכל עמא ידעין דרבי אלעזר תלמידיה דרבי יוחנן.

ומהו מיעבור קומי אדורי צלמא? אמר ליה: ומה את פליג ליה איקר? עבור קומוי ואסמי עיינוי. אמר ליה: יאות רבי לעזר עבד לך, דלא עבר קומך. אמר ליה: רבי יעקב בר אידי, יודע את לפייס.

As is well known, to be honored is an important aim for a man of letters. Literati place a high value on honor because it amounts to recognition by colleagues and students, which is the main criterion for achievement in their world. This could explain why, independently of one another, scholars studying the cultures of Babylonian and Palestinian rabbis against the backdrop of their surrounding local cultures have concluded that the pol-

92 Going West

itics of honor and shame lie at the heart of rabbinic actions.[32] Two well-known scholars of rabbinic culture in late antiquity, Seth Schwartz and Jeffrey Rubenstein, see honor/shame politics as its primary characteristic. Schwartz views the high value of honor and shame as a feature of Mediterranean society. Rubenstein regards the same value as something typically Sasanian-Babylonian culture, possibly influenced by the local oriental culture.[33] Schwartz discussed the above story as evidence for the Roman values held by Palestinian rabbis.[34] However, a reading of this text reveals that the dynamics of the acceptance of the internal Other outweigh the dynamics of incorporating the values of any distant Other. In all of its versions, our story appears immediately after a standard rabbinic account, which points out the rabbinic student's obligation to greet his master, at the very least, with the traditional phrase: Peace [be] with you, Rabbi!

When we bear this customary greeting in mind, the beginning of our story sounds very strange. The famous and venerable Rabbi Yoḥanan is walking on a street in Tiberias, leaning on the arm of a Rabbi Jacob bar Idi, his friend, and notices a student-disciple. He is a Babylonian named Rabbi Eleazar ben Pedat, who often appears near his master in stories and halakhic pericopae.[35]

When a master meets his student, he expects an expression of respect. Unexpectedly for this teacher, however, no greeting from the student is forthcoming. According to the narrator, the student even hid from the master. Despite the ambiguity of the language, it is evident that both rabbis were aware of the student's presence. Shortly afterward, the master, now a sufficient distance from the student, pours out his heart to his friend: "This Babylonian committed two wrongs against me; first, he did not greet me, and second, he did not recite a teaching in my name." In Rabbi Yoḥanan's dismay at his pupil's behavior, compounded by his Otherness, he refers to him as "the Babylonian": the rabbi implies that it is worse to be

---

32. See Schwartz, *Were the Jews a Mediterranean Society?*, 150–51.

33. See Rubenstein, *Culture of the Babylonian Talmud*, 67–79.

34. Honor and shame are pervasively important in the Yerushalmi's stories of intrarabbinic relations; what is less important, though still not wholly absent (see, e.g., the prayer of Rabbi Nehuniah ben Haqanah in y. Ber. 4:2, 7d), is the theme of dishonor resulting from defeat in an argument. This is perhaps because there are far fewer anecdotes about rabbinic arguments in the Palestinian than in the Babylonian Talmud. The two Talmudim are not opposites on this point but feature slightly different inflections of a shared set of themes. The real distinction between them is in their attitude not toward honor or shame but toward dialectical argumentation; see, e.g., David Brodsky, "From Disagreement to Talmudic Discourse: Progymnasmata and the Evolution of a Rabbinic Genre," in *Rabbinic Traditions Between Palestine and Babylonia*, ed. Ronit Nikolsky and Tal Ilan, Ancient Judaism and Early Christianity 89 (Leiden: Brill, 2014), 173–231.

35. Rabbi Eleazar (b. Pedat) was a third-generation (290–320 CE) Amora who studied with Rabbi Yoḥanan (see y. Sanh. 1:2, 18c; y. Ber. 2:1, 4b).

rejected by a foreigner than by a local resident. The teacher was distraught by being doubly wounded in public by his own student-disciple.³⁶

Rabbi Yoḥanan's companion begins with the second complaint. It was customary in the rabbinic community to attribute one's source of information to one's master. Y. Shabb. 1:2, 3a explicitly contrasts two approaches to this question:

Rabbi Hezekiah, Rabbi Jeremiah, Rabbi Ḥiyya in the name of Rabbi Yoḥanan: If you can trace the authority behind a tradition to Moses, do so, and if not, put the first [name you hear] first or the last last.	רבי חזקיה, רבי ירמיה, רבי חייא, בשם רבי יוחנן: אם יכול את לשלשל את השמועה עד משה, שלשלה, ואם לאו, תפוש או ראשון ראשון או אחרון אחרון.
What is the scriptural basis for the statement? "And teach them to your children and your grandchildren, especially concerning the day you stood before the Lord your God in Horeb" (Deut 4:9–10).	מה טעמא? "והודעתם לבניך ולבני בניך יום אשר עמדת לפני ה' אלהיך בחורב" (דברים ד ט-י).
Gidul said: Anyone saying a tradition from the mouth of the one who said it should see the author of the tradition as if he is standing before him.	גידול אמר: כל האומ' שמועה מפי אומרה, יהא רואה בעל השמועה כאלו הוא עומד כנגדו.

Rabbi Yoḥanan promotes the traditional view: since all traditions supposedly come from Moses anyway, it does not matter how a certain teaching was transmitted; one should cite it in the name either of the earliest rabbi or of the latest rabbi to whom the teaching is attributed. Neither the earliest nor the latest rabbi has a particular claim on the teaching—they are equal in Rabbi Yoḥanan's eyes. Gidul implies a different sense of attribution.³⁷ For him, teachings are intimately connected with whoever uttered them. Thus, when we cite a tradition, we are engaging not with all the generations of sages from Moses to our time but with the individual master who said it, a particular person we can imagine before our eyes, who can be called the "proprietor" (*ba'al*) of the tradition.³⁸ According

---

36. The story was analyzed recently by Hezser as an example of cultural misunderstanding between Babylonians and Palestinians regarding their body language (*Rabbinic Body Language*, 71–75).

37. This scholar is difficult to identify. It is possible that Gidul is a Rab Giddel, one of the bearers of this name mentioned in both Talmudim, see Albeck, *Introduction*, 194. In any case, this name is found only among the Babylonian rabbis, so it is possible that the teaching is of Babylonian origin.

38. See Moulie Vidas, "The Emergence of Talmudic Culture: Overview of a Work in Progress" (forthcoming).

to both Yoḥanan and Gidul, however, none of the rabbinic traditions can be expounded without the name of a sage from whom the teaching was received.

Thus, the Babylonian stranger, as depicted by Rabbi Yoḥanan, becomes unacceptable, not only because of his foreignness but also because of the Otherness of his behavior. However, in the words of Yoḥanan's companion, Rabbi Jacob, the stranger is consistently rehabilitated because of his native Babylonian upbringing. The Babylonians took the verse mentioned above from the book of Job—"Youths saw me and hid, elders arose and stood"—not quite literally. The verse implies that, when Job was strong and prosperous, along his route to his place at the city gate, young men sheepishly withdrew, and the aged were brought before him. However, according to this hypothetical Babylonian interpretation,[39] the youth expressed veneration for an elder by silently withdrawing from his presence or path. In the East, suggests Rabbi Jacob, people demonstrate respect not by words but by silence and detachment. Looking for evidence of this approach in the Babylonian Talmud, we find the following tradition:

b. Berakhot 27b

Rav Yehuda said in the name of Rab: A man should never pray neither next to his master nor behind his master	אמר רב יהודה אמר רב: לעולם אל יתפלל אדם לא כנגד רבו ולא אחורי רבו.
And it has been taught: Rabbi Eliezar says: One who prays behind his master, and one who greets his master, and one who returns a greeting to his master, and one who is in disagreement with the lesson of his master, and one who says something which he has not heard from his master causes the Divine Presence to depart from Israel.	ותניא: רבי אליעזר אומר: המתפלל אחורי רבו, והנותן שלום לרבו, והמחזיר שלום לרבו, והחולק על ישיבתו של רבו, והאומר דבר שלא שמע מפי רבו, גורם לשכינה שתסתלק מישראל.

This is a vigorous exhortation by the Babylonian redactor, forming the core of the relationship between students and master. The ruling "one who prays behind his master etc." is attributed to the ancient *tanna* Rabbi Eliezer. However, because there are no parallels to it in Tannaitic literature and in Palestinian Amoraic literature, it seems to be a Babylonian tradition.[40] Its Palestinian pedigree has been invented in order to increase

---

39. See also the usage of the verse in an enigmatic story in y. Mo'ed Qatan. 3:1, 81c, which I intend to discuss elsewhere.

40. The Babylonian Talmud is known to depict certain traditions as baraitot, whereas the Yerushalmi does not represent the parallel tradition as Tannaitic; see Jacob Nahum

the authoritativeness of the Babylonian norm. The "Babylonian baraita" underscores perfectly a Babylonian norm regulating a master–student relationship, according to which the student should keep a distance between himself and his master during prayer because otherwise the student would seem to be putting himself on the same level with the master. Thus, a student should not pray in the vicinity of his master, greet him, not to debate with him, or teach anything original but rather teach only the learning imparted to him by his master.

The late Babylonian treatise Kallah[41] elaborates this norm further.

Kallah 1:24[42]

| Rabbi Eliezer said: One who greets his master deserves mortal punishment. Ben Azai said: One who greets his master or answers his greeting or disagrees with his lesson—deserves mortal punishment. And everyone who says something attributed to the sage, but he never taught him that, he causes the Shekhina to depart from Israel and whoever says something in the name of the one who said it, he brings salvation to this world, as it is written: "Esther told the king in Mordecai's name" (Esth 2:22). | ר' אליעזר אומר: הנותן שלום לרבו חייב מיתה. בן עזאי אומר: כל הנותן שלום לרבו, ומחזיר לו, וחולק על ישיבתו, חייב מיתה, וכל האומר דבר מפי חכם שלא גמרו ממנו, גורם לשכינה שתסתלק מישראל, וכל האומר דבר בשם אומרו מביא גאולה לעולם, שנאמר "ותאמר אסתר למלך בשם מרדכי" (אסתר ב,כב). |

Epstein, *Introduction to the Mishnaic Text* [Hebrew] (Jerusalem: Magnes, 2000), 775-76, and Sussman, "Oral Torah," 273 n. 47.

41. There are two tractates with the title Kallah, a short one (Kallah) and a long one (Kallah Rabbati). Michael Higger, in his introduction to the edition of tractates, showed that the text of the short one is secondary to the long one; see *Massekhet Kallah Rabbati*, ed. Michael Higger (New York: Hotza·at De-vei Rabbanan, 1936), 32–33. The long one, according to Higger, is a post-talmudic Babylonian work. For a new study on that work, see David Brodsky, *A Bride without a Blessing: A Study in the Redaction and Content of Massekhet Kallah and Its Gemara*, TSAJ 118 (Tübingen: Mohr Siebeck, 2006). Brodsky (243–58) rejects Higger's conclusions, claiming that both works are complementary and from the same time. He proposes that the traditions of Kallah Rabbati 1–2 are genuine Babylonian Amoraic traditions. However, see the recent work of Yachin Epstein, "Studies in Massekhet Kalla Rabbati: Text, Redaction and Period" [Hebrew] (PhD diss., Hebrew University of Jerusalem, 2009), 361–84, which defends the traditional point of view on the late edition of this treatise.

42. See Higger, *Massekhet Kallah Rabbati*, 163–64. The same tradition appears in Kallah Rabbati 2:15, however with some changes. The first saying is attributed to Rabbi Eliezer ben Yaakov, the second to Eliezer ben Dehavai, namely, to other Tannaim. An interesting discussion, including an attempt to harmonize the above-mentioned norm with the reality, appears in one of the Kallah Rabbati's manuscripts; see Epstein, "Studies in Massekhet Kalla Rabbati," 82–83.

The formulation of this pseudo-Palestinian attribution is even stricter in this post-talmudic tractate than it is in the Babylonian Talmud itself. However, neither the Palestinian Talmud, nor any other Palestinian rabbinic composition, cites these strict "Tannaitic" regulations; the Yerushalmi insists that a student should greet his master.

y. Berakhot 2:1, 4b[43]

It was taught: [One who wishes to interrupt his recitation of the Shema'] to greet his teacher or [to greet] one who is greater than himself in Torah-learning, he is permitted to do so. From this rule, we deduce that a person must greet one who is greater than himself in Torah-learning.	תני: השואל בשלום רבו, או במי שהוא גדול ממנו בתורה, הרשות בידו. הדא אמרה: שאדם צריך לשאול במי שהוא גדול ממנו בתורה.

Michael Higger (1898–1952), in his introduction to Kallah, pointed out that this is just one of an extensive list of differences between Palestinian and Babylonian practices, which continued even into the early medieval period, as evidenced in Gaonic writings.[44]

Can we infer any differences between the cultures of the Palestinian Jews and the Babylonian Jews from their greeting customs, or does the narrator envision the "other" culture to be the antithesis of his own? The tradition suggests that, whereas the insiders are accustomed to ritualized, formulaic greetings at their meetings, the "Others" are more reserved in manner. What seems evident is that the narrator is putting his own desire to rehabilitate the Babylonian in the mouth of Rabbi Jacob, and perhaps also to preserve Rabbi Yoḥanan's honor, which involves justifying the Babylonian's behavior. This he does by not having Rabbi Eleazar address his master Rabbi Yoḥanan by name. Additionally, the fact that Rabbi Eleazar is a disciple of Rabbi Yoḥanan is undeniable, so that anything the student might say is supposed to be attributed to his teacher. This notion, however, is never uttered in rabbinic literature, and, as I have noted above,[45] in rab-

---

43. Academia ed., 3.

44. Higger, *Massekhet Kallah Rabbati*, 29. Ginzberg, in his commentary to y. Berakhot makes similar observations (*Commentary on the Palestinian Talmud*, 2:242). Moses Averbach, however, opines that not greeting the master was an ancient Palestinian custom that had been forgotten by the Amoraic period in Palestine but survived in Babylonia (*Jewish Education in the Mishnaic and Talmudic Period* [Hebrew] [Jerusalem: Reuven Maas; Baltimore: Hebrew College, 1983], 154), but this explanation seems dubious to me, and even Averbach himself does not insist on it; see 154.

45. See 94.

binic texts from the Land of Israel (e.g., y. Shabb. 1:2, 3a), students are urged to mention their teachers' names. In this sense, the Babylonian's apparent rudeness, by failing to mention his master's name, could be attributed not to his Otherness but to his adherence to the ethical habits of his homeland.

To be the Other means to be someone difficult to accept; now, however, with Rabbi Jacob's apology, Rabbi Eleazar is accepted. On the other hand, rules of social etiquette are loosened, and the dividing line between appropriate and inappropriate becomes blurred. The traditional etiquette of greetings is called into question.

The finishing touch to the Babylonian portrait was applied as if by chance, in a discussion about the details of a halakhic topic unrelated to the rude Babylonian student. In Tiberias, there was a famous statue called by the rabbis "Adori." According to some scholars, this name is a mistaken transcription of the name of Emperor Hadrian; according to others, it is a hard to identify Egyptian deity. In any case, it is a deified figure, whose veneration by Jews was forbidden.[46] Rabbi Jacob innocently asks if passing in front of the statue would be equivalent to worshiping it. According to the understanding of the nature of icons in late antiquity, the deity dwelling in the statue is meant to be honored. The existence of a foreign deity is not denied by this text, but its power and influence were not recognized by Jews and Christians, who regarded pagan gods as evil demons.[47] This made the question about the veneration of the gods and their public

---

46. As one can deduce from y. Avod. Zar. 3.8, 43b. The word was widely discussed, yet its meaning is still uncertain; in addition, it is not clear why it is דאדורי צילמא and not צילמא דאדורי. The statue is mentioned several times in the Talmud and seems to have been a well-known landmark, perhaps in Tiberias. Samuel Klein proposed that Adori = Adrianos (*Galilee: Geography and History of Galilee from the Return from Babylonia to the Conclusion of the Talmud* [Hebrew], 2nd ed. [Jerusalem: Mossad Harav Kook, 1967], 99–100), whereas Samuel Krauss suggested that it is Arueris, allegedly a Hellenistic-Egyptian deity—the transformation of the ancient Egyptian god Horus ("Ägyptische und syrische Götternamen im Talmud," in *Semitic Studies in Memory of Rev. Dr. Alexander Kohut*, ed. George Alexander Kohut [Berlin: Calvary, 1897], 339–53, here 345). Both ideas were rejected by Schwartz (*Were the Jews a Mediterranean Society?* 136) as unconvincing. Schwartz was more impressed by another suggestion of Krauss, who found a reading in Midrash Shmuel 19:4 (הרודים *harodim*) that may indicate that the statue portrayed Herod Antipas, who was the founder of the city in 19 CE. Indeed, the version in the Buber Edition (104) is צלמא דרודיס; and in the modern edition of B. Lifshitz the version is צלמא דרודוס (64). The version עלמין הרודים appears in the Parma Manuscript, see http://www.schechter.ac.il/.upload/Midrash/shmuel/%20%D7%99%D7%98.pdf. However, I cannot accept this corrupt version as the preferable one. See also Emmanuel Friedheim, *Rabbinisme et paganisme en Palestine romaine: Étude historique des realia talmudiques (Ier–IVème siècles)*, Religions in the Graeco-Roman World 157 (Leiden: Brill, 2006), 100 n. 343.

47. See, e.g., Tertullian, *Ad Scapulam*, 2 (http://www.tertullian.org/latin/ad_scapulam.htm) and Reuven Kiperwasser. "Rabba bar Bar Channa's Voyages" [Hebrew], *Jerusalem Studies in Hebrew Literature* 22 (2007–2008): 215–42, here 231 n. 60. And see recently Moshe Simon-Shoshan, "Did the Rabbis Believe in Agreus Pan? Rabbinic Relationships with Roman Power, Culture, and Religion in Genesis Rabbah 63," *HTR* 111 (2018): 425–50.

images on the streets rather urgent.⁴⁸ Rabbi Yoḥanan rules that to walk in front of the statue is not to worship it. While to face the statue is not to greet it or to worship foreign gods or the emperor, it does amount to devaluing the statue. One treats it as an insignificant object, thereby denying its iconic value.⁴⁹

Rabbi Jacob bar Idi points out that the Babylonian showed reverence toward Rabbi Yoḥanan by not passing in front of him and by standing still until after his teacher moved on. His explanation is couched in a negative analogy: although it is permitted to pass by foreign deities even though we do not intend to honor them, we do not act like this before our masters (i.e., pass by them), as we ought to honor them. Thus, our Babylonian, who was considered an ignorant, unfriendly Other by Rabbi Yoḥanan, turns out to have been quite an obedient rabbinic student, albeit with unconventional manners.

Once again, as in the story about Kahana and the same Rabbi Yoḥanan, an analogy is used to make a more profound point, which the rabbi who hears the analogy does not realize at first. The two stories seem to use the same literary device in order to criticize Rabbi Yoḥanan's approach to his students.⁵⁰

Rabbi Yoḥanan not only welcomes R. Jacob bar Idi's conciliatory rhetoric but also blesses his friend for his peacemaking. The silent Babylonian becomes a somewhat odd colleague, but otherwise acceptable. Once again, the insider culture draws boundaries while attempting to adopt the Other. To do this it has to compromise, but the house of study in Tiberias was governed by insiders who welcomed the peripatetic Other and reserved a place for him. The world they constructed could cope with the statue of Adori and with a silent Babylonian.

This raises the issue of empathy, embodied in these literary traditions. The Palestinian narrator was clearly sympathetic to his Babylonian brethren. Did this necessarily entail the will to minimize the Other's alterity and accept him as he was? Was this the immediate consequence of empathy?⁵¹ As Anna Freud reportedly said, empathy requires the ability to step

---

48. See Reuven Kiperwasser, "Encounters between the Iranian Myth and Rabbinic Mythmakers in the Babylonian Talmud," in *Encounters by the Rivers of Babylon: Scholarly Conversations between Jews, Iranians, and Babylonians*, ed. Uri Gabbay and Shai Secunda, TSAJ 160 (Tübingen: Mohr Siebeck, 2014), 285–304, here 293–95.

49. See Rachel Neis, "Religious Lives of Image-Things, Avodah Zarah, and Rabbis in Late Antique Palestine," *Archiv für Religionsgeschichte* 17 (2014): 91–121, here 107.

50. In the same manner, a story in b. Qid. 71b may be read as a mockery of Rabbi Yoḥanan; see further 163.

51. See Nils Bubandt and Rane Willerslev, "The Dark Side of Empathy: Mimesis, Deception, and the Magic of Alterity," *Comparative Studies in Society and History* 57 (2015): 5–34. Bubandt and Willerslev, in discussing two ethnographic cases, suggest the startling possibility that the alterity of the Other is not minimized but rather sometimes radicalized

into someone else's shoes and then to step out again.[52] Empathy means understanding the Other vicariously without losing one's own identity. Therefore, the story about the silent student misunderstood by the great Rabbi Yoḥanan, who retracts his criticism when his errors are pointed out, is a story that processes the transformation from sympathy to acceptance, from an identity formed by demarcation to one based on compassionate communion.

---

through empathy. See also Lauren Wispé, "The Distinction between Sympathy and Empathy: To Call Forth a Concept, a Word Is Needed," *Journal of Personality and Social Psychology* 50 (1986): 314–21.

52. See Mads Qvortrup, *The Political Philosophy of Jean-Jacques Rousseau: The Impossibility of Reason* (Manchester: Manchester University Press, 2003), 31.

5

The Appointment of Babylonians

We turn now to a story about the Other who comes to the city's gates. Without spending time on the streets, in butcher shops, or in bathhouses, he enters the Galilean house of study in search of a position. The host tries to keep the intruder near the gate, but the Other finally manages to find shelter, albeit relatively modest in quality. The ultimate acceptance of the Other sheds light on the previous events and gives new meaning to the host–guest relationship.

5.1 Something Good Can Come from a Babylonian

I propose a reading that focuses on a narrative tradition about the *minuy* (rabbinic appointment)[1] of the Babylonian expatriate Ḥanina bar Ḥama. I examine Palestinian reactions to Babylonian personalities, such as the fear and solidarity that are already familiar to us from other encounters with Babylonians. As I will elaborate below, the story represents the cautious attempt of the narrator to assess his integration as an Other in his own Palestinian cultural framework. As it is best read in light of accounts of the appointment of another, even more famous Babylonian, Hillel the Elder, to the position of Nasi (Patriarch),[2] we will begin with the following story.

---

1. מינוי is a term used in Palestinian rabbinic literature to denote ordination as a "licensed" sage, someone entitled to an exemption from fees and taxes specified by Roman law. See Lieberman, "Palestine in the Third and Fourth Centuries," 145. See also Lieberman, *Tosefta ki-fshuta*, 4:729 n. 40; and Catherine Hezser, *The Social Structure of the Rabbinic Movement in Roman Palestine*, TSAJ 66 (Tübingen: Mohr Siebeck, 1997), 425–27 (the sage's name cited by Hezser must be Ḥanina bar Ḥama).

2. On the image of Hillel in rabbinic literature and in the various stories about his rise to greatness from a historical point of view, see the recent work by Amram Tropper, *Rewriting Ancient Jewish History: The History of the Jews in Roman Times and the New Historical Method*, Routledge Studies in Ancient History 10 (London: Routledge, 2016), 163–79.

y. Pesahim 6:1, 33a

זו הלכה נעלמה מזקני בתירה. פעם אחת חל ארבעה עשר להיות בשבת ולא היו יודעין אם פסח דוחה את השבת אם לאו. אמרו: יש כאן בבלי אחד והלל שמו, ששימש את שמעיה ואבטליון, יודע אם פסח דוחה את השבת אם לאו. איפשר שיש ממנו תוחלת. שלחו וקראו לו. אמרו לו: שמעת מימיך כשחל ארבעה עשר להיות בשבת, אם דוחה את השבת אם לאו? אמר להן: וכי אין לנו אלא פסח אחד בלבד דוחה את השבת בכל שנה? והלא כמה פסחים ידחו את השבת בכל שנה ... אמרו לו: כבר אמרנו שיש ממך תוחלת. התחיל דורש להן מהיקש ומקל וחומר ומגזירה שוה.

מהיקש: הואיל ותמיד קרבן ציבור ופסח קרבן צבור, מה תמיד קרבן ציבו׳ דוח׳ שבת, אף פסח קרבן ציבור דוח׳ את השבת.

מקל וחומ׳: מה אם תמיד, שאין חייבין על עשייתו כרת, דוחה את השבת, פסח, שחייבין על עשייתו כרת, אינו דין שידחה את השבת? מגזירה שוה: נאמר בתמיד: "במועדו" (במדבר כח ב) ונאמר בפסח: "במועדו" (במדבר ט ב). מה תמיד, שנ׳ בו: "במועדו" דוחה את השבת, אף פסח, שנ׳ בו: "במועדו" דוחה את השבת.

אמרו לו: כבר אמרנו: אם יש תוחלת מבבלי? היקש שאמרת, יש לו תשובה. לא אם אמרת בתמיד, שכן יש לו קיצבה, תאמר בפסח, שאין לו קצבה. קל וחומר שאמרת, יש לו תשובה. לא אם אמרת בתמיד, שהוא קדשי קדשים, תאמר בפסח, שהוא קדשים קלין. גזירה שוה שאמרת, שאין אדם דן גזירה שוה מעצמו ...

אע״פ שהיה יושב ודורש להן כל היום לא קבלו ממנו עד שאמ׳ להן: יבוא עלי כך שמעתי משמעי׳ ואבטליון. כיון ששמעו ממנו כן, עמדו ומינו אותו נשיא עליהן. כיון שמינו אותו נשיא עליהן, התחיל מקנתרן בדברים, ואר׳: מי גרם לכם לצרך לבבלי הזה? לא על שלא שימשתם לשני גדולי עולם לשמעי׳ ואבטליון שהיו יושבין אצלכם?

כיון שקינתרן בדבריו׳ נעלמה הלכה ממנו. אמרו לו: מה לעשות לעם ולא הביאו סכיניהם: אמ׳ להן: הלכה זו שמעתי ושכחתי, אלא הניחו ליש׳. אם אינן נביאין, בני נביאים הן. מיד כל מי שהיה פסחו טלה, היה תוחבה בגיזתו; גדי, היה קושרה בין קרניו. נמצאו פסחיהן מביאין סכיניהן עמהן. כיון שראה את המעשה, נזכר את ההלכה. אמ׳: כך שמעתי משמעיה ואבטליון.

This law[4] was forgotten by the Elders of Betera. Once the fourteenth [of Nisan] fell on the Sabbath, and they did not know if the Passover sacrifice overrides the Sabbath or not. [They] said: There is here a certain Babylonian, and Hillel is his name, who served Shemaiah and Abtalion. [Perhaps he] knows whether a Passover sacrifice overrides the Sabbath or not. Possibly something good [can come] from him. [They] sent and called for him. They said to him: Have you ever heard when the fourteenth [of Nisan] falls on the Sabbath, whether [it] overrides the Sabbath or not? He said to them: Do we have only one Passover offering alone that overrides the Sabbath in the whole year? And are there not many Passover offerings that would override the Sabbath in the entire year? ... They said to him: We have already said that something good [can come] from the Babylonian. He started to expound for them from an analogy, and from an argument a fortiori and from an inference by analogy based on words' identity.

---

3. Academia ed., 529–30.
4. That is, the law in m. Pesah. 6:1 regarding the Passover sacrifice.

"From an analogy: Because the daily whole offering is a public offering, and the Passover sacrifice is a public offering. Just as the daily whole offering is a public offering and overrides the prohibition of the Sabbath, so the Passover sacrifice is a public offering and overrides the prohibition of the Sabbath.

From an argument, a fortiori: Now if the daily whole offering, on account of which people are not liable to extirpation, overrides the prohibitions of the Sabbath, the Passover sacrifice, on account of which people are liable to extirpation—is it not logical that it should override the prohibitions of the Sabbath?

From an inference by analogy based on the identity of words: Regarding the daily whole offering "its appointed season" (Num 28:2) is stated and regarding the Passover, "its appointed season" is stated (Num 9:2). Just as the daily whole offering, regarding which its season is stated, overrides the prohibition of the Sabbath, so the Passover sacrifice is a public offering and overrides the prohibition of the Sabbath.

And even though [Hillel] sat and expounded to them all day, [they] did not accept from him until he said: May [evil] befall me [if I lie]. Thus, I have heard from Shemaiah and Abtalion. As soon as they heard this from him, they stood up and appointed him Nasi over them. As soon as [they had appointed him Nasi over them,] he began to castigate them with words, saying: What caused you to need this Babylonian? Is it not because you failed to serve the two great men of the world, Shemaiah and Abtalion, who were sitting with you?

As soon as [Hillel] castigated them with words, a law escaped his memory, specifically: [They] said to him: What should [we] do for the people, for [before the Sabbath] they did not bring their knives [to slaughter the animal, which you have now demonstrated is permitted]? He said to them: This law I have heard but I have forgotten. Rather, [then,] leave Israel [alone]. If they are not prophets, they are the sons of prophets [and will know by themselves what to do]." Immediately whoever had as a Passover offering a lamb stuck the knife into its wool; if it was a kid, he tied it between his horns. As a result, the beasts they had designated for use as their Passover offerings brought their knives with them. When he saw this, he remembered the law. He said: So, I heard from Shemaiah and Abtalion.

Scholars have presented this story as a foundational narrative of the rabbinic movement (t. Pesah. 4:13–14).[5] It once happened that the day on

---

5. Cf. y. Pesah. 6:1, 33a; b. Pesah. 66a. For an analysis of the different versions of this story, see Fraenkel, *Aggadic Narrative*, 22–39; Menachem Katz, "The Stories of Hillel's Appointment as Nasi in the Talmudic Literature: A Foundation Legend of the Jewish Scholar's World" [Hebrew], *Sidra* 26 (2011): 81–116. See also Israel Ben-Shalom, *The School of Shammai and the Zealots' Struggle against Rome* [Hebrew], (Jerusalem: Yad Izhak Ben-Zvi and Ben-Gurion University of the Negev Press, 1993), 69–75, Jeffrey Rubenstein, *Rabbinic Stories*, Classics of Western Spirituality (New York: Paulist, 2002), 72–73, Richard Hidary, *Rabbis and*

which the Passover sacrifices were performed fell on the Sabbath. Rabbinic literature offers three different versions of this story: in t. Pesah. 4:14[6], in the Yerushalmi, and in the Babylonian Talmud. The story in Tosefta is only a short halakhic case. The story in the Bavli is an elaboration of the narrative tradition of the Yerushalmi.[7] The version in the Yerushalmi is a story of a significant celebration of acceptance of the Other, which reverberates in other Palestinian stories of the acceptance of a Babylonian. I am concerned here only with one crucial pattern of the story and its evaluation, but first let us briefly summarize the plot. The community leaders[8] were confounded by a halakhic question: Which should take precedence, the Sabbath (when slaughter, let alone roasting, is prohibited) or the Passover sacrifice? Should the sacrifice be postponed until after the Sabbath, or should the Sabbath be violated for the sake of the sacrifice? Hillel the Elder managed to win over the members of the rabbinic ruling group by claiming that he was the upholder of the oral tradition regulating this issue.[9] The story ends by stating that "on that very day they appointed Hillel as Nasi."[10] Thus, the unknown Babylonian immigrant demonstrated his intellectual superiority over the old elite circles, his hosts, and literally took their place. After admitting the stranger's authority, the Bnei Betera family simply left and disappeared into the narrative fog. Readers acquainted with how intellectual elites and their hierarchical structures function can appreciate the humility of this act, even putting aside the perhaps fictional role it plays in the narrative about the rise of Hillel's dynasty. However, because of this unusual twist in the plot, the story also illustrates the gracious self-control of the Bnei Betera sages, who voluntarily chose to make way for their former opponent. Interestingly, it appears that Hillel's oppo-

---

Classical Rhetoric: Sophistic Education and Oratory in the Talmud and Midrash (Cambridge: Cambridge University Press, 2017), 183–90.

6. See Saul Lieberman, *The Tosefta: According to Codex Vienna* (New York: Jewish Theological Seminary of America, 1995), 165–66; for English translation, see Jacob Neusner, *The Tosefta: Translated from the Hebrew with a New Introduction* (New York: Ktav, 1981), 137–38.

7. For comparison between Palestinian and Babylonian versions, see the thoughtful analysis of Fraenkel, *Aggadic Narrative*, 22–39.

8. In the Tosefta version it is not specified who posed the question to Hillel, but, in the versions of the Palestinian Talmud and the Babylonian Talmud, the conundrum is attributed to the patriarchal family at the time, Bnei Betera (= sons of Betera). This attribution could be the result of an attempt to bring t. Pesah. 4:13 into line with t. Sanh. 7:11. See Mira Balberg, *Blood for Thought: The Reinvention of Sacrifice in Early Rabbinic Literature* (Oakland: University of California Press, 2017), 147.

9. See Fraenkel, *Aggadic Narrative*, 22–32. Regarding the rhetorical details of the long exchange of opinion between two opponents, see Hidary, *Rabbis and Classical Rhetoric*, 190–93.

10. On the term *Nasi* and the rise and decline of the office of Nasi, see Martin Jacobs, *Die Institution des jüdischen Patriarchen: Eine quellen- und traditionskritische Studie zur Geschichte der Juden in der Spätantike*, TSAJ 52 (Tübingen: Mohr Siebeck, 1995), 307, 314–19.

nents, the family of Betera, were also not entirely indigenous residents of the Land of Israel. This name is perhaps first encountered in the writings of Flavius Josephus as the founder of a military colony of Babylonian Jews in the Land of Israel.[11] Other known carriers of this name are mentioned in the Tannaitic traditions.[12] It can be concluded that the *tannaim* were aware that the roots of this family originated in Mesopotamia,[13] and, as claimed by our narrator, they were teachers of the law and attained this status by studying with Shemaiah and Abtalion, the native sons of the Land of Israel. Their scholarship, however, did not pass the test of time and was recognized as inferior to Hillel's.

We are dealing here with a narrative tradition created and framed by Palestinian narrators. It is of particular interest that this tradition is highly sympathetic to the "Babylonian," whose foreignness is casually mentioned by his opponents. Their utterance "Possibly something good [can come] from a Babylonian," while generally benevolent, still distances the Other and puts him in a hierarchically inferior position. The reaction of these elders is quite close to the utterance of the proud Galilean Nathanael on hearing the news about the leadership of Jesus: "Can anything good come from Nazareth?" (John 1:46).[14] the rabbinic statement similarly aims to emphasize the future surprise about the acceptance of the outsider as a leader. The narrator has no doubt that Hillel is more significant and wiser than the rest of his colleagues—from the narrator's perspective, the founder of the rabbinic hierarchy in the Land of Israel must have been. The narrator's implication is that, on account of divine providence, it was none other than the Babylonian who continued and transmitted the work of the Land of Israel's deceased sages. A Babylonian guest became the host of the Palestinian rabbis' house of study.

But this transformation did not take place smoothly. At the end of the story, we learn that, after Hillel's election, the former outsider and stranger began to mock his former masters, the sages of the Betera family, who forgot their learning, for laziness in serving their masters. But after Hillel ascends to the position of head of sages, when faced with his first halakhic decision, for which the answer is simple enough, he forgets the halakhic answer. Salvation comes to the former outsider from outside—he sees the pilgrims coming to the temple. Their halakhically correct behavior, which he had forgotten, helps him remember and maintain his position. The narrator is aware of the violent consequences of such a quick

---

11. See Josephus, *Ant.* 17.23–28. See Tal Ilan and Vered Noam, in collaboration with Meir Ben Shahar, Daphne Baratz, and Yael Fisch, *Josephus and the Rabbis* [Hebrew], 2 vols., Between Bible and Mishnah (Jerusalem: Yad Ben Zvi, 2017), 1:451–52.
12. See Ilan and Noam, *Josephus and the Rabbis*, 1:73–74.
13. See ibid., 75.
14. This similarity was pointed out to me by Daniel Boyarin.

and radical transformation from guest to host.[15] In summary, this story is a major celebration of acceptance of the Babylonian Other, reaching its peak in the outsider's success. More than a simple retelling of the halakhic succession, it depicts a peaceful revolution of a very rare kind.

5.2. The Appointment of Ḥanina bar Ḥama

The next story is in an intertextual dialogue with the previous one. It is not a peaceful dialogue. The previous story is about great people whose behavior is noble; they are engaged in something important to society and are ready to sacrifice their own dignity. Even when they are mistaken, they are noble and prioritize society's needs. It is also a story favorable to the dynasty founded by Hillel. As is well known, the descendants of Rabbi Yehuda ha-Nasi headed the rabbinic hierarchy for almost three hundred years, and they claimed to be descendants of Hillel the Elder [16]

The following story is also about the descendants of Hillel, but their nobility and readiness to sacrifice their own dignity have now faded. The story, like the previous one, describes a collision between the learned foreigner and the local heads of the academic hierarchy.

y. Ta'anit 4:2, 78a[17]

ר' הוה ממני תרין מינויין. אין הוון כדיי היו מתקיימין, ואין לא, הוון מסתלקין. מדדמך, פקיד לבריה.
אמר: לא תעביד כן, אלא מני כולהון כחדא, ומני לרבי חמא בר חנינה בראשה.

ולמה לא מניתיה הוא? אמר רבי דרוסא: בגין דצווחין עלויי (בציפורין) ציפוראיי, ובגין צווחה עבדין.

---

15. Hillel is punished here with memory loss. About this story as evidence of the rabbinic approach to memory, see Reuven Kiperwasser, "The Art of Forgetting in Rabbinic Narrative," in *Rabbinic Study Circles: Aspects of Jewish Learning in Its Late Antique Context*, ed. Marc Hirshman and David Satran with the assistance of Anita Shtrubel; Studies in Education and Religion in Ancient and Pre-Modern History in the Mediterranean and Its Environs 8 (Tübingen: Mohr Siebeck, 2020), 67–85.

16. According to the relatively new approach of scholars, the title *Nasi* and the patriarchate as a form of socioreligious leadership began only with Rabbi Yehudah ha-Nasi; see Martin Goodman, *State and Society in Roman Galilee, A.D. 132–212*, 2nd ed., Parkes-Wiener Series on Jewish Studies (London: Vallentine Mitchel, 2000), 111-8 and Jacobs 1995, 99-123. On the portrait of this prominent figure in rabbinic literature, see Ofra Meir, *Rabbi Judah the Patriarch: Palestinian and Babylonian Portraits of a Leader* [Hebrew], Sifriyat "Helal Ben-Ḥayim" (Tel Aviv: Hakibbutz Hameuhad, 1999). For an attempt to reconstruct the historical figure from the literary traditions, see Aharon Oppenheimer, *Rabbi Judah ha-Nasi: Statesman, Reformer, and the Redactor of the Mishnah* (Tübingen: Mohr Siebeck, 2017). Regarding the claim of Patriarch's family to be descendants of Hillel the Elder, see Sacha Stern, who argues that Rabbi Yehuda ha-Nasi was not a son of Shimeon b. Gamliel but came from a different family of Galilean aristocracy ("Rabbi and the Origins of the Patriarchate," *JJS* 54 [2003]: 193–215).

17. See Academia ed., 728.

אמר רבי לעזר בי רבי יוסה: על שהשיבו טעם ברבים. רבי הוה יתיב מתני: "וזכרו פליטיהם אותי" (יחזקאל ו ט)ף "והיו אל ההרים כיוני הגיאיות כולם הומיות" (יחזקאל ז טז). אמר ליה: "הומות". אמר ליה: הן קריתה? אמר ליה: קדם רב המנונא דבבל. אמר ליה: כד תיחות לתמן, אמור ליה: דמנייתך חכים. וידע דלא מיתמני ביומוי.

Rabbi used to confer two appointments.[18] If they [the individuals] proved worthy, they remained, if not — they were removed. When he was about to die, he instructed his son, saying: Do not act so, but appoint them all one after another and Rabbi Ḥama bar Ḥanina first.

But why did he not do so himself? Said Rabbi Derosa:[19] It was because the people of Sepphoris cried out against him. And because of the crying out they did so?

Said Rabbi Lazar bar Rabbi Yose: It was because he publicly corrected what Rabbi had said. Rabbi was sitting and expounding the homily[20] "Then those of you who escape will remember me" (Ezek 6:9) "But those who escape from them at all, shall be on the mountains like doves of the valley, all of them moaning [*homiyot*]" (Ezek 7:16).

Rabbi Ḥanina said to him: The proper reading of the last word is "*homot.*" He said to him: Where did you study Scripture? He said to him: With Rab Hamnuna of Babylonia. He said: When you go back there, tell him that he appoints you a sage. So, Rabbi Ḥanina knew that he would never be appointed in Rabbi's time.

This story concerns competition between a learned foreigner and the local head of the academic hierarchy. The Babylonian newcomer is well educated and renowned for his knowledge, and he is naturally expected to be ordained as a rabbi. Although neither Hillel's name nor his ascendancy is openly mentioned in this story, Hillel's narrative should be borne in mind when we read it, because his descendants' arrogant behavior intertextually sheds light on the message of the narrative here.

Our story is preserved in two Palestinian sources, one (Eccl. Rab. 7:7[21]) relatively late and one (the Yerushalmi) quite early. The story about the long road that led Rabbi Ḥanina bar Ḥama[22] to his *minuy*[23] begins with a description of the situation before the appointment took place.

---

18. "Rabbi" without a name refers to Rabbi Yehuda ha-Nasi (ca. 165–220 CE).

19. Derosa is not a common name. It could be a corruption of "Dosa," the name of a well-known Palestinian Amora; see Albeck, *Introduction,* 232. However, considering the parallel version, we can hypothesize that the Yerushalmi here also had "Rabbi Jose," which because of copyists' errors became "Derosa" (ר' יוסא=דרוסא or ר' יוסא=דוסא, דר' יוסא).

20. See the explanation below, 109.

21. See the synoptic edition, http://www.schechter.ac.il/.upload/Midrash/kohelet%20raba/parasha7.pdf.

22. Initially, the Yerushalmi mentions Rabbi Ḥama bar Ḥanina, and then Rabbi Ḥanina; clearly the first version is a scribal error. The proper reading is Rabbi Ḥanina bar Ḥama.

23. See 101 n. 1 above.

According to the Yerushalmi, Rabbi would ordain two candidates; based on Ecclesiastes Rabbah, we know that this took place annually.[24] If the new appointees' performances were in order, he would permit them to remain in their positions. If not, the unsuccessful sages would have to depart (מסתלקין), and the vacancies would then be opened to other candidates. Before his death, Rabbi asked one of his sons to change the appointment procedure: rather than conferring both appointments at once, he should ordain the new sages one after the other, probably because of the declining number of candidates.[25] This explanation is based on my reading of the complex expression כולהון כחדא as כולהון בחדא. Lieberman's reading is different; he does not emend the text but explains that the expression means the decision to ordain all the young sages together (כולהון!). Therefore, he needs to hypothesize that, after every ordination procedure, a new appointment would occur only after the death of an appointee (כחדא).[26] In my view, this reading is overly complicated. My emendation simplifies the story because it halves the chance of becoming an ordained sage.[27]

In this story, we find two explanations of why Rabbi Ḥanina was ordained very late. According to the first, attributed in the Yerushalmi to Rabbi Dosa, Sepphoris's people opposed Rabbi Ḥanina's appointment.[28] This tradition is preserved in Ecclesiastes Rabbah in a more extended version and attributed to Rabbi Yose bar Zebid.[29] In this version, Rabbi Ḥanina wonders why the demand of the Sepphorians was taken into consideration, and Rabbi answers that if you consider someone's opinion in a favorable situation, then you must equally consider it in adverse situa-

---

24. It is not clear to what position and with what responsibilities they were appointed, but it must have given them some power and possibly some financial freedom.

25. See Lieberman, "Palestine in the Third and Fourth Centuries," 144.

26. Ibid., 144–45.

27. Unlike the Yerushalmi, Ecclesiastes Rabbah tells us that Rabbi would ordain two sages every year; if their work was not acceptable, they would die (דמכין). Strikingly, the later formulator made a mistake in interpreting the word מסתלקין, which could be understood literally as "leaving" and, more metaphorically, as "leaving this world, dying." Both usages occur in Yerushalmi; however, I would suggest, following Lieberman's note on this ("Palestine in the Third and Fourth Centuries," 144 n. 230), that our narrator implied the first meaning. Thus, the version in Ecclesiastes Rabbah is less reliable than the one in Yerushalmi.

28. According to Adolph Buchler (*The Political and the Social Leaders of the Jewish Community of Sepphoris in the Second and Third Centuries* [London: Jew's College 1909], 53–57) and Lieberman ("Palestine in the Third and Fourth Centuries," 144 n. 230), the expression "people of Sepphoris" refers to the Sepphorian mob, but Stuart S. Miller claims that this is a group of Sepphorian sages who, for political reasons, wished to prevent Rabbi Ḥanina's appointment ("R. Hanina bar Hama at Sepphoris," in *The Galilee in Late Antiquity*, ed. Lee I. Levine [New York: Jewish Theological Seminary of America, 1992], 175–200). See also Miller, *Sages and Commoners*, 100–106.

29. A Palestinian Amora of the fourth generation (320–350 CE); see Albeck, *Introduction*, 334.

tions. This is a benign explanation for Rabbi's behavior; on his deathbed he felt sorry for the Babylonian. Society was against him, not Rabbi.

But the story continues with another explanation for Rabbi Ḥanina's misfortune. The latter had once insulted the Nasi: Rabbi had delivered a sermon based on two verses from Ezekiel, and Rabbi Ḥanina corrected his reading in public. Rabbi's mistake did not alter the meaning of the verse. The word הומות is the plural form of הומה; the word הומיות is plural of הומיה; both actually mean the same.[30] It was considered inappropriate to correct mistakes made by the head of the rabbinic hierarchy, however slight. Our Babylonian, however, thought that the words of a prophet were more important than polite considerations; moreover, perhaps, in his culture it was appropriate for advanced students to correct their masters' mistakes.[31] At least this was the narrator's assumption.[32] To be both alien and to have an annoying foreign custom of correcting everyone, even your master, is reason enough not to be appointed to a high position. Rabbi's decision not to ordain him was expressed in his ironic question: Who is the problematic scholar's teacher? The teacher was, in fact, Rab Hamnuna, famous for his biblical erudition and pedantry.[33] The mention of Rab Hamnuna is meaningful. The name of a pedantic scholar is a marker of Babylonian identity in the Palestinian narrator's eyes. These Babylonians were exceptionally well versed in the Bible; they knew all the citations by heart. Therefore, they were dangerous in the house of study. Their presence threatened the sovereignty of the host.

The Babylonian's answer at first appears naïve, as the Babylonian did not detect the menacing undertone in Rabbi's voice. It is quite possible, however, that here the Babylonian was just proclaiming his right to do as he pleased, for he declared that he had been educated by a person with superb biblical knowledge. As the student of such a mentor, therefore, he

---

30. These are two different forms of the same root—the relatively rare הומיה is an active participle from המה. This form is sometimes found in poetry, e.g., Prov 1:21; 7:11; 9:13; Isa 22:2; and see Ludwig Koehler and Walter Baumgartner, *Hebrew and Aramaic Lexicon of the Old Testament* (Leiden: Brill, 1994), 250, s.v. המה. The form הומיות was known to Rabbi from other biblical verses, such as Prov 1:21, but the misreading was probably due to the phonetic influence of the preceding word גאיות.

31. See Averbach, *Jewish Education*, 76–79. There he proposes that Rabbi was angry with the Babylonian student because he corrected his mistake, which is less important than making a mistake in halakhic instruction.

32. Even though in the Babylonian Talmud itself we can find some restrictions about public questionings of rabbis in order to eliminate shaming; see Rubenstein, *Culture of the Babylonian Talmud*, 73–77, and 94 above.

33. On the term ספרא, see Zecharia Fraenkel, *Mabo ha-Yerushalmi* (Berlin: Berolini, 1922–1923), 118a; for the category of sages famous for their pedantic approach to the Bible, see David Rosenthal, "The Sages' Methodical Approach to Textual Variants within the Hebrew Bible" [Hebrew], in *Isac Leo Seeligmann Volume: Essays on the Bible and the Ancient World* 2, ed. Alexander Rofé and Yair Zakovitch; Jerusalem: Elchanan Rubinstein, 1983), 395–98.

had every right to correct the errors of Palestinian scholars.[34] The unlucky sage received from Rabbi the ironical advice to go from Palestine to Babylonia, to meet his teacher there and be ordained as a Palestinian sage, something that was of course impossible. Rabbi Ḥanina took this as implying that he would never be ordained as long as Rabbi's rulings remained in effect.[35] This account of Rabbi Ḥanina's rejection implies his non-acceptance as the Other. The guest left his position near the gate and felt himself quite at ease in the internal rooms of the house; but, after overstepping his role as guest, he was sent back to the gate, without being offered an opportunity to demonstrate his abilities by participating in the rabbinic discourse as an equal. The story then continues:

מן דדמך, בעא בריה ממניתיה ולא קביל עליה מתמנייא. אמ׳: לית אנא מקבל עלי מתמנייא, עד זמן דמתמני ר׳ פס דרומא קמיי. והוה תמן חד סב. אמ׳: אין חנינה קדמיי, אנא תיניין; אין ר׳ פס דרומיא קדמיי, אנא תיניין. וקביל עלוי רבי חנינה מיתמנייא תליתאי.

אמר ר׳ חנינה: זכית מארכה יומין אין בגין הדא מילתא. לית אנא ידע. אין בגין דהויית סליק מן טיבריא לציפורין והויינא עקים איסרטין מיעול מישאול בשלמיה דר׳ שמעון בן חלפותא בעין תינה. לית אנא ידע.

After he died, his son wished to appoint him, but he declined, saying: I shall not accept the appointment until you have first appointed Rabbi Pas of Daroma. There was an old man present who said: If R. Ḥanina is appointed first, I am second, and if Rabbi Pas of Daroma is first, I am second. Rabbi Ḥanina agreed to be appointed third.

Said Rabbi Ḥanina: I have merited living a long life. I do not know whether it is because of this incident or whether it is because when coming up from Tiberias to Sepphoris I took a roundabout route in order to greet Rabbi Shimeon ben Ḥalafta at Ayn Te'enah. I do not know.

The story continues: the Palestinian rabbis' leader dies, and it falls to the next descendant of Hillel to reward the Babylonian scholar. Yet, when Rabbi Yehuda ha-Nasi's son wishes to appoint our Babylonian, he declines because, according to his perceptions of honor and justice, his older college Rabbi Pas (or Apas) deserves to be selected first.[36] In the world of rabbinic academies of the time, however, another scholar had been disgraced by

---

34. Rabbi Ḥanina bar Ḥama as a representative of the Babylonian sages to Palestine is discussed in Schwartz, "Tension between Palestinian Scholars," 89; and Schwartz, "Patriotic Rabbi," 118–31.

35. The part of the verse cited to clinch the plot is not found in the Ecclesiastes Rabbah version. There is a lacuna in the first half of the story, which is nonetheless still attributed to R. Abun, unlike the attribution in the Yerushalmi.

36. For the analyses of the Babylonian parallel, see Amram Tropper, *Simeon the Righ-*

Rabbi Yehuda ha-Nasi. We do not know much about Rabbi Apas, except some of his teachings and the fact that he came from Daroma (the South), namely, from Judea, far from the Galilee, where most of our narrative accounts take place.[37] The narrative tradition we are looking at is Galilean, but apparently not very sympathetic to Sepphoris society and quite critical of Hillel's descendants. Rabbi Yehudah ha-Nasi could not suppress his anger toward noncompliant outsiders and thwarted their careers. He regretted some of his misdeeds, but even when he ordered his son to rectify the situation, he could do nothing in the face of local politics and human ambitions. A particular nameless candidate for ordination, simply called "one old man," did not want to postpone his appointment for anyone else, so our hero agreed to be appointed third and was forced to wait years for a vacancy. Now that we are nearing the punchline, the readers' gaze is probably focused on Rabbi Ḥanina's self-restraint. The actual message of the story, however, is more profound. It turns out that our hero was still alive long after the events described above. In rabbinic thought, longevity is a sign of a God-given blessing, a reward for righteousness and virtuous deeds.[38] Thus, in the epilogue to the story, the hero, in his old age, meditates on the virtuous deeds that merited him a long life. He posits two explanations for it: his first good deed may have been his refusal of the rabbinical appointment. His second good deed may have been his custom, whenever he returned from Tiberias to his hometown Sepphoris, to take a roundabout route and visit Rabbi Shimeon ben Ḥalafta, who lived out of his way in the village of Ayn Te'enah in the Sepphoris area.[39] He does not know which of these actions resulted in his longevity. To profess ignorance in this situation would have meant to admit that the acts were equal in value. Rabbi Shimeon ben Ḥalafta, an outsider living apart

---

teous in Rabbinic Literature: A Legend Reinvented, Ancient Judaism and Early Christianity 84 (Leiden: Brill, 2013), 179–83.

37. About the ties between Judea and (South) Galilee and their respective relationships to the Babylonian diaspora I will write further; see 132. Here I refer to previous discussions, first of all to Saul Lieberman, *Ha-Yerushalmi Kipshuto: A Commentary* (Jerusalem: Jewish Theological Seminary, 1935), 458; Abraham Goldberg, *Mishnah Shabbat* [Hebrew] (Jerusalem: Jewish Theological Seminary, 1976), 82; Schwartz, "Southern Judea and Babylonia," 188–97; Sussman, "We-shuv le-Yerushalmi Neziqin," 55–133; 96 n. 170.

38. See Jonathan Wyn Schofer, *Confronting Vulnerability: The Body and the Divine in Rabbinic Ethics* (Chicago: University of Chicago Press, 2010), 151-65.

39. About this extraordinary sage and his place in rabbinic narratives, see Kiperwasser, "Visit of the Rural Sage," 3–24. Regarding the village and its place, see Gottfried Reeg, *Die Ortsnamen Israels nach der rabbinischen Literatur*, Beihefte zum Tübinger Atlas des Vorderen Orients B.51 (Wiesbaden: Reichert, 1989), 483–84. According to this identification, the village was approximately 7 km east of Sepphoris. However, see the recent proposal of Uziel Leibner, "Appendix 3: The Map of the Toponyms" [Hebrew], in *Midrash Kohelet Rabbah* (Jerusalem: Schechter, 2016) 1–6, 120 n. 350, identifying the place with a former Arab village northeast of Sepphoris that is much closer.

from the rabbinic establishment of his period,⁴⁰ must have been very old by then. To visit an old sage living in solitude in a small village is a good deed, albeit insignificant. Yet it expresses a particular ideal. To visit a sage with no political influence is no less important than to be recognized by an academic institution or to receive a title from one of Hillel's descendants with real political clout. The final musing is subversive, for it expresses the longing for an alternative style of leadership based not on political power or money but on moral dignity and spiritual force. In the end, the guest succeeded, even though he had aimed to leave his designated place to play a role in his host's internal realm and was forcefully ejected and sent away. While he did not supplant the host, he did absorb the charisma of leadership from him. Now the host's house will continue to exist, but only in the shadow of the enduring moral values upheld by the guest.

5.3 A Babylonian Alive or Dead

The echoes of the prototypical story about the ascent of Hillel⁴¹ and the voluntary relinquishment of power by the Betera family resound in the next story, where we meet a formidable Babylonian who arouses decidedly mixed emotions among the Palestinian rabbis.⁴²

y. Kil'ayim 9:4, 32b⁴³

| Rabbi was very humble, and he said: Whatever anyone tells me to do I shall do, except for what the elders of Betera did on behalf of my forefather, for they gave up their position and appointed him in their place. If the Exilarch, Rab Huna, should come here, I should seat him above me because he comes from [the tribe of] Judah, while I come from [the tribe of] Benjamin, because he derives from the male and I from the female line.⁴⁴ | רבי הוה ענוון סגין והוה אמר: כל מה דיימר לי בר נשא אנא עביד, חוץ ממה שעשו זקני בתירה לזקני, דשרון גרמון מנשיאותיה ומנוניה. אין סליק רב חונא, ריש גלותא, להכא, אנא מותיב ליה לעיל מיניי, דהוא מן יהודה ואנא מבנימן; דהוא מן דכריא ואנא מן נוקבתא. |

---

40. See Kiperwasser, "Visit of the Rural Sage," 3–24.
41. See 101 above.
42. For a close parallel, see Gen. Rab. 33:3, Theodor-Albeck, 1:305–7, and also the commentary by Admiel Kosman (*Men's World*, 36–39). On the relationship of this story to the contexts in which it appears, see Shimon Fogel, "The Orders of Discourse in the House of Study (*beit midrash*) in Palestinian Rabbinic Literature: Organizing Space, Ritual and Discipline" [Hebrew] (PhD diss., Ben-Gurion University of the Negev, Beer Sheva, 2014), 315–18.
43. See Academia ed., 174. See y. Ketub. 12:2, 35a (1010).
44. See further 114 n. 49.

The Appointment of Babylonians   113

One time Rabbi Ḥiyya the Great came to him. He said to him: Lo, Rab Huna is here! Rabbi's face turned yellow. He said to him: His coffin has arrived. He said to him: Go see who wants you outside. He went out and found no one there, and he knew that Rabbi was angry with him. Then he did not go to see Rabbi for thirty days.

Said Rabbi Yose bar Rabbi Bun: During those thirty days, Rab learned from him all of the principles of the Torah.

At the end of the thirteen years and thirty days, Elijah came to him in the guise of Rabbi Ḥiyya the Great. He said to him: How is my lord doing? He said to him: I have a toothache. He said to him: Show me. And he showed it to him. [Elijah] put his finger on the tooth and healed it.

The next day Rabbi Ḥiyya the Great came to him. He said to him: How is my lord doing? As to your teeth, how are they doing? He said to him: From that moment when you put your finger on it, it has been healed. At that moment, [Ḥiyya] said: Woe for you, women in childbirth in the Land of Israel; Woe for you, pregnant women in the Land of Israel, [Ḥiyya] said: It was not I.[45] From that moment onward, Rabbi began to pay respect to Ḥiyya. When he came into the meeting house, he would say: Let Rabbi Ḥiyya the Great go in before me. Rabbi Ishmael bar Rabbi Yose said to him: Even before me? He said

חד זמן אעל רבי חייא רובא לגביה. אמר ליה: הא רב הונא לבר. נתכרכמו פניו של רבי. אמר ליה: ארונו בא. אמר ליה: פוק וחמי מאן בעי לך לבר. ונפק ולא אשכח בר נש, וידע דהוא כעיס עלוי. עבד דלא עליל לגביה תלתין יומין.

אמר רבי יוסי בר בון: כל אינון תלתויי יומיא, ילף רב מיניה כללא דאוריתא.

לסוף תלת עשרתי שניא ותלתתוי יומיא עאל אליהו לגביה בדמותי רבי חייא רובה. אמר ליה: מה מרי עביד? אמר ליה: חד שיניי מעיקה לי. אמר ליה: חמי לה לי, וחמי לה ליה. ויהב אצצעתיה עלה ואינשמת.

למחר עאל רבי חייה רובה לגביה. אמר ליה: מה עביד ר' האי שינך, מה היא עבידה? אמר ליה מן ההיא שעתא דיהב' אצצעתך עלה, אינשמת. באותה שעה אמר: אי לכם חיות שבארץ ישראל, אי לכם עוברות שבארץ ישראל. אמר ליה: אנא לא הוינא. מן ההיא שעתא הוה נהיג ביה ביקר. כד הוה עליל לבית וועדא, הוה אמר: יכנס רבי חייא רובא לפנים. אמר לו רבי ישמעאל בי רבי יוסי: לפנים ממני? אמר לו: חס ושלום. אלא ר' חייה רובה לפנים ורבי ישמעאל בי רבי יוסי לפני לפנים.

---

45. It is difficult to know if Ḥiyya understood what happened and why Elijah acted as he did or if he simply did not understand what the Patriarch was talking about and remained ignorant about what happened.

to him: "Heaven forbid. Rabbi Ḥiyya the Great is within, but Rabbi Ishmael bar Rabbi Yose is innermost."

The story begins by defining the protagonist as a humble man (*anav*). However, as I will show, the usage of this word here is highly sarcastic. The term *anav* is usually used in rabbinic literature to characterize a man honored by his local community, but who, despite or because of his good reputation, is ready to demean himself or refuse to be honored by others.[46] The epithet is often applied to the rabbinic community's central figures, such as Hillel or Rabbi Yehuda ha-Nasi. A narrative about a hero's humility (*'anava*) tends to focus on his trials and tribulations.[47] However, this story is different. Although he considers himself to be as humble as his ancestor Hillel, our hero is unwilling to do what the sons of Betera sages did, namely, to relinquish his post for someone else, a migrant from abroad, even if the newcomer was a much better scholar than he. Thus, he is not nearly as selfless as the Betera family. However, says our hero, in one situation, he would feel obliged to behave like Hillel—that is, if the current Exilarch of Babylonia, *Resh Galuta*, Rab Huna,[48] ever came to the Land of Israel, Rabbi would then voluntarily relinquish his position as Nasi for him. Here our protagonist betrays his sense of self-importance much more than his humility. He imagines that he will never be in the situation in which the Betera family found itself; he would never relinquish his throne for a stranger, because no such stranger existed among the inhabitants of the Land of Israel. Speaking boldly, he claims there is no one like himself. The only person whose esteem could be comparable to his is Rab Huna, peacefully dwelling in the Exilarch's house in Babylonia.[49] Thus, the only conceivable Hillel-like candidate for whom Rabbi would have left his office would have been the Babylonian, who already occupied the highest position in his own country and would therefore never

---

46. See Daniel Statman, "Some Resolutions of the Paradox of *Anava* in Jewish Sources" [Hebrew], *Iyun* 44 (1995): 355–70; and Admiel Kosman, "Some Notes on a Paradox of *Anava*" [Hebrew], *Iyun* 46 (1997): 209–20.

47. As, for example, in the story in Pesiq. Rab Kah. 18.5. See Bernard Mandelbaum, ed., *Pesikta de Rav Kahana: According to an Oxford Manuscript — with Variants from All Known Manuscripts and Genizoth Fragments and Parallels*, 2 vols. [Hebrew] (New York: Jewish Theological Seminary, 1987), 1:296–97, in which a humble (*anav*) sage is following an unknown, irritating youth for three full miles without complaint.

48. See Herman, *Prince without a Kingdom*, 94–100.

49. The explanation given by the protagonist for his willingness to relinquish his position to this Babylonian is his lineage. The Israelite ruler's scepter was wielded exclusively by males from the tribe of Judah. The protagonist sees in his rule a continuation of this biblical institution and therefore agrees that the candidate descended from Judah is his superior; see Julius Theodor, in Genesis Rabbah, ad loc.

leave it for distant Palestine. Yet, in a conversation with his Babylonian colleague-friend, Rabbi Ḥiyya, the humility of Rabbi is put to the test.[50] Rabbi Ḥiyya announces that the long-awaited Babylonian is already in Palestine and standing outside the Patriarch's house. Now, finally, Rabbi Yehuda ha-Nasi is expected to act like the sons of Betera. Our protagonist is bewildered, and the narrator is probably amused, commenting on his visibly humiliated yellow face. Only now does Ḥiyya expose the full truth of Rab Huna's alleged appearance. The Exilarch is only partially present—his body is here, but his soul has already left the world. Following the Babylonian custom of burial in the Holy Land, the Exilarch had organized his coffin's deliverance to the Land of Israel after his demise. His family, complying with the will of the deceased, had brought him to the Holy Land.[51] Thus, the Patriarch can continue to occupy his office after paying his respects to the deceased. Following Kosman, I claim that Ḥiyya's mockery places a mirror before Rabbi's eyes, so that, far from appearing as meek as his ancestor and opponents, he seems unbearably arrogant.[52] Finding himself thus humiliated, the Patriarch, who had been ironically described as humble at the outset of our story, avenges the mocker. Ḥiyya is sent out to see who is asking for him and finds that nobody is there, a portrait of his future isolation. As in the story about Ḥanina bar Ḥama, when the offender is sent to Babylonia to set off his insignificance and strangeness, and realizes that he has been rebuked, here Rabbi Ḥiyya feels the pain of being alone.[53] Both protagonists suffer, but the Babylonian, deprived of seeing the Palestinian, uses his thirty days of solitude to share his talmudic knowledge with a fellow Babylonian. Considering that this Babylonian student is Rab, the future founder of the main Babylonian Amoraic academy, it would seem that here the narrator has something very specific in mind. The education of a future Babylonian leader became possible because of the banishment of a Babylonian master from the sight of the Nasi. Also, let us note Rab's decision to spend the thirty-day period with Hiyya and not with Rabbi. The Nasi himself spent these days in pain, because of a toothache.[54] The Nasi's suffering would be explained later as a balancing factor in the sum of the sufferings of the population of the

---

50. Such a deed by Rabbi Ḥiyya would have represented an opposition to the arrogance of the patriarchate, as suggested by Gedaliah Alon, *The Jews in Their Land in the Talmudic Age, 70–640 C.E.*, trans. Gershon Levi, 2 vols. (Jerusalem: Magnes, 1980–1984), 2:722–25. For an interpretation of mockery in Lacanian psychoanalytic theory, see Kosman, *Men's World*, 38.

51. About burial in the Land of Israel, see above 44–46.

52. See and compare Kosman, *Men's World*, 38.

53. See ibid., 37 n. 12.

54. This detail seems more an embellishment in this story. It is quite possible, as suggested to me by Daniel Boyarin, that it is a relic from another story of Rabbi's toothache, which he was allotted as punishment for his inability to pity a calf who escaped from the slaughterhouse; see y. Ketub. 12:2, 35a.

Land of Israel. Here, the heavenly realm's reaction to his suffering is to send him Elijah the prophet, the favorite secondary hero of talmudic narrative. His main task in the structure of the rabbinic narrative is to resolve the complexities of the plot.[55] Elijah appears at the Nasi's house, however, in the guise of Rabbi Ḥiyya. Now the suffering Nasi sees before him not the mocking Babylonian, but the healing one. By touching the painful spot in Rabbi's mouth, he heals him and wins his sympathy.[56] Afterward, the Patriarch will honor his Babylonian colleague in his guise of the immortal prophet Elijah.

Interestingly, this tradition about the collision between a Galilean and a Babylonian, against the backdrop of the coffin of a Babylonian Exilarch named Huna arriving on the scene, is connected, in all of its occurrences, with another story about the coffin of a Babylonian Exilarch named Huna; the latter is told against the backdrop of a collision between Palestinians and Babylonians.[57]

y. Kil'ayim 9:4, 32b–c [58]

When Rab Huna, the Exilarch, died, they brought him up to here.	כד דמך רב הונא ריש גלותא אסקוניה להכא.
They said: Let us bring him to Rabbi Ḥiyya the Great, since he is one of them.	אמר: אן אנן יהבין ליה? אמרין: ניתיניה גבי ר' חייא רובה דהוא מן דידהון.
They asked: Who wishes to bring him there?	אמרין: מאן בעי מיהב ליה.

---

55. On Elijah in postbiblical literature, see Samuel Kohn, "Der Prophet Elia in der Legende," *MGWJ* 12 (1863): 241–96; Louis Ginzberg, "Die Haggada bei den Kirchenvätern und in der Apokryphischen Literatur," *MGWJ* 43 (1899): 76–80; Kristen H. Lindbeck, *Elijah and the Rabbis: Story and Theology* (New York: Columbia University Press, 2010).

56. Touching as a healing procedure is well known in Jewish and Christian healing stories; see, e.g., Matt 9:18–22; Mark 5:25–34; 10:46–52; Luke 8:43–48; 18:35–43; John 9:1–7. See Dov Noy, "The Talmudic-Midrashic 'Healing Stories' as a Narrative Genre," *Proceedings of Koroth* 9 (1988): 124–46.

57. The relationship between these traditions is "one of the most difficult puzzles in historical studies" (Shamma Friedman, "The Historical Aggadah in the Babylonian Talmud" [Hebrew], in *Saul Lieberman Memorial Volume*, ed. Shamma Friedman [Jerusalem and New York: Jewish Theological Seminary, 1993], 119–64, here 146), and their decipherment has been a challenge to all who have dealt with them, of whom I list here the following: Jacob Neusner, *A History of the Jews in Babylonia*, 5 vols., StPB 9, 11, 12, 14, 15 (Leiden: Brill, 1965–1970), 3:50–53; Gafni, *Land, Center and Diaspora*, 83–84; Goodblatt, *Monarchic Principle*, 149–54, 168–69, 280, 284. Recently the similarities in the plots of two stories were thoughtfully discussed by Herman, *Prince without a Kingdom*, 92–102.

58. See the Academia ed., 174; see 112 n. 43 above. Except for the above-mentioned parallel, the story has a parallel in Eccl. Rab. 9:10; see Kiperwasser, "Early and Late," 306–8.

Rabbi Haggai said: I shall enter and bring him there.	אמר רבי חגיי אנא עליל יהב ליה.
They said to him: You are surely seeking a pretext, since you are an old man, and you wish to enter and lie there.[59]	אמרו ליה: עילתך את בעי דאת גבר סב ואת בעי מיעול מיתב לך תמן.
He said to them: Put a rope on my leg, and if I delay there too long you can drag me out.	אמר לון: יהבון משיחתא ברגליי ואין עניית אתון גרשין.
He went in and found the coffin [*denin-gerona*].[60] Yehuda, my son, is after you, and no one else. Hezekiah, my son, is after you, and no one else. After you, Joseph, son of Israel, and no one else.[61]	עאל ואשכח תלת דנין: יהודה בני אחריך. ואין עוד. חזקיה בני אחריך. ואין עוד. אחריך יוסף בן ישראל. ואין עוד.

---

59. Namely, to rest there after your death.

60. The elliptical expression תלת דנין is extremely difficult to translate. According to some versions of the parallel in Ecclesiastes Rabbah, it should be coffins (ארונין). However, one of the versions in Ecclesiastes Rabbah reads as in the Yerushalmi. The suggestion of the commentators of the Yerushalmi, that it is an exposition of three boxes, is logical, though there is no other example of such a word usage; see Sokoloff, *Jewish Palestinian Aramaic of the Byzantine Period*, 148 (marked as uncertain). A way to explain the difficult language is that, immediately after the appearance of three casuistic sentences featured, perhaps the narrator refers to the plural of דין, that is, rules, or legal cases. I have explained it elsewhere in that way; see Kiperwasser, "Early and Late," but I am no longer sure of that explanation and wish to propose an emendation. The word גורנא/גורנה *gorna* is usually translated as "stone bath" (Sokoloff, *Jewish Palestinian Aramaic of the Byzantine Period*, 113). However, it is also defined as a "coffin, sarcophagus" in Syriac; see Sokoloff, *Syriac Lexicon*, 221. I suggest that the following chain of errors occurred— גורנא -גו רנא- גי רנא-ג׳ רניך- תלת דנין —and that originally it was a term for the burial place of a few deceased. That the burial place was inhabited by three deceased persons probably influenced the scribe to find the number "three" in the word *gorna*.

61. This sentence is an enigmatic one. In light of the development of the plot, it seems to me a polite salutation of a new guest, in which a host declares that the guests deserve to be a part of the feast together with Rabbi Ḥiyya's sons Yehuda and Hezekiah, declaring that he is worthy of joining them, as was nobody else. However, the final line is difficult to explain. Joseph the son of Israel is clearly the biblical Joseph and not one of the contemporaries of these rabbis. However, because the gathering of the sages takes place in some entrance to the netherworld, the inclusion of the deceased biblical personage in the group of deceased rabbis could be imagined. Some difficulty arises from the fact that, according to Josh 24:32, the remains of Joseph were buried in the vicinity of Sichem. Perhaps local Galilean tradition identified an ancient tomb there with the tomb of the son of Jacob. For such processes in ancient and medieval Galilee, see Elhanan Reiner, "Joshua Is Rabbi, Hatsor Is Meron: On Typology of a Galilean Foundation Myth" [Hebrew], *Tarbiz* 80 (2012): 179–218; Reiner, "From Joshua to Jesus: The Transformation of a Biblical Story to a Local Myth (A Chapter in the Religious Life of the Galilean Jew)" [Hebrew], *Zion* 71 (1996): 281–317. I will discuss this in more detail in another work.

He raised his eyes and looked. One said to him: Turn your face around	תלת עינוי מסתכלה. (איא). אית אמר ליה. אפיך אפיך.
He heard the voice of Rabbi Ḥiyya the Great telling Rab Yehuda, his son: Make room for Rabbi Huna to sit. But he did not accept being seated [next to Ḥiyya, the Elder].	שמע קליה דרבי חייא רבא אמר לרב יהודה בריה: נפיש לרב חונה יתיב ליה. ולא קביל עלוי מתיב ליה.
They say: Just as he did not agree to sit himself down, so his seed shall never cease.	אמרין: כמה דלא קביל עלוי מתיב ליה כן זרעיתיה לא פסקה לעולם.
[R. Haggai] left that place at the age of eighty years, and they doubled the number of his years.	ויצא משם והיה בן שמוני' שנה ונכפלו לו שניו.

The story begins with the Exilarch's death, and his coffin is about to be delivered to the Land of Israel. It is obvious to the narrator that Rab Huna, the Exilarch, will be buried alongside Rabbi Ḥiyya, since he is "one of them," a Babylonian. The choice of burial place is not incidental; it is the perfect solution to a problem. The Exilarch is worthy enough to lie alongside Rabbi Ḥiyya, in his grave. There is a problem, though: there are no deserving Palestinian rabbinic students to bring him into the burial cave. People are hesitant to enter this burial cave for fear of being harmed.[62] Finally, one brave old rabbi proposes to enter himself, but those around him suspect him of wishing to organize for himself an exclusive burial place that he would not otherwise deserve. Nonetheless, this Rabbi Haggai is generously rewarded, and he informs his colleagues of the miraculous atmosphere in Rabbi Ḥiyya's grave. It turns out that the deceased Babylonians of this family continue to exist in some form of life. They cannot leave the tomb because they are dead, but they are not entirely dead, because they retain their knowledge and speech.[63] They spend their time accepting visits from well-known biblical figures.[64] Rabbi Haggai is curious to see these formidable living-dead rabbis. Upon his entrance, however, he is commanded not to look at them so as to respect their privacy.[65] Then he hears Rabbi Ḥiyya tell his elder son Yehuda to make room for Rab Huna. In terms of the Mediterranean symposia culture, the scene

---

62. The same fear of being harmed by facing Rabbi Ḥiyya, even in a dream, is expressed in stories from y. Kil. 9:4, 32b–c, one of which I discuss below.

63. Some rabbinic meditations regarding whether a dead person is completely dead, or whether he is still able to follow earthly affairs, accompanied by a suggestion that extraordinary persons were able to maintain living features even after death, appear in rabbinic literature; see, e.g., y. Ber. 2:3, 4d; b. Ber. 18a.

64. See 117 n. 61 above.

65. It was probably a common belief that seeing the face of Rabbi Ḥiyya could be dan-

should be understood as the typical image of the afterlife—participation in an eternal funeral banquet.⁶⁶ By inviting the guest to take the place of his firstborn son, Rabbi Ḥiyya shows respect to his colleague. The latter, however, refuses.⁶⁷ Another person merely standing among the banquet participants is usually not an esteemed guest but a servant or, in the worst case, an intruder.⁶⁸ The humble Exilarch sees himself not as an equal participant in the feast of past generations' sages but as their servant. That is why he receives his reward, as it is related: "Just as he did not agree to sit himself down, so his seed shall never cease."

Let us consider these two stories and the reasons that they were compiled.⁶⁹ In the first story, Yehuda, the Patriarch, promises to step down for Rab Huna but is in no hurry to deliver on his promise when put to the test. His manner is far from humble. This story focuses on the competition between the Patriarchate and the Exilarchate, a topic that is hinted at also in the second story. The refusal of Rab Huna the Exilarch to take the seat of Yehuda son of Rabbi Ḥiyya is rewarded with a promise of successful progeny. The compiler expresses disdain for the dynasty of the Patriarch and praises the other dynasty. The contrast between the courtesy of the Exilarch and the behavior of the Patriarch indicates how proper leadership should look. It is unlikely that the leadership of the Exilarchs was humbler than that of the Patriarchs. Still, the humble Babylonian portrait in the second story was a model for how the leaders of the compiler's time should behave.⁷⁰ Here again, the image of the Babylonian has been used to shape the image of an alternative leadership to the Patriarchate.

The first story begins with the proud host freely proclaiming his readiness to relinquish his rule if the guest who appears at the gate possesses a more illustrious lineage than he. Apparently, though, the host does not want this to happen. The lie is exposed in the mockery of the guest,

---

gerous for a person who does not belong to a chosen group; see Kiperwasser, "Early and Late," 303–8.

66. See Herman, *Prince without a Kingdom*, 98.

67. For a similar gesture, see Lucian of Samosata, *Gallus 11*, *Symp.* 9; and, for a similar explanation of our story, see Herman, *Prince without a Kingdom*, 98.This motif is more developed in Ecclesiastes Rabbah; there, after that, the host tries to seat the guest in the place of his youngest son, but Rab Huna still refuses to take a place among the feasts and prefers to stay standing.

68. See Lucian of Samosata, *Symp.* 12–13.

69. Gafni had already wondered whether the three traditions on Rab Huna (including the parallel in Bavli, which I am not discussing here) were not created from one tradition alone. See Gafni, *Land, Center and Diaspora*, 83 n. 10. Herman assumes that the first story is derived from the second one; for his arguments, see*Prince without a Kingdom*, 99–100. I would like to suggest that they existed separately and that the elements of similarity were reinforced by the compiler for his purpose—to oppose the Exilarch's behavior to the behavior of the Patriarch. On the last point I completely agree with Herman's analyses.

70. See Herman, *Prince without a Kingdom*, 100.

another Babylonian whom the host never considered an appropriate candidate for the post. The trick played by the Babylonian Rabbi Ḥiyya sheds light on the weakness of the Palestinian host and damages his self-esteem. However, not without intervention from the heavenly realm, he is forced to embrace the mocking Babylonian and respect him as a revered insider. Thus, as in the previous story, the house of the host will continue to thrive, but only with the legacy of the enduring values upheld by the guest.

In sum: In the first of the stories analyzed in this chapter, the Babylonian comes to the Land of Israel when the senior members of the rabbinic community have forgotten the necessary knowledge. His arrival saves them from embarrassment. This story is set in the distant past, and therefore, apparently, the heroes behave in it as they should—they accept the stranger without any conditions, and the guest becomes the master of the "house of study." In the second story, close to the period of the narrator, things are not so perfect. The Babylonian comes from the outside, armed with learning and moral merit, which are unrecognized for many years, and the host rebukes the guest. The guest, however, will lead the community after the host's death, because he will become a figure worthy of imitation for the rabbis of the Land of Israel. In the third story, the guest, suffering from the host's anger, carries within himself the potential for salvation, ultimately realized through outside intervention.

Thus, we see the relationships between the leader of the Palestinian sages and his Babylonian brethren and, at the same time, the dependence of the Palestinian rabbinic leader on his Babylonian colleagues, both past and present. It seems that the Palestinian rabbinic community strove to maintain an ongoing dialogue with its Babylonian counterpart. Stories like these (all told by Palestinian narrators) are not informed by other Jewish communities because they did not engage in a continuous cultural exchange of Torah study with the home country. However, on the banks of the Babylonian rivers and in the Galilee hills, a meaningful discourse flourished and became crucial, in the fourth century, for shaping the identity of the Palestinian rabbinic communities.

6

"He is one of them!" Showing the Other His Place

The present chapter, like the previous ones, deals with Palestinian narrative traditions that present an apparently conventional encounter between the Insider and the Outsider. This time, however, there is a twist. Unlike the previous sympathetic treatments of the Other, the stories we are about to read reveal the narrator's antipathy toward the Other, leading the narrator to marginalize the Other eternally for the "historical crime" committed by his ancestors. This approach can be found in a short story from Shir ha-Shirim Rabbah, an anthology of exegesis on the biblical Song of Songs edited in the Land of Israel that probably dates to the end of the period of classical midrashic literature.[1] It is noteworthy that this tradition appears in a relatively marginal anthology and not in the Yerushalmi or Genesis Rabbah,[2] a fact that may indicate the marginality of this tradition in the rabbinic continuum. Nevertheless, as we will see, this tradition

---

1. On this work, see H. E. Steller, "Preliminary Remarks to a New Edition of *Shir Hashirim Rabbah*," in *Rashi 1040–1990: Hommage à Ephraïm E. Urbach; Congrès Européen des études juives*, ed. Gabrielle Sed-Rajna, Patrinoines (Paris: Cerf, 1993), 300–311; Günter Stemberger, *Introduction to the Talmud and Midrash* (Edinburgh: T&T Clark, 1996), 315–16; Tamar Kadari, "Song and Meaning: A New Look on Rabbinic Exegesis of the Song of Songs" [Hebrew], *Jerusalem Studies in Hebrew Literature* 28 (2016): 27–54. The tradition under consideration was discussed and compared with Babylonian parallels by Ben Shahar, "Restoration in Rabbinic Literature," 19–52; Yonatan Feintuch, "*Sanina le Ho* ..." [Hebrew], *Jewish Studies, an Internet Journal* 12 (2013): 1–23. Some of the following texts were analyzed by Ronit Shoshany, "People Suspected of Violating the Sabbatical Laws (*Bavli Sanhedrin* 26a): Analysis of the Story and the Attitude of the Babylonian Talmud to Resh Lakish," *Teuda* 24 (2012): 45–61. Richard Kalmin, *The Sage in Jewish Society of Late Antiquity* (London-New York: Routledge, 1999), 15–17.

2. On the relationship between these two works, see Hans-Jürgen Becker, *Die großen rabbinischen Sammelwerke Palästinas: Zur literarischen Genese von Talmud Yerushalmi und Midrash Bereshit Rabba*, TSAJ 70 (Tübingen: Mohr Siebeck, 1999); Becker, "Texts and History: The Dynamic Relationship between Talmud Yerushalmi and Genesis Rabbah," in *The Synoptic Problem in Rabbinic Literature*, ed. Shaye J. D. Cohen, BJS 326 (Providence, RI: Brown Judaic Studies, 2000), 145–61, Chaim Milikowsky, "On the Formation and Transmission of Bereshit Rabba and the Yerushalmi: Questions of Redactions, Text-Criticism and Literary Relationships," *JQR* 92 (2002): 521–67.

echoes in the Babylonian Talmud and seems to be considered by Babylonians as indicative of the relationship between Palestinians and their Babylonian brethren. The story records a confrontation with Otherness, but with a take that differs from the traditions found in other texts.

6.1 Rabbi Zeira at the Market Place

Once again, we encounter the Babylonian scholar Rabbi Zeira, following in the footsteps of his distant ancestors to seek a new life in the Land of Israel. As I noted above, the Palestinian storyteller, true to his community's cultural norms, is interested in these Babylonian brethren. As a host receiving guests, however, he is in a tricky situation. Recalling Derrida, perfect hospitality implies the absence of conditions: the host is ready to receive the guest as an equal, with no strings attached. But therein lies the danger that the demarcation line between guest and host will be erased, and the guest, the unknown stranger, will usurp the host's house. Thus, ideal hospitality does not exist, though the desire for it does. A host with guests always finds himself in a precarious situation: he wants to welcome the guest and maintain his place at the same time. Efforts to resolve this dissonance can lead the host to limit the guest's rights or, alternatively, voluntarily to waive his own rights. The best of hosts will perform an endless balancing act to reconcile his interrupted self. Our earlier story about the Galilean–Babylonian encounters featured the theme of uniting the interrupted self of the Galilean narrator, to whom the Babylonian is both a desired friend and a menacing stranger. In this story, however, a disconcerting attempt is made to justify a host's right to restrict his guest's freedom. In the previous case, the narrator tried to resolve the problem of accepting the Other while sympathizing with him. In contrast, this story provides a rationalization for the alienation of the Other. This lengthy introduction is intended to provide the backdrop for the following brief incident.

Song of Songs Rabbah 8:3

| Rabbi Zeira came to the market to buy something. He told a man on the weights: Weigh well. He answered him: Why don't you go away from us, Babylonian, whose forefathers destroyed (the Temple) at that time? Said Rabbi Zeira: Are my forefathers not your forefathers? He went into the study house. He heard the voice of Rabbi Illa, who was sitting while interpreting | רבי זעירא נפיק ליה לשוקא למיזבן מקומא (מאומה?). א"ל לדין דהוא תקיל: תקיל יאות. ואמר ליה: לית את אזיל לן מן הכא, בבלייא די חרבון אבהתיה (בית מוקדשא בההיא ענתה. אמר ר' זעירא: לית אבהתי כאבהתהון דהדין? על לבית וועדא ושמע קליה דרבי אילא יתיב דריש: "אם חומה היא" (שיר השירים ח, ט), אילו עלו ישראל חומה מן הגולה, לא חרב בית המקדש פעם שנייה. אמר: יפה לימדני עם הארץ. |

this verse: "… if she be a wall" (Song 8:3). Had Israel gone up (to the Land of Israel) like a wall from the diaspora, the Temple would not have been destroyed a second time. He said: The ignorant man had taught me well.

Once again, our hero Rabbi Zeira goes to the marketplace; there, he turns to a shopkeeper and asks him to weigh carefully—that is, to be accurate. This request seems odd, as it is difficult to imagine that ancients habitually reminded merchants not to cheat. Perhaps this man had been sloppy before. However, the seller—apparently a simple Galilean, not burdened by education but not unfamiliar with the cultural norms of his community—is offended by the stranger's implied criticism and answers back. The criticism expressed by an alien can easily be taken by an insider as insulting, arousing a desire to send the troublemaker back to where he came from. The angry vendor finds it necessary to present his perspective on Jewish history, in which our Babylonian is assigned the role of the villain. The merchant's words are based on an interpretation that appears in Song of Songs Rabbah immediately before this story:

Song of Songs Rabbah 8:3

This verse our masters interpreted about those returning from the diaspora.	:רבנן פתרי קרא בעולי גולה
"We have a little sister" (Song 8:9); these are people who came up from the diaspora.	"אחות לנו קטנה" (שיר השירים ח, ט) אלו עולי גולה.
"Little," for they were few. "She has no breasts," these are the five things that were lacking in the Second Temple, but were in the First: the Heavenly Fire, the anointing oil, the ark, the holy spirit, and the Urim and Tumim, as it is written "I may be pleased with it and be glorified (ואכבד)" (Hag 1:8).[3]	"קטנה", שהיו דלים באכלוסין, "ושדים אין לה", אלו חמשה דברים שהיה בית אחרון חסר מן הראשון, ואלו הן: אש של מעלה, ושמן המשחה, ארון, רוח הקדש, ואורים ותומים, הה"ד: "וארצה בו ואכבד" (חגי א ח), "ואכבד" כתיב חסר ה'.
"What shall we do for our sister (when she is spoken for) …" (Song 8:9). What shall we do on the day that it was	"מה נעשה לאחותנו" (ח, ט), מה נעשה ביום שנגזר: די עבר פרת עבר די לא עבר לא יעבור.

---

3. The method of interpretation is based on the strange spelling of the last word in the cited biblical verse: ואכבד, instead of ואכבדה. The absence of the letter ה from the verse alludes, according to this interpretation, to the absence of five items from the Second Temple. The numerical meaning of letter ה is 5, making this playful interpretation possible.

decreed: Those who crossed the Euphrates shall go forth, and those who did not cross it can no longer go forth."[4]

"If she be a wall" (Song 8:9), Had Israel gone up from Babylon as a wall, the Temple would not have been destroyed at that time, a second time.

"אם חומה היא" (שיר השירים ח, ט), אלו ישראל. העלו חומה מבבל לא חרב בית המקדש בההיא שעתא פעם שנית.

Song of Songs 8:3 is interpreted as referring to events of the era before the construction of the Second Temple, namely, events associated with the Jewish exiles who went up from Babylonia to the Land of Israel with Ezra the scribe. They again traveled the road once taken by Abraham and paved the way for future generations of Babylonian returnees. As is well known, only a small number of the Jews living in Babylon left to follow Ezra; these included the descendants of the exiled Israelites of various lineage categories. The fourth chapter of Mishnah Qiddushin famously lists ten lineage categories:

Ten family lines came up from Babylon: the priests, Levites, and Israelites, the impaired[5] priestly stocks, the proselytes, freedmen, mamzerim, and netinim[6] the shetuqi[7] and asufi[8]. (m. Qidd. 4:1)

עשרה יוחסין עלו מבבל: כהני, לויי, ישראלי, חללי, גירי וחרורי, ממזרי, נתיני, שתוקי ואסופי.

Now, the seeds of impending disaster were sown in the insufficient number of Babylonian immigrants who came with Ezra; that is, the

---

4. This refers to Cyrus's declaration; see Song of Songs Rab. 5:1, Esther Rab. petiḥta 8, Eccl. Rab. 10:1.

5. I follow Danby, 327. In the original language, חללי means literally "profaned"; such are the offspring of a union that transgresses the laws governing the marriage of the priestly stock.

6. Netin is an alleged descendant of the biblical Gibeonites; see Josh 9:27.

7. The meaning of the root is "to be silent"; he that is of *shetuki* stock is silent when reproached with his origin, according to the explanation in the following mishnaic paragraph; see 4:2.

8. The meaning of the root is "to gather." *Asufi* has thus the sense of "foundling." Regarding some of the categories mentioned here, see Baruch A. Levine, "Later Sources on the *Netinim*," in *Orient and Occident: Essays Presented to Cyrus H. Gordon on the Occasion of His Sixty-Fifth Birthday*, ed. H. A. Hoffner, AOAT 22 (Neukirchen-Vluyn: Neukirchener Verlag, 1973), 101–7, here 103 n. 8; Shaye J. D. Cohen, *The Beginnings of Jewishness: Boundaries, Varieties, Uncertainties*, Hellenistic Culture and Society 31 (Berkeley: University of California Press, 1999), 278–79; Meir Bar-Ilan, "The Attitude toward Mamzerim in Jewish Society in Late Antiquity," *Jewish History* 14 (2000): 125–70, here 152–53 nn. 34–35; Michael L. Satlow, *Jewish Marriage in Antiquity* (Princeton: Princeton University Press, 2001), 148–50.

origin of the Second Temple debacle lies in the Babylonians' reluctance to relocate to the land of their forefathers. The narrator most likely feels that the few repatriates, his direct progenitors, deserve praise—unlike those who chose to remain in rich Babylonia, bringing down divine wrath and eventually the Temple's destruction. It is hard to say whether the underlying rationale is that the Babylonians' failure to migrate to the Holy Land led to its underpopulation and consequently to its defeat in the war against the Romans, or whether the narrator is simply looking for a scapegoat on which to lay the blame for the destruction of the Temple. Perhaps it is both.

Let us now return to the story at hand. The merchant tells the Babylonian visitor, Zeira, a fourth-century CE rabbi, that his Babylonian ancestors are responsible for the destruction of the Second Temple in 70 CE, implying that he, too, is culpable for that disaster. In the trader's mind, even the lapse of several centuries does not expiate this crime. At first, Rabbi Zeira does not understand him and replies that he always believed that they both had the same forefathers, who were even more ancient than the generation of the return to Zion. Discouraged, he leaves the market and joins his fellow rabbis at a study-house. The plot is quite like that of Rabbi Zeira's return to the study-house after receiving a slap in the face from the angry butcher. In this story, however, the victim fares worse: in the study-house he hears the same theory about ancestral guilt, but now in the form of a sermon based on an interpretation of a verse from the Song of Songs. It turns out that a market vendor and a scholar are united in laying the blame for the Temple's destruction on the passive sixth-century BCE Babylonians and their descendants. To the vendor and the scholar, Babylonians like Rabbi Zeira ought to meekly accept such a view.

This part of the plot parallels the story in the Yerushalmi about Rabbi Zeira. There, he was slapped in the face by a commoner and went to the study-house, where, despite being a stranger, he was well received by the rabbis. Here, in the second Palestinian story, something quite different happens. This particular study-house shared the rank and file's attitudes toward Babylonians, supporting these views with biblical exegeses.[9]

To recall, at issue is the acceptance of learned Babylonians by the learned class of Palestinians. We cannot know how laypeople felt, because they did not leave us texts expressing their thoughts and feelings. We can only reconstruct their opinions from the narratives of those who recorded the views of their untutored brethren. Saul Lieberman read the first story that I analyzed above in light of the second story and concluded that only the simple folk were xenophobic; the Palestinian sages, he believed, sympathized with their Babylonian colleagues and tried to reconcile them

---

9. Ben Shahar, "Restoration in Rabbinic Literature," 39.

with the ordinary people. This reading is difficult to accept, although in the earlier story the narrator did try to distinguish between rabbis and their unlearned compatriots, sometimes by expressing features of solidarity with the new immigrants. Naturally, the playful butcher seemed more alien to the rabbis than the Babylonian scholar, who, despite his foreignness, was an intellectual, someone who was at home in the same textual community to which they belonged.

Nevertheless, as we saw in the analyzed text, the inner world of the rabbinic narrator sometimes depicts the elites and the common people as on the same team, opposing the Other. Some values of the textual Galilean community were shared by learned and unlearned men alike. In our case, the common value is a basic narrative about the Land of Israel and the generation of "returnees to Zion," that is, about the behavior of the repatriates of the Babylonian exile in the "Restoration" period.[10] The Palestinian narrator wishes to voice his opinion of what is "right." The stranger must be willing to accept the lessons of the unfamiliar environment, even those taught by the unlettered, however unflattering they are to him. He should look at himself through the eyes of his new friends and colleagues in the Land of Israel, learning how they view him as he tries to get along with them. The Palestinian narrator asks the sympathetic stranger to leave behind the features of his old identity and take on something new while condemning his Babylonian forebears.[11] We will likely never know how Babylonians were absorbed into the Palestinian culture. But since several Babylonian traditions had already been incorporated into the Yerushalmi and perhaps also into older rabbinic compositions, we may assume that their influence was not insignificant. Perhaps this led to a sense of inferiority on the part of the narrator and a desire to accord the Babylonians a social standing that was lower and more vulnerable than that of an insider.[12] The second story about Rabbi Zeira attempts to shape a different

---

10. On this generation in rabbinic literature, see Ben Shahar, "Restoration in Rabbinic Literature"; on the biblical portrait of the generation of the "Restoration," see Sara Japhet, *From the Rivers of Babylon to the Highlands of Judah: Collected Studies on the Restoration Period* (Winona Lake, IN: Eisenbrauns, 2006), 96–116.

11. This situation is familiar to anyone acquainted with the ups and downs of immigration. In her essay "We Refugees," Hannah Arendt depicts the German Jews wandering from country to country, fleeing from the spread of Nazism and all the while reconstructing their own identity. See Hannah Arendt, "We Refugees," in *Altogether Elsewhere: Writers on Exile*, ed. Marc Robinson; (San Diego: Harcourt Brace, 1996), 110–19. With some irony, Arendt notes that therein lay the danger of losing rather than regaining one's identity. See a contemporary, somewhat controversial explanation of this text by Giorgio Agamben, *Means without End: Notes on Politics*, Theory out of Bounds (Minneapolis: University of Minnesota Press, 2000), 114–19.

12. Here my approach departs from that of Lieberman. Although I share his desire to explain the situation in late antique Roman Palestine, I aim to do so not in terms of a reflec-

kind of Self based on a hierarchy between a stranger and an insider—the stranger should accept the insider's worldview.

To sum up these two stories in Palestinian rabbinic literature: in both, the sage's tribulations arouse the narrator's sympathy and, consequently, that of the implied reader. The story in Song of Songs Rabbah, however, reveals an attempt to justify the isolation of the Other. In contrast, the story from the Yerushalmi about Rabbi Zeira's first encounter with a native of the Land of Israel depicts the Other's situation sympathetically. In that story, Rabbi Zeira remains the Other, but the narrator tries to incorporate him into the insider milieu.

6.2 Angry Heart

In this subchapter, we remain in the textual tradition of Song of Songs Rabbah and observe how this text employs tactics of symbolic violence to distribute symbolic capital among the Galilean rabbis. Recall that, according to Bourdieu, when holders of symbolic capital use it against agents who hold less power of this sort, thereby seeking to alter their actions, they exercise symbolic violence. Here, as the bearers of prestige in the framework of their communities, local Galilean rabbis exercise this power toward Babylonian students. The Galileans impose their categories of thought and perception in order to establish their dominance. Song of Songs Rabbah continues with another story about ancient and later Babylonians.

Song of Songs Rabbah 8:10

Rabbi Yoḥanan and Rabbi Shmuel bar Naḥman: Rabbi Yoḥanan related: It is written: "The Lord will give you there an anguished heart" (Deut 28:65). When they went up, the anger went up with them. Rabbi Shmuel said: Only there they got the anguished heart, when they went up, they were cured.	רבי יוחנן ור' שמואל בר נחמן, ר' יוחנן אמר: כתיב: "ונתן ה' לך שם לב רגז" (דברים כח סה). כיון שעלו, רוגז ניתן ועלה עמהם. רבי שמואל אמר: שמה לב רגז. כיון שעלו, נתרפאו.
When Resh Laqish saw them gathering together on the streets, he said to them: disperse yourselves! He told (them): During your ascent you did not rise like a wall, and now you want to be a wall here?	ר"ל כד הוה חמי להון מצמתין בשוקא הוה אמר להון: בדרו גרמיכון. א"ל: בעליתכם לא נעשיתם חומה, וכאן באתם לעשות חומה?

---

tion of real events in rabbinic literature but as a reflection of real events in the inner world of the narrator—who transformed these events in his highly literary narratives.

When Rabbi Yoḥanan saw them, he used to rebuke them. He said: Just as the prophet rebukes them, saying: "My God will cast them away, because they did not hearken unto Him" (Hos 9:17) and I, should I not rebuke them?

ר' יוחנן כד הוה חמי להון הוה מקנתר להון. אמר: מה נביא מקנתר להון, שנאמר: "ימאסם אלהי כי לא שמעו לו" (הושע ט יז), ואנא לית אנא מקנתר להון?

This pericope is built around the verse: "Yet even among those nations you shall find no peace, nor shall your foot find a place to rest. The Lord will give you there an anguished heart and eyes that pine and a despondent spirit" (Deut 28:65). It describes Israel's suffering in its punishment by exile. The stress is on an "anguished heart," which literally means "angry heart." "Heart" in rabbinic thought is synonymous with "personality" or "mind."[13] According to Rabbi Yoḥanan, an "angry heart" was a feature of the exiled Jews' personality, which they retained even after their return to the promised land. This meant, so he claims, that if you see an angry person among your contemporaries, you can blame the anger on the exile and the generation of the Temple restoration period, who inherited it. According to Shmuel, the repatriates lost their anger upon entering the Holy Land; that is, if you now see an angry Palestinian man, he did not necessarily inherit his anger from his Babylonian ancestors. The two rabbis presented in our tradition disagree with each other regarding the fitting interpretation of Deut 28:65 but agree that anger is a trait of the diasporic Jewish personality.

Another, apparently independent text illustrates aspects of the "angry heart" behavior. Paradoxically, however, it is the Palestinian rabbis who behave angrily. One of them is the famous Rabbi Yoḥanan,[14] while the second is his colleague Resh Laqish. Both are depicted as lacking sympathy for the Babylonians and expressing their feelings boldly and even angrily.[15] Resh Laqish appears to be quite an aggressive character, who, upon meet-

---

13. See Reuven Kiperwasser, "Matters of the Heart: The Metamorphosis of the Monolithic in the Bible to the Fragmented in Rabbinic Thought," in *Judaism and Emotion: Texts, Performance, Experience*, ed. Sarah Ross, Gabriel Levy, and Soham Al-Suadi, Studies in Judaism 7 (Bern: Peter Lang, 2013), 43–59.

14. This version is problematic; variant spellings occur (Jonathan or Jona), but because he appears here together with Resh Laqish, one may assume that Rabbi Yoḥanan, his partner and friend, is intended.

15. In attempting to apologize for the anti-Babylonian tendencies in the Palestinian texts, Ronit Shoshany proposes that these are Palestinian reactions to attacks by Babylonians who were hostile to Resh Laqish because of his pronouncements, such as the views expressed in b. Yoma 9b ("People Suspected of Violating," 58–59). However, the anti-Babylonian sentiments of the above-mentioned rabbis were noticed already by Wilhelm Bacher, *Die Agada der Palästinensischen Amoräer*, 3 vols. (Strassburg: Karl J. Trübner 1892–1899; repr., Hildesheim: Olms, 1992) 2:350–53.

ing a gathering of Babylonians on the city streets, speaks insultingly to them, demanding that they disperse. His anger can be explained if a high concentration of Babylonian immigrants on the streets of Tiberias is unbearable to him because of the small number of Babylonians who had taken to the roads in the Restoration period. To punish that pitiably small number of former repatriates, the sage tells them not to congregate in noticeable groups when he is strolling on the street. Even if this saying is no more than a joke, it is rather aggressive in tone and appears aimed at discouraging strangers from forming pressure groups. The words of the second sage, the famous Rabbi Yoḥanan, are far from friendly: he used to rebuke (*meqanter*)[16] Babylonians in various unspecified ways.[17] The sage felt justified in his aggressive anti-Babylonian stance based on a biblical verse that parallels his mood: "My God will cast them away because they did not hearken unto Him, and they shall be wanderers among the nations" (Hos 9:17). In this verse, the prophet is speaking not about the Babylonians, past or present, but about some unidentified people who disobeyed God's command and were therefore cast away, destined to be wanderers forever. Rabbi Yoḥanan identifies the Babylonian Jews, born and raised in the diaspora, as the descendants of these outcasts. Both Rabbi Yoḥanan and Resh Laqish are unhesitating in their expression of animus toward the Babylonians. The narrator's rationalization of certain xenophobic tendencies of his own brethren is evident in this story. Although this tradition may be viewed as relatively marginal in the corpus of Palestinian rabbinic literature, it was accepted by the Babylonian Talmud, though in an inverted and edited form.

b. Yoma 9b

| Resh Laqish was bathing in the Jordan: Rabba bar bar Ḥana came to him and held out his hand. Resh Laqish said to him: I hate you (Babylonians), as it is written: "If she be a wall, we will build upon her a palace of silver; and if she be a door, we will enclose her with the boards of cedar" (Song 8:9). Had you made yourselves as a wall, and all come up in the days of Ezra, you would have been comparable to silver, upon which decay has no effect; now that you come as doors, you are like cedar, which is subject to decay. | ריש לקיש הוי סחי בירדנא. אתא רבה בר בר חנה. יהב ליה ידא. אמר ליה: אלהא! סנינא לכו, דכתיב: "אם חומה היא נבנה עליה טירת כסף ואם דלת היא נצור עליה לוח ארז" (שיר השירים ח ט). אם עשיתם עצמכם כחומה ועליתם כולכם בימי עזרא, נמשלתם ככסף, שאין רקב שולט בו. עכשיו, שעליתם כדלתות, נמשלתם כארז שהרקב שולט בו. |

---

16. See Sokoloff, *Jewish Palestinian Aramaic of the Byzantine Period*, 569.
17. We can read his words only in the *editio princeps*, because all manuscripts contain a homoioteleuton here from "rebuke" to "rebuke."

Here, we meet the old Palestinian sage bathing in the Jordan, as was customary for him in the Babylonian imagination,[18] while the foreigner—in this case, Rabba bar bar Ḥanna,[19] who is well known but not appreciated by his Babylonian colleagues—is trying to be polite to the elder and help him out of the water. But the sage refuses the proffered assistance, stating that he hates all Babylonians because of their ancestors' choice to stay in Mesopotamia during the Restoration period. This is clearly another late and tendentiously edited version derived from the tradition we saw in Song of Songs Rabbah. The Babylonian narrator is probably unaware of Rabbi Yoḥanan's anti-Babylonian sayings (or perhaps holds an apologetic view of him). Still, he is familiar with Resh Laqish's position, which is very close to the one related in the Palestinian source.[20] As this narrator does not wish to attribute blunt anti-Babylonian statements to the doyen of rabbinic literacy, he instead attributes them to Resh Laqish. But let us go to the end of this pericope.[21]

b. Yoma 9b-10a

| When [the latter] came to Rabbi Yoḥanan [and related to him what Resh Laqish had told him], he said: This is not the reason. If all had come with Ezra, even then the *Shekhina* would not have dwelt in the Second Temple, since it is written: "May God enlarge the boundaries of Japheth, and may he dwell in the tents of Shem" (Gen 9:27); that signifies, that although God enlarges the boundaries of Japheth, his *Shekhina* can only dwell in the tents of Shem. | כי אתא לקמיה דרבי יוחנן אמר ליה: לאו היינו טעמא, אי נמי סליקו כולהו בימי עזרא לא הוה שריא שכינה במקדש שני, דכתיב "יפת אלהים ליפת וישכן באהלי שם" (בראשית י ב). אף על גב דיפת אלהים ליפת – אין השכינה שורה אלא באהלי שם. |

---

18. Cf. the famous story from b. B. Metz. 84a about Rabbi Yoḥanan first meeting Resh Laqish while the latter was bathing in the Jordan River. On numerous scholarly discussions of this story, see Richard Kalmin, *The Sage in Jewish Society of Late Antiqity* (London: Routledge, 1999), 5, Boyarin, *Socrates and the Fat Rabbis*, 182–91.

19. See Kiperwasser, "Rabba bar Bar Channa's Voyages," 238.

20. I do not think that the Babylonian Talmud had a personal issue with Resh Laqish and for that reason created these stories about him, as proposed by Shoshany, "People Suspected of Violating," 58–59.

21. I am deliberately skipping the following discussion, which tries to attribute these bold sayings of Resh Laqish to Rabba bar bar Ḥanna and Zeiri, or to Rabbi Eleazar and Rabba bar bar Ḥanna. It is probably a later gloss.

Here, Rabbi Yoḥanan is proposing an alternative, less anti-Babylonian historiography. Rabbi Yoḥanan's interpretation comes from an exegesis on Gen 9:27, well known from the Palestinian parallel in Gen. Rab. 36:8[22] but not attributed there to Rabbi Yoḥanan.

Genesis Rabbah 36:8

"And he said: Blessed be the Lord, the God of Shem ... God enlarge Japeth" (Gen 9:27). This alludes to Cyrus, who decreed that the Temple be rebuilt, yet even so, "and he shall dwell in the tents of Shem" the Shekhina dwells only in the tents of Shem.	ויאמר: "ברוך י"י אלהי שם וגו' יפת אלהים ליפת" (בראשית ט, כז), זה כורש, שגזר שיבנה בית המקדש. אפעלפיכן "וישכן באהלי שם" (שם). אין שכינה שורה אלא באהלי שם.

The Babylonian narrator borrowed this textual tradition from the passage about the Persian emperor's role in erecting the Temple to adjust the anti-Babylonian tradition to a relatively neutral context.

As Yonatan Feintuch has keenly observed, the context of the Palestinian version of the tradition (or actually the two traditions) is an attempt to prove exegetically the historical guilt of the Babylonian Jews (Feintuch uses somewhat milder language, referring to the "critique of the Palestinians toward the Babylonians."[23] In the Babylonian Talmud, however, the context is a discussion of the fates of the two Temples; in fact, the text is filled with references to the ancient history of the Temples. Nevertheless, when discussing contemporary issues, the Babylonian editor is quite aware of the xenophobic background of the Palestinian tradition.

In the present context, Babylonians and Palestinians share the same tradition: while in the Land of Israel, the Babylonian scholar is confronted with local aggression, challenging the historical justification for his presence in the promised land. When the Babylonian turns to the study-house, however, the traditions part company. In the Palestinian tradition, the sage in the Academy justifies the hate speech of the street. In the Babylonian tradition, the editor mobilizes Rabbi Yoḥanan himself to purge the shame of the Babylonians. To the anti-Babylonian accusations, the sage replies, without considering the Babylonian deeds, that the Second Temple was unsuited to accommodate the *Shekhina* because the Persian emperor had built it. Aware of the lack of sympathy of his Palestinian brethren for the new immigrant, the Babylonian editor, unlike Rabbi Zeira in the Palestinian story, is unwilling to assume the role of the historical villain and

---

22. See Theodor Albeck, 1:342.
23. See Feintuch, "*Sanina le Ho ...*," 16.

proposes his own interpretation of past events, enlisting in this effort the head of the Palestinian sages.[24]

Here we first find the difficulties in resolving the dramatic conflict between the "insider" and the "internal Other" in the thought of the Babylonian sages and their colleagues in the Land of Israel. The Palestinian narrator is keen to set his own identity apart from that of the Other, who is painted in harsh colors. When the Babylonian narrator recounts the same conflict, he does not fully grasp its passionate nature and pragmatically seeks to justify it. I will return to this topic in Chapter 7.

6.3 They Are Haughty and Poor in Torah

Let us now leave the uncomfortably xenophobic passages of Song of Songs Rabbah and return to the pages of the Yerushalmi. Earlier, I suggested that the Galilean rabbinic community's strong aversion to the Babylonian Other was a marginal phenomenon and therefore not emphasized in the Yerushalmi but rather preserved only in the relatively peripheral Song of Songs Rabbah. Yet this is not the whole story, because the attempt to employ such symbolic violence can be found in the Yerushalmi as well, as we saw above. The Galileans' expressions of disdain toward the Babylonians, as well as the ethnic slurs, are usually milder in the Yerushalmi. However, in one particular tradition that records the discrimination experienced by a Babylonian scholar in a study-house, we see a rather intense, even shocking, expression of hatred. I refer to the following text:[25]

y. Pesahim 5:3, 32a[26]

Rabbi Simlai came before R. Yonatan [and] said to him: Teach me aggadah. [He] said to him: I have a tradition from my ancestors neither to teach aggadah to Babylonians nor to Southerners, for they are haughty and poor in Torah, and you are a Nehardean [by origin] and reside in the South and moreover a minor [who is likely to misunderstand]. He said to him: [At least] tell me one thing ...	רבי שמלאי אתא גבי רבי יונתן. אמר ליה: אלפן אגדה. אמר ליה: מסורת בידי מאבותי שלא ללמד אגדה לא לבבלי ולא לדרומי. שהן גסי רוח ומעוטי תורה. ואת נהרדעאי ודר בדרום {ועוד קטן}. אמר ליה: אמור לי חדא מילתא ...

---

24. Ben Shahar, "Restoration in Rabbinic Literature," 38–39.
25. See Melamed, *Introduction to Talmudic Literature*, 507.
26. See Academia ed., 525.

When in the Land of Israel, the Babylonian scholar, Rabbi Simlai[27] asks the Palestinian sage Rabbi Yonatan[28] to teach him the aggadah, a branch of the Oral Torah attractive to many masters, as well as to ordinary people. We might note, in this context, the oft-cited dictum of Rabbi Nehemiah: "the smiling face of the aggadah and the stern face of the halakhah" (Pesiq. Rab Kah. 12:25).[29] Our Babylonian is, in fact, a scholar of aggadah, most of his teachings being aggadic. Now he wishes to learn the specific aggadic instructions of Rabbi Yonatan. The latter, however, is unwilling to share his knowledge with Rabbi Simlai, and his reasoning is anything but friendly. For him, the art of aggadic teaching was off-limits to Babylonians or students from the South.[30] Just as a minor was excluded from aggadic study because of his social insignificance and doubts concerning his intellectual maturity, the internal Other, who is clearly not a Galilean but a Southerner and a Babylonian, was also excluded. Only narrowly defined halakhic teachings, but not aggadic lore, could be imparted to these Others. Like the previous tradition, this restrictive teaching tradition made its way to Babylonia and contributed to the Babylonians' views of their Palestinian brethren.

b. Pesahim 72b

Rabbi Simlai came before Rabbi Yoḥanan [and] said to him: Let the Master teach me the Book of Genealogies.[31] Said he to him, whence are you? He replied, From Lod.[32] And where is your dwelling? In Nehardea.[33] Said he to him: We do not discuss it either with the Lydians or with the Nehardeans, and how much more so with you, who are from Lod and live in Nehardea! But he urged him, and he consented Let us learn it in three months, he proposed. [Thereupon]	רבי שמלאי אתא לקמיה דרבי יוחנן, אמר ליה: ניתני לי מר ספר יוחסין. אמר ליה: מהיכן את? אמר ליה: מלוד. והיכן מותבך? בנהרדעא. אמר ליה: אין נידונין לא ללודים ולא לנהרדעים, וכל שכן דאת מלוד ומותבך בנהרדעא כפייה וארצי. אמר ליה: ניתנייה בשלשה ירחי. שקל קלא פתק ביה, אמר ליה: ומה ברוריה דביתהו דרבי מאיר, ברתיה דרבי חנניה בן תרדיון, דתניא תלת מאה שמעתתא ביומא משלש מאה

---

27. See Albeck, *Introduction*, 190.
28. It is difficult to say which of the rabbis named Jonathan is meant here.
29. This distinction between Halakhah and Aggadah is well known to modern Hebrew speakers as expressed by Chaim Nachman Bialik, who was paraphrasing an aphorism by Rabbi Nehemiah (Pesiq. Rab Kah. 12:25, Mandelbaum ed., 1:223).
30. See above, 111. Mentioning the youthfulness of our hero is apparently a late addition to this tradition, an attempt to soften the cruelty of the words of the Palestinian sage.
31. What this document is remains unclear. However, its existence correlates with the importance of the lineage in the Babylonian rabbinic culture; see Rubenstein, *Culture of the Babylonian Talmud*, 80–101.
32. Lod (Lydda) was an important city of the South; see 111 n. 37 above.
33. See 3 above.

| he took a clod and threw it at him, saying, If Beruriah, wife of R. Meir [and] daughter of R. Ḥanina b. Teradion, who studied three hundred laws from three hundred teachers in [one] day, could nevertheless not do her duty in three years, yet you propose [to do it] in three months! | רבוותא - ואפילו הכי לא יצתה ידי חובתה בתלת שנין, ואת אמרת בתלתא ירחי? |

In this story, the tradition underwent light editing upon its reception in Babylonia: aggadah has become the obscure Book of Genealogies, which likely ranks higher in importance than aggadah in the eyes of the Babylonian narrator.[34] In any case, an attempt is made to defuse the tension by claiming that the old master relented and agreed to teach the Babylonian. Even then, however, because of some comical disagreement regarding the following learning, the connection between the scholars goes bad.[35]

6.4. From Babylonia to Babylonia?

Rabbi Shimeon b. Laqish, whom we encountered in chapter 2 above, is the main protagonist in this discussion. Sharing the stage with Resh Laqish, the ultimate anti-Babylonian Galilean, is Rabbi Ḥiyya, the ultimate Babylonian patriot to sojourn in the Land of Israel. In the following text, we see how the formidable image of the great Babylonian, Rabbi Ḥiyya, is appropriated by Palestinian rabbinic culture. The sages of later generations take his figure as both a model and a source of reproach. In the following text, Rabbi Ḥiyya is already dead, yet he is somehow still present in the lives of Palestinians.

y. Kil'ayim 9:4, 32b–c[36]

| Rabbi Shimeon ben Laqish fasted three hundred fasts in order to see R. Ḥiyya the Great, but he did not see him. Finally, he began to be distressed. | רבי שמעון בן לקיש צם תלת מאוון צומין, למיחמי רבי חייה רובה ולא חמתיה. ובסופא שרא מצטער. |
| He said: Did he labor in learning of Torah more than I? | אמר: מה הוה לעי באוריתא סגין מניי? |

---

34. See 50–51 above and further 164.
35. As is evident, however, from the continuation of the story there in the Babylonian Talmud, he finally gave his Babylonian student not an aggadic lesson but a halakhic one, though I am not sure that this continuation is a part of above-mentioned narrative, but merely an addition.
36. Academia ed., 175.

They said to him: He brought Torah to the people of Israel to a greater extent than you have, and not only so, but he even went into exile.	אמ' ליה: ריבץ תורה בישראל יותר ממך, ולא עוד אלא דהוה גלי.
He said to them: And did I not go into exile too?	אמר לון: ולא הוינא גלי?
They said to him: You went into exile only to learn, but he went into exile to teach others.	אמרין ליה: את הויתה גלי מילף, והוא הוה גלי מלפה.

This story reflects the widespread folk belief that the deceased can be contacted in a dream. As we have seen, however, it takes more than one's will to make this happen. As is evident from other stories in this chain, Rabbi Ḥiyya could be seen only by select dreamers. Here, the dreamer is the famous Rabbi Shimeon ben Laqish, but although he has already fasted for three hundred days,[37] the deceased refuses to reveal himself. Resh Laqish expresses his exasperation by arguing that he is no less learned than the deceased. However, respondents pose a bold and seemingly rhetorical question to Resh Laqish. Its formulation evades the claim of equal erudition by pointing out the greatness of the deceased Babylonian scholar in that he not only achieved his outstanding knowledge, with which the Palestinian rabbi demands to be compared, but he was eager to share his knowledge with other people and labored toward this end. But the list of Rabbi Ḥiyya's superior merits is not yet exhausted. He left his homeland and settled in a foreign place, albeit a very special foreign place—the Land of Israel. Our proud Palestinian then continues the competition. He demands his share among the select contingent of exiled sages: "And did I not go into exile too?" The answer runs: "You went into exile only to learn, but he went into exile to teach others." This answer is the punch line: the Babylonian is still greater than the Palestinian because the reason for his exile was to bring his learning to the new place of his sojourn. Thus, we are informed that the famous learning partner of the formidable Rabbi Yoḥanan went into temporary exile to become a student but not to spread his learning. Where he went is not mentioned.

Let us consider the meaning of this last sentence in the story, which probably reveals where the tradition comes from. The conscious juxtaposition of the Palestinian sage to the Babylonian, in which the Babylonian is someone who brings with him his learning to share it with the locals and the Palestinian is nothing more than a student who goes to a distant land for what he lacks, is a typology designed to raise the authority of the Bab-

---

37. This is probably a stereotypical motive; see 81–82 above.

ylonian and devalue the Palestinian. Is this the basic Palestinian approach to Babylonian learning, which developed in the generations after Rabbi Yoḥanan and his disciples? The Palestinians may have seen themselves as wholly independent and self-sufficient but nevertheless seem to have preferred to see in the genesis of their scholarship a foundation laid by the Babylonians—and perhaps this really was the case. The narrator is quite critical of Resh Laqish, albeit in a restrained manner.[38] Yet the reader wonders: Why was Rabbi Shimeon ben Laqish so proud of his exile experience, and where did he go? Perhaps the following selection of texts can help us unravel this mystery.

y. Shevi'it 6:1, 36d[39]

Rabbi Shimeon ben Laqish went to Bosra. They came to him and said: Find us a man who will deliver sermons, judge, teach Bible, be a sexton and fulfill all our needs.[40]	ר' שמעון בן לקיש אזל לבוצרה. אתון לגביה. א"ל: חמי לן בר נש דריש, דיין, ספר, חזן, עביד כל צורכינן.
He saw a Babylonian and said to him: I have found you a good place.	חמא חד בבליי. אמר ליה: חמית לך חד אתר טב.
He came before Rabbi Yoḥanan. He said to him: From Babylonia to Babylonia?	אתא לגבי רבי יוחנן. אמר ליה: מן בבל לבבל?
Said Rabbi Jacob bar Abba: On the basis of what did Rabbi Yoḥanan say to him "from Babylonia to Babylonia"? This implies that he who purchases (land) there is not obligated (to keep the agricultural rules)?	אמר יעקב בר אבא: מן מה דאמר רבי יוחנן, "מן בבל לבבל"? הדא אמרה: הקונה שם אינו מתחייב.
Rabbi Yoḥanan considered, "Bezer in the wilderness" (Deut 4:43) and asked Rabbi Shimeon ben Laqish: Is Bezer Bosra?	סבר רבי יוחנן מימר: "את בצר במדבר" (דברים ד מג). שאל לרבי שמעון בן לקיש: בצר בוצרה?

This small pericope in the Yerushalmi is elliptical. The story is conceptually related to other stories in which priests and laymen ask Rabbi Yoḥanan if it is permitted to go to various places that are technically outside the Land of Israel but in its vicinity. There the toponym Bosra is first mentioned in the following rule: "Priests are accustomed to going as far as Daray. And regarding the border of Bosra, priests are accustomed to going as far as the orchard." Note that this appears again in the story

---

38. However, in a much later version of the story, preserved by Ecclesiastes Rabbah, the critical hints of the ancient narrator are exposed and developed further.
39. See Academia ed., 198–99
40. See Sokoloff, *Jewish Palestinian Aramaic of the Byzantine Period*, 197.

about Rabbi Yasa and his mother, which I discussed earlier.⁴¹ Now we have this story told about the visit of Rabbi Shimeon ben Laqish in Bosra, obviously the very city mentioned above. The Jewish inhabitants of this city ask him to find them a person able to meet all of their community's religious needs.⁴² Sometime later, Rabbi Shimeon meets someone who fulfills this criterion. Neither the place nor the time of this discovery is disclosed, but the fact that he is a Babylonian is emphasized. The final decision about the question is now brought to Rabbi Yoḥanan; it is not clear whether he is approached by his Palestinian colleague or by the Babylonian candidate. The rabbi's laconic response? "From Babylonia to Babylonia." Is this delivered with an exclamation mark? Or perhaps as a question? Did the master express his consent, or his discontent, or perhaps his anger? While we cannot know for sure, the fact that in the previous cases he ruled in the negative might indicate that he did so here as well. But what does "From Babylonia to Babylonia" mean? Since the discussion touches on places in the vicinity of the border of the promised land, how could it be called Babylonia? A possible answer is that the term Babylonia is taken here in a very wide metaphorical sense, as the commentators of the Yerushalmi understood it. Indeed, in the ensuing discussion, Rabbi Yoḥanan identifies Bosra with the biblical Betzer, a city in Transjordan, again emphasizing that the point is that Bosra is simply outside of the Land of Israel, not that it is literally in Babylonia.⁴³ Thus, Resh Lakish regarded the Syrian Bosra as part of the Greater Land of Israel (and therefore it needs to follow the laws regarding the Land of Israel). R. Yoḥanan, for his part, rejected this identification and therefore regarded it as beyond the borders of the Land of Israel (חוץ לארץ).

Turning now to the late parallel of this tradition, we will see how the geographical realities were understood in Deuteronomy Rabbah.⁴⁴ The

---

41. See 32 above.

42. For a very similar motive in the story about the people of Simonia applying to Rabbi Yehuda the Patriarch for such an educator for their community, see y. Yevam. 12:6, 13a.

43. The place-name בְּצְרָה, mentioned in the biblical narrative, is usually identified by some as one of the sites adjacent to the modern town of Bouseira (بصيرا) in modern Jordan. The most likely identification of Bosra is with the ancient capital of Edom, which still existed in Roman and Byzantine times as Bostra, quite close to the border of the promised land. If that were the case, however, no satisfactory explanation for "From Babylonia to Babylonia" can be provided. Even though we have now found a place to which Rabbi Shimeon ben Laqish went into exile, it does not seem to be a place where a rabbinic student from Tiberias would go to obtain knowledge.

44. Deuteronomy Rabbah (Saul Lieberman, *Midrash Devarim Rabbah* [Jerusalem: Bambreger and Wahrman, 1965]), also called the Spanish version of Deuteronomy Rabbah according to M. B. Lerner, is a combination of an unknown Yelamdenu Midrash and a selection of the standard version of Tanhuma. See Miron B. Lerner, "New Light on the Spanish Recension of Deuteronomy Rabbah (1): The Evolution of ed. Lieberman" [Hebrew], *Teuda* 11 (1996): 107–45; Lerner, "New Light on the Spanish Recension of Deuteronomy Rabbah (2):

story appears in the context of a discussion regarding the so-called cities of refuge, designated by biblical law as shelters for those who commit involuntary murder. Discussing different cities of refuge, the midrash mentions that the first cities of this kind were founded in the area of the tribe of Reuben. To illustrate this point, it quotes the verse Deut 4:43, "The cities were these: Bezer in the wilderness plateau, for the Reubenites, etc." An explanatory remark is added: "this means that Bezer is on its (own) behalf and Bosra is on its (own) behalf," namely, that they are separate entities. Then, to support the claim that Bezer and Bosra are different cities, the text cites a tradition parallel to that found in the Yerushalmi passage discussed above:

Deuteronomy Rabbah, *vaethanan*[45]

Rabbi Shimeon ben Laqish went to Bosra. They asked him: Have you not seen a man who will sit among us and be a Bible teacher, a Mishnah teacher, a sexton, and a scribe and will be in all of these things? He told them: Say that you are looking for Rabbi Yoḥanan?	רשב״ל אזל לבוצרה. אמרי ליה: לית את חמי חד בר נש דיתיב גבן, דיהוי ספר, ומתניין, וחזן, וכתב, ויהוי בכל (אילין) מיליא? אמ' להון: תאמרון דיהבתון עיניכון בר' יוחנן.
He went into his house and saw a Babylonian who possessed all these attributes that they asked in Bosra. He asked him: Would you like to go to Bosra, and to set up for us there this and that, of time and to settle for us there? He said to him: A Babylonian came from Babylonia and you want to settle him there? From impure Land to impure Land!	אתא לגו ביתיה, וחמא חד בבלייא דהוו ביה כל אילין מיליא, דאמרין ליה בבוצרה. א״ל: בעי את מייתי לבצרה ומיתב לן כדן וכדן ומיתב לן גביהון? אמ' ליה: ייתי בבלייא מן בבל, ולבבל את בעי למיתב [ליה]? מן ארעא מסאבתא לארעא מסאבתא.
Rabbi Shimeon (ben Laqish) came to Rabbi Yoḥanan and said to him: I went to Bosra and they told me: Did you see a man who will sit among us and be a Bible teacher, a Mishnah teacher, a	אתא ר״ש אמ' לר' יוח', אזלית לבצרה, ואמרין לי: חמית חד בר נש דיהוי ספר ומתניין וחזן וכתב? חמית חד בבלא ואמרית ליה: בעי את מייתי לך לבוצרה? ואמ' לי: מן בבל אייתית ולבבל את בעי מתיב לי?

On the Origins of Pericopes *Vaethanan-Eqev*" [Hebrew], *Tarbiz* 70 (2001): 417–27. But there is no doubt that, however late the final redaction of the collection, the tradition under discussion, which has no parallels anywhere except here, may well be quite ancient.

45. Lieberman ed., 60–61

sexton and a scribe and I saw a Babylonian and I asked him, Would you like to settle in Bosra? And he said to me, The Babylonian came from Babylonia and you want to settle him there?

Rabbi Yoḥanan said to him: He answered you correctly! And is there a Bosra in Babylonia?! It is not part of the Land of Israel nor is it from the cites of refuge, as it is written: "The cities were these: Bezer in the wilderness plateau" (Deu 4:43). This is not Bosra.

א״ל ר׳ יוחנן יאות אמ׳ לך,

ואית לך בצרה בבבל. לית היא מן ארעא דישראל, ואינה מערי מקלט, דכתיב: "את בצר במדבר" (דברים ד מג). ואין זו בצרה.

The story likely stems from the same nucleus that y. Shev. 6:1, 36d stems from, but in this later retelling,[46] the narrator adds detail, in which he tries to explain the story from his point of view. Rabbi Shimeon indeed went to Bosra, and the locals indeed asked him for an educator with many qualities. The wish list is slightly modified; they now want a teacher for Mishnah as well as a scribe. Rabbi Shimeon reads this request as an attempt on the part of the locals to persuade the famous Rabbi Yoḥanan to move to their area, because who else could be so versatile and knowledgeable?[47] However, coming home, probably to Tiberias, he encounters a Babylonian who is endowed with the requisite pedagogical traits. Rabbi Shimeon proposes the position at Bosra to the Babylonian. And the Babylonian, who is utterly silent in the Yerushalmi version, here is unexpected and bold. When Resh Lakish offers the Babylonian, who has recently arrived in the Land of Israel, the opportunity to go and teach in Bosra, the latter replies cynically, "From Babylonia to Babylonia?" That is, he does not consider Bosra to be part of the Land of Israel, and therefore going there is equivalent to returning to Babylonia, which he has so recently left. The Babylonian's response is in accord with the opinion of R. Yoḥanan, who indeed endorses it, based on his rejection of Bosra's identification with Bezer. The indifferent hero of the talmudic story voices his point of view and shows his perception of reality. He left his spiritually polluted birthplace for purely religious reasons to live in his own pure and sacred land. He understands that Rabbi Shimeon wants him to settle on "impure land."[48] As we can surmise from Rabbi Shimeon's bewilderment when recounting

---

46. Due to the late dating of the compilation, though the tradition itself could be from the early post-Amoraic period and is undoubtedly a Palestinian one.

47. Compare y. Yevam. 12:6, 13a, where the locals ask Rabbi Yehuda the Patriarch to send them a man like him.

48. This detail resembles the story about the death of Ulla; see 198 below.

the story to his master, the Babylonian's objection is surprising. The master, however, admits that justice is with the stranger.

If these identifications are correct and the tradition in Deuteronomy Rabbah indeed accounts for the Yerushalmi's tradition, the exile of Rabbi Shimeon of Laqish was to Transjordan, which is rather close to the Land of Israel. However, the main figure here is a Babylonian, who is an ideal internal Other for a Palestinian narrator—once he has arrived in the promised land, no "impure land," regardless of its proximity to the Land of Israel, can lure him away.

Summing up, we saw in the above traditions the tendency to put the Other in his place and erect necessary barriers between the storyteller and the Other. These attempts to contain the Babylonians within the boundaries demarcated by the will of their benevolent Palestinian hosts are acts of symbolic violence, expressed here in language and in forms of exegetic discourse. They aim to form a particular structured field and prevent individuals from leaving its borders. Although it is only language-based, this form of violence is very potent; it is capable of producing social domination and even incite physical attack.[49] What is more, in the last of the traditions analyzed above, the idea appears that a Babylonian stranger has never become an integral part of the community of sages of the Land of Israel; therefore, if needed, he could easily be replaced and sent back to the place "where he belongs." The Babylonian himself, however, seems to feel differently.

These traditions are probably marginal in the polyphonic choir of rabbinic meditations on the place of the internal Other. Their presence, however, should not remain unnoted. Having become known to the Babylonians and accepted by the editors of the Babylonian Talmud, these minor traditions shaped Babylonians' self-perceptions and their relations to their Palestinian brethren.

Narratives, as products of a culture, express the tensions and perturbations of that culture. Rabbinic culture specifically has produced a profusion of stories, among them an important narrative about the collision between self and Other. The narratives offered above imbricate self and society, representing a vital resource for shaping identities and forging relationships between members of rabbinic communities and laypersons. These narratives bring multiple partial selves to life, and the intersection between these selves afforded narrators opportunities to impose order on otherwise disjointed events, linking past, present, and future. Accordingly, the Palestinian narrator of y. Ber. 2:8, 5c draws an image of a Babylonian in conflict with a local commoner: no matter how playful the local may be, in the narrative, he appears unworthy of imitation. This

---

49. See Slavoj Žižek, *Violence: Six Sideways Reflections*, Big Ideas (London: Profile Books, 2009), 1.

narrator is interested in a republic of letters in which the disciples of Palestinian and Babylonian sages exchange opinions as equals. In the story, he manages to forge a unity of disparate territories and origins. Despite his concern for the newcomer, however, the Palestinian narrator prefers a hierarchical model of society in which Palestinians assume pride of place, and Babylonians, given the shortcomings of their progenitors, are an inferior group. Hence, he adopts a hierarchical model whose presence at the time is justified by what took place in the past.

7

Going West but Remaining at Home

Chapters 1–6 of this book analyzed Palestinian narratives about Babylonian rabbis' encounters with local inhabitants in the Land of Israel. But how was this phenomenon of Babylonians moving to the Land of Israel seen in Babylonia? Were the Babylonian narrators aware that the Palestinian narrators tended to depict an uneasy acceptance of Babylonians in the Land of Israel, and did they share these story lines? Here I will show how some of these travel tales were reflected in the Babylonian Talmud.[1] As a rule, in these later traditions, the Babylonian narrators tended to minimize conflict, despite their evident awareness of Palestinian perceptions of Babylonians as outsiders and the occasional portrayal of a Babylonian as a comic figure.[2] Still, "ascendance" to the Land of Israel had strong religious connotations for them. It thus remained essential to the Babylonian Talmud narrators, who, as we shall see, sometimes infused their portrayals of migrant Babylonians with an ironic twist.[3]

7.1 Rabbi Zeira Redux

We begin with the Babylonian version of the story about Rabbi Zeira's arrival, which has little in common with its Palestinian counterpart. Let us recall that in the Palestinian sources, Rabbi Zeira is an illustrious sage who is often the object of derision. The Babylonian narrators, however, generally portray him as worthy of veneration. The following texts, which present Zeira's first visit to the Land of Israel, show a different side of the matter.

---

1. See 55 and 61 above.
2. See above 39 and 121.
3. See further 152, 166, 189. The list of examples could have been prolonged.

b. Ketubbot 112a[4]

| When Rabbi Zeira went up to the Land of Israel and could not find a ferry wherein to cross [the river], he grasped a rope and was crossing. Thereupon a certain heretic sneered at him: Hasty people, that put your mouths before your ears, you are still, as ever, clinging to your hastiness. The former replied: Moses and Aaron were not worthy [of entering the Land of Israel]; who could assure me that I am worthy [of entering]? | ר' זירא כי הוה סליק לארץ ישראל לא אשכח מברא למיעב' נקט במצרא וקעבר אמ' לי' ההוא מינא עמא פזיזא דקדמיתו פומייכו לאוזניכו אכתי בפזיזותייכו קיימיתו אמ' ליה דוכת' דמשה ואהרן לא זכו לה אנא מי יימ' דזכינא לה |

Rabbi Zeira has taken the hard way from Mesopotamia to the Land of Israel. The narrator assumes that he traveled through Transjordan, following Moses and Aaron's footsteps, and now, to reach the Holy Land, he must cross the Jordan. In the Babylonian narrator's imagination, the Jordan is as vast as the Euphrates and the Tigris, and hence the rabbi must cross it with a ferry. This seems to have been the so-called cable ferry, which moves across the water while held by ropes leading to the shore. Though the passenger is already on board, the ferryman is not in a hurry to launch the simple mechanism into action. Perhaps he is waiting for additional passengers to show up, or perhaps the weather conditions are unfavorable. Our traveler is not willing to wait any longer. Grabbing the rope with his hands, he manages to bridge the gap between the ferry and the promised land on his own.

But behind the scenes, someone is watching—a *min*, a heretic.[5] The Other here is an external one[6] who turns out to be a real opponent—argumentative and skeptical. He makes a pointed reference to the famous agga-

---

4. For the talmudic text, I follow Soncino's *editio princeps*.

5. The identity of the *minim* remains debated; see Stuart S. Miller, "The 'Minim' of Sepphoris Reconsidered," *HTR* 86 (1993): 377–402; Martin Goodman, "The Function of 'Minim' in Early Rabbinic Judaism," in *Geschichte – Tradition – Reflexion: Festschrift für Martin Hengel zum 70. Geburtstag*, ed. Hermann Lichtenberger, 3 vols. (Tübingen: Mohr Siebeck, 1996), 1:501–10; Adiel Schremer, *Brothers Estranged: Heresy, Christianity, and Jewish Identity in Late Antiquity* (Oxford: Oxford University Press, 2010), 102–3, 210 n. 9; Daniel Boyarin, *Border Lines: The Partition of Judaeo-Christianity*, Divinations (Philadelphia: University of Pennsylvania Press, 2004), 221.

6. The story has a parallel in b. Shabb. 88a that is quite close in form and structure but differs in content. This story mentions neither Zeira nor the Land of Israel but is nonetheless akin to our story. I would suggest that the similarities of the versions indicate that the narrator in b. Ketubbot borrowed the story's ending from Shabbat and adjusted it to his new story. I intend to show elsewhere that a comparison with the parallel story in

dic tradition interpreting the words spoken by the children of Israel when the Torah was about to be read to them at Mount Sinai: "All that God has said we would do and hear" (Exod 24:7). According to this tradition, the children of Israel immediately and zealously accept the entire package of commandments prescribed by God for future generations, as witnessed in the biblical text by the word sequence "we will do and hear," emphasizing a willingness to fulfill the law even before having heard it. The *min* provocatively suggests that hearing is part of a thought process; in fact, it is its beginning. On this and other points, he criticizes what he views as a precipitous decision to act (*na'ase*) when that decision is not preceded by the necessary understanding. According to this apostate's rationale, the Jews acted rashly, according to their hearts, and were therefore unable to think clearly. Had they known that this alliance would condemn them to a life of veritable enslavement to commandments, they might have reconsidered. Rabbi Zeira, pulling the rope, acts out of love for the promised land, closing his ears, that is, his faculty of reason, to the danger of drowning. The apostate bystander rebukes Jews as a community for their irrational, fanatical, and precipitous behavior at Mount Sinai, disparaging them as the "hasty people."

Here, the narrator has the heretic articulate the Babylonian rabbis' ideas about their own identity. Where is the line drawn between the selflessly absurd, though admirable, actions of Rabbi Zeira and those of a reasonable person? With a competent but not particularly sympathetic Other as his spokesman, I suggest, the rabbinic narrator expresses his embarrassing doubts. To formulate such concerns outside of a fictional story about figures from the distant past would be too controversial. While the narrator cannot wholly reject the apostate's commonsense arguments, neither can he wholeheartedly concur with his condemnation of the rabbi's commitment to ascend to the Land of Israel. The response of Rabbi Zeira is the answer of the Babylonian narrator to the apostate's retort: the biblical past parallels the present. The heretic likens Rabbi Zeira to the Israelites at Mount Sinai, and the rabbi then compares himself to Moses and Aaron. Born in the distant diaspora, these two biblical figures guided Israel's people through the wilderness to the promised land but died upon approaching it, thus failing to enter. Zeira perceives this as a paradigm for his own exodus. According to the apostate, the foundational Jewish myth is the reception of the Torah at Mount Sinai; for Rabbi Zeira it is the exodus of the Jews, hastily embarked upon, which led them to freedom. He acknowledges that this less-than-logical behavior fails the test of common sense. If the divinely chosen leaders of Israel, the brothers Moses and

---

b. Shabbat makes evident that the altercation in the story was originally not between the Babylonian sage and a Palestinian apostate but between Raba and a heretical opponent.

Aaron, found their final resting place on the threshold to the promised land, he does not know what will happen to him. Our hero, however, believes that he should act. Aware of the risk entailed in grasping the rope at the pier, he is nevertheless intent on fulfilling the goal of attaining the Holy Land. To do so he is willing to risk being drowned—and, perhaps equally important in this context—to appear ridiculous to the rational skeptics who stare scornfully down on him from the deck. The reader is left hanging about the physical fate of the rabbi.

Moreover, this outcome is immaterial to the narrator. The reader and everyone else know that Rabbi Zeira set foot on the soil of the promised land, where he was welcomed—albeit not without painful humiliation.[7] For the storyteller, the point was to expose the conflict inherent in talmudic culture, the eternal dispute between piety and common sense, between the Other's cold rationality and the emotional irrationality of the self. Such conflicts do not appear to be resolved but are replicated, wisely and aesthetically, in the mirror of a humorous narration.

The Babylonian story, then, is so far removed from its Palestinian parallels that it cannot possibly derive from a common prototype, or else the prototype has been so utterly transformed by the Babylonian narrator that any common features have become unrecognizable. While the humorous Yerushalmi account offers a bold reflection on the run-in between the Palestinian insider and Babylonian Other, in the Babylonian story, we find Zeira, the quintessential "our Babylonian," as the protagonist arriving in the Land of Israel. Thus, the conflict here is not between Babylonians and Palestinians, but rather between religious exaltation and cold rationality in the Babylonian narrator's inner world—between two different models of the Babylonian self. The story in b. Ketubbot serves to bolster the Babylonians' position in their internal dialogue vis-à-vis religious exaltation. This is a much more pressing theme for them than the trials and tribulations of their brethren in the promised land.

This narrator is preoccupied with the paradigm of arrival in the promised land as a model of religious piety. His achievement lies in attaining absolute continuity with a distant biblical past, thus imbuing the present with profound spiritual meaning.

7.2 Kahana Redux

Another one of the three stories of y. Berakhot discussed above[8] is distantly mirrored in the Babylonian Talmud—the account of the dramatic

---

7. There are numerous stories about the life of Zeira in the Land of Israel in the Babylonian Talmud (e.g., b. B. Metz. 85a; b. Avod. Zar. 16b; b. Sanh. 14a) and one about his death and the eulogy recited at his grave in Tiberias (b. Meg. 6a).

8. See 61 above.

migration of Rab Kahana to the Land of Israel. This story has attracted the attention of many scholars[9] who recognize its relevance to the issue of the emergence of the Babylonian academy. It presents a robust debate between the head of the Palestinian sages and a Babylonian visitor, which ends with a pyrrhic victory for the Babylonian, who dies but is ultimately presented as superior to his violent host.[10] Other scholars have taken special interest in the Persian elements incorporated by the late Babylonian narrator.[11] The story seems to belong to the last redactional layer of the Babylonian Talmud in its present form.[12] I wish to focus on the possible attitude of the late Babylonian narrator to the Yerushalmi story analyzed above by following Shamma Friedman's reading; at the same time, I will also try to explain why the narrator embellished the story with such an abundance of exotic details and what purposes were served by the narrative's construction. Here is the text of this unusually long story.[13]

---

9. See Daniel Sperber, *Magic and Folklore in Rabbinic Literature*, Bar-Ilan Studies in Near Eastern Languages and Culture (Ramat Gan: Bar-Ilan University Press 1994), 145–64; Isaiah M. Gafni, "The Babylonian *Yeshiva* as Reflected in Bava Qamma 117a," *Tarbiz* 49 (1980): 292–301; Gafni, *Jews of Babylonia*, 194–97; Adiel Schremer, "'He Posed Him a Difficulty and Placed Him': A Study in the Evolution of the Text of TB Bava Kama 117a" [Hebrew], *Tarbiz* 66 (1997): 403–15; Friedman, "Further Adventures," 247–71; Friedman, "The Talmudic Narrative about Rav Kahana and R. Yoḥanan (Bava Kamma 117a–b) and Its Two Textual Families," in *Annual of Bar-Ilan University: Studies in Judaica and the Humanities* 30–31 (2006), *In Memory of Prof. Meyer Simcha Feldblum*, 409–90; Geoffrey Herman, "The Story of Rav Kahana (b. Baba Qamma 117a-b) in Light of Armeno-Persian Sources," in *Irano-Judaica VI: Studies Relating to Jewish Contacts with Persian Culture throughout the Ages*, ed. Shaul Shaked and Amnon Netzer (Jerusalem: Ben-Zvi Institute, 2008), 53–86; and see quite recently Haim Weiss and Mira Balberg, "'Raise My Eyes for Me': Gazing at Old Age in a Talmudic Narrative," *Oqimta* 6 (2020): 41–81.
10. As opposed to this consensus, see Eliezer Shimshon Rosenthal, who focused his attention mostly on the first scene ("For the Talmudic Dictionary: Talmudica Iranica," in *Irano-Judaica 1: Studies Relating to Jewish Contacts with Persian Culture throughout the Ages*, ed. Shaul. Shaked [Jerusalem: Ben-Zvi Institute, 1982], 38–134, here 86). He held that the story had existed independently of the rest, finding support in Geonic works that contain only it. He also resolutely defended the story's historicity. For a more nuanced reading, see Herman, "Story of Rav Kahana," 54-58, and other articles mentioned in previous note.
11. Sperber (*Magic and Folklore*) demonstrated the story's Babylonian provenance despite its mostly Palestinian setting, proved its late date of composition although the protagonists belong to an earlier period, and noted its overall tendentious character, while emphasizing the artistic literary quality in its usage of Persian elements. This last aspect was continued and developed by Herman, who adduced that Persian and Armenian sources resonate most strikingly when sounded against the common version of the talmudic story.
12. See Herman "Story of Rav Kahana," 53–86.
13. The version of the story examined here is the common version. This is not the version rendered by MS Hamburg 165 and the Leningrad-Antonin 861 Genizah Fragment. See Gafni, "Babylonian *Yeshiva*," 292–301; Schremer, "'He Posed Him a Difficulty,'" 403–15; and finally Friedman "Talmudic Narrative," 409–90. The latter has made a strong case for the primacy of the common version over the "short version branch."

b. Bava Qamma 117 a–b[14]

A certain man who intended to reveal his neighbor's straw[15] came before Rab. He said to him: You shall certainly not reveal [it]. He said to him: I shall and will reveal it. Rab Kahana sat before Rab. He tore out his windpipe. Rab recited over him: "Your sons lie in a swoon at the corner of every street like an antelope caught in a net" (Isa 51:20).[16] Just as this antelope, once it has fallen into a net, one has no mercy on it, so, too, the wealth of Israel, once it has fallen into the hands of Gentiles, one has no mercy on it. He said to Rab Kahana: Until now there were Greeks[17] who did not take account of bloodshed, but now there are Persians who take account of bloodshed [and call out: MRDYN! MRDYN!][18] Arise, go up to the Land of Israel, and accept upon yourself not to pose challenging questions before Rabbi Yoḥanan for seven years.

ההוא גברא דהוה בעי אחוויי אתיבנא דחבריה. אתא לקמיה דרב. א"ל: לא תחוי ולא תחוי. א"ל: מחוינא ומחוינא. יתיב רב כהנא קמיה דרב. שמטיה לקועיה מיניה. קרי רב עילויה: "בניך עולפו שכבו בראש כל חוצות כתוא מכמר" (ישעיה נא כ), מה תוא זה, כיון שנפל במכמר אין מרחמין עליו, אף ממון של ישראל, כיון שנפל ביד עובדי כוכבים, אין מרחמין עליו. א"ל רב: כהנא, עד האידנא הוו פרסאי, דלא קפדי אשפיכות דמים. והשתא איכא יוונאי, דקפדו אשפיכות דמים, ואמרי: מרדין מרדין. קום סק לארעא דישראל, וקביל עלך דלא תקשי לרבי יוחנן שבע שנין.

He went and found Resh Laqish sitting revising the literary unit[19] [of Talmud] of the day for the rabbis. He [Kahana] said to them: "Where is Resh Laqish?" They said to him: Why? He told them this and that difficulty, and this and that solution. They told Resh Laqish.

אזיל אשכחיה לריש לקיש דיתיב וקא מסיים מתיבתא דיומא לרבנן. אמר להו: ריש לקיש היכא? אמרו ליה: אמאי? אמר להו: האי קושיא והאי קושיא, והאי פירוקא והאי פירוקא. אמרו ליה לריש לקיש. אזל ריש לקיש א"ל לרבי יוחנן: ארי עלה מבבל, לעיין מר במתיבתא דלמחר.

---

14. I am following Geoffrey Herman's translation with some minor changes.
15. This means that he was an informer to the Persian authorities.
16. The translation is from *Tanakh* תנ"ך: *The Holy Scriptures: The New JPS Translation according to the Traditional Hebrew Text* (Philadelphia: Jewish Publication Society, 1985), 730.
17. In all the manuscripts the order is wrong: in the beginning "Greeks" and then "Persians." In the translation, I corrected the text according to the editio princeps. The usual approach of scholars to this textual peculiarity is to propose that this text hints at the government change from Arsacid to Sasanian. But see Herman, who proposed that this transformation hints at the change from the Sasanian reign to the early Muslim era ("Story of Rav Kahana," 54 n. 2, 74).
18. See Sperber, *Magic and Folklore*, 145-64.
19. Sokoloff, *Jewish Babylonian*, p. 683 §2 with references.

Resh Laqish went [and] said to Rabbi Yoḥanan: A lion has come up from Babylonia. The Master should examine carefully tomorrow's literary unit [of Talmud].

On the morrow they sat him on the first row before Rabbi Yoḥanan. (Rabbi Yoḥanan) said a tradition but (Rav Kahana) advanced no difficulty with it; a[nother] tradition, but he advanced no difficulty with it. (Rav Kahana) was lowered back seven rows until they sat him on the last row. Rabbi Yoḥanan said to Rabbi Shimeon ben Laqish: The lion you spoke of has become a fox!

(Rav Kahana) said: May it be Your will that these seven rows be in place of the seven years that Rab bid me. He rose to his feet and said: Would the Master return to the beginning. (Rabbi Yoḥanan) said a tradition, and (Rav Kahana) raised a difficulty. They placed him in the first row. He said a tradition and he raised a difficulty. Rabbi Yoḥanan was seated upon seven mattresses. They pulled out one mattress from below him. (Rabbi Yoḥanan) said a tradition and (Rav Kahana) raised a difficulty, until they had pulled out all the mattresses from below him, until he was sitting on the ground.

Rabbi Yoḥanan was an old man, and his eyebrows drooped over [his eyes]. He said to them: Lift up my eyes that I may behold him. They lifted them up with a silver stick. He saw that his lips were split [and] thought that he was laughing at him. He was grieved, and (Rav Kahana) passed away.

The next day Rabbi Yoḥanan said to the rabbis: Did you see how that Babylonian acted? They said to him: That is

למחר אותבוה בדרא קמא קמיה דר' יוחנן. אמר שמעתתא ולא אקשי, שמעתתא ולא אקשי. אנחתיה אחורי שבע דרי עד דאותביה בדרא בתרא. א"ל רבי יוחנן לר"ש בן לקיש: ארי שאמרת נעשה שועל!

אמר: יהא רעוא דהני שבע דרי להוו חילוף שבע שנין דאמר לי רב. קם אכרעיה, א"ל: נהדר מר ברישא. אמר שמעתתא ואקשי; אוקמיה בדרא קמא; אמר שמעתתא ואקשי. ר' יוחנן הוה יתיב אשבע בסתרקי, שלפי ליה חדא בסתרקא מתותיה. אמר שמעתתא ואקשי ליה, עד דשלפי ליה כולהו בסתרקי מתותיה, עד דיתיב על ארעא.

רבי יוחנן גברא סבא הוה ומסרחי גביניה, אמר להו: דלו לי עיני ואחזייה, דלו ליה במכחלתא דכספא, חזא דפרטיה שפוותיה, סבר אחוך קמחייך ביה, חלש דעתיה ונח נפשיה.

למחר אמר להו רבי יוחנן לרבנן: חזיתו לבבלאה היכי עביד? אמרו ליה: דרכיה הכי. על לגבי מערתא. חזא דהוה הדרא ליה עכנא.

his nature. He entered the [burial] cave [and] saw that a snake was encircling it. He said to it: Oh, snake! Oh snake! Pray open your mouth so that the master may visit the pupil, but he did not open; that the colleague may visit the colleague, but he did not open; that the pupil may visit his master, and he opened. He prayed and raised him [back to life]. He said to him: If I had known that this is the Master's nature I would not have been grieved. Now, may the Master come together with us?" He said to him: If you can pray that I shall not die again, I shall go, but if not, I shall not go. Since the hour had passed, it had passed. He asked him all the doubts he had, and he solved them. And this is why Rabbi Yoḥanan was wont to say: Your [i.e., the Babylonian] (sages) say it is theirs.[20.]

א״ל: עכנא, עכנא, פתח פומיך ויכנס הרב אצל תלמיד, ולא פתח. יכנס חבר אצל חבר, ולא פתח. יכנס תלמיד אצל הרב, פתח ליה. בעא רחמי ואוקמיה. א״ל: אי הוה ידענא דדרכיה דמר הכי לא חלשא דעתי, השתא ליתי מר בהדן. א״ל: אי מצית למיבעי רחמי דתו לא שכיבנא אזילנא, ואי לא, לא אזילנא. הואיל וחליף שעתא חליף. תיירה, אוקמיה, שייליה כל ספיקא דהוה ליה ופשטינהו ניהליה. היינו דאמר ר׳ יוחנן: דילכון אמרי, דילהון היא.

This story, compiled in a typical threefold structure, begins with an explanation of what led the young Kahana to make the decision to migrate, a detail that the Yerushalmi does not provide.[21] After killing an informer, Rab Kahana was advised by Rab to flee to Palestine. There he became involved in an academic duel in Rabbi Yoḥanan's academy that culminated in his own death. In Kahana's burial cave, the last scene features an impressive conversation between the deceased Rab Kahana, now freshly revived, and the living Rabbi Yoḥanan. Shamma Friedman's analysis of this narrative uses an intertextual approach to the talmudic sources and argues for the late Babylonian narrator's alteration of other talmudic sources during the retelling of his story. The editor combined aspects of two different Babylonian rabbis: both were named Kahana, and both were affiliated with Rab, went to Palestine, and became involved with Rabbi Yoḥanan. One is a young and insignificant student, as reflected in the already analyzed story from y. Ber. 2:8, 5c,[22] and the other, as in y. Rosh Hashanah (4:1, 59b) (and its parallels), is a great master from whom Rabbi

---

20. That is, the Torah comes from the Babylonians; see Friedman, "Further Adventures," 264–65; Friedman, "Historical Aggadah," 163–64.

21. See 56 above.

22. See Friedman, "Further Adventures," 253–56.

Yoḥanan sought wisdom.[23] Analyzing the story in depth, Friedman concluded that the first scene, in which we meet the culprit's defiant attitude toward Rab and the latter's death (with a torn windpipe as the mode of killing), is borrowed from an anecdote in b. Yoma 87a. Kahana besting Resh Laqish, in the middle scene, finds its parallel in y. Kil. 1:6, 27a.[24] The primary literary source is, according to Friedman, b. B. Metz. 84a–b, the famous Rabbi Yoḥanan–Resh Laqish and Rabbi Eleazar bar Rabbi Shimeon cycles.[25] The sources of evidence are thematic agreements, the adaptation of whole phrases, and common metaphors that reveal the secondary nature of b. Bava Qamma 117 a–b compared to the b. Metz. tradition.[26]

Accepting Friedman's reading of the story as a compilation of ancient motifs made by a late narrator, I wish to understand the narrator's intention in choosing to retell this story in such a manner so differently from the source material. By embedding the Palestinian story's nucleus about a Babylonian named Kahana, who was humiliated by locals but defeated them in verbal sparring, in a thin layer of elements borrowed from different narrative traditions, the narrator adds something new and significant for both himself and his readers. The intellectual duel, the death of the Babylonian hero, his revival, and his second death correlate directly with the image of the Babylonian's antagonist, Rabbi Yoḥanan. By juxtaposing these two iconic sages in opposition, the narrator is saying something about his own Babylonian identity. Of all the Babylonian stories analyzed in this chapter, this one is the most significant: an identity coalesces through a direct encounter with the Other. At the story's climax, the end of the duel, Rabbi Yoḥanan grasps the Babylonian guest's superiority and wants to see his face.[27] Misinterpreting the Babylonian's facial expression

---

23. See Pesiq. Rab Kah. 23, 11 (Mandelbaum ed., 1:345); Lev. Rab. 29 (Margulis ed., 684); Friedman, "Further Adventures," 257–59. I mentioned this older contemporary of Rab and Samuel above, 10 n. 56.

24. The parallel in y. Kil'ayim offers a bold saying by Rabbi Jose: "Here Kahana has cast his net over Rabbi Shimeon ben Laqish and caught him"; see Friedman, "Further Adventures," 267.

25. On these cycles, see Friedman, "Historical Aggadah," 119–63; and Friedman, "Development and Historicity in the Aggadic Narrative of the Babylonian Talmud: A Study Based upon B.M. 83b-86a," in *Continuity and Culture: Essays in Jewish Studies in Honor of the Ninetieth Anniversary of the Founding of Gratz College*, ed. N. M. Waldman (Philadelphia: Gratz College, 1987), 67–80.

26. Friedman, "Further Adventures," 260–64. To Friedman's detailed list of correspondences between the two sources, Herman added a comparison of the seven mattresses upon which Rabbi Yoḥanan sat with the sixty mattresses mentioned in b. B. Metz. 84b.

27. It should not be understood that Rabbi Yoḥanan kills Rab Kahana by gazing at him. When the rabbinic narrator wants to kill someone with a glance, he does not hesitate to express this by mentioning the act of gazing, as in b. B. Bat. 75a (= b. Sanh. 100a), or Rab Sheshet in b. Ber. 58a; b. Shabb. 34a; and see 77 above.

as mirth,[28] the doyen of the Palestinian sages becomes angry — an emotion often associated with him in the Babylonian Talmud. This anger causes the death of the person who provoked it.

We find an inversion or an inverted mirroring of this situation in y. Berakhot.[29] In the Palestinian stories, the jeering attack on the Babylonian leads to the offending Palestinians' death. Here the Babylonian is the victim, whereas the Palestinian is the cause of wrathful divine intervention on behalf of the Babylonian. The Palestinian rabbi is mocked throughout the story, literally downgraded from the highest to the lowest position.[30] On the next day, however, upon discovering that the Babylonian is already dead and buried, he goes to his tomb. He is put to the test so that he will recognize his true status vis-à-vis the deceased Babylonian. The test is carried out with the help of magical snakes guarding Kahana's tomb. The Palestinian master of the sages obtains permission to enter only after he admits that he is a disciple of the deceased, meaning that he is inferior to him.

Rabbi Yoḥanan is still powerful enough to revive his opponent and engage him in a short scholarly discussion. In this part of the story, a number of lines appear damaged, and the precise wording varies slightly from manuscript to manuscript. It seems, however, that the plot runs as follows: Rabbi Yoḥanan invites Rab Kahana back to the academy. The latter agrees on the condition that his reviver pray for him not to die again. It is at this point that the confusion sets in. Rabbi Yoḥanan is incapable of fulfilling this condition; there follows a comment that the hour has passed, but it is unclear whose words these are. Few scholars have dealt with this passage, and a reliable textual restoration is probably impossible.[31] I would suggest that these are the narrator's ironic words in summing up the story. The Palestinian sage cannot promise that he will never be angry again, nor that he will never again cause anyone to die. As in the famous story about him and Resh Laqish (b. B. Metz. 84a-b), he is unable to prevent his friend's death, so here he cannot avoid the second death of the Babylonian, whose superiority he has recently acknowledged. The comparison goes further: as in the Resh Laqish story, where his sense of honor and inability to control his emotions cause the death of his companion, here the same traits bring about Kahana's death. Thus, in penance for allowing the Babylonian to die, the Palestinian master will be bound for the rest of his life to the last

---

28. Compare this with a similar motif above, 91–92. I owe this observation to Amram Tropper.

29. I owe this observation to Judith von Bresinsky.

30. For the famous motif of the cushions taken from beneath his throne, see n. 26 above.

31. See Sperber, *Magic and Folklore*, 86 n. 21; Rubenstein, "Coping with the Virtues," 112, 275 n. 6. Earlier readings, assuming that Rab Kahana did not return to his grave, follow Rashi's commentary, on which see Friedman, "Further Adventures," 253–54.

lesson he received from his dead and resurrected colleague. Our story is a product of Babylonian polemics against the Palestinian rabbis.[32]

But there is more: the story is also highly critical of what the Babylonian narrator regards as bedrock features of Palestinian rabbinic culture: the claim of superiority and the trouble with accepting the Other, especially the Babylonian Other. This is true despite the fact that the Palestinians themselves are unable to set up the academic process without reference to Babylonian learning, already deeply rooted in Palestinian teachings. Thus, from this narrative, a new Babylonian identity emerges, conceived of as complementary to the Palestinian one. In this process, which took place among the first generations of Palestinian Amoraim, an ancient conflict was resolved, not without pain and bloodshed, by incorporating Babylonian wisdom into Palestinian law and lore.

7.3 Rab Safra Goes West

Now we will turn to a different kind of Babylonian "going West" story, one that is not a creative retelling of a Palestinian narrative nucleus. The following stories have no Palestinian parallel and are apparently genuine Babylonian creations. They present encounters between hosts and guests, which, as was noted above, contain the seeds of violence. The following case concerns a Babylonian who went West and there found unfriendly locals who beat him up—a hostile encounter not only with the internal but with the external Other.

b. Avodah Zarah 4b[33]

| R. Abbahu commended Rab Safra to the *minim* as a great man, thus exempting him from paying taxes for thirteen years.[34] One day, on coming | משתבח להו ר' אבהו למיני ברב ספרא, דאדם גדול הוא. שבקו ליה מיכסא דתליסר שנין. יומא חד אשכחוהו. אמרו ליה: כתיב: "רק אתכם ידעתי מכל משפחות האדמה על כן |

---

32. See Sperber, *Magic and Folklore*, 86 n. 21; and Kalmin, *Sage in Jewish Society*, 5.
33. The story and its historical evidence were discussed by Robert Travers Herford, *Christianity in Talmud and Midrash* (London: Williams & Norgate, 1903), 266–70; Efraim E. Urbach, "The Repentance of the People of Nineveh and the Discussions between Jews and Christians" [Hebrew], *Tarbiz* 20 (1949): 118–22; Adiel Schremer, "Stammaitic Historiography," in *Creation and Composition: The Contribution of the Bavli Redactors (Stammaim) to the Aggadah*, ed. Jeffrey L. Rubenstein, TSAJ 114 (Tübingen: Mohr Siebeck, 2005), 219–37, here 224; Michal Bar-Asher Siegal, *Early Christian Monastic Literature and the Babylonian Talmud* (New York: Cambridge University Press, 2013), 5–9.
34. This detail is uncertain. Does it mean that he received the money as an honorarium for his work either (a) as a teacher to the *minim* (Herford, *Christianity in Talmud*, 267) or (b) as an assistant collector of imperial revenues (Bacher, *Die Agada*, 2:96) or (c) simply as a scholar; see the Babylonian motif about scholars accepting a salary as recorded in b. B. Bat. 8b.

across him, they said to him: It is written: "You only have I known [or loved] from all the families of the earth; therefore, I will visit upon you all your iniquities" (Amos 3:2); if one is in anger does one vent it on one's friend? But he was silent and could give them no answer; so, they wound a scarf around his neck and tortured him. When Rabbi Abbahu came and found him [in that state], he said to them: Why do you torture him? Said they: Have you not told us that he is a great man? He cannot explain to us the meaning of this verse! Said he: I may have told you [that he was learned] in Tannaitic teaching; did I tell you [he was learned] in Scripture? They said to him: How is it then that you know it? He replied: We, who are frequently with you, set ourselves the task of studying it thoroughly, but others do not study it as carefully. Said they: Will you then tell us the meaning? He said to them: I will explain it by a parable. To what may it be compared? To a man who is the creditor of two persons, one of them a friend, the other an enemy; from his friend, he will accept payment little by little, whereas from his enemy, he will exact payment in one sum.

אפקוד עליכם את כל עונותיכם" (עמוס ג ב).
מאן דאית ליה סיסיא ברחמיה מסיק ליה?
אישתיק ולא אמר להו ולא מידי. רמו ליה
סודרא בצואריה וקא מצערו ליה. אתא רבי
אבהו. אשכחינהו. אמר להו: אמאי מצעריתו
ליה? אמרו ליה: ולאו אמרת לן דאדם גדול
הוא? [ולא ידע למימר לן פירושא דהאי
פסוקא]. אמר להו: אימר דאמרי לכו בתנאי,
בקראי מי אמרי לכו? אמרו ליה: מ"ש אתון
דידעיתון? אמר להו: אנן דשכיחינן גביכון,
רמינן אנפשין ומעיינן, אינהו לא מעייני. אמרו
ליה: לימא לן את. אמר להו: אמשול לכם משל,
למה"ד? לאדם שנושה משני בנ"א, אחד אוהבו
ואחד שונאו. אוהבו נפרע ממנו מעט מעט,
שונאו נפרע ממנו בבת אחת.

It is known from the Babylonian Talmud that our Babylonian protagonist, Rab Safra (fourth century), traveled to Palestine and back a number of times.[35] Learned and prominent, he was deemed a "great man."[36] The story relates how this figure, highly regarded in Babylonia, reacts to "great-man" expectations in the Land of Israel. The Babylonian rabbi is welcomed by his Palestinian colleague Rabbi Abbahu of Caesarea, a city that was populated by many Christians in the fourth century, under the

---

35. See b. Hul. 110b; b. Pesah. 52b; b. B. Qam. 104b.
36. See above, and b. B. Bat. 144a.

rule of the eastern Roman Empire; the *minim* mentioned in the story are Christians, and the narrator indicates that the newcomer's residence in the city, together with a tax exemption, was arranged by the Palestinian host and the Christian city officials.

Our Babylonian is set upon by *minim* and subjected to a kind of intellectual trial. They demand that he interpret the prophetic verse: "You only have I known from all the families of the earth; therefore, I will visit upon you all your iniquities" (Amos 3:2).[37] The sectarian interprets the expression "you only have I known" to mean "you are the only beloved one," thus raising the question: how could someone who is angry misuse the beloved by venting his anger on him? One answer to this question, and probably the expected one, is that love is not mentioned in the verse at all, but because of His exact knowledge of the nature of this selected tribe, God decided to follow His flock and punish it deservedly. Rab Safra, however, is unwilling to accept such teaching, perhaps because it would create the impression that he believes that God does not love His chosen people. Nonetheless, the sage cannot provide an alternative interpretation that corresponds to the traditional rabbinic instruction on this topic. He is thus tortured by the questioners until his Palestinian host arrives and solves the problem by demonstrating a "convincing" interpretation in the form of a parable. The people of Israel are the beloved chosen of God, who, in punishing them, is showing proof of divine love for His earthly partner. Others, who are less important in His eyes, will receive their punishment only once in the afterlife and suffer proportionately much more.[38]

But let us leave aside theology and return to Rabbi Abbahu, Rab Safra, and the *minim*. Rabbi Abbahu tells the *minim* that "we" Palestinian rabbis live in close proximity to you and study Scripture to be able to engage in polemics with your Bible experts. In contrast, the Babylonians do not know you and thus ignore such matters. This interpretation has been accepted at face value by some readers.[39] However, the Babylonian narrator is not implying that Babylonians are ignorant of biblical verse interpretation; they run into trouble only when these verses are taken out of context and applied to an altogether different, speculative field, such as religious propaganda. This intriguing difference between Babylonian and Palestinian biblical interpretation appears only in the Babylonian Talmud.[40] As we saw above, the Yerushalmi narrator sees Babylonians

---

37. This verse has not attracted much exegetical attention; except for our passage from b. Avodah Zarah, it appears only in late Midrash and does not seem to have been understood as something with dangerous interpretative potential, see Aggadat Bereshit 8, Tanna Devei Eliyahu 16.

38. Herford, *Christianity in Talmud*, 270.

39. See ibid.; and Urbach, "Repentance of the People," 118–22.

40. See Schremer, *Brothers Estranged*, 226 n. 57; Schremer, "Stammaitic Historiography," 223–24.

as more biblically knowledgeable than Palestinians.[41] I agree with Adiel Schremer that it would be a mistake to take this story as implying that controversial disputes between the rabbis and Christians did not occur in Babylonia.[42] There is plenty of evidence that lively polemics flourished between rabbis and Christians in Sasanian Babylonia, as echoed in patristic writings and also in the Babylonian Talmud itself.

Nonetheless, I disagree with Schremer on a different point, namely, that this passage was "a warning directed to Babylonian students to be vigilant to study Scripture, precisely because they might be called to reply to a 'word of *minut*' in their own place, in Babylonia."[43] According to this reasoning, the story aimed to advise Babylonian students to learn how to manipulate verses used in Christian anti-Jewish polemic in order to avoid being attacked by *minim*. I take a different view of the matter. In my opinion, the narrator wants his readers to avoid the wildly militant polemics highlighted here, the transgressive, potentially dangerous verse manipulation/interpretations, because of their foreign, if deceptively appealing, nature. Leave these activities to the Palestinians, who may be facing fanatical and violent Christians, he advises—it is not the Babylonian way of learning.[44] This story's message is close to the pericope's idea about Rabbi Itzhak and Rab Naḥman from b. Ta'an. 5b, which I will analyze in the following chapter.[45] Both there and in our current context, the narrators distinguish between their exegetical methods and those of their internal Others; in other words, they delineate the dividing line between Palestinian scholars and themselves.

If one analyzes this story in terms of the relationship between host and guest, it turns out that the Babylonian narrator is quite sympathetic toward the figure of his Palestinian host. While the collision between host and guest in the story leads to violence, the host is not entirely responsible for this outcome. In this way, the narrator tells his readers that their hosts in Palestine are not wholly in possession of their homes because dangerous tenants inhabit them. Perhaps the narrator is already aware that Jews are no longer heirs to their Land, but that a new and violent owner allows them to sojourn there.

---

41. See 109 above.

42. Contra Herford, *Christianity in Talmud*; and Urbach, "Repentance of the People," 118–22.

43. Schremer, *Brothers Estranged*, 226 n. 57. See also Daniel Boyarin, "The Christian Invention of Judaism: The Theodosian Empire and the Rabbinic Refusal of Religion," *Representations* 85 (2004): 21–57.

44. This, of course, does not mean that such polemics were only common in Palestine, but it reflects more the situation in Babylonia. I suppose that the Babylonian narrator is projecting the situation of polemics witnessed by him in his own land onto Palestine but imagines it to be even more violent.

45. See 184 above.

7.4 Bar Bavel Goes West

The next case is also about a Babylonian "going West," but this story lacks a parallel in the Palestinian rabbinic literature.[46] This narrator is quite critical of his main protagonist, a Babylonian, while displaying more sympathy for his Palestinian heroine. His chief focus, however, is not a Babylonian–Palestinian confrontation but, as I will try to show, an altogether different sort of clash.

b. Nedarim 66b[47]

A man from Babylonia went up to the Land of Israel and married a woman [there]. He said to her: Cook for me a couple [תרי] of lentils. She cooked him [only] two [תרי] lentils. He was furious with her.[48] The next day he said to her: Cook me a sack-full [גריוה] [of lentils]. She cooked a sack-full [גריוה]. He said to her: Go, bring	ההוא בר בבל דסליק לארעא דישראל. נסיב איתתא. אמר לה: בשילי לי תרי טלפחי. בשילה ליה תרי טלפחי. רתח עלה. למחר אמר לה: בשילי לי גריוא. בשילה ליה גריוא. אמר לה: זילי אייתי לי תרי בוציני. אזלת ואייתי ליה תרי שרגי. אמר לה: זילי תברי יתהון על רישא דבבא. הוה יתיב בבא בן בוטא אבבא וקא דאין דינא. אזלת ותברת יתהון על רישיה. אמר לה: מה הדין דעבדת? אמרה ליה: כך ציוני

---

46. This story has attracted scholars with differing points of view; see Ilan, "Joke in Rabbinic Literature," 57–75; David Sperling, "Aramaic Spousal Misunderstanding," *JAOS* 115 (1995): 205–9; Dina Stein, "The Untamable Stew: Language and Women as Institutional Makers" [Hebrew], *Jerusalem Studies in Hebrew Literature* 22 (2007–2008): 243–61; Ido Hevroni, "The Midrash as Marriage Guide," *Azure* 29 (2007): 103–20; David Brodsky, "Why Did the Widow Have a Goat in Her Bed? Jewish Humor and Its Roots in the Talmud and Midrash," in *Jews and Humor*, ed. Leonard J. Greenspoon, Studies in Jewish Civilization 22, Proceedings of the Twenty-Second Annual Symposium of the Klutznick Chair in Jewish Civilization, Harris Center for Judaic Studies, October 25–26, 2009 (West Lafayette, IN: Purdue University Press, 2011), 13–32; and Reuven Kiperwasser, "Wives of Commoners," 418–45.

47. See Moshe Hershler and Joshua Hutner, eds., The Babylonian Talmud with Variant Readings: *Tractate Nedarim*, 2 vols. (Jerusalem: Institute for the Complete Israeli Talmud, 1985–1991), 1:172–73.

48. The text above follows the new edition of tractate Nedarim, taking into consideration manuscripts and Genizah fragments versions (see Hershler and Hutner, *Babylonian Talmud with Variant Readings: Nedarim*, 1:171, apparatus criticus to line 18 (above n. 47). In some manuscripts the textual witnesses state that the unfortunate wife mistook טלפי ("hooves," which is a Hebrew word that usually does not appear in Aramaic texts) for טלפחי ("lentil"; see Michael Sokoloff, *A Dictionary of Jewish Babylonian Aramaic of the Talmudic and Geonic Periods*, 2nd ed. [Ramat Gan: Bar-Ilan University Press, 2021], 459–60). Some readers prefer this version, according to which a substantial meal of two bovine hooves requested by the husband is replaced by two lentils only; see Sperling, "Aramaic Spousal Misunderstanding," 207 n. 22; and Stein, "Untamable Stew," 245 nn. 10–11. Other readers—in my opinion, quite correctly—prefer the "two lentils" version, and the explanation in the commentary of *Babylonian Talmud with Variant Readings*. The *talpuhei* /*talpei* version was proposed by Rashi, and therefore it is quite logical to assume that later copyists were influenced by him.

me two melons [בוציני]. She went and bought him two lamps. He told her to break them on the head of the gate [רישא דבבא]. Baba [בבא] ben Buta was sitting at the gate [אבבא], deciding legal cases. She went and broke them on his head. He (Baba ben Buta) told her: Why have you done this? She told him: My husband commanded me! He said to her: You performed the will of your spouse; may God grant you two sons like Baba ben Buta.

בעלי. אמר: את עשית רצון בעליך. המקום יוציא ממך שני בנים כבבא בן בוטא.

The Bavli editor chose this story as the final text in the eighth chapter of tractate Nedarim, which discusses vows.[49] Perhaps designed to amuse the reader, it conveys, as such stories often do, an additional didactic message. Both the narrator and the protagonist are Babylonian, but presumably the former never did what the latter does—travel to the distant promised land. He is sure, however, that the Aramaic of the Land of Israel's inhabitants is different from his own. Moreover, the narrator has transplanted the plot to the distant past, which is also unknown territory to him. Our Babylonian migrant arrives in a new land to begin a new life with a new native-born wife.[50] The narrator suggests that the husband and wife differ regarding attitudes toward words and their meanings. The language of the husband and, by extension, of the Babylonians is chock-full of idioms and other figures of speech. The wife and, by extension, the Palestinians are led astray precisely because of their insistence on the literal meaning of words. While the husband and the Babylonians are prone to ambiguity, the wife and the Palestinians are prone to concision and literalness. The husband uses a masculine language in which words mean something other than what they seem to say.[51] The woman, for her part, fulfills her

---

49. The story seems to have no direct relationship to the rules of vows. Instead, it deals with peace within the family, something customary in traditional Jewish preaching, and, as I claim in "Wives of Commoners," 437–41, it also conveys a subtle polemical message elevating the Babylonian Talmud above its Palestinian counterpart.

50. Dina Stein has proposed that the story expresses the negative attitude of Babylonians to immigration to the Land of Israel and intermarriage with Palestinian Jews ("Untamable Stew," 246). I agree that certain conflicts between Palestinians and Babylonians underlie the story; see further 160, but I do not take these to be the focus of the tale. In fact, it seems here that the narrator even slightly idealizes life in the Land of Israel in the distant Tannaitic past.

51. This, I think, is the main conflict of the story, a view also expressed by Stein ("Untamable Stew," 248 n. 22), but later she preferred to read the story as having been built

husband's requests in a literal way. In her upbringing, obedience to her spouse, like obedience to God, has clarity of concrete purpose. The narrator mocks this behavior, and, by way of allusion, he also mocks a literalistic understanding of the Torah. At the start of the story, the newlywed husband orders his wife to prepare a modest dinner, asking for a small portion ["a couple"] of lentils. To his dismay, however, she understands this figure of speech literally and prepares only two lentils. The plot is an ancient literary topos known, for example, from the ancient Greek "Life (Romance) of the Fabulist Aesop," a work dating from approximately the second century CE, presumably of Greco-Egyptian provenance, and widely known in Greek-speaking areas.[52] Aesop was a slave whose master, Xanthus, asked him to cook "lentil" for him without using the word's plural form. The slave carefully, and perhaps maliciously, prepared a single lentil, which he then served to his master, much to the amusement of Xanthus's guests.[53]

The Aesop Romance, 39–41[54]

When Xanthus found some of his friends at the bath, he told Aesop to give the robes to their servants and said to him: "Aesop, go on home, and since my wife trampled the vegetables in her temper, go out and cook us lentil. Put it in the pot, put some water in with it, put it on the cooking hearth, put some wood under it, and light it; if it starts to go out, blow on it. Now, do as I say.... " When the drink had been going around for some time, Xanthus said: "Aesop, is the lentil cooked?" Aesop said: "Yes." Xanthus said: "Let me see if it is done." Aesop brought the one lentil on a spoon and gave it to Xanthus. Xanthus ate the one lentil and said: "It's done. Bring it in and serve it." Aesop put on a plate, poured the soup, and said, "Dinner is served!" Xanthus said: "Why there is nothing but soup you've served. Where is the lentil?" Aesop said: "Why you ate the lentil." Xanthus said: "Did you cook just one?" Aesop said: "Yes. Did you not tell me to 'cook lentil' and not 'lentils'? The one is singular and another plural."

---

on the discrepancies between dialects and geographical realties, which I fail to find here. See below n. 52.

52. See William Hansen, ed., *Anthology of Ancient Greek Popular Literature* (Bloomington: Indiana University Press, 1998), 107–10. The comparison with this Greek source was already proposed by Brodsky, "Why Did the Widow Have a Goat," 31 n. 28, but I was not aware of this publication in my 2017 publication. However, his treatment of the parallels here differs from mine.

53. In the continuation of Aesop's story, the master ordered the slave to prepare bovine legs for him, a problematic demand for the slave. Maybe the appearance of the "leg" in certain manuscript versions of our talmudic story, which circulated in medieval Europe, was influenced by Aesop's story; see Hansen, *Anthology of Ancient Greek*, 110.

54. I cite from the translation by Lloyd W. Daily as published in Hansen, *Anthology of Ancient Greek*, 128–29.

In Aesop's tale, we see an intellectual slave's revenge on his philosophically narrow-minded owner. The narrator elicits subversive sympathy for the wisdom of the oppressed slave over that of the oppressive owner. Does our Palestinian heroine prepare her husband's dinner with neither malice nor intent to teach him a lesson? If that is the case, then we must wonder how she nevertheless emerges at the end as the mistress of the situation.[55]

As I read the story, the angry husband understands the linguistic basis for his wife's mistake but probably attributes the miscommunication to female stupidity or to the general simplicity of Palestinian Jews. In his view, such an obedient but dim-witted creature must genuinely believe that two lentils could satisfy the hunger of a Babylonian man. He still does not comprehend that, faced with a cultural and gender divide, he should change *his* approach to words and their meanings. Next time, when requesting his favorite lentils, he informs his wife that he needs many lentils to be satisfied. Still caught in the Babylonian tendency to play with words, though, rather than saying "a lot," he specifies a measure, namely, a *griva*, which is roughly the equivalent of ten liters.[56] An English-language equivalent of this expression might be to ask for a "ton" of chocolate, only to be unprepared to consume such an amount. Lo and behold, the Babylonian receives exactly what he ordered—ten kilograms of lentils cooked by his diligent spouse who, no doubt, mobilized others to help in this absurd task. Yet again, the husband is forced to face the consequences of his actual words.

But he has not yet learned his lesson. To the delight of the reader, our

---

55. Hevroni does not hesitate here to proclaim that our heroine is a "feminist" who in her own way fights against the norms of the androcentric community to which she belongs: "… this reading leads us to the conclusion that the story's heroine is a kind of proto-feminist waging a war of self-liberation against the marriage norms of the period" ("Midrash as Marriage Guide," 110). Although the formulation seems to me far-fetched, I also tend to see here a subversive protest tactic.

56. Here I would like to correct my error in my above-mentioned article ("Wives of Commoners," 440), from one ton to ten liters; see Adrian D. H. Bivar, "Weights and Measures," *Encyclopaedia Iranica*, https://brillonline.com/entries/encyclopaedia-iranica/weights-and-measures-i-pre-islamic-period-COM_10392?s.num=14http://www.iranicaonline.org/articles/weights-measures-i. I am grateful to Simcha Gross for his correction. I understand *griva* as a volume measure, according to its first appearance in Sokoloff's dictionary (see Sokoloff, *Jewish Babylonian Aramaic*, 246), and not according to his comment in the following entry, for it is consistent with the wordplay that I see here. Sperling points out that the "husband spoke a dialect rich in loanwords of Iranian origin, *grw* means 'neck', 'throat', 'self' and 'soul'" ("Aramaic Spousal Misunderstanding," 208 and n. 38) based on D. N. Mackenzie, *A Concise Pahlavi Dictionary* (London: Oxford University Press, 1971), 37. But, as Sperling notes there, a homonym *grw* meaning a grain measure also exists in Pahlavi. Therefore, in a close reading of the text it is quite possible to understand the word as referring only to different amounts of lentils and not to meat. Stein ("Untamable Stew," 245) accepts Sperling's reading of this word.

Babylonian continues to urge his young wife to prepare his long-awaited dinner. This time, he wants to eat *botsina*-gourds, and he carefully indicates that he is simply asking for a couple of these vegetables. However, in Babylonian (but not Palestinian) Aramaic, this plant's name is homonymous with the Aramaic word "lamp," and the latter meaning of the word was far more widespread than the former one.[57] Yet again, the wife interprets her husband's instructions literally: at the end of the day, our Babylonian will return home to find nothing but two oil-filled lamps standing on the dinner table.[58]

The now-enraged husband next instructs his wife to break the vessels on the "head" of the gate, that is, the upper part of the gate. Obedient as ever, the wife goes to the city gate—the place where the rabbinical court gathers and where the venerable Palestinian sage, Baba ben Buta, is sitting. This *tanna*, who lived in Jerusalem before the destruction of the Second Temple, was a disciple of Shammai. Little is known about him apart from his extreme piety. The narrator chose this ancient sage from the remote past for his own narratological purposes: his name is similar to the word that our Babylonian protagonist used to designate the gate on which his wife should break the lamps.[59] The charm of the wordplay (Baba ben Buta—*a-de-baba*) is hopelessly lost in translation. As in the previous episode, these wordplay elements of the story are possible only in Babylonian Aramaic.

Of interest is this last venue: the city gate is a liminal space, and liminal areas are charged and dangerous.[60] Our heroine will arrive at the gate vulnerable and weak, but, having once passed the gate, she will assume a new social role.[61] The husband sends his wife to the threshold of their house, namely, tries to keep her under his ownership. Instead, she goes to the city's gates, thus escaping his sphere of influence and bringing their case to the attention of the community.

A conflict is now inevitable. Rather than breaking her lamps on the head or the top of the city gate, the poor woman smashes them with all

---

57. Ironically, *botsina* is the only Aramaic word in the story that does not have a double meaning in Palestinian Aramaic—it means only "gourd." I doubt, however, that the Babylonian narrator was aware of this difference.

58. As proposed by Stein, the lamp has a certain sexual connotation ("Untamable Stew," 250). Indeed, the translation of "gourds" to "lamps" expresses somewhat the mood of the woman, probably feeling deprived of her husband's love. Interestingly, lamps also appear in the story from the Yerushalmi; see ibid., nn. 34–36; and Galit Hasan-Rokem, "Rabbi Meir, The Illuminated and Illuminating," in *Current Trends in the Study of Midrash*, ed. Carol Bakhos, JSJSup 106 (Leiden: Brill, 2006), 236–38.

59. See also Sperling, "Aramaic Spousal Misunderstanding," 205 n. 5.

60. See Barton, *Sorrows of the Ancient Romans*, 168–72. See 69 above.

61. I prefer to see here the liminality of the gate as relevant for understanding the story; however, the biblical model of the city gates as the location of courts of law probably also adds an intertextual meaning for this element of the plot.

her might on the head of the unfortunate city judge, whose name actually means "gate."[62] As befits a wise man, however, the sage remains calm and inquires about the bizarre behavior.

This drama is reminiscent of Grimms' fairy tale about Hans—(*Der gescheite Hans*—Clever Hans)—the unlucky, dutiful son. Hans blindly follows his mother's instructions, in the process destroying everything in his path and losing his bride. Yet, disturbing as the story is, it is meant merely to amuse. In the realm of narrative, the outrageous behavior of an oppressed character—slave, son, or wife—not only provokes laughter but also erases, if only briefly, the boundaries that confine the character.[63] Nevertheless, once the laughter dies down, enslavement returns. Aesop is beaten, and Hans is forced to make restitution for the damage he has caused.

Our heroine, however, receives an unexpected vindication. The sage learns that she was led to her deplorable action by her blind devotion to her spouse. Without inquiring into the husband's backstory, the wise man recognizes the woman's needs.[64] With such a stereotypical Babylonian as a husband, she needs sons (two of them, in fact, complementing the two lentils, the two gourds, and the two lamps), and they will both have to be as wise and as gentle as Baba ben Buta. They will not indulge in fantasies about imbecilic but obedient wives. Moreover, they will not react in anger to misunderstandings with their spouses. Spiritually, they will be sons of the sage, not of the Babylonian, neither commoners nor foreigners. In this story, sages and women turn out to be minority groups on the margins of a society controlled by laymen. As Dina Stein notes, in our story "generative competence" is transferred from the husband to the rabbi through a fictional device that is useful for resolving vows: Baba ben Buta's insight concerning the wife's desire to be reconciled with her husband.[65] Nevertheless, the rabbinic narrator consoles the female protagonist, providing

---

62. Gate in Palestinian Aramaic is תרעאה, while בבא is Babylonian Aramaic, derived from Akkadian; see Sokoloff, *Jewish Babylonian Aramaic*, 119. The name Baba, probably meaning father, grandfather, or elder, is widespread in all Aramaic dialects (see, e.g., Sokoloff, *Syraic Lexicon*, 115), but it is not attested in Galilean Aramaic. That the Palestinian women "misunderstood" the word baba-gate as the sage named Baba, namely, according to the Palestinian dialect, is the one and only proof of a real dialectal difference between the Babylonian and his Palestinian wife, and fits Sperling's and Stein's theses. See above n. 444.

63. The list of parallels can certainly be continued; see the discussion by Hansen, *Anthology of Ancient Greek*, 111 n. 11, about African American tales involving John and Old Master, a striking counterpart in a modern tradition to the contentious and wily relationship of Aesop and Xanthus in the ancient Greek context. See Roger D. Abrahams, *Afro-American Folktales* (New York: Pantheon 1985), 263–95.

64. I see a parallel between this story and the story about R. Meir allowing a woman to spit in his eye; see Kiperwasser, "Wives of Commoners," 423–25; and see Hasan-Rokem, "Rabbi Meir," 236–38.

65. Stein, "Untamable Stew," 252.

her with the sages as allies and granting her a certain vicarious involvement in the rabbinic realm through her two promised sons.

For the narrator, women, as the ultimate internal Other, have the potential to effect change. Fundamentally different from and subservient to men, women are nonetheless capable of conveying a significant message to the rabbinic community. The rabbinic narrator readily allies himself with this oppressed woman against her husband. He seems to believe that women can behave better than commoners, about whom he has no illusions. Therefore, in the story about a Babylonian, he contrasts not Palestinians and Babylonians but rabbis and laymen. Our Babylonian, who wanted to live in the land of his ancestors, probably typifies the narrator's opinion of Babylonian "Zionists," who he thinks were not the best representatives of his rabbinic community, if not to say total outsiders. A reader might justifiably wonder whether this story is about Babylonians and Palestinians—or, alternatively, whether it is using the distinction to orchestrate comical misunderstandings between a husband and wife. The Palestinian Other is only a minor issue in the story, which presents the Palestinian heroine quite sympathetically and displays neither fear nor self-doubt vis-à-vis the Palestinian Other.

7.5 Carrying Rabbi Yoḥanan

In the previous case, we analyzed a humorous narrative from the Babylonian Talmud. Now we will get a taste of the Babylonian sense of humor. The following story does not belong to the "Going West" type. If we consider the other stories in this chapter to be in dialogue with the stories analyzed in chapter 3, this one recalls chapters 1 and 5. An implicit attempt is made to restrict the space for the Palestinian Other in the universe of Babylonians. The internal Other is similarly alienated in this story, but the Palestinian way of coping with the Other differs from what we saw in chapter 6. There, a serious attempt was made to manipulate the conscience of the reader; here we observe good-natured and reciprocal mockery. Beneath the joking, however, lies quite a serious matter: the relationship between the groups to whom the mocker and the ridiculed belong.

b. Qiddushin 71b[66]

Ze'iri was evading Rabbi Yoḥanan, who was urging him: Come, marry my daughter. One day they were strolling	זעירי הוה משתמיט מיניה דר' יוחנן, דאמ' ליה: תא נסיב ברתאי. יומא חד הוו קא אזלי בארחא. כי מטו לעורקמא דמיא, אתא זעירי

---

66. According to MS Oxford Opp. 248 (367).

on the road, when they came to a pool of water. Thereupon he placed Rabbi Yoḥanan on his shoulders and carried him across. Said he to him: Our learning is fitting but our daughters are not fitting?

ארכביה אכתפיה לר' יוחנן ומעבר ליה. אמ' ליה אורייתין כשרה, בנתין לא כשרה?

Once again we meet Rabbi Yoḥanan, this time accompanied by his student, the Babylonian Ze'iri, not to be confused with our old friend Zeira.[67] Ze'iri is a scholar of Babylonian origin who relocated to Roman Palestine in his youth, studied there, and then returned to Babylonia.[68] Our story appears in the context of a discussion on the recurrent theme of the Babylonians' lineage.[69] It seems that the elderly master, Rabbi Yoḥanan, and his young student, Ze'iri, have been traveling together, and they have now reached a stream of water.[70] Following the conventions of respect, the narrator has the sage cross the stream on the shoulders of his disciple. We might note here that the old man, sitting astride the young man's shoulders, is probably already a humorous image. Moreover, the name, or nickname, of the latter may allude to his smallness or frailty, which reinforces the comic effect. But the peak of the comedic situation is found in the dialogue that accompanies it. While still in the middle of the water the rabbi rebukes his Babylonian student for being so committed to safeguarding his lineage that he refuses to marry his master's daughter. In my view, this is a comic presentation of the great sage humiliating himself. Alternatively, however, it might be a self-mocking act on the part of the Babylonian narrator, who seems to be saying: we are so obsessed with our genealogy that even the daughter of the illustrious Rabbi Yoḥanan is not good enough for us. In any case, this anecdote reveals the basic model of the relationship between the Babylonian narrator and his Babylonian

---

67. See the reading of this story in Oppenheimer, *By the Rivers of Babylon*, 92–94. He sees in this story historical evidence for the eagerness of Babylonians in fourth-century Palestine to preserve their lineage and not to mix with the Palestinian "rabble."

68. See Albeck, *Introduction*, 173–74.

69. See 50–51, 133 above; and Rubenstein, *Culture of the Babylonian Talmud*, 84–86.

70. See Sokoloff, *Jewish Babylonian Aramaic*, 854, for ערקומא. The word is unique, and the etymology is uncertain. It appears in b. Meg. 15a as an interpretation of Esth 4:17: "So Mordecai went away and carried out." Regarding the term "carried out," Shmuel proposes that "he carried across the pool of water" without specifying what or whom he carried. This is an interesting parallel usage of the expression, but a little difficult to understand. Does it have a metaphorical meaning or just a literary one? This uncertain water source reappears in the story of an anonymous scholar who helps Resh Laqish cross this pool on his shoulders; see b. Meg. 28b. In both stories, the old master is honored by a young man who carries him across a water pool on his shoulders. I own this observation to Daniel Boyarin, who drew my attention to this parallel.

audience: despite our profound appreciation of the knowledge of Palestinian rabbis and especially their authorities (such as Rabbi Yoḥanan), we must still maintain distance. Here, I believe that the narrator empathizes with the poor Palestinian for his bad lineage but, at the same time, leaves him outside, alienating him—albeit without malice. In like manner, the Babylonians make a benevolent attempt to appropriate the great figures from the Palestinian pantheon, but not without some mockery (revised hierarchies can be found in the pericope below).[71]

b. B. Metzi'a 85b[72]

| Rabbi Zeira said: Last night Rabbi Yose son of Rabbi Ḥanina appeared to me, and I asked him, Near whom are you seated [in the Heavenly Academy]? [He answered]: Near Rabbi Yoḥanan. And Rabbi Yoḥanan near whom? [Near] Rabbi Yannai. And Rabbi Yannai? Near Rabbi Ḥiyya. Said I to him: And is not Rabbi Yoḥanan [worthy of a seat] near Rabbi Ḥiyya? He replied to me: In the place of fiery sparks and flaming tongues, would one let the smith's son [bar nappaḥa] enter there? | אמ' ר' זירא אמש נראה ליר' יוסי בר' חנינא. אמרתי לו: אצל מי אתה תקוע? אצל ר' יוחנן. ור' יוחנן אצל מי? אצל ר' ינאי. ור' ינאי אצל מי? אצל ר' חייא. ור' יוחנן אצל ר' חייא לא? אמ' לי: באתר דזיקוקין דנור ובעורין אישא, מאן מעייל בר נפחא לתמן? |

In this brief story, narrated by none other than our old acquaintance Rabbi Zeira, the narrator communicates with his deceased friend, apparently in a dream.[73] The dead friend, Rabbi Yose bar Ḥanina, informs him that in the next world, apparently in the heavenly academy, which the sages conceived of as their lot in the other world, he holds the especially honorable right to sit beside Rabbi Yoḥanan, who had been his master during his lifetime.[74] This esteemed master sits beside Rabbi Yannai,[75] a sage from the previous generation and master of Rabbi Yoḥanan,[76] who in turn sits beside the formidable Rabbi Ḥiyya.[77] All the sages are seated according

---

71. For my previous analyses of this text and its comparison to its parallel in Ecclesiastes Rabbah 9:10, see Kiperwasser, "Early and Late," 308–9.
72. According to MS Escorial G-I-3.
73. About this trope and custom, see Hasan-Rokem, "Communication with the Dead," 213–32.
74. On Yose bar Ḥanina and his discipleship, see Albeck, Introduction, 185.
75. Ibid., 161–62.
76. In the printed edition, Rabbi Yannai sits beside Rabbi Ḥanina bar Ḥama, another Babylonian, on whom see 106 above. This order is probably even more logical, listing two Palestinians accompanied by two Babylonians; however, it is absent in manuscripts.
77. See 112, 116, 134 above.

to hierarchical order by generations—the young one beside the old, the disciple beside the teacher. The narrator seems to have in mind an ancient symposium or study session, in which the participants recline one beside the other. An unexpected question is then raised (apparently not by Rabbi Zeira, but by the editor): why is Rabbi Yoḥanan not seated next to Rabbi Ḥiyya? The import of the question is probably: why not break the hierarchy of generations and seat the most important of the Palestinian rabbis in the vicinity of the most important of the Babylonians? The answer is somewhat ironic in nature, and the narrator indicates that the question was a rhetorical one. A folk maxim is provided: "In the place of fiery sparks and flaming tongues, would one let the smith's son [*bar Nappaḥa*][78] enter there?" In a literal sense, this proverb implies that the fiery workplace of a blacksmith is not an appropriate place for his inexperienced son. But the narrator plays with the proverb, knowing that Rabbi Yoḥanan's full name is "Yoḥanan bar Nappaḥa" and that the wisdom of Rabbi Ḥiyya is compared to fire.[79] The Babylonian narrator questions the hegemony of Palestinian scholarship and states that Rabbi Yoḥanan's wisdom and the wisdom of his disciples are based on Babylonian foundations. For the Babylonian narrator, Palestinians will forever be apprentices of their Babylonian masters. Rabbi Yoḥanan is one of the most popular Palestinian masters in the Babylonian Talmud. Many of his teachings are quoted there, and many important Babylonian traditions are attributed to him. The desire to appropriate the formidable Palestinian goes hand in hand with the fear of exalting him overly much.

Summary

The narrative texts in the Babylonian Talmud about Babylonians going to the promised land are less dramatic than the parallel Palestinian texts. Since the plot of "ascendance" to the Holy Land is not particularly prominent in this literature, it does not serve to shape the Babylonian's identity vis-à-vis the Palestinian Other as such.

---

78. See Sokoloff, *Jewish Babylonian Aramaic*, 725.

79. Likening his learning to fire is a leitmotif in this pericope in the Bavli; see b. B. Metzi'a 85b. The story under consideration should be compared to the story in b. Hul. 137b in which Rabbi Yoḥanan humbly relates being a student and witnessing the scholarly discussions between Rabbi Yehuda ha-Nasi and Rab, which were described as inducing זיקוקין דנור, "fiery sparks," from the mouth of the master to the mouth of the student and vice versa. Thanks go to Geoffrey Herman for reminding me of this tradition. See also the story about Rabbi Abin in y. Ber. 5:1, 9a, in which assassins who plan to murder the sage are frightened by sparks of fire (זיקוקין דנור) coming out from his neck.

The Bar Babel narrative is the Babylonian variant of the "Going West" stories of Palestinian origin. However, the inglorious arrival of Bar Babel in the Holy Land is more comedic than dramatic in tone. Like many jokes, this one does not feature a great deal of sympathy—in this case for the Babylonian. Nonetheless, the story's focal point is not a competition between the Babylonian protagonist and the Palestinian Other, but rather a powerful reflection by the Babylonian narrator on gender politics and the possibility of sages cooperating with women in confronting the Other, an untutored man. Therefore, the Babylonian's primary internal Other is a compatriot layman, not a remote Palestinian.

In the Babylonian Talmud, Rabbi Zeira's glorious arrival in the Holy Land is converted into a modest narrative about the theological differences between a local Babylonian and a vaguely distant Other. The no-less-glorious visit of Rab Kahana to Rabbi Yoḥanan's city does, however, echo in the Babylonian Talmud. There we finally find a plot that enables the narrator to build his own identity in some correlation with the Palestinian image, which, it is worth noting, fails to provoke strong feelings in him. He is fascinated by significant figures of the Palestinian past, above all by Rabbi Yoḥanan and Resh Laqish, both known by contemporaries as not particularly sympathetic toward their Babylonian brethren.[80] But the Babylonian narrator constructs his Palestinian Other only from remnants and fragments of literary traditions, not from real-life historical figures. He wishes to put into perspective the fourth century's migration processes, which aroused passionate arguments and demanded self-reflection.

Some elements of mockery, like those analyzed in chapter 2, do appear in the Babylonian Talmud. Certain pseudo-historical speculations intended to explain the present, as discussed in chapter 6, could be explored in Babylonian narratives as well. Both Babylonians and Palestinians agree about the substantial incorporation of Babylonian knowledge into Palestinian learning.

---

80. See 122–34.

8

Going East

Alongside the stream of Babylonians going to the Land of Israel, quite a substantial flow of Palestinian rabbis moved in the opposite direction, to Babylonia, an enormously rich and promising country.[1] This movement was depicted by both Palestinian and Babylonian narrators. It seems that the Palestinians generally did not view these "descending" protagonists particularly positively. Nonetheless, some of them became popular with the Babylonian narrators. I will investigate whether the Babylonian portrait of the migrating Palestinian rabbi in his encounter with the Babylonians can serve as evidence for the processes of xenophobia and philoxenia in the mind of the Babylonian narrators. My sense is that the Palestinian Other did not evoke the same strong emotions among the Babylonians as the Babylonian aroused among the Palestinians.

Before us is one main task: to analyze the journeys in the opposite direction from the previous ones, namely, the Palestinians coming to Babylonia and facing the local human environment.

8.1. Going East as a Galilean: The Nephew of Rabbi Yehoshu'a Goes East

In Tannaitic times, a few Palestinian scholars are said to have sojourned in, or visited, Babylonia. A common religious reason for this journey was to intercalate the year. For example, Rabbi Aqiva traveled to Nehardea to intercalate the year, according to m. Yevam. 16:7. Perhaps the most remarkable case of "going East" for this purpose is that of Ḥananiah, the nephew of Rabbi Yehoshu'a.[2] There are two narrative traditions about the reasons for Ḥananiah's departure and his deeds in Babylonia.[3] According

---

1. Scholarly journeys between Palestine and Babylonia in Tannaitic times are listed and analyzed by Hezser, *Jewish Travel*, 333–38.
2. Academia ed., 1037.
3. Previously discussed by scholars; see Gafni, *Land, Center and Diaspora*, 107–9; Sacha Stern, *Calendar and Community: A History of the Jewish Calendar, Second Century BCE–Tenth*

170 Going West

to one of these traditions, represented in both Talmudim, his emigration led to the establishment of a fully independent rabbinic authority in Babylonia:[4]

y. Nedarim 40a, 6:8 [5]

Hananiah, the nephew of Rabbi Yehoshu'a intercalated[6] outside the Land. Rabbi [Yehuda ha-Nasi] sent him three letters with Rabbi Itzhak and Rabbi Nathan; in the first, he wrote: To his Holiness Hananiah. In the second, he wrote: The kids that you have left behind have become billy goats. In the third, he wrote: If you don't accept [our authority], go out in the wilderness of the bramble, and you be the slaughterer and Nehunion the sprinkler.[7]

He read the first and honored them; the second and honored them. When he read the third, he wished to discredit them. They said to him: You cannot, as you have already honored us! Rabbi Itzhak stood up and read in the Torah: These are the festivals of Hananiah, the nephew of Rabbi Yehoshu'a." They said to him: "These are festivals of the Lord" (Lev 23:4). He said to them: By us. Rabbi

חנניה בן אחי רבי יהושע עיבר בחוצה לארץ. שלח ליה רבי תלת איגרן גבי רבי יצחק ורבי נתן. בחדא כתב: לקדושת חנניה. ובחדא כתב: גדיים שהינחתה נעשו תיישים. ובחדא כתב: אם אין את מקבל עליך צא לך למדבר האטד ותהא שוחט ונחונינון זורק.

קדמיתא ואיקרון. תינייתא ואיקרון. תליתייא בעי מבסרתון. אמרין ליה: לית את יכיל דכבר איקרתנון. קם רבי יצחק וקרא: כתיב באוריתא: "אלה מועדי חנניה בן אחי רבי יהושע". אמרין ליה: "מועדי יי'" (ויקרא כג ד). אמ' לון: גבן. קם רבי נתן ואשלם: "כי מבבל תצא תורה ודבר יי' מנהר פקוד". אמרין ליה: "כי מציון תצא תורה ודבר יי' מירושלם" (ישעיהו ב ג). אמ' לון: גבן.

Century CE (Oxford: Oxford University Press, 2001), 247–49; Hezser, *Jewish Travel*, 334; Boyarin, *Traveling Homeland*, 49–51.

    4. See Boyarin, *Traveling Homeland*, 49.

    5. See Academia ed., 1037 (appears here with some corrections of clear scribal errors). A doublet of this tradition appears in y. Sanh. 1:2, 19a (1269). The story is discussed by Boyarin, *Traveling Homel*and, 48–51, whose translation I roughly follow here.

    6. Meaning, added a month to the year to keep the solar and lunar calendars synchronized.

    7. Nehunion the priest is a name by which the Yerushalmi refers to a historical figure—the priest Onias, known to us from Josephus (*Ant.* 13.72), who was a high priest in the Egyptian Temple of God of Israel in Elephantine, see Rafael Yankelevitch, "The Identity of Nehunion Ahia" [Hebrew], *Milet* 2 (1984): 137–41. It is difficult to know why they changed his name. "Onias" means Hananiah; it is possible that the change in name is there to distinguish between the two Hananias; see Ilan and Noam, *Josephus and the Rabbis*, 219, on the question of whether there is a joke involved in the name.

Nathan got up and completed: "For from Babylon will go out the Torah, and the Word of the Lord from river Paqod." They said, "For from Zion will go out the Torah, and the Word of the Lord from Jerusalem" (Isa 2:3). He said: By us.

[Ḥananiah] went and complained about them to Rabbi Yehuda ben Betera in Nisibis. He said to him: After them ... after them ....[8] He said to him: Do I not know what is over there? What tells me that they are masters of calculating the calendar like me? Since they are not so well informed as I am in calculating the calendar, let them listen to what I say. [He replied:] And since they [now] are masters of calculation as much as you, you must listen to them. He rose up and mounted his horse. Places which he reached, he reached, [and there he retracted his intercalation,] and the ones he did not reach observed the holy days in error.

אזל וקבל עליה גבי רבי יהודה בן בתירה לנציבין. אמר ליה: אחרי[ה]ם, אחריהם. אמר ליה: לינה ידע מה שבקית תמן. מאן מודע לי דאינון חכמין מחשבה דכוותי! מכיון דו אמר: לא חכמין דכוותי, ישמעון ליה. מכיון שאינון חכמין מחשבה דכוותי, ישמע להון. קם ורכב סוסיא. הן דמטא מטא. הן דלא מטא נוהגין בקילקול.

It is written: "[These are the words of the letter which Jeremiah the prophet sent from Jerusalem] to the rest of the elders of the exiles" (Jer 29:1). Said the Holy One, blessed be he: The elders of the exile are most valuable to me. [Yet] more beloved to me is the smallest circle which is in the Land of Israel, more than a great Sanhedrin located outside of the Land.

כתיב "ואל יתר זקני הגולה" (ירמיהו כט א). אמר הקדוש ברוך הוא: ביותר הן חביבין עלי זקני הגולה. חביבה עלי כת קטנה שבארץ ישראל מסנהדרין גדולה שבחוצה לארץ.

This story appears in the context of a discussion on permission to intercalate the calendar outside of the Land of Israel. The text concludes that, when the intercalation in the Holy Land is impossible, intercalation abroad is permitted, as is evident from the cases of the prophets Jeremiah and Ezekiel, who, according to the Yerushalmi, conducted such

---

8. Meaning that the protagonist must accept the authority of the Palestinian sages.

procedures while in exile. Following this ruling, the story presented above appears; in it, the protagonist, far from being a prophet, intercalates a year in Babylonia, while all his colleagues are alive and well in the Land of Israel. Following Daniel Boyarin, I see this narrative as full of disdain against those who "go East" and try to build there some alternative to the "West."[9] Ḥananiah, having left the Holy Land, sets himself up to perform the commandment of intercalating the calendar in Babylonia, which had previously been an exclusive prerogative of the Patriarch's court. Rabbi Yehuda ha-Nasi, hearing of this, sends along letters with messengers to dissuade him from this rebellious act of setting up an independent rabbinic authority.[10] The first letter is simply a letter of praise to him, so he praises and honors the messengers in return. In the second letter, the messengers are praised by the sender. Those who were young kids when Ḥananiah left are now full-grown billy goats, a metaphor for great Talmud scholars. Naturally, the receiver is now obliged to praise the messengers again. The third letter contains the trap. First, he is told that if he persists in his "rebellion," he should go out into the desert and rule over the brambles and thorn bushes;[11] second, he is compared to another Ḥananiah, Onias, a powerful figure of schism, who built a Temple in Egypt to compete with the Temple in Jerusalem. At this point, Ḥananiah tries to discredit the couriers but cannot, as they have already been credited. These now press the attack, parodying the verse "These are the festivals of the Lord" (Lev 23:4) when one is called up to read from the Torah, reading it: "These are the festivals of Ḥananiah." In other words, he implies that Ḥananiah's calendar is inconsistent with the holy calendar of the Lord and replaces it with a profane one. The people, not quite getting the point, reply that the verse says, "These are the festivals of the Lord!" to which Rabbi Itzhak responds: Yes, that is what is written in our Torah, but apparently in yours (you Babylonians), it says, "The festivals of Ḥananiah." The ruse is repeated when Rabbi Nathan reads the portion from the Prophets and recites, "For from Babylon will go out Torah and the Word of the Lord from the river Paqod."[12] Once again, the people are tricked into supplying the correct reading and receive a sarcastic explanation. The narrator presents the Babylonians as simpletons who do not understand the sarcastic interpretations of the biblical verses

---

9. See Boyarin, *Traveling Homeland*, 49–50.

10. On sending letters, see Lutz Doering, *Ancient Jewish Letters and the Beginnings of Christian Epistolography*, WUNT 298 (Tübingen: Mohr Siebeck, 2012), 343–76.

11. Perhaps brambles (אטד) here is an allusion to Yotam's parable from the book of Judges, 9:14.

12. This biblical toponym (see Jer 50:21) in Babylonia is seldom mentioned in rabbinic literature; see Aharon Oppenheimer, *Babylonia Judaica in the Talmudic Period* (Wiesbaden: L Reichert, 1983), 300–305.

by the Palestinians due to their poor sense of humor, requiring the Palestinians to explain to these dolts the punchline of their jokes.

In the next paragraph, we learn that Ḥananiah's calendar was not merely independent of that of Palestine but also substantially different, for when it was rescinded, the more distant communities that could not be informed in time, following Ḥananiah's calendar, observed a festival on the wrong date.[13] Interestingly, as a punishment for Ḥananiah's misconduct, the narrator sends him to Nisibis, to the famous Rabbi Yehuda ben Betera.[14]

Following the description of Ḥananiah's unsuccessful attempt to annul his own calendar, a few lines of exegesis on Jer 29:1 are presented, in which the exegete states that any decision made by Palestinian sages, even if they are in the minority and weaker than their Babylonian brethren, is preferable and supported by divine acclamation.[15] This story expresses the Palestinians' fears about the rising authority of the Babylonian academy. It includes an etiological explanation for the appearance of the Babylonian tendency to assert independence vis-à-vis Palestine—a rebellious Palestinian rabbi initiated it. Thus, the tendency was bad from the beginning. However, the Babylonians tell the same story differently:

b. Berakhot 63a–b:	
Rav Safra said: Rabbi Abbahu used to relate: When Ḥanina, nephew of Rabbi Yehoshu'a, went down to the diaspora, he used to intercalate years and determine the beginning of months outside the Land. They sent after him two sages: Rabbi Yose ben Kipar and the grandson of Zechariah ben Qabutal. When he saw them, he said to them: Why have you come here? They said: To learn Torah we	אמר רב ספרא, רבי אבהו הוה משתעי: כשירד חנינא בן אחי רבי יהושע לגולה היה מעבר שנים וקובע חדשים בחוצה לארץ. שגרו אחריו שני תלמידי חכמים רבי יוסי בן כיפר ובן בנו של זכריה בן קבוטל. כיון שראה אותם, אמר להם: למה באתם? אמרו ליה: ללמוד תורה באנו. הכריז [עליהם]: אנשים הללו גדולי הדור הם, ואבותיהם שמשו בבית המקדש ....

---

13. See Stern, *Calendar and Community*, 247. Taking into consideration the exact language of the narrator, they continue to observe the festival according to the wrong date in the present.

14. Rabbi Yehuda ben Betera is, strictly speaking, not really a Babylonian but the dweller of a Roman city only recently annexed by the Sasanian rulers of Persia. In terms of his education and subordinance, he belongs more to the community of the Palestinian rabbis than to the community of the Babylonians; see Oppenheimer, *By the Rivers of Babylon*, 76–77.

15. This point of view is very far from the famous Babylonian view about the preferability of independent rabbinic regulation to divine intervention in human deeds, boldly expressed in the celebrated story of "Akhnai's oven," b. Ber. 19a; see Rubenstein, *Talmudic Stories*, 34–63.

have come. He declared concerning them: These men are the giants of their generation, and their fathers served in the Temple! . . .

[Ḥanina] began to declare something impure, and they declared it pure; he declared that something was permitted, and they declare forbidden. He declared of them: These men are worthless, and they are *tohu*! They said to him: You have already built; you may not tear down. You have already fenced in; you may not break down the fence. He said to them, what is the reason that what I declare impure, you declare pure and what I declare forbidden, you declare permitted? They said to him, because you intercalate years and determine months outside the Land. He said to them: But did Aqiva ben Yosef not intercalate years and determine months outside the Land? They said to him: Leave Rabbi Aqiva aside, for he had not left behind him in the Land of Israel anyone as great as he was. He said: Also, I have not left behind me in the Land of Israel anyone as great as I. They said: The kids that you have left behind have become billy goats with horns, and it is they who sent us after you, and they said to us, go and say to him in our name: If he obeys, it is good, and if not, he will be excommunicated. And say to our brothers in the exile: If they obey, it is good, and if not, they should go up to a mountain where Ahia will build an altar, Ḥanina will play the harp, and all will apostatize and say they have no portion in the god of Israel! All the people began to low and cry and

התחיל הוא מטמא והם מטהרים, הוא אוסר והם מתירים. הכריז עליהם: אנשים הללו של שוא הם, של תהו הם. אמרו לו: כבר בנית, ואי אתה יכול לסתור, כבר גדרת, ואי אתה יכול לפרוץ. אמר להם: מפני מה אני מטמא ואתם מטהרים, אני אוסר ואתם מתירים? אמרו לו: מפני שאתה מעבר שנים וקובע חדשים בחוץ לארץ. אמר להם: והלא עקיבא בן יוסף היה מעבר שנים וקובע חדשים בחוץ לארץ. אמרו לו: הנח רבי עקיבא, שלא הניח כמותו בארץ ישראל. אמר להם: אף אני לא הנחתי כמותי בארץ ישראל. אמרו לו: גדיים שהנחת נעשו תישים בעלי קרנים, והם שגרונו אצלך. וכן אמרו לנו: לכו ואמרו לו בשמנו: אם שומע, מוטב, ואם לאו, יהא בנדוי. ואמרו לאחינו שבגולה: אם שומעין, מוטב, ואם לאו, יעלו להר, אחיה יבנה מזבח, חנניה ינגן בכנור, ויכפרו כולם ויאמרו: אין להם חלק באלהי ישראל. מיד געו כל העם בבכיה ואמרו: חס ושלום! יש לנו חלק באלהי ישראל. וכל כך למה? משום שנאמר: "כי מציון תצא תורה ודבר ה' מירושלים" (ישעיה ב ג).

said: God forbid; we do have a portion in the god of Israel! And why all this fuss [on the part of the Palestinians]? Because it says: "for from Zion will go out Torah and the word of the Lord from Jerusalem!"

Sharing the common nucleus of a narrative with the Palestinian story, this story is the product of a transformation that took place on its way from the Palestinian to the Babylonian Talmud. According to the Palestinian version, Ḥananiah had performed one act: intercalation, that is, the occasional proclamation of a second month of Adar in a certain year; according to the Babylonian version, Ḥananiah both intercalated years and declared a new month. This would be a different story altogether, as it would have meant that he had taken charge of the setting of the entire calendar.[16] If the Palestinian version assumes the primacy of Palestinian calendrical authority to be permanent and intrinsic to the Land of Israel, according to the Babylonian version, it is contingent on the more extraordinary erudition of the Palestinian sages.[17] The Palestinian visitors still prevail, and the Palestinian emigrant is clearly understood by the narrator to be a rebellious son of the rabbinic community. Yet a crucial ideological difference lies behind the text. In the Yerushalmi, the phrase "The kids you have left behind have become billy goats" is a compliment to Rabbi Ḥananiah: those young pupils you trained have become talmudic scholars in their own right. Initially, Rabbi Ḥananiah treats the statement as a positive one; then he realizes that by doing so he has empowered some very hostile emissaries. In the Babylonian Talmud, the story involves a kind of contest regarding where the more significant Torah scholars are to be found — in Babylonia or Palestine — and the emissaries from Palestine are made to claim that the young students whom Ḥananiah had left behind have become great scholars, and, therefore, his claim to be able to intercalate in Babylonia (as the greatest scholar in the world) is invalid. Underlying this text is the idea that the center of the Torah, the new Zion, is not necessarily in the place of geographical Zion but in the place where the greatest scholars are to be found.[18] As it happens, in the case of Ḥananiah, namely, in the distant past of our narrator, the real Zion was still identical with the Zion of proper

---

16. Stern, *Calendar and Community*, 248
17. Gafni, *Land, Center and Diaspora*, 107–11.
18. Such dynamics are typical of the metamorphosis of traditions between Palestine and Babylonia; see, e.g., Rubenstein, "Coping with the Virtues," 159–88; Isaiah M. Gafni "How Babylonia became 'Zion': Shifting Identities in Late Antiquity," in *Jewish Identities in Antiquity: Permutations and Transformations; International Conference in Memory of Menachem Stern, June 25–27, 2007*, ed. L. I. Levine and D. R. Schwartz (Tübingen: Mohr Siebeck,

learning. However, the narrator is inclined to locate the new Zion in contemporary Babylonia.

According to the Yerushalmi's version of the story, Palestine is always and forever the only Holy Land and the sole center of authority: "For from Zion will go out Torah and the word of the Lord from Jerusalem." No metaphoric understanding of Zion, no transformation of the center to the diaspora, or vice versa, is possible.

The son of the Land of Israel, who preferred "the bosom of the stepmother," is depicted as a rather sinister figure. In the late Palestinian tradition, however, he will become more than sinister—he will become a heretic. Now let us see how the image of Ḥananiah metamorphosed in a late Palestinian narrative.

Ecclesiastes Rabbah 1:9[19]

Ḥanina the son of the brother of Rabbi Yehoshu'a went to Capernaum and the heretics cast on him a "spell" and put him on a donkey on the Shabbat. Rabbi Yehoshu'a, his uncle, went there, and anointed and healed him. He said to him: Because the wine of that evil one is awake in you, you cannot stay in Land of Israel. He went down to Babylonia, where he died.	חנינא בן אחי ר׳ יהושע אזל להדא כפר נחום, ועבדין ליה מינאי מילא, ועלון יתיה רכיב חמרא בשבתא. אזל לגבי ר׳ יהושע חביביה, ויהב עלוי משח ואסיתיה. אמ׳ ליה: מכיון דאתער בך חמרא דההוא רשיעא, לית אנא יכיל שרי בארעא דישראל. נחת ליה מן תמן לבבל ודמך תמן.

This short story is a part of a chain of accounts expounding the verse "all things are exhausting" (Eccl 1:8). Among other things, the story discusses the exhausting futile power of the *minut*, namely, heresies, and all sorts of associated practices.[20] Ḥanina the nephew of Rabbi Yehoshu'a vis-

---

2009), 333–48; Tal Ilan, "Heaven and Hell: Babylonia and the Land of Israel in the Bavli," in Nikolsky and Ilan, *Rabbinic Traditions between Palestine and Babylonia*, 158–72.

19. See Marc G. Hirshman, ed., *Midrash Kohelet Rabbah 1–6: Critical Edition based on Manuscripts and Genizah Fragments* (Jerusalem: Midrash Project of the Schechter Institute of Jewish Studies, 2016), 76; see also the commentary, 79–80. My commentary on this story is different from his. I discussed this story briefly in Kiperwasser and Ruzer, "The Holy Land and Its Inhabitants in the Pilgrimage Narrative of the Persian Monk Bar-Sauma" [Hebrew], *Cathedra* 148 (2013): 51 (for an English version see Kiperwasser and Ruzer, "Competition for the Sacred Space," 190–91). See also Moti (Mordechai) Arad, *Sabbath Desecrators with Parresia: A Talmudic Legal Term and Its Historic Context* [Hebrew] (New York: Jewish Theological Seminary of America, 2009), 294–308.

20. The identity of the *minim* remains contested; see Miller, "'Minim' of Sepphoris," 377–402; Goodman, "Function of 'Minim,'" 501–10; Adiel Schremer, *Brothers Estranged*, 102–3, 210 n. 9; Boyarin, *Borderlines*, 221. In our story, however, these *minim* are most likely Christians; see further 177.

its Capernaum, a Christian stronghold in Galilee,[21] where he falls victim to heretics, who bewitch him with an utterance (*mila*).[22] Enchanted, he violates the Shabbat by riding a donkey, demonstrating his departure from the Jewish community of faith.[23] For this reason, his uncle, Rabbi Yehoshu'a, goes to where his nephew violated Shabbat and heals him with oil. At first sight, the form of healing seems odd, but it becomes more comprehensible when we view it from a comparative perspective. Scented oil and wine were ingredients of the religious procedure of conversion to Christianity in this period.[24] After baptism, the neophyte's body was covered with a specially scented oil, whose odor was compared to the scent of salvation. This oil, named chrism, was sweet-smelling, a mixture of aromatics and olive oil, and—according to Tertullian and, later, Isidore of Seville—made one a Christian.[25] Describing the conversion of the Jews of Clermont, the poet Fortunatus proposed a dual model of odors; according to this model, the odor of the unconverted was foul by contrast to the sweet smell of the newly baptized, who have been sealed with the chrism and thus exude a new spiritual odor.[26] The procedure is not mentioned explicitly in rabbinic literature. The use of the aromatic scent as a euphemistic expression for conversion to Christianity appears in early post-talmudic literature of Palestinian origin—the so-called *ma'asim* literature.[27]

Following the anointment, the new convert partook of the wine, a

---

21. See Stanislao Loffreda, "Capernaum," *OEANE* 1:416–9; Benni Arubas and Rina Talgam, "Jews, Christians and 'Minim': Who Really Built and Used the Synagogue at Capernaum – A Stirring Appraisal," in *Knowledge and Wisdom: Archaeological and Historical Essays in Honor of Leah Di Segni*, ed. Giovanni C. Bottini, L. Daniel Churpcala, and Joseph Patrich, Collection maior 54 (Milan: Edizioni Terra Santa, 2014), 237–74. Eyal Ben-Eliyahu suggests that the polemic in rabbinic literature against the Christian tendency to sanctify places might explain the relatively few references to Bethlehem, and the absence of Nazareth in rabbinic literature ("The Rabbinic Polemic against Sanctification of Sites," *JSJ* 40 [2009]: 260–80). This is one of the exceedingly rare mentions of a city which at the time of the narrator was already entire Christian.

22. On *milah* as a magical saying, see Sperber, *Magic and Folklore*, 60–66.

23. See Arad, *Sabbath Desecrators*, 255–56, 296.

24. See Susan Ashbrook Harvey, *Scenting Salvation: Ancient Christianity and the Olfactory Imagination*, Transformation of the Classical Heritage 42 (Berkeley: University of California Press, 2006), 67.

25. See Tertullian, *De Baptismo* 7 (CCSL 1:282, http://www.tertullian.org/works/de_baptismo.htm). Cf. Isidore, *Etymologiae* 6.50 (PL 82:256). We have no sixth-century description of the making of the chrism, but Pseudo-Germanus (ca. 700) links the aromatic in the oil to the cross of Christ. He claims that the chrism was made with balsam; the balsam came from the tree called *lentiseus*, which tradition says was used for the pieces of the cross; see *Expositio Antiquae Liturgiae Gallicanae*, ed. J. J. Quasten (Munster: Aschendorff, 1934), 27.

26. See Harvey, *Scenting Salvation*, 332.

27. See Hillel I. Newman, *The Ma'asim of the People of the Land of Israel: Halakhah and History in Byzantine Palestine* [Hebrew] (Jerusalem: Yad Ben-Zvi: 2001), 107–8. Another euphemistic expression for the conversion in this literature is יצא ידי עולמו, "left his world," which at first appears in late midrash. See Newman, *Ma'asim of the People*, 105.

metaphorical substitute for Christ's blood.[28] I would suggest that the reference to heretical magic in our story refers to the Christian use of the sacramental wine and the chrism oil. The oil used by the rabbinic healer was meant to neutralize the influence of the Christian sacrament. However, the oil used here by Rabbi Yehoshu'a was probably less scented.[29] The substitution of the oil of Christian salvation with its Jewish antidote may be read in light of another struggle between two different oils. In a story of the conversion of Jews of Clermont in the sixth century,[30] we are told that at Easter 576, as a recent convert from Judaism was proceeding from the baptistry through the city gate, one of the Jews of the town tipped a quantity of rancid oil on him. In this instance, the offender escaped stoning by a Christian mob only through the bishop's intervention.[31] Bernhard Blumenkranz has suggested that this story intended to mock this Christian use of sweet-smelling oil.[32] Returning to our case with this Clermont account in mind, I suggest that the oil of Rabbi Yehoshu'a functions as an antidote to neutralize the spell of the Other. The wine's effect, which is identified with "that evil man," seems to be a reference to the wine sacrament. In this sense, the late, but possibly independent, version of this story, as it appears in the medieval Exempla of Rabbis,[33] is even more remarkable: "Rabbi Yehoshu'a put on him some oil and said on him some words," meaning that he performed a standard procedure that was parallel but opposite to the Christian one performed on him earlier.[34] Apparently "that evil one" is Jesus. Now, why cannot the effect of the wine of the sacrament be canceled? R. Yehoshu'a explains that it is "awake" in his nephew—meaning that it is alive, having become one with his living person. This is in fact the Christian theology behind the sacrament. When the Christian partakes of the body and blood of Christ, it becomes one with his own body and blood and transforms him into a member of the body of Christ (as one flesh). Apparently, our narrator was aware of the Christian claim that identity with Christ is effected by the sacrament. This explains why Ḥanina must leave the Holy Land—he has become an embodiment

---

28. See John Halliburton, "Anointing in the Early Church," in *The Oil of Gladness: Anointing in the Christian Tradition*, ed. Martin Dudley and Geoffrey Rowell (London: SPCK; Collegeville, MN: Liturgical Press1993), 77–91.

29. See further n. 32.

30. See Brian Brennan, "The Conversion of the Jews of Clermont in AD 576," *Journal of Theological Studies* NS 36 (1985): 321–37.

31. Ibid., 321.

32. Bernhard Blumenkranz, *Juifs et Chrétiens dans le monde occidental, 430–1096*, Études juives 2 (Paris: Mouton, 1960), 140, 270.

33. On this, see Reuven Kiperwasser, "Midrash ha-Gadol, The Exempla of the Rabbis (*Sefer Ma'asiyot*) and Midrashic Works on Ecclesiastes: A Comparative Approach" [Hebrew], *Tarbiz* 75 (2006): 409–36.

34. See Gaster, *Exempla of the Rabbis*, the story n. 213, 140.

or perhaps a temple of the wicked Christ, an object of idolatrous worship, and as such he must be uprooted from the Land. Therefore, the enchanted rabbi is sent into exile to Babylonia, where he will be far away from his magical encounters. Here, the religious struggle takes on the form of a battle between two healing methods, where the healing material is contrasted with the rival religion's ritual material.[35]

In the eyes of the Palestinian narrator, Babylonia is a place that is relatively free of heresies, enabling exile to constitute an effective antidote.[36.] Thus, at least some of the Babylonian rabbinic instructors, and especially those who made Babylonia independent of the center in Palestine, were former Palestinians who were forced to leave their homeland under questionable circumstances.

8.2. Beaten Galileans

In this chapter, I continue to portray the flow of Palestinian rabbis who moved to Babylonia; however, this time clearly for mercantile reasons. This particular case of misfortune of Galileans visiting Babylonia was depicted by both Palestinian and Babylonian narrators. In this plot about Galileans going to Babylonia, the Palestinians were not only not warmly accepted in their new place — they were beaten there.[37]

y. Qiddushin 3:5, 64a[38]

| A story: Rabbi Dosethai bar Rabbi Yannai and Rabbi Yose ben Kipar went down there [i.e., to Babylonia] to collect [debts] for the sages. Ill-[rumors] were said of them. They [the Babylonians] sought [now] not to give to them anything.[39] They came and sought to take back from | דלמא. ר׳ דוסתי ביר׳ ינאי ור׳ יוסי בן כיפר נחתון למגביה לחבריא תמן. איתאמר עליהון לישנא בישא. הוון בעיין דלא יהויין כלום. אתון בעון מיפקא מינהון. אמרין לון: [כבר זבנון אמרן לון]: ומנן. אמרין לון: מנן בעי תקמינון טבאות. אמרין לון: שומרי חינם אנחנו. אזלון לגבי ר׳ דוסתי ביר׳ ינאי. אמ׳ לון: אהן הוא כולא. נסבון לר׳ יוסי בן כיפר וכפתון ואפקון מיניה. |

---

35. See the comparison of the two, as in the case of Barsauma, Kiperwasser and Ruzer, "Competition for the Sacred Space," 190–91.

36. Probably this suggestion displays a consensus between the Palestinian and Babylonian storytellers; see b. Avod. Zar. 4b, discussed below, 153 and 156.

37. See Geoffrey Herman, "Midgets and Mules, Elephants, and Exilarchs: On the Metamorphosis of a Polemical Amoraic Story," in Nikolsky and Ilan, *Rabbinic Traditions between Palestine and Babylonia*, 117–32.

38. According to the printed edition it is 3:4, however it is based on 3:5. See the Academia ed., 1172. There is a parallel in y. Git. 1:5, 43d. Some errors are corrected based on a comparison between the two versions.

39. This phrase, missing in the Gittin parallel, makes little sense and seems to be corrupt.

them [what they had already given]. They said to them: We have already acquired possession [of the money]. They said to them: We want you to undertake liability [for any loss]. They replied: We are in the status of unpaid guardians [who have no legal liability for loss]. They went over to Rabbi Dosethai bar Rabbi Yannai. He said to them: Here is the lot. They took Rabbi Yose ben Kipar and bound him and [forcibly] took [the money] from him.

When they went up here [i.e., to Palestine], [i.e., Rabbi Yose ben Kipar] came before [Dosethai's] father. He said to him: See what your son did to me? He asked him: What did he do to you? He answered: Had he agreed with me, they would not have taken anything from us. [Dosethai's father] said to [his son]: Why did you act in this way? [Dosethai] replied: I saw them; a proper court[40] and their hats a cubit high, and they were speaking from their middle, and Yose, my brother, bound, and the whip rising and coming down, and I asked [myself]: Does my father have another Dosethai?

כד סלקון להכא, אתא לגבי אבוי. אמ' ליה: [חמי] מה עבד(ת כן) [לי ברך]. אמ' ליה: מה עבד לך? אמ' ליה: אילו אשוי עימי לא הוון מפקה מינן כלום. אמ' ליה: מה עבדת כן? אמ' ליה: ראיתי אותן בית דין שוה וכובעיהן אמה ומדברין מחציין ויוסה אחי כפות ורצועה עולה ויורדת. ואמרתי: שמא דוסתי אחר יש לאבא?

Two rabbinic students are sent to Babylonia to collect debts for the Palestinian sages.[41] They run into trouble and are required to surrender the money that they collected. After a brief exchange of a halakhic nature, one of the sages declares his refusal to cooperate with the locals and is conse-

---

40. On שוה, see Saul Lieberman, *Greek in Jewish Palestine: Studies in the Life and Manners of Jewish Palestine in the II–IV Centuries C.E.*, 2nd ed. (New York: Feldheim, 1965), 176–77; cf. Neusner, *History of the Jews in Babylonia*, 2:303. See also Rosenthal, "For the Talmudic Dictionary," 86. Herman proposes that the Babylonian redactor was not interested in attaching to the Exilarchate the quality of a law court ("Midgets and Mules," 119).

41. See Alon, *Jews in Their Land*, 248–52; Moshe Beer, "Torah and Derekh Eretz," *Bar-Ilan* 2 (1964): 148–51. Alon found evidence here for a delegation collecting contributions for the support of the rabbis in Palestine. As observed by Herman, however, the term למגבי relates to the collection of debts and not donations ("Midgets and Mules, 122).

quently beaten. The second rabbi cooperates with the locals and remains unharmed. Upon their return to Palestine, they speak about this Babylonian experience. The second rabbi defends his action while describing the intimidating court judges and his fear of personal injury. The Palestinian narrator clearly wishes to depict the Babylonian Jews as collaborators with the Persian authorities, treacherous individuals who torture their own Palestinian brethren after breaking their word. This story is anti-Babylonian. As Herman put it:

> The Yerushalmi is an anti-Babylonian story. Its Palestinian perspective has full articulation. It relates a journey from Palestine to a foreign land of two distinguished Palestinian rabbis. When false accusations undermine their mission, they apply acceptable Jewish legal principles but are countered by intimidation. A feeling of foreignness pervades all that relates to Babylonia. That country is seen as a dangerous place, the law there is arbitrary, and the external appearance and manner of the people is distinctly odd.[42]

Therefore, the appearance of a variant of this story, unsympathetic to Persian rule, in the Babylonian Talmud elicits the question, Why did the Babylonian narrator think that it deserved to be retold at all? We will now consider the Babylonian version and attempt to answer this question.

b. Gittin 14a–b[43]

| Rabbi Aḥai bar Rabbi Yoshiah had a silver goblet in Nehardea. He said to Rabbi Dosethai bar Rabbi Yannai and to Rabbi Yose bar Kipar: When you come [there], bring it [back to me]. They went and retrieved it. [The Nehardeans] said to them: Make [legal] acquisition from us. They replied to them: No. [The Nehardeans] said to them: [Then] return it to us! Rabbi Dosethai bar Rabbi Yannai said to them: Yes. Rabbi Yose bar Kipar said to them: No. They bound him [Rabbi Yose bar Kipar]. They were tormenting him, saying: Does Sir observe how things are done [here]? [Rabbi Dosethai bar Rabbi Yannai] said to them: Beat him well! | ר' אחי בר' יאשיה הוה ליה איסקפא דכספא בנהרדעא. אמר להו לר' דוסתאי בר' ינאי ולר' יוסי בר כיפר: בהדי דאתיתו, אייתוה ניהליה. אזול יהביה ניהליה. אמרי להו: נקני מינייכו. אמרי להו: לא. אמרי להו: אהדריה ניהלן. ר' דוסתאי ברבי ינאי אמר להו: אין. ר' יוסי בר כיפר אמר להו: לא. כפתוה. הוו קא מצערי ליה. א"ל: חזי מר היכי קא עביד? אמר להו: טב רמו ליה. |

---

42. Herman, "Midgets and Mules," 125–26.
43. The source is presented here according to the *editio* princeps with limited changes on the basis of the manuscripts.

When they came to [Rabbi Aḥai bar Rabbi Yashiah, Rabbi Yose bar Kipar] said: Does Sir note that not only did [Rabbi Dosethai] not help me, but he said "beat him well"? He said: Why did you act in this way? [Rabbi Dosethai bar Rabbi Yannai] said: Those people were a cubit (high), and their hats a cubit (high), and they spoke from their middle, and their names are outlandish: Arda, Arta, and *Pili barish*. [If] they say: Bind [him], they [surely] bind [him]. If they say: Kill him, they would [surely] kill! Had they killed Dosethai, who would give Yannai my father a[nother] son like me? [Rabbi Aḥai] said to him: Are those people close to the sovereign powers? He said: Yes. Do they possess horses and mules that run after them? He replied: Yes. [Rabbi Aḥai then said:] If so, you acted well.

כי אתו לגביה, א"ל: חזי מר לא מיסתייה, דלא סייען. אלא אמר להו: טב רמו ליה? א"ל: אמאי עבדת הכי? א"ל אותן בני אדם, הן אמה, וכובען אמה, ומדברין מחצייהן, ושמותיהן מבוהלין: ארדא, וארטא, ופילי בריש. אומרין: כפותו, כופתין. אומרין: הרוגו, הורגין. אילו הרגו את דוסתאי, מי נתן לינאי אבא בן כמותי? א"ל: בני אדם הללו קרובים למלכות הן? א"ל: אין. יש להן סוסים ופרדים שרצים אחריהן? אל: אין. אי הכי שפיר עבדת.

In the Bavli, the plot is somewhat different. The same two rabbis are sent to retrieve a silver goblet belonging to a third sage, Rabbi Aḥai bar Rabbi Yoshiah,[44] during their short sojourn in Nehardea. Once the object is collected, the locals demand its return. After their initial joint refusal (the halakhic discussion differs from that in the Yerushalmi version and is briefer) one of the two sages consents to hand over the item while the other, who refuses, is beaten by the locals, cheered on by his colleague. Upon their return to Rabbi Aḥai bar Rabbi Yoshiah, the sage who was beaten, complains about his colleague's behavior. The second sage defends himself by describing the intimidating nature of the locals. Rabbi Aḥai bar Rabbi Yoshiah's inquiries lead him to the conclusion that these Babylonians are "close to the sovereign powers." Our Palestinian visitor understands that their power is based on their connection to the Parthian court.

This story has been celebrated among scholars for its vivid portrayal of the Babylonians.[45] With its apparent capacity to carry out both corporal

---

44. See b. Shabb. 152b; b. Qidd. 72a. He seems to have originated in Palestine; see Aharon Hyman *Sefer Toldoth Tanna'im ve-Amora'im* [Hebrew], 3 vols. (Jerusalem: Machon Pri Haaretz, 1987), 1:136. Neusner thought that he dwelled in Palestine at the time that the story is set (*History of the Jews in Babylonia*, 1:94–97).

45. See Alon, *Jews in Their Land*, 1:249; Moshe Beer, *The Babylonian Exilarchate* [Hebrew] (Tel Aviv: Devir, 1976), 45, 58–60; Neusner, *History of the Jews in Babylonia*, 94–97, 100–103; Rosenthal, "For the Talmudic Dictionary," 86–87; Goodblatt, *Monarchic Principle*, 140 n. 43;

and capital punishment, a Babylonian court of law is particularly striking. The dress and personal names of the Jews are markers of a remarkably acculturated, Persianized Jewry. Mention of horses and mules suggests that these Babylonian Jews were part of the elite, perhaps fulfilling a role in the region's military makeup.[46]

It seems, however, that the main object of this story is different from that of the Palestinian version. As Herman put it:

> The Bavli indeed shares some of these details. It, too, features the same pair of sages from Palestine, but nothing is said of a journey from Palestine—they are already in Babylonia from the beginning. Their Palestinian origin functions differently, introducing naïve characters unfamiliar with the local scene. They, too, are roughly treated, here by the Nehardeans. However, they do not return to Palestine, but to Rabbi Aḥai, who sent them. He reveals his own familiarity with the villains. In this version, then, the focus is not Babylonia but Nehardea.[47]

The Babylonian narrator extends the story, making significant additions to the Yerushalmi version that advance his objective. Thus, he takes a story that served the Palestinians in their teachings against the Babylonians and transforms it into a teaching against a particular sort of Babylonian—the Nehardeans—in his own intra-Babylonian polemic. The Palestinians as the Other are not particularly important for the purpose of this narration. Their visit becomes a private matter for a local resident. The main hero becomes Rabbi Aḥai bar Rabbi Yoshiah, a well-known figure connected elsewhere to Babylonia.[48] In this version of the legal case, the pledge and its owner have switched identities: now it refers to money that

---

Ahron Oppenheimer, "Enforcement in Palestine and in Babylonia in the Late Tannaitic Era," in *The Paths of Peace: Studies in Honor of Israel Friedman Ben-Shalom*, ed. D. Gera and M. Ben-Zeev (Beer-Sheva: Ben Gurion University of the Negev Press, 2005) 366–70.

46. On this source as evidence for the success of the Jews in integrating into the Parthian nobility, and likewise, on the weakness of rabbinic authority in Babylonia in the second century, and generally for the Parthian era, see Neusner, *History of the Jews in Babylonia*, 1:94–97, 100. However, see Herman, who agrees, "Indeed elephants, typically associated with the army, might also be hinted at, more generally, the allusion to Babylonian Jews in close contact with the kingdom suggests a striking degree of confidence and autonomy" ("Midgets and Mules," 123). He continues, however: "The Babylonian villains of the story have usually been identified with the Exilarchate. Set in the second century CE, this story has served as a potent source for the early history of the Exilarchate and for Babylonian Jewry as a whole. Taken at face value it might suggest that this exilarchic authority enjoyed at this point in time a status unparalleled in the course of the talmudic era, perhaps with a military role and a mandate for capital punishment." But he refutes this understanding further on.

47. See Herman, "Midgets," 126. On the competition between Babylonian cities that had a Jewish population, see Gafni, *Jews and Judaism in the Rabbinic Era*, 247–56.

48. See Herman, "Midgets and Mules," 122 n. 38; and Hyman, *Sefer Toldoth Tannaim*, above, n. 44.

a local sage, Rab Sheshet, has in Mehoza. He asks Rab Yoseph bar Ḥama to collect it when he next passes through.[49] The dialogue appended to the end steadily draws the audience closer to the story's actual targets, which are not just Nehardeans, but those bearing such foreign names as Arda and Arta and with equestrian habits. The Babylonian Talmud is branding specific segments in the Nehardean Jewish community. It marks them culturally with distinctive names and other details linking them to the powers that distanced them from the rabbis and their legal system. Beaten Palestinians are not such an issue here.

Both stories about Palestinians going East are related by Palestinian narrators and then retold by Babylonian ones. The Palestinian narrators are not fond of their countrymen going to Babylonia. The first story is about bad behavior on the part of a former Palestinian; generations after its first appearance, Palestinians are still unhappy with it and make the hero into a Christian heretic, a highly suspicious figure. All the narration surrounding the figure of Ḥananiah serves to shape Palestinian rabbinic identity by erecting a fence between them and the Babylonians and powerfully proclaiming the centrality of their own academic milieu. The same story retold by the Babylonian narrator, despite his attempt to keep the plot's main structure intact, now subversively claims that the center is not in the Land of Israel but in the place that boasts more significant scholarship.

If the editor of the Babylonian Talmud made any attempt to construct a Babylonian identity in this story, it was not effected by creating a direct conflict between the Palestinians and Babylonians. For this late narrator, the conflict was already resolved, and now he only benevolently revises the old Palestinian plot.

The beaten Palestinians' story is an anti-Babylonian story, told by the Palestinian narrator, marked by sarcasm and even antipathy toward the Babylonians. The depiction of Babylonia and the Babylonians is a dystopic one, and the fence erected between the insider and the Other is very clearly marked. Going East from the Palestinian narrator's point is a meaningful and tragic journey in search of (a false) identity. Mirroring these plots in the Babylonian narration converts and inverts them into entirely new story lines.

8.3. Going East in the Babylonian Talmud: Rabbi Itzhak goes East

Now I turn to stories from the Babylonian Talmud about Babylonians accepting Palestinians in their land in Mesopotamia. By facing the Other,

---

49. See Herman, "Midgets and Mules," 127.

the Babylonian narrator comes to understand in what ways a Babylonian differs from a Palestinian or how the Babylonian shapes his own identity by distinguishing himself from the Other. One example is a long story about the encounter between Rabbi Itzhak and Rab Naḥman, in which the Other is honored and admired. However, even in this paean to a Palestinian's creativity, the self-reflection of the Babylonian narrator is evident. Even while admiring the specific qualities of the Palestinian, the Babylonian finds himself quite content with his own traits. He will draw the borders of his own identity at some distance from the supposed model of Palestinian literacy.

This pericope in b. Ta'an. 5a–6a[50] consists of several narrative units, of which only a few are relevant for my discussion here and will be quoted below. In this story, shaped as a dialogue between a Babylonian rabbi and his Palestinian guest, the Babylonian humbly addresses the Palestinian and no less humbly accepts his rather extravagant exegetical suggestions.[51] All teachings provided by the Palestinian as answers are attributed to Rabbi Yoḥanan, who was the most renowned authority in Palestine and an iconic representative of the Palestinian sages in the Babylonian Talmud.[52] From the beginning, the Babylonian narrator contrasts the Palestinian with the Babylonian. The Babylonian host is modest and humble, and during their exchange of opinions, he positions himself as a student of the guest. The guest is well spoken, free, and daring. In the beginning of the story, which I omit here, the Babylonian asks about the verse in Joel 2:23 and receives a comprehensive exegesis on this verse from the Palestinian. Then he asks about 2 Kgs 8:1; then about Jer 10:8. Every answer is built around a sophisticated passage of purely exegetical nature. Without going into the content of this exegesis, I propose that the purpose of this dialogical prologue is to present a typological introduction of the protagonists and an exposition of their relationship. The Palestinian is a student of the famous Rabbi Yoḥanan and is good at aggadic interpretations. The Babylonian, who sits next to him, should, in his opinion, ask questions and learn from his wise words. In the next narrative component of the story, some identity markers are provided.

---

50. For the critical edition of this text, see Henry Malter, *The Treatise Ta'anit of the Babylonian Talmud* (New York: American Academy for Jewish Research, 1930), 11–14. For an English translation, see Malter, *The Treatise Ta'anit of the Babylonian Talmud* (Philadelphia: Jewish Publication Society of America, 1967), 48–63.

51. See Isaac Heinemann, *Darkhei HaAggadah* (The Methods of the Aggadah) [Hebrew], (Jerusalem: Magnes, 1953) 192–93; Joseph Heinemann, *Aggadot ve-Toledotehen* (Aggadah and Its Development) [Hebrew] (Jerusalem: Keter, 1974), 163–65; Chaim Milikowsky "Midrash as Fiction and Midrash as History: What Did the Rabbis Mean?," in *Ancient Fiction: The Matrix of Early Christian and Jewish Narrative*, ed. Jo-Ann A. Brant, Charles W. Hedrick, and Chris. Shea, SymS 32 (Atlanta: Society of Biblical Literature, 2005), 117–27.

52. See Melamed, *Introduction to Talmudic Literature*, 454. See also 32, 92, and 163 above.

b. Ta'anit 5b[53]

Rab Naḥman and Rabbi Itzhak were sitting at a meal, and Rab Naḥman said to Rabbi Itzhak: Let the Master expound something. He replied: Thus, said Rabbi Yoḥanan: One should not converse at meals lest the food goes down his windpipe and his life will thereby be endangered. After they ended the meal, R. Yoḥanan: Jacob added, our forefather is not dead. He [Rav Naḥman] objected: Was it then for naught that he was mourned and embalmed and buried? The other replied: I am exegeting a verse [in *midrash*], as it is said: "Fear thou not, O Jacob, My servant, says the Lord; neither be dismayed, O Israel, for lo, I will save thee from afar and thy seed from the land of their captivity" (Jer 30:10). The verse likens him [Jacob] to his seed [Israel]; as his seed will then be alive, so he too will be alive.

רב נחמן ורבי יצחק הוו יתבי בסעודתא, אמר ליה רב נחמן לרבי יצחק: לימא מר מילתא! אמר ליה: הכי אמר רבי יוחנן: אין מסיחין בסעודה, שמא יקדים קנה לושט ויבא לידי סכנה. בתר דסעוד אמר ליה: הכי אמר רבי יוחנן: יעקב אבינו לא מת. אמר ליה: וכי בכדי ספדו ספדניא וחנטו חנטייא וקברו קברייא? אמר ליה: מקרא אני דורש, שנאמר: "ואתה אל תירא עבדי יעקב נאם ה' ואל תחת ישראל כי הנני מושיעך מרחוק ואת זרעך מארץ שבים" (ירמיה ל י). מקיש הוא לזרעו. מה זרעו בחיים, אף הוא בחיים.

I would like to point out two distinct elements in this short story. The Babylonian, who has already sampled this sage's aggadic learning, is eager to ask more and more, and attempts to ask questions during the meal. However, his guest refuses, and provides a quite natural explanation for his refusal—to talk during the meal is a bad custom that can lead to dangerous consequences for the speaker's health.

This exchange of opinions, as rightly observed by Geoffrey Herman,[54] is not without irony, since in expounding this teaching of Rabbi Yoḥanan, the transmitter must violate it. However, despite this piece of wisdom, attributed to Rabbi Yoḥanan, there is no trace in Palestinian rabbinic literature of the notion of the importance of silence during a meal. The rationale behind this halakhic norm appears in the Tosefta (t. Ber. 4:12; Lieberman, 20–21), but in a different setting and for another purpose. There it appears

---

53. For the text see Malter, *Treatise Ta'anit* (1930), 14. In translation, I am following Malter with some changes.

54. Geoffrey Herman, "Table Etiquette and Persian Culture in the Babylonian Talmud" [Hebrew], *Zion* 77 (2012): 149–88, esp. 180–81.

as an explanation for why, if new wine is served during a feast, which requires an additional blessing, every guest utters the blessing, instead of one uttering the blessing on behalf of all the others, and them answering Amen. The reason for the answer is that, if this were not done, some guests might be caught with food in their mouths and suddenly choke or suffocate. Suppose, however, that the Palestinian tradition deals with the behavior of a person caught in a spontaneous situation. In that case, the Babylonian tradition presents this requirement not to speak while eating as an established custom, even if the act of speech comes in the form of wise teachings and sermons. The only source in rabbinic literature that highly values the silent meal is the Babylonian Talmud, especially the pericope in b. Ber. 46b,[55] which not only attests to the prevalence of the custom of silent meals among Babylonian Jews but also indicates a local, Persian source for this custom. Scholars who deal with traces of Iranian influences in the Babylonian Talmud have recently proposed that Iranian mythological perceptions about the nature of defilement lie behind that norm of silent meals. Surprisingly, Babylonian Jews accepted this Iranian norm but provided a different rationale for it.[56] Here in b. Ta'anit, the rationalization of the Iranian cultural custom is attributed to the head of the Palestinian sages to neutralize its Iranian color and propose it as an authentically Jewish tradition from the Land of Israel.

Let us now turn to the next component of the story, which scholars have recently analyzed as a representative example of provocative rabbinic exegesis.[57] In this story, the Palestinian guest finally surrenders to the host's requests to teach him some Torah by saying that Jacob, our father, never died. Rab Naḥman, taking the bait, asks in bewilderment how could it be that the patriarch did not die, even though it is written in scripture that Egyptian professionals embalmed him. Rabbi Itzhak responds by saying: מקרא אני דורש, *miqra ani doresh*, which means "I am engaged in Bible interpretation." Here he is alluding to the interpretation method in which he is engaged. He quotes Jer 30:10, in which God asks Jacob not to be dismayed when he calls him again by the name of "Israel," when promising that his descendants will be rescued from the land of their exile. Jacob will again have peace and security, and no one will frighten him.

Then the midrashist goes on to say that Israel, or Jacob, is compared to his seed; as his seed, namely, his descendants, is alive, he too is alive. The interpretation is purely metaphorical and therefore does not contradict the embalming plot. As Milikowsky has noted, Rabbi Itzhak's sermon is

---

55. Carefully analyzed in ibid., 180–82.
56. Herman, "Table Etiquette," 181–82; Shaul Shaked, "'No Talking during a Meal': Zoroastrian Themes in the Babylonian Talmud," in *The Talmud in Its Iranian Context*, ed. Carol Bakhos and M. Rahim Shayegan, TSAJ 135 (Tübingen: Mohr Siebeck, 2010), 161–77.
57. See Milikowsky, "Midrash as Fiction," 124–25.

actually more complicated, and the statement denying the death of the patriarch is based not only on the verse from Jeremiah but also on some other intertextual connections.[58] There are three biblical scenes of dying patriarchs: Abraham (Gen 25:8), Isaac (35:29), and Jacob (49:33). In the death scenes of the first two, the word *died* is mentioned explicitly, but it is absent in Jacob's death scene. All the descriptions of these scenes state that the hero expired and was gathered to his people. These verses were known to both participants of the dialogue. In the absence of a broader explanation, however, Rab Naḥman understood his Palestinian guest's first statement as a proposition to make Jacob like Elijah—an eternal living holy figure wandering between the worlds. Yet, according to Rabbi Itzhak, we are dealing not with a reality of any sort but with midrash. Midrash is a narrative that is embedded in the biblical text, though not explicitly. According to Rabbi Itzhak, God has excluded from the Torah any mention of death from Jacob's death scene to hint at the message of Jeremiah— that the descendants of Jacob will have eternal life. Therefore, Jacob's life will not be interrupted. This example epitomizes the nature of midrash. It is a sort of narrative that is extrapolated from a text by experienced and learned readers, such as Rabbi Itzhak himself, and God himself grants it. The ability to reconstruct this sacral fiction is given to only a chosen few, and Rab Naḥman clearly lacks the skills of Rabbi Itzhak. He is educated enough to comprehend his Palestinian colleague's exegetical exercise, but his ability to construct that sort of narrative from the biblical texts is limited. In other words, he is less able than his Palestinian colleague to grasp allusions and further develop them.[59]

What is important in the present context is that a new and bold typological difference between the two rabbis is here emphasized. For the first time, the Palestinian guest selects the topic of discussion. He knows that Rab Naḥman is interested in the biblical past and reads the verses not literally but as connected to one continuous narrative. The Palestinian takes the biblical text as a continuum of hints, helping him reconstruct the Jewish people's divine message. Does this distinction between Babylonian and Palestinian readings of the biblical past necessarily reflect a historical situation, or is it an attempt by the Babylonian narrator to define Babylonian identity markers compared to an imagined Palestinian iden-

---

58. Milikowsky, "Midrash as Fiction," 124–25.

59. See Hayes, "Displaced Self Perceptions," 249–89. Hayes argued that rabbinic authors/redactors of late antiquity felt a deep ambivalence about noncontextual, nonrational methods of exegesis (midrash). She further argued that the rabbinic authors of an aggadic passage in the Babylonian Talmud deployed various nonrabbinic "others"—heretics, sectarians, and Romans—in order to voice and thus grapple with their own radical doubt about their noncontextual (nonrational) methods of exegesis. In this example, we can see that to express their attitudes toward some unusual, though not completely nonrational methods of midrash, they can also employ a Palestinian rabbi, that is, the internal Other.

tity, and somehow to poke fun at this identity? The exchange of opinions between the rabbis seems ironic, and the narrator ironizes the relatively simple approach of the Babylonians to biblical interpretation. However, he distances himself slightly from the Palestinian's exegetical acrobatics, which makes his teachings enigmatic and addressed to only a small audience of scholars.

The self-irony of the Babylonian comes to a crescendo in the following section:

Said Rabbi Itzhak: Whoever says Rahab, Rahab, immediately has a seminal emission. Said Rab Naḥman to him: I say it and am not in any way affected. He said to him: This I told regarding those who know her and are her acquaintances (and call her name).[60]	אמר רבי יצחק: כל האומר רחב רחב מיד נקרי. אמר ליה רב נחמן: אנא אמינא, ולא איכפת לי! אמר ליה: כי קאמינא: ביודעה ובמכירה (ובמזכיר את שמה).

In continuation of the previous paradoxical statement, "the patriarch Jacob never died," comes another no less paradoxical statement, namely, that anyone who says the name of the biblical harlot Rahab[61] twice will become sexually aroused and ejaculate.[62] Once again, we expect the guest to trump the host. And indeed, Rab Naḥman is exceptionally naive. First, he tries to experiment on his own body and is surprised at the results: reciting the famous harlot's name twice does not, in fact, sexually arouse him. His guest remarks this woman's name has such an influence only on men who were close to her and knew her intimately. This can refer only to the male inhabitants of Jericho, who bought Rahab's sexual services, and they all died by the sword of Yehoshu'a's soldiers,[63] allowing the woman to begin her life anew, without witnesses to her previous professional experience.[64]

---

60. The words in parentheses are bracketed also in Malter's edition and are absent in many versions.

61. For example, according to the Aramaic Targum of Judg 2:1, she was a "food seller." Josephus declares that she was an innkeeper (*Ant*.5.12–15). In rabbinic Judaism, Rahab is a prostitute who ultimately repented; see b. Zevah. 116a–b. On the image of Rahab in the Babylonian Talmud in comparison with the Palestinian rabbinic literature, see Ilan, *Massekhet Ta'anit*, 94–96.

62. For a parallel version, see b. Meg. 15a.

63. Beyond the males of Jericho, the clients of Rahab who were aware of her profession included two unnamed spies, identified in rabbinic tradition with Caleb and Pinchas (Tanhuma Shelah 16:1).

64. I assume that even this odd statement about Rahab has exegetical roots in biblical verses that are not cited here and therefore cannot be reconstructed. The possible connec-

When they were about to part, [Rav Naḥman] said: Master, bless me. He replied: Let me tell you a parable: To what may this be compared? To a man who was journeying in the desert; he was hungry, weary and thirsty, and he lighted upon a tree the fruits of which were sweet, its shade pleasant, and a stream of water flowing beneath it; he ate of its fruits, drank of the water, and rested under its shade. When he was about to continue his journey, he said: Tree, O Tree, with what shall I bless you? Shall I say to thee: May thy fruits be sweet? They are sweet already; that your shade be pleasant? It is already pleasant; that a stream of water may flow beneath you? Lo, a stream of water flows already beneath thee; therefore, [I say]: May it be [God's] will that all the shoots taken from you be like unto you.' So also, with you. With what shall I bless you? With [the knowledge of the Torah?] You already possess [knowledge of the Torah]. With riches? You have riches already. With children? You have children already. Hence [I say]: May it be [God's] will that your offspring be like unto you.

כי הוו מיפטרי מהדדי אמר ליה: ליברכן מר. אמר ליה: אמשול לך משל, למה הדבר דומה. לאדם שהיה הולך במדבר והיה רעב ועיף וצמא, ומצא אילן שפירותיו מתוקין וצלו נאה, ואמת המים עוברת תחתיו. אכל מפירותיו, ושתה ממימיו, וישב בצילו. וכשביקש לילך, אמר: אילן אילן, במה אברכך? אם אומר לך שיהו פירותיך מתוקין, הרי פירותיך מתוקין; שיהא צילך נאה, הרי צילך נאה, שתהא אמת המים עוברת תחתיך, הרי אמת המים עוברת תחתיך. אלא: יהי רצון שכל נטיעות שנוטעין ממך יהיו כמותך. אף אתה, במה אברכך? אם בתורה - הרי תורה, אם בעושר - הרי עושר, אם בבנים - הרי בנים. אלא: יהי רצון שיהיו צאצאי מעיך כמותך.

In this final passage, the two rabbis are parting, and the guest has to bless the host before leaving. The blessing is well formulated and elegant; it reaffirms the advantage of the host, who was lightly ridiculed just a moment ago, and confirms that his chosen path is correct and does not need to be changed. The borders between the Palestinian and Babylonian are drawn—the stranger from Palestine has a sharp tongue; he is a joker and a brilliant manipulator of aggadic passages. This is the status quo. The ideal Babylonian may be clumsy in aggadah as a teacher, but he is superior to

---

tion to the previous story is that the "eternal life" of Jacob was not a part of "reality" but an element of a "virtual reality" or "fiction," just as the sex appeal of the biblical harlot is still valid, but only among the personages of the biblical narrative.

the Palestinian because he is an insider.⁶⁵ Or, returning to Derrida's terminology, the guest appears at the gates of the Host; he is politely welcomed and, soon after, honorably sent home. I do not detect here many hints of what we have called the interrupted self of the narrator. The Babylonian narrator seems to be at peace with his own self. He still needs the Palestinian Other to shape his own identity, but the collision between the host and the Other here is less dramatic and less painful than the collisions we witnessed in chapter 3.⁶⁶

8.4 Ulla: Life and Death in Babylonia

Now I continue to deal with stories about Babylonians accepting Palestinians in their land in Mesopotamia. The going East of a certain Ulla received attention not only in the Bavli but also in Palestinian texts. Ulla was a Palestinian scholar born in the Land of Israel who spent his life traveling between his homeland and Babylonia.⁶⁷ For this reason, he was called in the Palestinian Talmud Ulla Nahota, literally, "Ulla who goes down" (y. Kil. 9:3, 32d). Even though he is remembered as having spent much more time in Babylonia than in the Land of Israel, he remained a stranger in Babylonia; in the Babylonian narratives, he plays the role of a stranger or an internal Other, in comparison to whom the definitive features of the insider become clearer. In the following, several episodes about him will be analyzed.

b. Ta'anit 9b⁶⁸

Ulla chanced to be in Babylonia and observed light clouds. He told them: Remove the garments, for rain is now coming. However, no rain fell, and he exclaimed: As the Babylonians are liars, so too is their rain.	עולא איקלע לבבל. חזא פורחות. אמר להו: פנו מאני, דהשתא אתי מיטרא. לסוף לא אתי מיטרא. אמר: כי היכי דמשקרי בבלאי, הכי משקרי מיטרייהו.

---

65. Another typological collision between Rab Naḥman, as the ultimate Babylonian, in contrast to his Palestinian brethren could be learned from b. Hul. 124a, analyzed by Boyarin, *Traveling Homeland*, 60–65.

66. See the explanation of Christine Hayes, "'In the West, They Laughed at Him': The Mocking Realists of the Babylonian Talmud," *Journal of Law, Religion and State* 2 (2013): 137–67: In the rhetorical function of the phrase "in the west [the Land of Israel], they laughed at him/it" found in dialectal halakhic contexts in the Babylonian Talmud and here as well, the Palestinian Other serves the Babylonian narrator in shaping his own identity. See also Redfield, "Redacting Culture, 29–80

67. Albeck, *Introduction*, 302–3.

68. The doublet of this part of the tradition appears in in b. Pesah. 88a.

Ulla chanced to be in Babylonia and, observing that a basketful of dates was being sold for a zuz,[69] he exclaimed: A basketful of honey for a zuz and yet the Babylonians do not occupy themselves with the study of the Torah? During the night, he was in agony [from eating the dates], and he then exclaimed: A basketful of knives for a zuz and yet the Babylonians occupy themselves with the study of the Torah?

עולא איקלע לבבל, חזי מלא צנא דתמרי בזוזא. אמר: מלא צנא דדובשא בזוזא ובבלאי לא עסקי באורייתא? בליליא צערוהו. אמר: מלא צנא דסכינא בזוזא ובבלאי עסקי באורייתא?

The reader is faced here with a typical narrative mocking the Other. In the first story, the stranger from the distant Holy Land observes some known natural phenomenon, namely, light clouds, called *porehot*, a precursor to rain in his own country. The guest is so sure that this is the case in Babylonia as well that he demands of the host to collect all the garments scattered outside to protect them from the coming rain.[70] However, he fails to consider that he is now located in a different climate zone, as everyone probably knows. Ulla, who is Palestinian, is portrayed as naïve, a little like the unnamed Babylonian newcomer we observed earlier, who became breakfast for the lion he had revived.[71] Ulla does not know the obvious thing about Babylonia, and he fails to learn from his failures. Stymied, he reacts in a way that is probably typical of a Palestinian Other in the narrator's eyes. He is angered not only by the unpredictable weather of Babylonia but also by his Babylonian brethren. According to him, they are liars, and their country's climate is as treacherous as they are. Rumors about Palestinians hating the Babylonians, which we saw in the traditions discussed above, seem to have made their way to Babylonia and impressed our narrator. In this humorous depiction, the Other is gullible, harmful, and readily serves the narrator as a marker of the border separating himself from the Other.[72]

The second story is also humorous, but much more complicated. In his first days in Babylonia, Ulla is surprised by the prosperity demonstrated by the low price of such an essential fruit as dates, a significant component of the ancient menu. However, it is not enough for the Palestinian to admit the local market's benefits, for he adds something a bit

---

69. See Sperber, *Roman Palestine*, 103–7 and n. 70.
70. For a similar motif, see the story about Honi the rainmaker, m. Ta'an. 3:8.
71. See 43 above.
72. See Boyarin, *Traveling Homeland*, 56–57.

offensive. If the Babylonians could so easily satiate themselves, why do they not dedicate more time to Torah study? In other words, he implies, had we Palestinians been so wealthy and well-fed as you Babylonians, we would be much more learned than you are. Here the narrator is mocking the Palestinian's admiration of the Babylonians' wealth and his expressions of their superiority. But Ulla receives his comeuppance in the course of events. After over-indulging in Babylonia's wonderful fruits, he suffers from stomach upset. Following the typology of a mocked protagonist, he concludes that the local fruits' irresistible low price tempts the buyer to overeat. This allows reconciliation with the image of the despised Babylonian. Despite eating such dangerous food, these people make some progress in Torah learning and deserve to be praised for it. The gullible Palestinian is put in his place, and some elements of local patriotism are adjusted. The Babylonian claim is that they eat fruits that are much better and cheaper than in Palestine, and they learn Torah as diligently as the Palestinians, if not more so.

As we observed in our Palestinian cases, we see here too that the narrator sets up a comparison between Palestinians and Babylonians in order to define his own identity. This good-natured mockery does not make the Palestinian less honorable, at least in the case of Ulla, whose teachings are numerous in the Babylonian Talmud. What is new here is that the Babylonian narrator is aware of the Palestinians' ill feelings toward their Babylonian brethren, and he sees himself as obliged to respond. The Babylonian rabbis' awareness of their Palestinian brethren's hostility toward them, as well as their knowledge of the typical ethnic slurs directed again Babylonians, are explicitly presented in the following text.

b. Ketubbot 68a

| Said Abaye: And one of them is as good as two of us. Said Raba: When one of us, however, goes up there he is as good as two of them. For [you have the case of] Rabbi Jeremiah who, while here, did not understand what the Rabbis were saying, but when he went up there, he referred to us as stupid Babylonians.[73] | אמר אביי: וחד מינייהו עדיף כתרי מינן. אמר רבא: וחד מינן, כי סליק להתם, עדיף כתרי מינייהו. דהא רבי ירמיה, דכי הוה הכא, לא הוה ידע מאי קאמרי רבנן. כי סליק להתם, קרי לן בבלאי טפשאי. |

This short dialogue's participants are dated much later than Ulla and the other protagonists of our stories, but they are probably close in time to the narrator. The first interlocutor is full of admiration for the inhabitants of

---

73. Cf. b. Menah. 42a.

the Land of Israel, concluding that one of them is as good as two Babylonians. The second interlocutor does not disagree but adds that Babylonians, when they arrive in the study houses of the Land of Israel, are twice as good as the locals. He then describes the case of Rabbi Jeremiah, who was a less-than-outstanding student during his time in Babylonia. Still, when he arrived in the Land of Israel and became a learned man there, he began calling his former brethren "stupid Babylonians," meaning that he distanced himself from his own people and perceived himself as wiser than them.[74] Perhaps even further-reaching overtones can be detected here: for the Babylonian narrator, this new Palestinian, who is so eager to mock the Babylonians, was unable to understand anything when he was in their school, meaning that he was not so bright himself when he was among his Babylonian contemporaries. This limited student went to the Land of Israel and became so influential among the Palestinians that he could mock his former brethren, who had been his superiors when he was with them.[75]

Let us turn now to other narratives of Ulla's experiences on Babylonian soil.

b. Berakhot 51b

Ulla was once at the house of Rab Naḥman. They had a meal, and he said grace, and he handed the cup of benediction to Rab Naḥman. Rab Naḥman	עולא אקלע לבי רב נחמן. כריך ריפתא, בריך ברכת מזונא, יהב ליה כסא דברכתא לרב נחמן. אמר ליה רב נחמן: לישדר מר כסא דברכתא לילתא? אמר ליה: הכי אמר רבי יוחנן: אין פרי

---

74. On this sage in the Babylonian Talmud and in later rabbinic literature, see Hannan Gafni, "The Image of R. Jeremiah in the Nineteenth Century Haskalah Literature" [Hebrew], in *Between Babylonia and the Land of Israel: Studies in Honor of Isaiah M. Gafni*, ed. Geoffrey Herman, Meir Ben Shahar, and Aharon Oppenheimer (Jerusalem: Zalman Shazar, 2017), 419–36. Rabbi Jeremiah is mentioned in the Babylonian Talmud among those Babylonian rabbis who found their place in the Land of Israel in their youth (b. Ketub. 65a). A few dozen halakhic teachings of this rabbi are dispersed throughout the Babylonian Talmud. He is, however, especially famous for his extremely negative expressions toward his Babylonian brethren, which are not completely devoid of mockery (see, e.g., b. Pesah. 34b). Commonplace in all his anti-Babylonian sayings is that Babylonian learning is unclear and inferior in comparison with Palestinian learning (see b. Sanh. 24a). Interestingly, these sayings were carefully preserved in the Babylonian Talmud, probably evidencing the Babylonians' proclivity for self-criticism (as suggested by Beer Goldberg, "These are Words of BG …," *Hamagid* 11 (1887): 261; see also Gafni, "Image of R. Jeremiah," 422–23). The Babylonians were aware of their own preference for obscure scholasticism and were ready to poke fun at themselves for it, by collecting the venomous sayings of their own renegade.

75. Critical remarks against Babylonians who go to the Land of Israel are quite typical among Babylonian narrators; see 193 above and the story about Abaye and Rabbin in b. Ber. 47a and its analysis in Eliashiv Fraenkel, "Meetings and Conversations of Sages in Stories Regarding Halakhic Background in the Babylonian Talmud" [Hebrew] (PhD thesis, Bar-Ilan University, Ramat-Gan, Israel, 2015), 156–59.

said to him: Please send the cup of benediction to Yalta. He said to him: Thus, said Rabbi Yoḥanan: The fruit of a woman's body is blessed only from the fruit of a man's body since it says: "He will also bless the fruit of thy body" (Deut 7:13). It does not say "the fruit of her body," but "the fruit of thy body." It has been taught similarly: Whence do we know that the fruit of a woman's body is only blessed from the fruit of a man's body? Because it says: "He will also bless the fruit of thy body" (Deut 7:13). It does not say "the fruit of her body," but "the fruit of thy body." Meanwhile, Yalta heard, got up in a passion, entered the wine cellar, and broke four hundred jars of wine. Rab Naḥman said to him: Let the Master send her another cup? He sent it to her with a message: All that wine can be counted as a benediction. She returned answer: "Gossip comes from peddlers and vermin from rags."

בטנה של אשה מתברך אלא מפרי בטנו של איש, שנאמר: "וברך פרי בטנך" (דברים ז יג). "פרי בטנה" לא נאמר, אלא "פרי בטנך". תניא נמי הכי: רבי נתן אומר: מנין שאין פרי בטנה של אשה מתברך אלא מפרי בטנו של איש? שנאמר: "וברך פרי בטנך". "פרי בטנה" לא נאמר, אלא "פרי בטנך". אדהכי שמעה ילתא, קמה בזיהרא ועלתה לבי חמרא ותברא ארבע מאה דני דחמרא. אמר ליה רב נחמן: נשדר לה מר כסא אחרינא? שלח לה: כל האי נבגא דברכתא היא. שלחה ליה: ממהדורי מילי וממסמרטוטי כלמי.

The event described in this story is rather mundane. Nonetheless, it has much to tell us about gender roles in rabbinic society and causes the storyteller to doubt their justification.[76] Let us first introduce the cast of characters. Ulla takes advantage of his business trips to import and export knowledge and wisdom between the academies of Palestine and Babylonia. Here again, our hero finds himself in Babylonia. He is an important guest hosted by the venerable sage Rab Naḥman, whose wife is an independent and strong-minded woman named Yalta.[77]

Here, it seems that the guest is reclining in the company of the host, Rab Naḥman, but the host's spouse is silently present in the same room or in the vicinity. At the end of the meal, the guest, as dictated by etiquette, says the blessing after receiving the wine cup,[78] which he then passes

---

76. See the thoughtful commentary of Tal Ilan, *Mine and Yours Are Hers: Retrieving Women's History from Rabbinic Literature*, AGJU 41 (Leiden: Brill, 1997), 121–29.

77. Ilan claims that Yalta is actually not the wife of Rab Naḥman but an independent woman and an associate (*Mine and Yours Are Hers*, 121–22). This interesting proposition still deserves discussion.

78. The cup of blessing is a technical term in the Babylonian Talmud, which has a sig-

politely to the host. This return action—receiving the cup from the hands of the host and returning it to him—is an exchange of courtesies between the two protagonists, in which the host proclaims the guest as a good and honorable man.[79] However (probably unexpectedly for the guest), the host asks him to send the cup to Yalta, indicating that she is an important person who is worthy of honor. I suggest that this act is necessary because Rab Naḥman wants to emphasize that his wife should be rewarded for her act of hospitality. But his guest has a different view of gender relations. Being a learned man, he naturally does not respond directly to the host, claiming that women are not accorded such honor among Palestinians. Instead, he expresses this idea in the form of a scholastic construction, perhaps hoping that in this coded, erudite form his refusal will be lost on the mistress of the house.

How does Ulla respond? As usual, he cites a teaching of his mentor, Rabbi Yoḥanan. This teaching is unconnected to the current context of blessing after a meal but is instead an argument from the field of embryology. A child is often referred to as the fruit of the womb, and everyone knows that means a female's womb. Nevertheless, Ulla argues that the "blessing" that leads to the conception of a newborn is not in the mother's womb but rather in the father's loins. The woman bears the fetus, but the vital element comes from the man.[80]

This argument reaches the ears of the hostess, who strolls into the cellar and smashes every vessel in it (the number 400 is hyperbolic). The message to the guest seems to be that this was the last drink you will ever receive in my home.

Rab Naḥman, who appears nonplussed by the behavior of his wife, insists that the guest show her some respect. Now the guest is obliged to send a conciliatory message. However, it seems that he sends it after having left the host's house. Roughly, the message runs: "The other day

---

nificant body of definitions and discussions attached to it; see, e.g., b. Ber. 52a, 55a; b. Shabb. 76a; and b. Eruv. 29b, for halakhic definitions of the cup's size and contents. See also b. Pesah. 105b, for a discussion of the halakhot related to this cup during the ritual meal on the first night of Passover.

79. According to b. Sotah 38b, "R. Joshua b. Levi said: We only give the cup of blessing over which is recited the Grace after Meals to one who has a good eye, as it says, 'the generous man [man of good eye] is blessed, for he gives of his bread to the poor' (Proverbs 22, 9) Read it as 'shall bless.'" (About the good and evil eye see 77 n. 90 above.) Here in b. Sotah, there is a connection between the recitation of the Grace after Meals on the cup of blessing and the goodness of the person who is the reciter. The host here is boldly publicizing the good qualities of the guest.

80. The ancients (both Jews and Greeks) exaggerated the father's role in embryogenesis, being completely unaware of the existence of the ovum. See Reuven Kiperwasser, "Three Partners in a Person: The Metamorphoses of a Tradition and the History of an Idea," *Irano-Judaica 8: Studies Relating to Jewish Contacts with Persian Culture throughout the Ages*, ed. J. Rubanovich and G. Herman (Jerusalem: Ben-Zvi Institute, 2019), 393–438.

I did not send the blessings of the cup of wine to you. So, let all the wine that you spilled that day be the blessing of the wine, and things will return to their place." Yalta's answer is prompt and cutting: ממהדורי מילי ומסמרטוטי כלמי. The first expression, translated above as "gossip," literally means "dragging of words." She is probably hinting that dragging words is a profession of our Palestinian, who expects some financial support in exchange for them.[81] But the dragging of words is also a destructive process, like insects creeping out of rags. Yalta's response leaves the hapless guest with no hope.

The finale of the story, as persuasively shown by Tal Ilan, seems to be a daring paraphrase of a verse from the book of Ben Sira 42:13: "From a garment [בגד] comes a moth [עש, סס] and from a woman the wickedness of women."[82] Ben Sira, a sage of the Second Temple period, whose book was known in Babylonia, was known for his misogynistic outlook. In this chapter, he claims that women's bad qualities can be compared to a process akin to that of a moth destroying garments. The narrator, who has presumably read Ben Sira, puts into the mouth of Yalta a mirror image of Ben Sira's phrase. In that mirror, men who produce words devoid of value are likened to insects swarming in old clothes.

Through Yalta, the talmudic narrator criticizes a widespread male prejudice, namely, making alliances with a woman.[83] Yalta here enters into dialogue not only with the moderate misogyny of Ulla but also with the acerbic misogyny of Ben Sira. In her intertextual manipulation of this Second Temple text, she demonstrates that a woman can enter the ring with the sages and emerge the victor.[84]

Let us now turn to a story about the death of this Palestinian in Babylonia.

b. Ketubbot 111a	y. Kil'ayim 9:4, 32c[85]
עולא הוה רגיל דהוה סליק לארץ ישראל. נח נפשיה בחוץ לארץ. אתו אמרי ליה לרבי אלעזר. אמר: אנת עולא "על אדמה טמאה תמות" (עמוס ז, יז). אמרו לו: ארונו בא. אמר להם: אינו דומה קולטתו מחיים לקולטתו לאחר מיתה.	עולא נחותא הוה אי[ת]דמך תמן. שרי בכי. אמרין ליה מה לך בכי. אנן מסקין לך לארעא דישראל. אמר לון ומה הנייה לי. אנא מובד מרגליתי גו ארעא מסאבתא. לא דומה הפולטה בחיק אמו לפולטה בחיק נכריה.

---

81. The same verb could be used to mean harassing a woman.

82. See Tal Ilan, *Integrating Women into Second Temple History*, TSAJ 76 (Tübingen: Mohr Siebeck 1999), 176–79.

83. On the formation of alliances between rabbis and women, see Kiperwasser, "Wives of Commoners."

84. Another possible explanation, suggested to me by Daniel Boyarin, is that both Yalta and Ben Sira are using a common proverb.

85. Academia ed., 76.

Ulla was in the habit of traveling to the Land of Israel. He died outside the Land of Israel. When people came and reported this to Rabbi Eleazar, he exclaimed, You Ulla, "you yourself will die on impure land" (Amos 7:17).[86] His coffin, they said to him, has arrived. Receiving a man in his lifetime, he replied, is not the same as receiving him after his death.	Ulla, who goes down [*nahota*], was about to die there (i.e., in Babylonia). He began to weep. They asked him: Why are you crying? Will we not bring your body to be buried there? He said to them: And what good does it do me if I lose my pearl [my soul] in an unclean land? One who gives it up in the bosom of one's mother is not the same one who exudes it in the bosom of a foreign woman.

The same plot is retold here by two different narrators—one in Palestine and one in Babylonia—but it has a shared nucleus. Ulla, the traveler, dies during his travels.[87] However, the Yerushalmi shows the dying person himself at a moment of distress, crying. He is upset to end his life far away from his homeland.[88] The people around his deathbed, namely, the Babylonians, do not understand the sorrow of the Palestinian; for them, the chief value of the Land of Israel is as a place in which to be buried. The Palestinians often mocked this peculiar belief.[89] They understood Ulla's sorrow—dying in Babylonia and then suffering the long route to the promised land in the eschatological era. However, the real reason for his weeping is different. The explanation resembles the parable mentioned above of the motherland and the stepmother-land.[90] Ulla compares his death to a precious stone falling out of his body, which had been a storage place for that treasure.[91] To lose the soul abroad, on contaminated foreign soil, is, according to Ulla, much worse than to lose it in the soil of the Land of Israel. To die overseas is like going to the bosom of the stepmother, literally, to a foreign woman. To die in the Land of Israel is to put your soul in the bosom of a birth mother. I think that behind this metaphoric usage lies an interpretation of Job 1:21: עָרֹם יָצָתִי מִבֶּטֶן אִמִּי, וְעָרֹם אָשׁוּב שָׁמָּה: "Naked

---

86. This is a paraphrase of Amos 7:17: וְאַתָּה, עַל-אֲדָמָה טְמֵאָה תָּמוּת, "[Your land will be measured and divided up], and you yourself will die in an impure land."

87. The Yerushalmi unambiguously notes that Ulla is an expatriate in Babylonia, whereas the wording of Babylonian Talmud is evasive: Ulla used to wander between the two countries. It is possible, as proposed to me by Geoffrey Herman, that the Babylonian narrator is trying to assign to Ulla Babylonian citizenship.

88. Sorrow of dying far from the place where a person was born is a leitmotif of this passage in the Yerushalmi; and see Kiperwasser, "Elihoref and Ahiah," 255–73.

89. See 46 above.

90. See 60, 78, 176 above.

91. Up to this point my explanation is quite like the one proposed recently by Hezser, *Rabbinic Body Language*, 220–21, which I came across only after writing this chapter.

I came from my mother's womb, and naked shall I return." Ulla understands death as an opportunity to reunite with his ancestors' land, not by being buried in it but through the departure of soul from body there.

It is doubtful whether all these arguments are known to the Babylonian narrator. In his story, the plot begins after Ulla has already died in Babylonia. Some Babylonians coming to the Land of Israel visit a local sage (R. Eleazar ben Pedat, the former Babylonian?) and tell him the sad news about Ulla's death. The Palestinian rabbi laments his colleague's death using the same simile used by Ulla in the Palestinian story—it is terrible to drop the precious stone of the soul in an impure foreign land. However, if we analyze the nature of the lament, its meaning turns out to be critical of the deceased. The Palestinian uses the saying of the bitter prophet Amos against his enemy, the false prophet Amaziah, stating, "Therefore thus says the Lord: Your wife shall be a harlot in the city, and your sons and your daughters shall fall by the sword, and your land shall be divided by line, and you yourself shall die in an unclean land, and Israel shall surely be led away captive out of his land" (Amos 7:17). Therefore, lamenting a colleague, the Palestinian implies that the deceased was punished for his deeds. He is not at all sympathetic to the *naḥotei* wandering between the Land of Israel and Babylonia.[92] He considers this occupation doubtful and leaving the Land of Israel for that purpose dangerous and sinful.[93] The lament includes confirmation of the fact that the deceased was practically cursed for his lifestyle. The Babylonians, however, who brought the sad news to the Palestinian colleague, still suppose that the truly dreadful thing about dying in a foreign land is being buried there. Therefore, they announce to their host that they have brought the deceased to be buried in the pure soil. They do not understand that the rabbi is opposed to spending one's life and giving up one's soul in an impure land. For him, to bring the body of the deceased to the pure Land is entirely unnecessary. Moreover, the explanation of the burial as a return to the mother's bosom is completely absent in the Babylonian Talmud narrative. For Babylonians, the Land of Israel, despite all its holiness, is not a mother.[94] What is a part of their tradition is that a Palestinian rabbi is depicted here as indifferent to the destiny of one of the most prominent *naḥotei*. The Babylonian narrator is aware of Palestinians' lack of appreciation for the importing of Palestinian literacy to Babylonia and their lack of sympathy for Babylonians' burial customs. Perhaps, then, we are reading a Babylonian expression of sympathy toward the wandering Palestinian. The narrator intends to relate that, while Ulla was a stranger in Babylonia all his life, when his dead body was finally brought to the Holy Land, according to the Babylo-

---

92. On *naḥotei*, see 6–7 above.
93. See 34 above.
94. See 36–37 above.

nian rabbinic practice, he was treated by his compatriots as a stranger and was cursed rather than blessed.

In this chapter, we have seen the Palestinian narrator send his heroes East, and the Babylonian narrator receive Palestinians in the East. The Palestinian narrator tends to lack sympathy for either his protagonists or the journey's destination. Babylonia, despite being rich and attractive, is still a dystopian place. Retelling the violent collisions between Palestinians and Others, the narrators do not even try to unite the Palestinian's interrupted self. Going East is a dreadful thing in their minds, and there is no need to sympathize with the border-crossers. In the mirror image provided by Babylonian narration, the same Palestinian newcomer is an important figure, almost as a Babylonian newcomer is in Palestine. This is not surprising, considering that Palestinians and Babylonians share a common cultural value—Torah study. However, the Palestinian is presented as gullible and weak enough for the narrator to distance himself from him, even while expressing a necessary sympathy. In this distance, the borderline between the insider and the Other is drawn and the shaping of local identity takes place. The Babylonian local identity, as distinct from the identity of the Palestinian, is predicated on minor differences in literacy and the use of the language. The Babylonian narrator, who can admire the brilliance of the Palestinians' exegetic speculations and their sense of humor, presents the local as dull, punctilious, and unable to understand a joke. There is a Babylonian "importance of being earnest," a quality that does not jive with what we find in the Babylonian Talmud's literary tradition (which is, in fact, full of humor).[95] Some Babylonian literary passages are quite playful. Still, the Babylonian self-representation as a serious person fits well with his fictional character as constructed by the Babylonian narrator. Moreover, the Babylonian narrator presents independent women who take their importance seriously. This impulse is much less present with the Palestinian narrator.

---

95. See Boyarin, *Socrates and the Fat Rabbis*, 191–92.

Epilogue

Going Back and Forth

This book began with the East–West trajectory, but in the course of my wanderings through narrative spaces, I discovered that the dynamics of the rabbinic universe are not fully illuminated without the reverse trajectory. Accordingly, in these seven chapters, we have migrated with our Babylonian heroes to the Roman Land of Israel and with our Palestinian strangers to Sasanian Babylonia. I introduced my study as a narratological inquiry and defined my aim as exploring how, behind the stories of acceptance of Jewish migrants in the communities of the Land of Israel and Babylonia, we find the contours of the self of the rabbinic narrators. In the first chapter, I analyzed humorous stories that mock the Other. I tried to show how behind these stories lies a painful misunderstanding between the insider and the outsider. As in the tale of the Babylonian fool devoured by a lion, the Other was brought to the host's gate; after a humorous but violent situation, his remains were left there. In Derrida's terminology, the mocking stories about Babylonian immigrants are attempts by the narrator to protect himself from possible interruption. In ridiculing the Other, he keeps him at bay and his own role as host intact.

In the second chapter, I presented the narratives of an ongoing dialogue between two important loci in the Palestinian narrator's symbolic geography. As is to be expected, the Land of Israel is more significant for Palestinian narrators than places abroad. However, when describing Babylonia's inferiority and embellishing it with dystopian features, the narrator is preoccupied with defining how Babylonians will never be able to become full Palestinians even if they relocate to the Holy Land. Their learning is inferior; they are not only unfamiliar with the commandments of the Holy Land, but they do not even know the proper usage of the bath. They are so narrow-minded that they cannot even find the shortcut to the Holy Land, concealed in their own country.

Moreover, as I showed in chapter 6, Babylonians remain, at least according to a minority opinion, culpable for the sins of their ancestors, who were unwilling to return to the Holy Land in the time of Ezra. Nonetheless, they are desirable dialogue partners for the Palestinian narrator. For him, the Babylonian figure evokes sympathy, and the Palestinian makes a modest attempt to embrace the stranger, as I discussed in chapters 2 and 3. Aside from the necessity of accepting the significant Other generously, one cannot forget that Babylonia is the land of Abraham and, in a manner of speaking, the homeland of Judaism. The powerful metaphor of a mother vis-à-vis a stepmother was thus invented, serving both participants in the intercultural dialogue. Palestinians were aware of cultural differences between them and the Babylonian immigrants and described how these differences often led to inconveniences and misunderstandings. At least some of them, however, were no less aware of the cultural richness of the Babylonians and thus showed an openness to absorbing Babylonian cultural features, as shown in chapter 4. The Land of Babylonia and the Land of Israel remained connected in the perception of all by numerous cultural commonalities. The connection between these two essential loci was permanently supported by ambassadors traveling back and forth. This traffic formed and transformed the identity of these groups. Through the process of comparison, new forms of identity came into existence. Thus, it turns out that in Palestinian rabbinic literature, in numerous narrative collisions between Palestinian rabbis and their Babylonian colleagues, another Other appears—the unlearned Palestinian man. Some of these stories serve the Palestinian narrators as demarcations between their own identity and the identity of their unlearned compatriots, who are even more distant than the Babylonian foreigner. Comparably, in the Babylonian Talmud, some of the collision stories between Palestinians and Babylonians become stories in which the mainstream Babylonians demarcate themselves from other Babylonians—the bad-mannered inhabitants of Nehardea.

Traveling in the narrated universe, wherever one starts—whether it is from West to East or East to West—one ends up at the very center of the narrator's universe, namely, in his own self. Having started with the Palestinian narrator's split self, I will conclude with it as well. We will complete our wanderings through the narrative expanses of the East and the West by analyzing a short story in which the traffic of the desirable but dangerous Babylonians from the East to the West receives its worthiest embodiment from the Palestinian narrator. In other words, the split parts of the Palestinian narrator's self finally come together.

y. Sanhedrin 3:9 (3:6), 20d[1]

Rabbi Yehoshu'a ben Levi said: One may receive witnesses, not in the parties' presence and issue a decision.	ר' יהושע בן לוי אמר: מקבלין העדות בלא בעל דין ועבדין ליה גזר דין.

---

1. Academia ed., 1285.

As the following: Kahana died and had willed his estate to Rabbi Yoshiah. Rabbi Leazar heard witnesses, not in the presence (of the heirs), and handed the estate to Rabbi Yoshiah. Furthermore, the estate contained books (scrolls?). Rabbi Leazar wrote to (Kahana's) heirs: Books that came into the possession of the Land of Israel cannot be taken outside the Land [of Israel].

כהדא: כהנא דמך ושבק ירתו לר' יאשיה וקביל רבי לעזר סהדו דלא באפוי וזכי לר' יאשיה. ולא עוד אלא דשבק ספרים. כתב רבי לעזר לירתוי: ספרים שזכת בהן ארץ ישראל אין מוציאין אותן חוצה לארץ.

This is a halakhic story with a modest purpose—to illustrate the ruling formulated by Rabbi Yehoshu'a ben Levi that a court can decide on a case even in the absence of one of the parties.[2] A story follows to support this ruling, about a foreigner, apparently a Babylonian, named Kahana who died in the Land of Israel and willed his estate to his colleague, a rabbi named Joshia. Even though the name is a typical Palestinian one, the Rabbi Joshia mentioned in the Yerushalmi is usually one of the students of Rabbi Yoḥanan,[3] meaning that he belonged to the same generation as the Kahana we met earlier. Therefore, if this identification is correct, it brings us to an unexpected and exciting epilogue to the story of Kahana's migration to the Land of his ancestors. It may be inferred that he returned to the Promised Land and lived or at least died there. Even though the deceased had relatives in Babylonia, he decided to leave his estate to another rabbi, another student of their shared master, Rabbi Yoḥanan. This decision was probably not enthusiastically accepted by the family of the deceased, who accordingly applied to the court for restitution.

As is customary according to Palestinian halakhah, the judge, Rabbi Leazar,[4] decided to uphold Kahana's will and ruled that the inheritance would go to his Palestinian friend. Up to this point, everything in this story was no more than a halakhic illustration supporting the previous discussion. Immediately following this part of the story, however, the narrator mentions a significant portion of the estate—the deceased's library. This addition plays no role in the halakhic discussion. Books, as material items with a specific value, are part of the estate, and if all the estate should be given to the friend of the deceased, why should the judge mention these items separately? Apparently, the books here figure as the sym-

---

2. This is completely forbidden by Babylonian halakhah; see b. B. Qam. 112b.
3. Albeck, *Introduction*, 243.
4. It is difficult to know which one of the bearers of this name in this generation of scholars is meant here. It could either be Eleazar ben Pedat, a former Babylonian whom we already met, or it could be any other contemporaneous rabbi; see Albeck, *Introduction*, 224, 227.

bolic inheritance of the dead Babylonian rabbi. These books, which are not Torah scrolls, are the personal library of the sage. We know little about such libraries. Scholars' prevailing tendency is to see rabbinic culture, in the East and the West, as predominantly oral. At the same time, book possession and book collecting are sporadically mentioned in rabbinic literature.[5] It is my belief that this story about the death of such an iconic figure as Kahana was introduced here not only for halakhic purposes but also to allude to Kahana's cultural heritage. This is why the books are not lumped together with the rest of the estate but rather are viewed as something special and separate. The narrator must now leave aside his everyday Aramaic language and formulate a ruling on the books in the much more poetic Hebrew: "Books that came into possession by the Land of Israel cannot be taken outside the Land." Suddenly, the story about the estate of one particular foreigner who dies without close descendants in the Land becomes the story about how the Land of Israel is awarded an inheritance of great cultural value. The symbolic mother and stepmother as metaphors for the Land of Israel and Babylonia are nowhere to be seen here. Yet the story is framed with that very assumption: that for the Palestinian narrator the Babylonian Other belongs to him, to his Land, to his culture, to his textual community. This is the reason why the Palestinian narrator is not satisfied with the dead bones of Babylonians who are so annoyingly eager to be buried in the Holy Land; he wants them as part and parcel of life in the Land of Israel. He needs the books of the Babylonians to be on the shelves of his libraries; he needs their gullible presence at the markets and in the bathhouses; he needs the Babylonians' erudition to be incorporated into his own; he needs the Babylonian's oft-derided figure for the construction of his own identity. As a good host, he knows that real hospitality is unconditional; therefore, he needs to embrace the Other, causing the interruption mentioned above of his own self. The books of the deceased, if someone does not throw them into the fire, find their way to library shelves, and their fate is either to be taken over by the culture whose frameworks they inhabit or to be rejected by that culture. Kahana's library, in accordance with his will, is now in the possession of his friend, but, according to the judge's poetic ruling, the books have in fact become the possession of the Land of Israel, which not so long ago was defined by the deceased as a cruel mother.

According to both Talmudim, Kahana found his final resting place in the land of his ancestors. The Palestinian rabbinic tradition records an

---

5. See Shlomo Na'eh, "The Structure and Division of Torat Kohanim A (Scrolls)," *Tarbiz* 66 (1997): 507–12; Na'eh, "The Craft of Memory: Memory Structures and Textual Patterns in Rabbinic Literature," *Mehqerei Talmud III: Talmudic Studies Dedicated to the Memory of Professor Ephraim E. Urbach* [Hebrew], ed. Y. Sussman and D. Rosenthal (Jerusalem: Magnes, 2005), 543–59, here 555–56.

unrequited love story in which love is stronger than death. Not only does Kahana find his eternal rest in the Land of Israel, but his cultural heritage becomes incorporated into it. The narrators of the Babylonian Talmud claim neither his bones nor his books because they believe that Kahana belongs to them, as does the Torah, despite the Palestinians' view of the matter.

Returning to the idea of culture as a machine that continuously produces meaning,[6] we have seen how two related rabbinic cultures generated production while constructing relations with each other. The above stories show that the Palestinian rabbis' culture contains some harsh xenophobic expressions. Still, this culture is drawn to the Other and strongly desires his approval and incorporation. The Babylonian rabbis' culture expresses fewer xenophobic utterances toward the Palestinians, and in general is much more tolerant. Yet this culture, too, seems to need an internal Other for constructing its own identity, albeit not necessarily a Palestinian one.

The central premise of this book is that the narratives of Going West and Going East not only reflect the ongoing and intensive interaction between the rabbinic elites of Palestine and Babylonia throughout late antiquity; rabbinic figures from the "other" rabbinic center also served as "internal Others" through whom rabbinic authors articulated the nature and legitimacy of their scholastic practices, knowledge, and authority. Scholarship has demonstrated that rabbinic literature deploys the figure of the religious or ethnic "Other" as a means of articulating the rabbinic self; it stands to reason that the "internal other" would loom particularly large in the rabbinic imagination. A host of scholars have demonstrated that Jewish non-rabbis, pagan Romans, Christians of various kinds, Sasanian Persians, Jewish heretics, and so on, all feature prominently in rabbinic narratives that aim to delineate the boundaries of rabbinic communities, modes of piety, and theological commitments. If that is the case, how indeed might one group of rabbis have responded to other rabbis whose styles of learning, norms of comportment, and speech patterns reflect a different cultural context and scholastic milieu? I suggest that the sheer volume of interest in the "internal Other" decreases rabbinic engagement with the more distant Other. The number and range of sources focusing on this intra-rabbinic encounter bolster scholars' core contention that the "internal Other" was pivotal in the rabbinic construction of self. Derrida's hermeneutic model provides a useful framework for understanding the expression of cultural values in the rabbinic stories I discuss. His guest/host terminology perfectly suits the contents of the stories analyzed above and helps shape the discussion about the acceptance of the Other in rab-

---

6. See 12 above.

binic culture. Above, I explore stories about a particular Babylonian foreigner who enters a Galilean city. Following convention, the hosts must accept him, accord him equal rights, and not treat him as a stranger. If the guests are equal members of the same textual community, they are also the promised land's heirs. In this case, though, the hospitality leads to violence and the construction of the narrator's interrupted self. This painful interruption of the self ultimately becomes a way of obtaining a new self, a new identity. In this way, I identify three different selves of the rabbinic narrator regarding acceptance of the internal Other, namely, the Babylonian in his sojourn in the Land of Israel. The first two are strongly attracted to the Babylonian Other because they shape their own identity in relation to his. The third, as conveyed by the Babylonian narrator, mostly maintains his distance.

1. The empathic self of the Palestinian narrator appears in a series of three stories in y. Berakhot and related texts. This self, a tortured one, discloses an internal conflict. He is torn between xenophobia and philoxenia. He seeks a compromise between the obligation to embrace the other and the need to put him in his place—that is, to establish distance. The third chapter's stories are narrated from the perspective of this interrupted self of the Palestinian narrator. There, we found no attempt to balance the discontinuity of the self by restricting the guest's freedom or alienating him.

2. Palestinian rabbinic culture also produced another self, however, which found expression in one single, rather late work of Palestinian rabbinic literature, namely, Song of Songs Rabbah. This work's self is fully consolidated, allowing its xenophobia to triumph over its philoxenia, segregating the Other and justifying this segregation. This self is also interrupted by its nature. Still, its discontinuity, in this case, is counterbalanced by an attempt to restrict the Other's rights and to estrange the guest by scrutinizing his genealogy.

3. The third self is the benevolent one of the Babylonian narrators, as was fixed in b. Ketubbot 112a. It does not suffer the dilemma of embracing or rejecting, but it is not a self that permits alienating the inner Other. The Babylonian self belongs to a confident narrator who has long ago constructed his personality, and the Palestinian Other serves only to add nuance to some features of his identity.[7] This self, too, is partially interrupted—but is also much more complacent.

Both rabbinic cultures, then, use the figure of the internal Other to reflect on their own identity. Yet there is a notable difference: the Babylonian Other was more significant for constructing the Palestinian self than the Palestinian was for the Babylonians.

---

7. Gruen, too, argues for a diasporic self-confidence and claims that diasporic Jewish literature uses humor and irony as analytical tools (*Diaspora*, 180–81, 193, 210–12).

Bibliography

Abrahams, Roger D. *Afro-American Folktales*. New York: Pantheon, 1985.
Agamben, Giorgio. *Means without End: Notes on Politics*. Theory out of Bounds. Minneapolis: University of Minnesota Press, 2000.
Albeck, Chanoch. *Introduction to the Talmud, Bavli and Yerushalmi* [Hebrew]. Tel Aviv: Dvir, 1969.
———. "Studies in Babylonian Talmud" [Hebrew]. *Tarbiz* 9 (1938): 163–78.
Alexander, Elizabeth Shanks. *Transmitting Mishnah: The Shaping Influence of Oral Tradition*. Cambridge: Cambridge University Press, 2006.
Alon, Gedaliah. *The Jews in Their Land in the Talmudic Age, 70–640 C.E.* Translated by Gershon Levi. 2 vols. Jerusalem: Magnes, 1980–1984.
Amit, Aharon. "The Epithets ברפחין, בן פיחה and ברפחתי and Their Development in Talmudic Sources" [Hebrew]. *Tarbiz* 72 (2003): 489–504.
Anderson, Benedict. *Imagined Communities: Reflections on the Origin and Spread of Nationalism*. London: Verso, 1983.
Arad, Moti (Mordechai). *Sabbath Desecrators with Parrhesia: A Talmudic Legal Term and Its Historic Context* [Hebrew]. New York: Jewish Theological Seminary of America, 2009.
Arendt, Hannah. "We Refugees." Pages 110–19 in *Altogether Elsewhere: Writers on Exile*. Edited by Marc Robinson. San Diego: Harcourt Brace, 1996.
Arubas, Benni, and Rina Talgam. "Jews, Christians, and 'Minim': Who Really Built and Used the Synagogue at Capernaum – A Stirring Appraisal." Pages 237–74 in *Knowledge and Wisdom: Archaeological and Historical Essays in Honor of Leah Di Segni*. Edited by Giovanni C. Bottini, L. Daniel Chrupcala, and Joseph Patrich. Milan: Edizioni Terra Santa, 2014.
Averbach, Moses. *Jewish Education in the Mishnaic and Talmudic Period*. Jerusalem: Reuven Maas; Baltimore: Hebrew College, 1983.
Bacher, Wilhelm. *Die Agada der Palästinensischen Amoräer*. 3 vols. Strassburg: Karl J. Trübner, 1892–1899. Repr., Hildesheim: Olms, 1992.
———. *Tradition und Tradenten in den Schulen Palästinas und Babyloniens: Studien und Materialien zur Entstehungsgeschichte des Talmuds.*

Schriften herausgegeben von der Gesellschaft zur förderung der Wissenschaft des Judentums. Leipzig: Gustav Fock, 1914.

Baker, Cynthia. "Bodies, Boundaries, and Domestic Politics in a Late Ancient Marketplace." *Journal of Medieval and Early Modern Studies* 26 (1996): 391–418.

Bakhos Carol. "Reading against the Grain: Humor and Subversion in Midrashic Literature." Pages 71–80 in *Narratology, Hermeneutics, and Midrash: Jewish, Christian, and Muslim from Late Antiquity through to Modern Times*. Edited by Gerhard Langer and Constanza Cordoni. Poetik, Exegese und Narrative. Göttingen: Vandenhoeck & Ruprecht, 2014.

Balberg, Mira. *Blood for Thought: The Reinvention of Sacrifice in Early Rabbinic Literature*. Oakland: University of California Press, 2017.

Balberg, Mira, and Haim Weiss. "'That Old Man Shames Us': Aging, Liminality, and Antinomy in Rabbinic Literature." *JSQ* 25 (2018): 17–41.

Bank, L. "Rabbi Zeira et Rab Zeira." *Revue des études Juives* 38 (1899): 47–63.

Bar-Ilan, Meir. "The Attitude toward Mamzerim in Jewish Society in Late Antiquity." *Jewish History* 14 (2000): 125–70.

Barton, Carlin A. *The Sorrows of the Ancient Romans: The Gladiator and the Monster*. Princeton: Princeton University Press, 1995.

Beard, Mary. *Laughter in Ancient Rome: On Joking, Tickling, and Cracking Up*. Sather Classical Lectures 71. Berkeley: University of California Press, 2015.

Becker, Hans-Jürgen. *Die großen rabbinischen Sammelwerke Palästinas: Zur literarischen Genese von Talmud Yerushalmi und Midrash Bereshit Rabba*. TSAJ 70. Tübingen: Mohr Siebeck, 1999.

———. "Texts and History: The Dynamic Relationship between Talmud Yerushalmi and Genesis Rabbah." Pages 145–61 in *The Synoptic Problem in Rabbinic Literature*. Edited by Shaye J. D. Cohen. BJS 326. Providence, RI: Brown Judaic Studies, 2000.

Beer, Moshe. *The Babylonian Amoraim: Aspects of Economic Life* [Hebrew]. Ramat-Gan: Bar Ilan University Press, 1982.

———. *The Babylonian Exilarchate* [Hebrew]. Tel Aviv: Devir, 1976.

———. "Torah and Derekh Eretz." *Bar-Ilan* 2 (1964): 148–51.

Ben-Eliyahu, Eyal. "The Rabbinic Polemic against Sanctification of Sites." *JSJ* 40 (2009): 260–80.

Benjamin, Isaac. *The Invention of Racism in Classical Antiquity*. Princeton: Princeton University Press, 2004.

Benovitz, Moshe. *Talmud Ha-Igud: BT Berakhot, Chapter 1, With Comprehensive Commentary* [Hebrew]. Jerusalem: Union for Interpretation of the Talmud, 2006.

Ben Shahar, Meir. "The Restoration in Rabbinic Literature: Palestine and Babylonia from Past to Present" [Hebrew]. *Zion* 79 (2014): 19–52.

Ben-Shalom, Israel. *The School of Shammai and the Zealots' Struggle against*

Rome [Hebrew]. Jerusalem: Yad Izhak Ben-Zvi and Ben-Gurion University of the Negev Press, 1993.
Bergson, Henri. *Laughter: An Essay on the Meaning of the Comic.* Translated by Cloudesley Brereton and Fred Rothwell. London: Macmillan, 1900.
Besa. *The Life of Shenoute.* Edited by David N. Bell. Kalamazoo, MI: Cistercian Publications, 1983.
Binyamin, Elizur. "Pesikta Rabbati: Introductory Chapters" [Hebrew]. PhD diss., Hebrew University, 2000.
Bivar, Adrian D. H. "Weights and Measures," *Encyclopaedia Iranica online.* https://brillonline.com/entries/encyclopaedia-iranica/weights-and-measures-i-pre-islamic-period-COM_10392?s.num=14
Blumenkranz, Bernhard. *Juifs et Chrétiens dans le monde occidental, 430–1096.* Études juives 2. Paris: Mouton, 1960.
Bohman, James. "Reflexivity, Agency and Constraint: The Paradoxes of Bourdieu's Sociology of Knowledge." *Social Epistemology* 11 (1997): 171–86.
Bond, Helen. "You'll Probably Get Away with Crucifixion: How Brian (and Jesus) Ended Up on a Roman Cross." Pages 113–26 in *Jesus and Brian: Exploring the Historical Jesus and His Times via Monty Python's Life of Brian.* Edited by Joan E. Taylor. London: Bloomsbury T&T Clark, 2015.
Bourdieu, Pierre. *The Logic of Practice.* Translated by Richard Nice. Stanford, CA: Stanford University Press, 1990.
———. *Outline of a Theory of Practice.* Translated by Richard Nice. Cambridge Studies in Social Anthropology 16. New York: Cambridge University Press, 1977.
———. "Social Space and Symbolic Power." *Sociological Theory* 7 (1989): 14–25.
Boyarin, Daniel. *Border Lines: The Partition of Judaeo-Christianity.* Divinations. Philadelphia: University of Pennsylvania Press, 2004.
———. "The Christian Invention of Judaism: The Theodosian Empire and the Rabbinic Refusal of Religion." *Representations* 85 (2004): 21–57.
———. *A Traveling Homeland: The Babylonian Talmud as Diaspora.* Divinations. Philadelphia: University of Pennsylvania Press, 2015.
———. *Socrates and the Fat Rabbis.* Chicago: University of Chicago Press, 2009.
Braude, William G. *Pesikta Rabbati: Discourses for Feasts, Fasts, and Special Sabbaths.* 2 vols. Yale Judaica Series 18. New Haven: Yale University Press, 1968.
Brennan, Brian. "The Conversion of the Jews of Clermont in AD 576." *Journal of Theological Studies* NS 36 (1985): 321–37.
Brodsky, David. *A Bride without a Blessing: A Study in the Redaction and*

Content of Massekhet Kallah and Its Gemara. TSAJ 118. Tübingen: Mohr Siebeck, 2006.

———. "From Disagreement to Talmudic Discourse: Progymnasmata and the Evolution of a Rabbinic Genre." Pages 173–231 in *Rabbinic Traditions between Palestine and Babylonia.* Edited by Ronit Nikolsky and Tal Ilan. Ancient Judaism and Early Christianity 89. Leiden: Brill, 2014.

———. "Why Did the Widow Have a Goat in Her Bed? Jewish Humor and Its Roots in the Talmud and Midrash." Pages 13–32 in *Jews and Humor.* Edited by Leonard J. Greenspoon. Studies in Jewish Civilization 22. Proceedings of the Twenty-Second Annual Symposium of the Klutznick Chair in Jewish Civilization, Harris Center for Judaic Studies. West Lafayette, IN: Purdue University Press, 2011.

Brody, Robert. "The Epistle of Sherira Gaon." Pages 253–64 in *Rabbinic Texts and the History of Late-Roman Palestine.* Edited by M. Goodman and P. Alexander. Oxford: Oxford University Press, 2010.

Bubandt, Nils, and Rane Willerslev. "The Dark Side of Empathy: Mimesis, Deception, and the Magic of Alterity." *Comparative Studies in Society and History* 57 (2015): 5–34.

Buchler, Adolph. *The Political and the Social Leaders of the Jewish Community of Sepphoris in the Second and Third Centuries.* London: Jew's College, 1909.

Clarke, John R. *Looking at Laughter: Humor, Power, and Transgression in Roman Visual Culture, 100 B.C.–A.D. 250.* Berkeley: University of California Press, 2007.

Cohen, Shaye J. D. *The Beginnings of Jewishness: Boundaries, Varieties, Uncertainties.* Hellenistic Culture and Society 31. Berkeley: University of California Press, 1999.

Coleman, Katheleen M. "Fatal Charades: Roman Executions Staged as Mythological Enactments." *Journal of Roman Studies* 80 (1990): 44–73.

Cook, John Granger. "Crucifixion as Spectacle in Roman Campania." *NovT* 54 (2012): 68–100.

———. "Envisioning Crucifixion: Light from Several Inscriptions and the Palatine Graffito." *NovT* 50 (2008): 262–85.

———. "Roman Crucifixions: From the Second Punic War to Constantine." *ZNW* 104 (2013): 1–32.

Critchley, Simon. *On Humour.* Thinking in Action. London: Routledge, 2011.

Danby Herbert, ed. *The Mishnah.* Oxford: Clarendon, 1933.

Derrida, Jacques. *Acts of Religion.* Translated by Gil Anidjar. New York: Routledge, 2002.

———. *Adieu: To Emmanuel Levinas.* Translated by Pascale-Anne Brault and Michael Naas. Meridian. Stanford, CA: Stanford University Press, 1999.

———. *Of Hospitality*. Translated by Rachel Bowlby. Cultural Memory in the Present. Stanford, CA: Stanford University Press, 2000.
Diamond, Eliezer. "But Is It Funny? Identifying Humor, Satire, and Parody in Rabbinic Literature." Pages 33–53 in *Jews and Humor*. Edited by Leonard J. Greenspoon. Studies in Jewish Civilization 22. Proceedings of the Twenty-Second Annual Symposium of the Klutznick Chair in Jewish Civilization Harris Center for Judaic Studies. West Lafayette, IN: Purdue University Press, 2011.
———. *Holy Men and Hunger Artists: Fasting and Asceticism in Rabbinic Culture*. Oxford: Oxford University Press, 2004.
Doering, Lutz. *Ancient Jewish Letters and the Beginnings of Christian Epistolography*. Tübingen: Mohr Siebeck, 2012.
Dor, Zwi Moshe. *The Teaching of Eretz Israel in Babylon* [Hebrew]. Tel Aviv: Dvir, 1971.
Dundes, Alan. *From Game to War and Other Psychoanalytic Essays on Folklore*. Lexington: University Press of Kentucky, 1997.
———. "A Study of Ethnic Slurs: The Jew and the Polack in the United States." *Journal of American Folklore* 84, 332 (1971): 186–203.
Eagleton, Terry. *Culture*. New Haven: Yale University Press, 2016.
Efrati, Shlomi. "Pesiqata of Ten Commandments and Pesiqta of Matan Torah: Text, Redaction and Tradition Analysis" [Hebrew]. PhD diss., Hebrew University in Jerusalem, 2019.
Eliav, Yaron Z. "Baths." Pages 432–34 in *The Eerdmans Dictionary of Early Judaism*. Edited by John J. Collins and D. C. Harlow. Grand Rapids: Eerdmans, 2010.
———. "Bathhouses as Places of Social and Cultural Interactions." Pages 605–22 in *The Oxford Handbook of Jewish Daily Life in Roman Palestine*. Edited by Catherine Hezser. Oxford: Oxford University Press, 2010.
———. "Catherine Hezser, *Jewish Travel in Antiquity*." *JAOS* 133 (2013): 382–84.
———. "Did the Jews at First Abstain from Using the Roman Bath-House?" [Hebrew]. *Cathedra* 75 (1995): 3–35.
———. "The Material World of Babylonia as Seen from Roman Palestine: Some Preliminary Observations." Pages 153–85 in *The Archaeology and Material Culture of the Babylonian Talmud*. Edited by Markham J. Geller. IJS Studies in Judaica 16. Leiden: Brill, 2015.
———. "Pylè – Puma – Sfat Medinah and a Halakha Concerning Bathhouses" [Hebrew]. *Sidra* 11 (1995): 5–19.
———. "The Roman Bath as a Jewish Institution: Another Look at the Encounter between Judaism and the Greco-Roman Culture." *JSJ* 31 (2000): 416–54.
———. "A Scary Place: Jewish Magic in the Roman Bathhouse" [Hebrew]. Pages 88–97 in *Man near a Roman Arch: Studies Presented to Prof. Yoram*

Tsafrir. Edited by Leah Di Segni et al. Jerusalem: Israel Exploration Society, 2009.

———. "What Happened to Rabbi Abbahu at the Tiberian Bath-House? The Place of Realia and Daily Life in the Talmudic Aggada" [Hebrew]. *Jerusalem Studies in Jewish Folklore* 17 (1995): 7–20.

Elledge, Casey D. "Future Resurrection of the Dead in Early Judaism: Social Dynamics, Contested Evidence." *Currents in Biblical Research* 9 (2011): 394–421.

Epplett, Chris. "Spectacular Executions in the Roman World." Pages 520–32 in *A Companion to Sport and Spectacle in Greek and Roman Antiquity*. Edited by Paul Christesen and Donald G. Kyle. Blackwell Companions to the Ancient World: Literature and Culture. Malden, MA: Wiley-Blackwell, 2013.

Epstein, Jacob Nahum. *Introduction to the Mishnaic Text* [Hebrew]. Jerusalem: Magnes, 2000.

———. *Prolegomena ad Litteras Amoraiticas, Talmud Babylonicum et Hierosolymitanum* [Hebrew]. Edited by Ezra Zion Melamed. Jerusalem: Magnes, 1962.

Epstein, Yachin. "Studies in Massekhet Kalla Rabbati: Text, Redaction and Period" [Hebrew]. PhD diss., Hebrew University of Jerusalem, 2009.

Feintuch, Yonatan. "*Sanina le Ho* …" [Hebrew]. *Jewish Studies, an Internet Journal* 12 (2013): 1–23.

Fishbane, Simcha. *Deviancy in Early Rabbinic Literature: A Collection of Socio-Anthropological Essays*. Brill Reference Library of Judaism 27. Leiden: Brill, 2007.

Floor, Willem M. "Bathhouses." Pages 863–69 in vol. 3 of the *Encyclopædia Iranica*. Edited by E. Yarshater. 16 vols. London: Routledge & Kegan Paul; Leiden: Brill, 1982–2019. http://www.iranicaonline.org/articles/bathhouses.

Fogel, Shimon. "The Orders of Discourse in the House of Study (*beit midrash*) in Palestinian Rabbinic Literature: Organizing Space, Ritual and Discipline" [Hebrew]. PhD diss., Ben-Gurion University of the Negev., Beer Sheva, 2014.

Foxhall, Lin. "Introduction." Pages 1–15 in *When Men Were Men: Masculinity, Power and Identity in Classical Antiquity*. Edited by Lin Foxhall and John B. Salmon. Leicester-Nottingham Studies in Ancient Society 8. London: Routledge, 1998.

Fraenkel, Eliashiv. "Meetings and Conversations of Sages in Stories Regarding Halakhic Background in the Babylonian Talmud" [Hebrew]. PhD thesis, Bar-Ilan University Ramat-Gan, Israel, 2015.

Fraenkel, Yonah. *The Aggadic Narrative: Harmony of Form and Content* [Hebrew]. Tel Aviv: Hakibbutz Hameuḥad, 2001.

———. *Darkhei ha-Agadah ve-Hamidrash* [Hebrew]. Givatayim: Dvir, 1991.

———. *Studies in the Spiritual World of the Aggadic Narrative* [Hebrew]. Tel Aviv: Hakibbutz Hameuḥad, 1981.
Fraenkel, Zecharia. *Mabo ha-Yerushalmi*. Berlin: Berolini, 1922–1923.
Friedheim, Emmanuel. *Rabbinisme et paganisme en Palestine romaine: Étude historique des realia talmudiques (Ier–IVème siècles)*. Religions in the Graeco-Roman World 157. Leiden: Brill, 2006.
Friedman, Shamma. "Development and Historicity in the Aggadic Narrative of the Babylonian Talmud: A Study based upon B.M. 83b-86a." Pages 67–80 in *Continuity and Culture: Essays in Jewish Studies in Honor of the Ninetieth Anniversary of the Founding of Gratz College*. Edited by N. M. Waldman. Philadelphia: Gratz College, 1987.
———. "The Further Adventures of Rav Kahana: Between Babylonia and Palestine." Pages 247–71 in vol. 3 of *The Talmud Yerushalmi and Graeco-Roman Culture*. Edited by Peter Schäfer. 3 vols. TSAJ 71, 79, 92. Tübingen: Mohr Siebeck, 2002.
———. "The Historical Aggadah in the Babylonian Talmud" [Hebrew]. Pages 119–64 in *Saul Lieberman Memorial Volume*. Edited by Shamma Friedman. Jerusalem and New York: Jewish Theological Seminary, 1993.
———. "The Talmudic Narrative about Rav Kahana and R. Yoḥanan (Bava Kamma 117a-b) and Its Two Textual Families." Pages 409–90 in *Annual of Bar Ilan University: Studies in Judaica and the Humanities* 30–31 (2006), *In Memory of Prof. Meyer Simcha Feldblum*.
Furstenberg, Yair. "Am Ha-Aretz in Tannaitic Literature and Its Social Contexts" [Hebrew]. *Zion* 78 (2013): 287–319.
Gafni, Hannan, "The Image of R. Jeremiah in the Nineteenth Century Haskalah Literature" [Hebrew]. Pages 419–36 in *Between Babylonia and the Land of Israel: Studies in Honor of Isaiah M. Gafni*. Edited by Geoffrey Herman, Meir Ben Shahar, and Aharon Oppenheimer. Jerusalem: Zalman Shazar, 2017.
Gafni, Isaiah M. "The Babylonian *Yeshiva* as Reflected in Bava Qamma 117a." *Tarbiz* 49 (1980): 292–301.
———. "How Babylonia became 'Zion': Shifting Identities in Late Antiquity." Pages 333–48 in *Jewish Identities in Antiquity: Permutations and Transformations; International Conference in Memory of Menachem Stern, June 25–27, 2007*. Edited by L. I. Levine and D. R. Schwartz. Tübingen: Mohr Siebeck, 2009.
———. *Jews and Judaism in the Rabbinic Era: Image and Reality – History and Historiography*. TSAJ 173. Tübingen: Mohr Siebeck, 2019.
———. *The Jews of Babylonia in the Talmudic Era* [Hebrew]. Jerusalem: Zalman Shazar Center, 1990.
———. *Land, Center and Diaspora: Jewish Constructs in Late Antiquity*. JSPSup 21. Sheffield: Sheffield Academic, 1997.
———. "'Scepter and Staff': Concerning New Forms of Leadership in the

Period of the Talmud in the Land of Israel and Babylonia," Pages 84–91 in *Priesthood and Monarchy: Studies in the Historical Relationships of Religion and State* [Hebrew]. Edited by I. Gafni and G. Motzkin. Jerusalem: Zalman Shazar Center, 1986–1987.

Garnsey, Peter. *Social Status and Legal Privilege in the Roman Empire.* Oxford: Clarendon, 1970.

Gaselee, Stephen. *The Golden Ass: Being the Metamorphoses of Lucius Apuleius.* LCL. London: William Heinemann; New York: Macmillan, 1915.

Gasparov, Michail. *Zapiski I Vipiski* [Russian]. Moskow: Novoe Lit. Obozrenie, 2001.

Gaster Moses. *The Exempla of the Rabbis: Being a Collection of Exempla, Apologues, and Tales.* London: Asia Publishing Co., 1924.

Geller, Markham J. "Bloodletting in Babylonia." Pages 305–24 in *Magic and Rationality in Ancient Near Eastern and Graeco-Roman Medicine.* Edited by Herman Frederik J. Horstmanshoff and Marten Stol. Studies in Ancient Medicine 27. Leiden: Brill, 2004.

Ginzberg, Louis. *A Commentary on the Palestinian Talmud* [Hebrew]. 4 vols. Texts and Studies of the Jewish Theological Seminary of America 10–12, 21. New York: Jewish Theological Seminary, 1941–1961.

———. "Die Haggada bei den Kirchenvätern und in der Apokryphischen Literatur." *MGWJ* 43 (1899): 76–80.

Goldberg, Abraham. "The Babylonian Talmud." Pages 325–33 in vol. 1 of *The Literature of the Sages.* 2 vols. Edited by Shmuel Safrai. CRINT 1. Philadelphia: Fortress, 1987).

Goldberg, Abraham. "Rabbi Zeira and Babylonian Custom in Palestine" [Hebrew]. *Tarbiz* 36 (1964): 319–41.

Goldberg, Abraham. *Mishnah Shabbat* [Hebrew]. Jerusalem: Jewish Theological Seminary, 1976.

Goldberg, Beer. "These Are Words of BG ..." *Hamagid* 11 (1887), http://jpress.org.il/Olive/APA/NLI_heb/?action=tab&tab=browse&pub=MGD&_ga=2.191151786.1096076318.1531032740-1039970139.1524989680#panel=document.

Goodblatt, David M. *The Monarchic Principle: Studies in Jewish Self-Government in Antiquity.* Tübingen: Mohr Siebeck, 1994.

Goodman, Martin. "The Function of 'Minim' in Early Rabbinic Judaism." Pages 501–10 in *Geschichte – Tradition – Reflexion: Festschrift für Martin Hengel zum 70. Geburtstag.* Edited by Hermann Lichtenberger. 3 vols. Tübingen: Mohr Siebeck, 1996.

———. *State and Society in Roman Galilee, A.D. 132–212.* 2nd ed. Parkes-Wiener Series on Jewish Studies. London: Vallentine Mitchel, 2000.

Gottlieb, Erika. *Dystopian Fiction East and West: Universe of Terror and Trial.* Montreal: McGill-Queen's University Press, 2001.

Gray, Alyssa M. *A Talmud in Exile: The Influence of Yerushalmi Avodah Zarah*

on the Formation of Bavli Avodah Zarah. BJS 342. Providence, RI: Program in Judaic Studies, Brown University, 2005.
Gross, Simcha. "When the Jews Greeted ʿAlī: Sherira Gaon's Epistle in Light of Arabic and Syriac Historiography." *JSQ* 24 (2017): 122–44.
Gruen, Erich S. *Diaspora: Jews amidst Greeks and Romans*. Cambridge: Harvard University Press, 2002.
Gruen, Erich S. *Rethinking the Other in Antiquity*. Martin Classical Lectures, New Series. Princeton: Princeton University Press 2011).
Halliburton, John. "Anointing in the Early Church." Pages 77–91 in *The Oil of Gladness: Anointing in the Christian Tradition*. Edited by Martin Dudley and Geoffrey Rowell. London: SPCK; Collegeville, MN: Liturgical Press, 1993.
Hansen, William, ed. *Anthology of Ancient Greek Popular Literature*. Bloomington: Indiana University Press, 1998.
Harvey, Susan Ashbrook. *Scenting Salvation: Ancient Christianity and the Olfactory Imagination*. Transformation of the Classical Heritage. Berkeley: University of California Press, 2006.
Hasan-Rokem, Galit. "Communication with the Dead in Jewish Dream Culture." Pages 213–32 in *Dream Cultures: Explorations in the Comparative History of Dreaming*. Edited by D. Shulman and G. G. Stroumsa. Oxford: Oxford University Press, 1999.
———. "Rabbi Meir, The Illuminated and Illuminating." Pages 236–38 in *Current Trends in the Study of Midrash*. Edited by Carol Bakhos. JSJSup 106. Leiden: Brill, 2006.
———. *Web of Life: Folklore and Midrash in Rabbinic Literature*. Contraversions. Stanford, CA: Stanford University Press, 2000.
Hayes, Christine. "The Complicated Goy in Classical Rabbinic Sources." Pages 147–67 in *Perceiving the Other in Ancient Judaism and Early Christianity*. Edited by Michal Bar-Asher Siegal, Wolfgang Grünstäudl, and Matthew Thiessen. WUNT 394. Tübingen: Mohr Siebeck, 2017.
———. "Displaced Self Perceptions: The Deployment of Minim and Romans in Bavli Sanhedrin 90b-91a." Pages 249–89 in *Religious and Ethnic Communities in Later Roman Palestine*. Edited by H. Lapin. Lanham: University Press of Maryland, 1998.
———. "'In the West, They Laughed at Him': The Mocking Realists of the Babylonian Talmud." *Journal of Law, Religion and State* 2 (2013): 137–67.
———. "The 'Other' in Rabbinic Literature." Pages 243–69 in *The Cambridge Companion to the Talmud and Rabbinic Literature*. Edited by Charlotte Elisheva Fonrobert and Martin S. Jaffee. Cambridge Companions to Religion. Cambridge: Cambridge University Press, 2007.
Heinemann, Isaac. *Darkhei HaAggadah* [The Methods of the Aggadah] [Hebrew]. Jerusalem: Magnes, 1953).

Heinemann, Joseph. *Aggadot ve-Toledotehen* [Aggadah and Its Development] [Hebrew]. Jerusalem: Keter, 1974.

Hengel, Martin. *Crucifixion in the Ancient World and the Folly of the Message of the Cross*. London: SCM, 1977.

Herford, Robert Travers. *Christianity in Talmud and Midrash*. London: Williams & Norgate, 1903.

Herman, Geoffrey. "Babylonia: A Diaspora Center." In *Oxford Handbook of the Jewish Diaspora*. Edited by H. R. Diner. Oxford: Oxford University Press, forthcoming.

———. "Midgets and Mules, Elephants, and Exilarches: On the Metamorphosis of a Polemical Amoraic Story." Pages 117–32 in *Rabbinic Traditions between Palestine and Babylonia*. Edited by Ronit Nikolsky and Tal Ilan. Ancient Judaism and Early Christianity 89. Leiden: Brill, 2014.

———. *A Prince without a Kingdom: The Exilarch in the Sasanian Era*. TSAJ 150. Tübingen: Mohr Siebeck, 2012.

———. "The Story of Rav Kahana (b. Baba Qamma 117a–b) in Light of Armeno-Persian Sources." Pages 53–86 in *Irano-Judaica VI: Studies Relating to Jewish Contacts with Persian Culture throughout the Ages*. Edited by Shaul Shaked and Amnon Netzer. Jerusalem: Ben-Zvi Institute, 2008.

———. "Table Etiquette and Persian Culture in the Babylonian Talmud" [Hebrew]. *Zion* 77 (2012): 149–88.

Hershler, Moshe, and Joshua Hutner, eds. *The Babylonian Talmud with Variant Readings: Tractate Nedarim*. 2 vols. Jerusalem: Institute for the Complete Israeli Talmud, 1985–1991.

Hevroni, Ido. "The Midrash as Marriage Guide." *Azure* 29 (2007): 103–20.

Hezser, Catherine. "Crossing Enemy Lines: Network Connections between Palestinian and Babylonian Sages in Late Antiquity." *JSJ* 46 (2015): 224–50.

———. *Jewish Travel in Antiquity*. TSAJ 144. Tübingen: Mohr Siebeck, 2011.

———. "The Mishnah and Ancient Book Production." Pages 167–92 in vol. 1 of *The Mishnah in Contemporary Perspective*. Edited by J. Neusner and A. J. Avery-Peck. 2 vols. HdO 1.65, 87. Leiden: Brill, 2002–2006.

———. *Rabbinic Body Language: Non-verbal Communication in Palestinian Rabbinic Literature of Late Antiquity*. JSJSup 179. Leiden: Brill, 2017.

———. "Samuel Krauss' Contribution to the Study of Judaism, Christianity, and Graeco-Roman Culture within the Context of *Wissenschaft* Scholarship." *Modern Judaism* 33 (2013): 1–31.

———. *The Social Structure of the Rabbinic Movement in Roman Palestine*. TSAJ 66. Tübingen: Mohr Siebeck, 1997.

Hidary, Richard. *Rabbis and Classical Rhetoric: Sophistic Education and Oratory in the Talmud and Midrash*. Cambridge: Cambridge University Press, 2017.

Higger, Michael. *Massekhet Kallah Rabbati*. New York: Hotza·at De-vei Rabbanan, 1936.
Hirshman, Marc, ed. *Midrash Kohelet Rabbah 1–6: Critical Edition based on Manuscripts and Genizah Fragments*. Jerusalem: Midrash Project of the Schechter Institute of Jewish Studies, 2016.
Hope, Valerie M. *Death in Ancient Rome: A Sourcebook*. London: Routledge, 2007.
Hyman, Aharon. *Sefer Toldoth Tanna'im ve-Amora'im* [Hebrew]. 2 vols. Jerusalem: Machon Pri Haaretz, 1987.
Ilan, Tal. "Dance and Gender in Massekhet Ta'anit." Pages 217–25 in *A Feminist Commentary on the Babylonian Talmud: Introduction and Studies*. Edited by Tal Ilan et al. Tübingen: Mohr Siebeck, 2007.
———. *Feminist Commentary on the Babylonian Talmud*. Vol. 2.9, *Massekhet Ta'anit*. Tübingen Mohr Siebeck, 2008.
———. "Heaven and Hell: Babylonia and the Land of Israel in the Bavli." Pages 158–72 in *Rabbinic Traditions between Palestine and Babylonia*. Edited by Ronit Nikolsky and Tal Ilan. Ancient Judaism and Early Christianity 89. Leiden: Brill, 2014.
———. *Integrating Women into Second Temple History*. TSAJ 76. Tübingen: Mohr Siebeck, 1999.
———. "The Joke in Rabbinic Literature: Home-born or Diaspora Humor?" Pages 57–75 in *Humor in Arabic Culture*. Edited by Georges Tamer. Berlin: de Gruyter, 2009.
———. *Mine and Yours Are Hers: Retrieving Women's History from Rabbinic Literature*. AGJU 41. Leiden: Brill, 1997.
Ilan, Tal, and Vered Noam, in collaboration with Meir Ben Shahar, Daphne Baratz, and Yael Fisch. *Josephus and the Rabbis* [Hebrew]. 2 vols. Between Bible and Mishnah. Jerusalem: Yad Ben-Zvi, 2017.
Jacobs, Martin. *Die Institution des jüdischen Patriarchen: Eine quellen- und traditionskritische Studie zur Geschichte der Juden in der Spätantike*. TSAJ 52. Tübingen: Mohr Siebeck, 1995.
———. "Römische Thermenkultur im Spiegel des Talmud Yerushalmi." Pages 219–311 in vol. 1 of *The Talmud Yerushalmi and Graeco-Roman Culture*. Edited by Peter Schäfer. 3 vols. TSAJ 71, 79, 92. Tübingen: Mohr Siebeck, 1998–2002.
Japhet, Sara. *From the Rivers of Babylon to the Highlands of Judah: Collected Studies on the Restoration Period*. Winona Lake, IN: Eisenbrauns, 2006.
Kadari, Tamar. "Song and Meaning: A New Look on Rabbinic Exegesis of the Song of Songs" [Hebrew]. *Jerusalem Studies in Hebrew Literature* 28 (2016): 27–54.
Kalmin, Richard. "Genealogy and Polemics in Literature of Late Antiquity." *HUCA* 67 (1996): 77–94.
———. *Migrating Tales: The Talmud's Narratives and Their Historical Context*. Berkeley: University of California Press, 2014.

———. *The Sage in Jewish Society of Late Antiquity*. London: Routledge, 1999.

Katz, Menachem. "The Stories of Hillel's Appointment as Nasi in the Talmudic Literature: A Foundation Legend of the Jewish Scholar's World" [Hebrew]. *Sidra* 26 (2011): 81–116.

Kiperwasser Reuven. "The Art of Forgetting in Rabbinic Narrative." Pages 67–85 in *Rabbinic Study Circles: Aspects of Jewish Learning in Its Late Antique Context*. Education and Religion in Ancient and Pre-Modern History in the Mediterranean and Its Environs 8. Tübingen: Mohr Siebeck, 2020.

———. "Body of the Whore, Body of the Story and Metaphor of the Body." Pages 305–19 in *Introduction to Seder Qodashim*. Edited by Tal Ilan, Monika Brockhaus, and Tanja Hidde. Feminist Commentary on the Babylonian Talmud 5. Tübingen: Mohr Siebeck, 2012.

———. "Early and Late in Kohelet Rabbah: A Study in Redaction-criticism." [Hebrew]. Pages 291–312 in *Bible and Its World, Rabbinic Literature and Jewish Law and Jewish Thought*. Edited by Baruch J. Schwartz, Abraham Melamed, and Aharon Shemesh. Iggud: Selected Essays in Jewish Studies 1. Jerusalem: Magnes, 2008.

———. "Elihoref and Ahiah – The Metamorphosis of the Narrative Tradition from the Land of Israel to the Sassanian Babylonia." Pages 255–73 in *Rabbinic Traditions between Palestine and Babylonia*. Edited by Ronit Nikolsky and Tal Ilan. Ancient Judaism and Early Christianity 89. Leiden: Brill, 2014.

———. "Encounters between the Iranian Myth and Rabbinic Mythmakers in the Babylonian Talmud." Pages 285–304 in *Encounters by the Rivers of Babylon: Scholarly Conversations between Jews, Iranians, and Babylonians*. Edited by Uri Gabbay and Shai Secunda. TSAJ 160. Tübingen: Mohr Siebeck, 2014.

———. "Matters of the Heart: The Metamorphosis of the Monolithic in the Bible to the Fragmented in Rabbinic Thought." Pages 43–59 in *Judaism and Emotion: Texts, Performance, Experience*. Edited by S. Ross, G. Levy, and S. Al-Suadi. Bern: Peter Lang, 2013.

———. "Midrash ha-Gadol, The Exempla of the Rabbis (*Sefer Ma'asiyot*) and Midrashic Works on Ecclesiastes: A Comparative Approach" [Hebrew]. *Tarbiz* 75 (2006): 409–36.

———. "The Misfortunes and Adventures of Elihorepf and Ahiah in the Land of Israel and in Babylonia: The Metamorphosis of a Narrative Tradition and Ways of Acculturation." Pages 232–49 in *Rabbinic Traditions between Palestine and Babylonia*. Edited by Ronit Nikolsky and Tal Ilan. Ancient Judaism and Early Christianity 89. Leiden: Brill, 2014.

———. "Narrating the Self: Stories about Rabbi Zeira's Encounters in Land of Israel." Pages 353–72 in *Self, Self-Fashioning, and Individuality in Late Antiquity: New Perspectives*. Edited by Maren R. Niehoff and Joshua Levinson. Culture, Religion, and Politics in the Greco-Roman World 4. Tübingen: Mohr Siebeck, 2019.

———. "Narrative Bricolage and Cultural Hybrids in Rabbinic Babylonia: On the Narratives of Seduction and the Topos of Light." Pages 23–45 in *The Aggada of the Babylonian Talmud and Its Cultural World*. Edited by Jeffrey L. Rubenstein and Geoffrey Herman. BJS 362. Providence, RI: Brown Judaic Studies, 2018.

———. "Rabba bar Bar Channa's Voyages" [Hebrew]. *Jerusalem Studies in Hebrew Literature* 22 (2007–2008): 215–42.

———. "Sons of a Stepmother versus a Mother's Children." *Frankel Institute Annual* (2015): 42–45.

———. "Three Partners in a Person: The Metamorphoses of a Tradition and the History of an Idea." Pages 393–438 in *Irano-Judaica 8: Studies Relating to Jewish Contacts with Persian Culture throughout the Ages*. Edited by J. Rubanovich and G. Herman. Jerusalem: Ben-Zvi Institute, 2019.

———. "The Visit of the Rural Sage: Text, Context and Intertext in a Rabbinic Narrative" [Hebrew]. *Jerusalem Studies in Jewish Folklore* 26 (2009): 3–24.

———. "Wives of Commoners and the Masculinity of the Rabbis: Jokes, Serious Matters and Migrating Traditions." *JSJ* 48 (2017): 418–45.

Kiperwasser, Reuven, and Serge Ruzer. "Competition for the Sacred Space: Barsauma's Vita and Rabbinic Traditions." Pages 181–216 in Aryeh Kofsky and Serge Ruzer, in collaboration with Reuven Kiperwasser, *Reshaping Identities in Late Antique Syria-Mesopotamia: Christian and Jewish Hermeneutics and Narrative Strategies*. Judaism in Context 19. Piscataway, NJ: Gorgias, 2016.

———. "To Convert a Persian and to Teach Him the Holy Scriptures: A Zoroastrian Proselyte in Rabbinic and Syriac Christian Narratives." Pages 91–127 in *Jews, Christians and Zoroastrians: Religious Dynamics in a Sasanian Context*. Edited by G. Herman. Piscataway, NJ: Gorgias Press, 2014.

———. "The Holy Land and Its Inhabitants in the Pilgrimage Narrative of the Persian Monk Bar-Sauma" [Hebrew]. *Cathedra* 148 (2013): 41–70.

Kister, Menachem. "Addenda to the Talmudic Lexicon" [Hebrew]. Pages 431–47 in *Mehqerei Talmud II: Talmudic Studies Dedicated to the Memory of Professor Eliezer Sh. Rosenthal*. Edited by M. Bar-Asher and D. Rosenthal. Jerusalem: Magnes, 1993.

Klein, Samuel. *Galilee: Geography and History of Galilee from the Return from Babylonia to the Conclusion of the Talmud* [Hebrew]. 2nd ed. Jerusalem: Mossad Harav Kook, 1967.

Koehler, Ludwig, Walter Baumgartner, Johann Jakob Stamm, Mervyn E. J.

Richardson. *Hebrew and Aramaic Lexicon of the Old Testament*. Leiden: Brill, 1994.

Kohn, Samuel. "Der Prophet Elia in der Legende." *MGWJ* 12 (1863): 241–96.

Koltun-Fromm, Naomi. "A Jewish-Christian Conversation in Fourth-Century Persian Mesopotamia," *JJS* 47 (1996): 45–63.

Kosman, Admiel. *Gender and Dialogue in the Rabbinic Prism*. Studia Judaica 50. Berlin: de Gruyter, 2012.

———. *Men's World: Reading Masculinity in Jewish Stories in a Spiritual Context*. Translated by Edward Levin. Würzburg: Ergon, 2009.

———. "Some Notes on a Paradox of *Anava*" [Hebrew]. *Iyun* 46 (1997): 209–20.

Kovelman, Arkady B. *Between Alexandria and Jerusalem: The Dynamic of Jewish and Hellenistic Culture*. Brill Reference Library of Judaism 21. Leiden: Brill, 2005.

Kraus, Björn. *Erkennen und Entscheiden: Grundlagen und Konsequenzen eines erkenntnistheoretischen Konstruktivismus für die Soziale Arbeit*. Weinheim: Beltz Juventa, 2013.

Krauss, Samuel. "Ägyptische und syrische Götternamen im Talmud." Pages 339–53 in *Semitic Studies in Memory of Rev. Dr. Alexander Kohut*. Edited by George Alexander Kohut. Berlin: Calvary, 1897.

———. *Griechische und Lateinische Lehnwörter im Talmud, Midrasch und Targum*. Berlin: S. Calvary, 1898–1899.

———. *Kadmoniot Ha-Talmud* [Hebrew]. 4 vols. Berlin and Vienna: Benjamin Herz, 1896–1948.

———. *Persia and Rome in Talmud and Midrash* [Hebrew]. Jerusalem: Mossad ha-Rav Kook, 1948.

Kushelevsky, Rella. "The Function of Humor in Three Versions of the Theme 'Rabbi Joshua Ben Levi and the Angel of Death'" [Hebrew]. *Jerusalem Studies in Jewish Folklore* 19–20 (1998): 329–44.

Leibner, Uziel. "Geographical Essay" [Hebrew]. Pages 116–25 in *Midrash Kohelet Rabbah 1–6*. Edited by M. Hirshman. Jerusalem: Schechter, 2016.

Levine, Baruch A. "Later Sources on the *Netinim*." Pages 101–7 in *Orient and Occident: Essays Presented to Cyrus Gordon on the Occasion of His Sixty-Fifth Birthday*. Edited by H. A. Hoffner. AOAT 22. Neukirchen-Vluyn: Neukirchener Verlag, 1973.

Levine, David. "Holy Men and Rabbis in Talmudic Antiquity." Pages 45–57 in *Saints and Role Models in Judaism and Christianity*. Edited by Marcel Poorthuis and Joshua Schwartz. Jewish and Christian Perspectives 7. Leiden: Brill, 2004.

Levinson, Joshua. "Athlete of Faith and Fatal Fictions" [Hebrew]. *Tarbiz* 68 (1998): 61–86.

———. "Bodies and Bo(a)rders: Emerging Fictions of Identity in Late Antiquity." *HTR* 93 (2000): 343–72.
———. "Post-Classical Narratology and the Rabbinic Subject." Pages 81–107 in *Narratology, Hermeneutics, and Midrash: Jewish, Christian, and Muslim from Late Antiquity through to Modern Times*. Edited by Gerhard Langer and Constanza Cordoni. Poetik, Exegese und Narrative. Vienna: Vienna University Press, 2014.
Levitsky, Joseph. "The Illegitimate Child (Mamzer) in Jewish Law," *Jewish Bible Quarterly* 18 (1989): 6–12.
Lewis, Paul. *Comic Effects: Interdisciplinary Approaches to Humor in Literature*. Albany: State University of New York Press, 1989.
Licht, Chaim. *Ten Legends of the Sages: The Image of the Sage in Rabbinic Literature*. Hoboken, NJ: Ktav, 1991.
Lieberman, Saul. "As It Was, So It Will Be" [Hebrew]. Pages 331–38 in *Studies in Palestinian Talmudic Literature*. Edited by D. Rosenthal. Jerusalem: Magnes, 1991.
———. *Greek in Jewish Palestine: Studies in the Life and Manners of Jewish Palestine in the II–IV Centuries C.E.* 2nd ed. New York: Feldheim, 1965.
———. *Ha-Yerushalmi Kipshuto: A Commentary*. Jerusalem: Jewish Theological Seminary, 1935.
———. *Midrash Devarim Rabban*. Jerusalem: Bamberger and Wahrman, 1965.
———. "Palestine in the Third and Fourth Centuries." Pages 112–79 in *Texts and Studies*. New York: Ktav, 1974.
———, ed. *The Tosefta: According to Codex Vienna*. New-York: Jewish Theological Seminary of America, 1995.
———. *Tosefta ki-fshuta: A Comprehensive Commentary on the Tosefta*. 10 vols. in 9. New York: Jewish Theological Seminary, 1955–1988.
Lindbeck, Kristen H. *Elijah and the Rabbis: Story and Theology*. New York: Columbia University Press, 2010.
Loffreda Stanislao. "Capernaum." Pages 416–19 in vol. 1 of *The Oxford Encyclopedia of Archaeology in the Near East*. Edited by Eric M. Meyers. New York: Oxford University Press; 1997.
Mackenzie, D. N. *A Concise Pahlavi Dictionary*. London: Oxford University Press, 1971.
Malter, Henry, ed. *The Treatise Ta'anit of the Babylonian Talmud* [Hebrew]. New York: American Academy for Jewish Research, 1930.
Mandelbaum, Bernard, ed. *Pesikta de Rav Kahana: According to an Oxford Manuscript – with Variants from All Known Manuscripts and Genizoth Fragments and Parallels* [Hebrew]. New York: Jewish Theological Seminary, 1987.
Marcus, Joel. "Crucifixion as Parodic Exaltation." *JBL* 25 (2006): 73–87.
Margaliot (Margulies), Mordechai. *Encyclopedia of the Sages of the Talmud and the Geonim* [Hebrew]. 2 vols. (Tel Aviv: Chechik, 1969).

———. *Midrash Wayyikra Rabbah: A Critical Edition based on Manuscripts and Genizah Fragments with Variants and Notes*. 5 vols. New York: JTS Press, 1972.

Martineau, William H. "A Model of the Social Functions of Humor." Pages 101–25 in *The Psychology of Humor: Theoretical Perspectives and Empirical Issues*. Edited by Jeffrey H. Goldstein and Paul E. McGhee. New York: Academic Press, 1972.

Masterson, Mark. "Studies of Ancient Masculinity." Page 19–32 in *A Companion to Greek and Roman Sexualities*. Edited by Thomas K. Hubbard. Blackwell Companions to the Ancient World 100. Chichester: Wiley, 2014.

Meir, Ofra. *Rabbi Judah the Patriarch: Palestinian and Babylonian Portraits of a Leader* [Hebrew]. Sifriyat "Helal Ben-Ḥayim." Tel Aviv: Hakibbutz Hameuhad, 1999.

Melamed, Ezra Zion. *An Introduction to Talmudic Literature* [Hebrew]. Jerusalem: Galor,1972/1973 .

Mez, Adam. *Die Renaissance des Islams*. Heidelberg: C. Winter, 1922.

Milikowsky, Chaim. "Midrash as Fiction and Midrash as History: What Did the Rabbis Mean?" Pages in 117–27 in *Ancient Fiction: The Matrix of Early Christian and Jewish Narrative*. Edited by Jo-Ann A. Brant, Charles W. Hedrick, and Chris Shea. SymS 32. Atlanta: Society of Biblical Literature, 2005.

———. "On the Formation and Transmission of Bereshit Rabba and the Yerushalmi: Questions of Redactions, Text-Criticism and Literary Relationships." *JQR* 92 (2002): 521–67.

Miller, Stuart S. "The 'Minim' of Sepphoris Reconsidered." *HTR* 86 (1993): 377–402.

———. "R. Hanina bar Hama at Sepphoris." Pages 175–200 in *The Galilee in Late Antiquity*. Edited by Lee I. Levine. New York: Jewish Theological Seminary of America, 1992.

———. *Sages and Commoners in Late Antique 'Erez Israel: A Philological Inquiry into Local Traditions in Talmud Yerushalmi*. TSAJ 111. Tübingen: Mohr Siebeck, 2006.

———. *Studies in the History and Traditions of Sepphoris*. Leiden: Brill, 1984.

Mitchell, Alexandre G. Review of *Looking at Laughter: Humor, Power, and Transgression in Roman Visual Culture, 100 B.C.–A.D. 250*, by John R. Clarke. *Bryn Mawr Classical Review* 2008.09.55, http://bmcr.brynmawr.edu/2008/2008-09-55.html.

Momigliano, Arnaldo. *Alien Wisdom: The Limits of Hellenization*. Cambridge: Cambridge University Press, 1975.

Moreshet, Menachem. *A Lexicon of the New Verbs in Tannaitic Hebrew* [Hebrew]. Ramat Gan: Bar-Ilan University Press, 1980.

Na'eh, Shlomo. "The Craft of Memory: Memory Structures and Textual Patterns in Rabbinic Literature" [Hebrew]. Pages 543–59 in vol. 2 of

Mehqerei Talmud III: Talmudic Studies Dedicated to the Memory of Professor Ephraim E. Urbach. Edited by Y. Sussman and D. Rosenthal. Jerusalem: Magnes, 2005.

———. "From the Bible to Talmud (and Back): Lexical Studies in Hebrew and Aramaic" [Hebrew]. Pages 133–50 in *Hebrew through the Ages: In Memory of Shoshanna Bahat.* Edited by Mosheh Bar-Asher. Jerusalem: Academy of the Hebrew Language, 1997.

———. "The Structure and Division of Torat Kohanim A (Scrolls)." *Tarbiz* 66 (1997): 483–515.

———. "Talmud Yerushalmi of the Academy of the Hebrew Language." *Tarbiz* 71 (2002): 569–603.

Neis, Rachel. "Religious Lives of Image-Things, Avodah Zarah, and Rabbis in Late Antique Palestine." *Archiv für Religionsgeschichte* 17 (2014): 91–121.

———. *The Sense of Sight in Rabbinic Culture: Jewish Ways of Seeing in Late Antiquity.* Greek Culture in the Roman World. New York: Cambridge University Press, 2013.

Neusner, Jacob. *A History of the Jews in Babylonia.* 5 vols. StPB 9, 11, 12, 14, 15. Leiden: Brill, 1965–1970.

———. *The Tosefta: Kodoshim.* New York: Ktav, 1979.

———. *The Tosefta: Translated from the Hebrew with a New Introduction.* New York: Ktav, 1981.

Newman, Hillel I. "Closing the Circle: Yonah Fraenkel, the Talmudic Story, and Rabbinic History." Pages 105–35 in *How Should Rabbinic Literature Be Read in the Modern World?* Edited by Matthew Kraus. Judaism in Context 4. Piscataway, NJ: Gorgias Press, 2006.

———. *The Ma'asim of the People of the Land of Israel: Halakhah and History in Byzantine Palestine* [Hebrew]. Jerusalem: Yad Ben-Zvi, 2001.

Nickelsburg, George W. E. *Resurrection, Immortality, and Eternal Life in Intertestamental Judaism.* Cambridge: Harvard University Press, 1972.

Nikolsky, Ronit, and Tal Ilan, eds. *Rabbinic Traditions between Palestine and Babylonia.* Ancient Judaism and Early Christianity 89. Leiden: Brill, 2014.

Noy, Dov. "The Talmudic-Midrashic 'Healing Stories' as a Narrative Genre." *Proceedings of Koroth* 9 (1988): 124–46.

Ochs, Elinor, and Lisa Capps. "Narrating the Self." *Annual Review of Anthropology* 25 (1996): 25–43.

Oppenheimer, Aharon. *Between Rome and Babylon: Studies in Jewish Leadership and Society.* Edited by Nili Oppenheimer. TSAJ 108. Tübingen: Mohr Siebeck, 2005.

———. *By the Rivers of Babylon: Perspectives on the History of Talmudic Babylonia* [Hebrew]. Jerusalem: Zalman Shazar Center, 2017.

———. "Enforcement in Palestine and in Babylonia in the Late Tannaitic Era." Pages 366–70 in *The Paths of Peace: Studies in Honor of Israel Fried-*

man Ben-Shalom. Edited by D. Gera and M. Ben-Zeev. Beer-Sheva: Ben Gurion University of the Negev Press, 2005.

———.*Rabbi Judah ha-Nasi: Statesman, Reformer, and the Redactor of the Mishnah*. Tübingen: Mohr Siebeck, 2017.

Petrides, Antonis K. "Lucian's 'On Dance' and the Poetics of the Pantomime Mask." Pages 433–50 in *Performance in Greek and Roman Theatre*. Edited by George W. M. Harrison and Vayos Liapis. Mnemosyne Supplements 353. Leiden: Brill, 2013.

Preuss, Julius. *Biblical and Talmudic Medicine*. Translated by F. Rosner. New York: Ktav, 1971. German original, 1911.

Qvortrup, Mads. *The Political Philosophy of Jean-Jacques Rousseau: The Impossibility of Reason*. Manchester: Manchester University Press, 2003.

Redfield, James Adam. "Redacting Culture: Ethnographic Authority in the Talmudic Arrival Scene." *Jewish Social Studies* 22 (2016): 29–80.

Reeg, Gottfried. *Die Ortsnamen Israels nach der rabbinischen Literatur*. Beihefte zum Tübinger Atlas des Vorderen Orients B.51. Wiesbaden: Reichert, 1989.

Reiner, Elhanan. "From Joshua to Jesus: The Transformation of a Biblical Story to a Local Myth (A Chapter in the Religious Life of the Galilean Jew)" [Hebrew]. *Zion* 71 (1996): 281–317.

———. "Joshua Is Rabbi, Hatsor Is Meron: On Typology of a Galilean Foundation Myth" [Hebrew]. *Tarbiz* 80 (2012): 179–218.

Robinson, Tom. Review of *Diaspora: Jews amidst Greeks and Romans*, by Erich S. Gruen, *Bryn Mawr Classical Review* 2002.10.33, https://bmcr.brynmawr.edu/2002/2002.10.33/.

Roniger, Luis, and Michael Feige. "From Pioneer to Freier: The Changing Models of Generalized Exchange in Israel." *European Journal of Sociology* 33.2 (1992): 280–307.

Rosenblum, Oded. "The Activities of the Nehutei, Ulla and Rav Dimi, According to Sugiot in the Babylonian Talmud." PhD diss., Haifa University, 2007.

Rosenfeld, Ben-Zion, and Joseph Menirav. *Markets and Marketing in Roman Palestine*. Translated by Ch. Cassel. Leiden: Brill, 2005.

Rosenthal, David. "The Sages' Methodical Approach to Textual Variants within the Hebrew Bible" [Hebrew]. Pages 395–98 in vol. 2 of *Isac Leo Seeligmann Volume: Essays on the Bible and the Ancient World*. 2 vols. Edited by Alexander Rofé and Yair Zakovitch. Jerusalem: Elchanan Rubinstein, 1983.

Rosenthal, Eliezer Shimshon. "For the Talmudic Dictionary: Talmudica Iranica." Pages 38–134 in *Irano-Judaica 1: Studies Relating to Jewish Contacts with Persian Culture throughout the Ages*. Edited by Sh. Shaked. Jerusalem: Ben-Zvi Institute, 1982.

Rosenthal, Yoav. "Transportations: Text and Reality." *AJS Review* 41.2 (2017): 333–73.

Rosen-Zvi, Ishay, and Adi Ophir. *Goy: Israel's Others and the Birth of the Gentile*. Oxford Studies in the Abrahamic Religions. Oxford: Oxford University Press, 2020.

Rubenstein, Jeffrey L. "Coping with the Virtues of the Land of Israel: An Analysis of 110b–112a" [Hebrew]. Pages 159–88 in *Israel–Diaspora Relations in the Second Temple and Talmudic Periods*. Edited by Isaiah M. Gafni. Jerusalem: Shazar Institute, 2004.

———. *The Culture of the Babylonian Talmud*. Baltimore: Johns Hopkins University Press, 2003.

———. *Stories of the Babylonian Talmud*. Baltimore: Johns Hopkins University Press, 2010.

———. *Talmudic Stories: Narrative Art, Composition, and Culture*. Baltimore: Johns Hopkins University Press, 1999.

Safrai, Shmuel. *In the Days of the Temple and in the Days of the Mishnah: Studies in the History of Israel* [Hebrew]. 2 vols. Jerusalem: Magnes, 1994.

Samuelsson, Gunnar. *Crucifixion in Antiquity: An Inquiry into the Background and Significance of the New Testament Terminology of Crucifixion*. WUNT 2/310. Tübingen: Mohr Siebeck, 2011.

Satlow, Michael L. *Jewish Marriage in Antiquity*. Princeton: Princeton University Press, 2001.

Schlüter, Margarete. *Auf welche Weise wurde die Mishna geschrieben? Das Antwortschreiben des Rav Sherira Gaon, mit einem Faksimile der Handschrift Berlin Qu. 685 (or. 160) und des Erstdrucks Konstantinopel 1566*. Texts and Studies in Medieval and Early Modern Judaism 9. Tübingen: Mohr Siebeck, 1993.

Schofer, Jonathan Wyn. *Confronting Vulnerability: The Body and the Divine in Rabbinic Ethics*. Chicago: University of Chicago Press, 2010.

Schoville, Keith N. "Dance." Pages 374–86 in vol. 1 of *Dictionary of Daily Life in Biblical and Post-Biblical Antiquity*. Edited by Edwin M. Yamauchi and Marvin R. Wilson. Peabody, MA: Hendrickson, 2014.

Schremer, Adiel. *Brothers Estranged: Heresy, Christianity, and Jewish Identity in Late Antiquity*. Oxford: Oxford University Press, 2010.

———. "'He Posed Him a Difficulty and Placed Him': A Study in the Evolution of the Text of TB Bava Kama 117a" [Hebrew]. *Tarbiz* 66 (1997): 403–15.

———. *Male and Female He Created Them* [Hebrew]. Jerusalem: Zalman Shazar Center, 2004.

———. "Stammaitic Historiography." Pages 219–37 in *Creation and Composition: The Contribution of the Bavli Redactors (Stammaim) to the Aggadah*. Edited by Jeffrey L. Rubenstein. TSAJ 114. Tübingen: Mohr Siebeck, 2005.

Schwartz, Joshua. "*Aliya* from Babylonia during the Amoraic Period (200–500 C.E.)" [Hebrew]. *Jerusalem Cathedra* 3 (1983): 58–69.

———. "Babylonian Commoners in Amoraic Palestine." *JAOS* 101 (1981): 317–22.
———. "Southern Judaea and Babylonia." *JQR* 72 (1982): 188–97.
———. "The Patriotic Rabbi: Babylonian Scholars in Roman Period Palestine." Pages 118–31 in *Jewish Local Patriotism and Self-Identification in the Graeco-Roman Period*. Edited by Siàn Jones and Sarah. Pearce. JSJSup 31. Sheffield: Sheffield Academic, 1998.
———. "Tension between Palestinian Scholars and Babylonian Olim in Amoraic Palestine." *JSJ* 11 (1980): 78–94.
Schwartz, Seth. *Imperialism and Jewish Society, 200 B.C.E. to 640 C.E.* Jews, Christians, and Muslims from the Ancient to the Modern World 32. Princeton: Princeton University Press, 2002.
———. *Were the Jews a Mediterranean Society? Reciprocity and Solidarity in Ancient Judaism*. Princeton: Princeton University Press, 2009.
Segal, Alan F. *Life after Death: A History of the Afterlife in the Religions of the West*. New York: Doubleday, 2004.
Segev, Tom. *The Seventh Million: The Israelis and the Holocaust*. Translated by Haim Watzman. New York: Straus & Giroux, 1993.
Setzer, Claudia. *Resurrection of the Body in Early Judaism and Early Christianity: Doctrine, Community, and Self-Definition*. Leiden: Brill, 2004.
Simon-Shoshan, Moshe. "Did the Rabbis Believe in Agreus Pan? Rabbinic Relationships with Roman Power, Culture, and Religion in Genesis Rabbah 63." *HTR* 111 (2018): 425–50.
Shaked, Shaul. "'No Talking During a Meal': Zoroastrian Themes in the Babylonian Talmud." Pages 161–77 in *The Talmud in Its Iranian Context*. Edited by Carol Bakhos and M. Rahim Shayegan. TSAJ 135. Tübingen: Mohr Siebeck, 2010.
Shapira, Anita. *Visions in Conflict* [Hebrew]. Tel Aviv: Am Oved, 1989.
Shoshany, Ronit. "People Suspected of Violating the Sabbatical Laws (*Bavli Sanhedrin* 26a): Analysis of the Story and the Attitude of the Babylonian Talmud to *Resh Lakish*." *Teuda* 24 (2012): 45–61.
Siegal, Michal Bar-Asher. *Early Christian Monastic Literature and the Babylonian Talmud*. New York: Cambridge University Press, 2013.
Smith, Jonathan A., Paul Flowers, and Michael Larkin. *Interpretative Phenomenological Analysis: Theory, Method and Research*. London: Sage, 2009.
Sokoloff, Michael. *A Dictionary of Jewish Babylonian Aramaic of the Talmudic and Geonic Periods*. 2nd ed. Ramat Gan: Bar-Ilan University Press, 2021.
———. *A Dictionary of Jewish Palestinian Aramaic of the Byzantine Period*. 3rd rev. ed. Ramat Gan: Bar-Ilan University Press, 2017.
———. *A Syriac Lexicon: A Translation from the Latin; Correction, Expansion, and Update of C. Brockelmann's Lexicon Syriacum*. Winona Lake, IN: Eisenbrauns 2009.

Sperber, Daniel. "Inflation in Fourth Century Palestine." *ArOr* 34 (1966): 54–66.

———. *Magic and Folklore in Rabbinic Literature*. Bar-Ilan Studies in Near Eastern Languages and Culture. Ramat Gan: Bar-Ilan University Press, 1994.

———. *Roman Palestine, 200–400: Money and Prices*. Bar-Ilan Studies in Near Eastern Languages and Culture. Ramat Gan: Bar-Ilan University Press, 1974.

———. "The Value of '*manah*'" [Hebrew]. *Talpioth* 9 (1970): 591–611.

Sperling, David. "Aramaic Spousal Misunderstanding." *JAOS* 115 (1995): 205–9.

Statman, Daniel. "Some Resolutions of the Paradox of *Anava* in Jewish Sources" [Hebrew]. *Iyun* 44 (1995): 355–70.

Stein, Dina. "Following Goats: Text, Place and Diasporas." Pages 523–37 in *Talmudic Transgressions: Engaging the Work of Daniel Boyarin*. Edited by Charlotte ElishevaFonrobert et al. JSJSup 181. Leiden: Brill, 2017.

———. *Textual Mirrors: Reflexivity, Midrash, and the Rabbinic Self*. Divinations. Philadelphia: University of Pennsylvania Press, 2012.

———. "The Untamable Stew: Language and Women as Institutional Makers" [Hebrew]. *Jerusalem Studies in Hebrew Literature* 22 (2007–2008): 243–61.

———. "The Wild Goat Chase Models of Diaspora and Salvation" [Hebrew]. *Jewish Studies* 51 (2016): 93–130.

Steller, H. E. "Preliminary Remarks to a New Edition of *Shir Hashirim Rabbah*." Pages 300–311 in *Rashi 1040–1990: Hommage à Ephraïm E. Urbach; Congrès Européen des études juives*. Edited by Gabrielle Sed-Rajna. Patrinoines. Paris: Cerf, 1993.

Stemberger, Günter. *Introduction to the Talmud and Midrash*. Edinburgh: T&T Clark, 1996.

Stern, Sacha. *Calendar and Community: A History of the Jewish Calendar, Second Century BCE–Tenth Century CE*. Oxford: Oxford University Press, 2001.

———. "Rabbi and the Origins of the Patriarchate." *JJS* 54 (2003): 193–215.

Stock, Brian. *The Implications of Literacy: Written Language and Models of Interpretation in the Eleventh and Twelfth Centuries*. Princeton: Princeton University Press, 1983.

Stroumsa, Guy. "'Caro salutis cardo': Shaping the Person in Early Christian Thought." *History of Religions* 30 (1990): 25–50.

———. "Interiorization and Intolerance in Early Christianity." Pages 168–82 in *Die Erfindung des inneren Menschen: Studien zur Religiösen Anthropologie*. Edited by Jan Assmann. Studien zum Verstehen fremder Religionen 6. Gütersloh: Mohn, 1993.

Sussman, Yaakov. "Masoret Limmud u-Mesoret Nusah shel ha-Talmud ha-Yerushalmi: Le-Verur Nusha'otehav shel Yerushalmi Masekhet

Sheqalim" [Hebrew]. Pages 12–76 in *Research in Talmudic Literature: A Study Conference in Honour of the Eightieth Birthday of Sha'ul Lieberman*. Jerusalem: Israel Academy of Sciences and Humanities, 1983.

———. "Torah Shebe'alpeh' Peshutah Kemashma'ah: Kokho shel Kotzo shel Yud" ['Oral Torah' Literally—The Power of the Tip of Yod] [Hebrew]. Pages 209–384 in vol. 1 of *Mehqerei Talmud III: Talmudic Studies Dedicated to the Memory of Professor Ephraim E. Urbach*, 2 vols.. Edited by Y. Sussman and D. Rosenthal. Jerusalem: Magnes, 2005.

———. "We-shuv le-Yerushalmi Neziqin" [Hebrew]. Pages 55–133 in vol. 1 of *Mehqerei Talmud I: Talmudic Studies*. 2 vols. Edited by Y. Sussman and D. Rosenthal. Jerusalem: Magnes Press, 1989–1990.

Sysling, Harry. *Tehiyyat Ha-Metim: The Resurrection of the Dead in the Palestinian Targums of the Pentateuch and Parallel Traditions in Classical Rabbinic Literature*. TSAJ 57. Tübingen: Mohr Siebeck, 1996.

Talmud Yerushalmi According to Ms. Or. 4720 (Scal.3) of the Leiden University Library. Jerusalem: Academy of the Hebrew Language, 2001.

Taylor, Charles. *Sources of the Self: The Making of the Modern Identity*. Cambridge: Harvard University Press, 1989.

Tropper, Amram. "From Tatlafush to Sura" [Hebrew]. *Oqimta* 2 (2014): 1–16.

———. *Like Clay in the Hands of the Potter: Sage Stories in Rabbinic Literature* [Hebrew]. Jerusalem: Zalman Shazar Center, 2011.

———. *Rewriting Ancient Jewish History: The History of the Jews in Roman Times and the New Historical Method*. Routledge Studies in Ancient History 10. London: Routledge, 2016.

———. *Simeon the Righteous in Rabbinic Literature: A Legend Reinvented*. Ancient Judaism and Early Christianity. Leiden: Brill, 2013.

Turán, Tamás. "'Wherever the Sages Set Their Eyes, There Is either Death or Poverty': On the History, Terminology and Imagery of the Talmudic Traditions about the Devastating Gaze of the Sages." *Sidra* 23 (2008): 137–205.

Turner, Victor. *Ritual Process: Structure and Anti-Structure*. Lewis Henry Morgan Lectures 1966. Chicago: Aldine, 1969.

Urbach, Efraim E. "The Repentance of the People of Nineveh and the Discussions between Jews and Christians" [Hebrew]. *Tarbiz* 20 (1949): 118–22.

Valler, Shulamit. *Women and Womanhood in the Talmud*. Translated by B. Sigler Rozen. Atlanta: Scholars Press, 1999.

Vermès, Géza. *The Resurrection*. New York: Doubleday, 2008.

Vice, Samantha. "Literature and the Narrative Self." *Philosophy* 78 (2003): 93–108.

Vidas, Moulie. "The Bavli's Discussion of Genealogy in Qiddushin IV." Pages 285–326 in *Antiquity in Antiquity: Jewish and Christian Pasts in the Greco-Roman World*. Edited by Gregg Gardner and Kevin L. Osterloh. TSAJ 123. Tübingen: Mohr Siebeck, 2008.

Vidas, Moulie. "The Emergence of Talmudic Culture: Overview of a Work in Progress." Forthcoming.

Wasserman, Mira B. *Jews, Gentiles, and Other Animals: The Talmud after the Humanities*. Divinations. Philadelphia: University of Pennsylvania Press, 2019.

Weiss, Haim, and Mira Balberg. "'Raise My Eyes for Me': Gazing at Old Age in a Talmudic Narrative." *Oqimta* 6 (2020): 41–81.

Werman, Cana. "Was Hillel a Pharisee?" Pages 66–104 in *Sources and Interpretation in Ancient Judaism: Studies for Tal Ilan at Sixty*. Edited by Meron M. Piotrkowski, Geoffrey Herman, and Saskia Dönitz. Ancient Judaism and Early Christianity 104. Leiden: Brill, 2018.

Westmoreland, Mark W. "Interruptions: Derrida and Hospitality," *Kritike* 2.1 (2008): 1–10.

Wilfand, Yael. "Did the Rabbis Reject the Roman Public Latrine?" *Bulletin Antieke Beschaving: Annual Papers on Mediterranean Archaeology* 84 (2009): 183–96.

———. *Poverty, Charity and the Image of the Poor in Rabbinic Texts from the Land of Israel*. Social World of Biblical Antiquity 9. Sheffield: Sheffield Phoenix, 2014.

Wispé, Lauren. "The Distinction between Sympathy and Empathy: To Call Forth a Concept, a Word Is Needed." *Journal of Personality and Social Psychology* 50 (1986): 314–21.

Yankelevitch, Rafael. "The Identity of Nehunion Ahia" [Hebrew]. *Milet* 2 (1984): 137–41.

Yegül, Fikret K. *Bathing in the Roman World*. Cambridge: Cambridge University Press, 2010.

Žižek, Slavoy. *Violence: Six Sideways Reflections*. Big Ideas. London: Profile Books, 2009.

Zylko, Boguslaw. "Culture and Semiotics: Notes on Lotman's Conception of Culture." In "Reexamining Critical Processing." Special issue, *New Literary History* 32.2 (2001): 391–408.

Index of Selected Passages

Hebrew Bible
Genesis
1:2 — 29
9:27 — 130–31
10:2 — 130
11:4 — 59 n. 22
11:9 — 25, 60 n. 22
18:19 — 81
25:7 — 81

Leviticus
23:4 — 170

Numbers
9:2 — 103
28:2 — 103

Deuteronomy
4:9–10 — 93
4:43 — 136, 138
7:13 — 195
28:65 — 128
32:43 — 46

Judges
8:8–9 — 60 n. 22

2 Kings
2:11 — 86

Isaiah
2:3 — 171
28:22 — 67
42:5 — 44
44:27 — 27
51:20 — 148

Ezekiel
6:9 — 107
7:16 — 107
37:14 — 44

Jeremiah
2:7 — 46
29:1 — 171
51:49 — 27

Hosea
9:17 — 128, 129
13:14 — 36

Amos
3:2 — 154, 155
7:17 — 198

Haggai
1:8 — 123

Psalms
116:9 — 44

Job
1:21 — 198
28:23 — 36
29:8 — 91

Proverbs
1:21 — 80

Song
8:9 — 123, 124, 129

Esther
2:22 — 95

Ezra
7:6 — 23

Rabbinic Literature and Targums

Mishnah
Qiddushin
4:1 — 124

Tosephta
Berakhot
2:20 — 69 n. 57

Pesahim
4:13–14 — 103

Shabbat
15:8 — 4

Bava Qama
2:11 — 4
7:3 — 23, 60

Arakhin
4:26–27 — 64

Palestinian Talmud
Berakhot
2:1, 4b — 90, 92 n. 35, 96
2:8, 5c — 34, 53, 55, 61, 66
3:1, 6a–b — 32

Index of Selected Passages

Berakhot (cont.)
4:1, 7a   26
4:1, 7b   27, 28, 29, 30
4:2, 7d   92 n. 34
5:1, 9a   166 n.79

Pe'ah
1:1, 15d   79

Kil'ayim
9:4, 32b   112–13
9:4, 32b–c   116–18, 134
9:4, 32c   46, 197

Ma'aser Sheni
5:2, 56a   30

Shevi'it
6:1, 36d   136

Shabbat
1:2, 3a   93, 96

Pesahim
5:3, 32a   132
6:1, 33a   102

Sheqalim
2:6, 47a   90 n. 31

Ta'anit
2:13, 76a   81 n. 6
4:2, 78a   106

Megillah
2:4, 63b   83 n. 13

Mo'ed Qatan
3:1, 71c   33
3:7, 83c   90

Yevamot
12:6, 13a   139 n. 47

Ketubbot
2:6, 26a   3
12:2, 35a   112 n. 42, 115 n. 54
12:2, 35b   44

Nedarim
40a, 6:8   170–71

Qiddushin
3:5, 64a   179
3:12, 84c   47, 48

Sanhedrin
1:2, 18c   92 n.35
3:9 (3:6), 20d   202–3

Avodah Zarah
3:1, 42c   81
3:8, 43b   97 n. 46

Midrash
Genesis Rabbah
11:4   9
36:8   131
37:4   29
38:11   25
59:4   79

Leviticus Rabbah
22:4   42
32:72   47

Pesiqta de Rav Kahana
12:25   133 n.29
18:5   114 n. 47
23:11   151 n. 23

Deuteronomy Rabbah, vaethanan   138

Ecclesiastes Rabbah
1:9   176
3:2   57, 58
9:10   116 n.58, 165 n. 77
10:1   124 n.4

Ecclesiastes Zuta
7, 7   26 n. 9

Song of Songs Rabbah
5:1   124 n. 4
8:3   122, 123
8:10   127

Esther Rabbah
pt. 8   124 n. 4

Tanhuma, Shelah
16:1   189 n. 63

Babylonian Talmud
Berakhot
27b   94
51b   193–94
58a   151 n. 27
63a–b   173

Shabbat
29a   3
34a   151 n. 27
41a   69 n. 55
88a   144 n. 6
147a   66 n. 49
152b   182 n. 44

Eruvin
39b   66 n. 49

Pesahim
52b   154 n. 35
72b   133
86b   20
87b   36

Yoma
9b   129, 130

Betzah
24b   3

Ta'anit
5b   186, 189–90
9b   191–92

Megillah
6a   146 n.7
29a   3
15a   164 n. 70, 189 n. 62

Yevamot
96b–97a   90 n. 31

Index of Selected Passages   233

Ketubbot		Zevahim		Isidore	
16b–17a	84	116a-b	189 n. 61	*Etymologiae*	
17a	81, 88			6.50	177 n.25
68a	193	Menahot			
103b	3	42a	193 n. 73	Tertullian	
111a	197			*De Baptismo*	
112a	144	**Kalla Tractates**		7	177 n. 25
		Kallah Rabbati		*Ad Scapulam*	
Nedarim		9:1	84	2	97 n. 47
66b	157				
		Kallah		**Josephus**	
Gittin		1:24	95	*War*	
6a	7			3.321	74
14a–b	181–82	**Targum**			
		2 Kings		*Antiquities*	
Qiddushin		2:11	86	5.12–15	189 n. 61
71b	163–64			13.72	170 n. 7
72a	182 n. 44	Judges		17.23–28	105 n. 11
		2:1	42 n. 14,		
Bava Qamma			189 n. 61	**Greco-Roman Literature**	
80a	7 n.33			*Aesop Romance*	
104b	154 n. 35	**Medieval Jewish**		39–41	159
112b	203 n. 1	**Literature**			
117a	5 n. 19, 56	Epistle of Rab Sherira		Apuleius	
117a–b	56, 59 n. 22,	Gaon	2, 3	*Metamorphoses*	
	147, 151–52			*(Golden Ass)*	57
		Christian Literature		3:1–11	58 n. 18
Bava Metzi'a		Matthew			
84a	130 n. 18,	9:18–22	116 n. 56	Petronius	
	146 n. 7			*Satyricon*	67 n. 52
85a	81	Mark			
85b	165–66	5:25–34	116 n. 56	Strabo	
		10:46–52	116 n. 56	*Geography*	
Bava Batra		14:65	73	3.4.18	74
75a	151 n.27	15:16–20	73	Cicero	
144a	154 n. 36	15:29–32	73	*Pro Murena*	
				6.13	87
Sanhedrin		Luke			
14a	146 n. 7	7:32	58 n. 19	Plutarch	
		8:43–48	116 n. 56	*Moralia*	
Avodah Zarah		18:35–43	116 n. 56	9:15	87
4b	153				
16b	146 n. 7	John		Lucian	
		1:46	105	*De saltatione*	87
Hullin		9:1–7	116 n. 56	*Gallus*	
95b	6			11	119
110b	154 n. 35	Besa		*Symposia*	
137b	6	*The Life of Shenoute*	71	9	119
				12–13	119

General Index

Abaye, R., 5, 6
Abbahu, R., 153, 154, 155, 173
Adori, 91, 97
Aesop, 159, 162
am ha-aretz, 14–15, 64
angry heart, 127–28
archon, 67, 70
Ayn Te'enah , 110–11

Babylonian Synagogue, 4
Baker, Cynthia, 14
Bakhtin, Mikhail, 76, 77
Balberg, Mira, 88
bar paḥin, 57, 75
Barton, Carlin, 69, 161
bat qol, 80, 85–86
bathhouse (Roman institution), 28–29, 66–68, 69–71, 78
Beard, Mary, 40–41
Berekhiah, R., 48–50
Bergson, Henry, 76
Betera family, 102, 104–5, 112, 114–15
Bezer, 136, 138–39
bloodletting, 62
Bond, Helen, 72–73
books, 203–5
Bosra, 32–33, 136–39
Bourdieu, Pierre, 24, 55, 127
Boyarin, Daniel, 8, 37, 40, 105, 170–72, 191, 200
burial place, tomb, 44, 45, 46, 117, 118, 150, 152
butcher, 61–62, 64–66

Caesarea, 44–45, 154

Capernaum, 176–77
chrism, 177–78
Critchley, Simon, 41
crucifixion, 66, 71–74

dance, 83–84, 87–88
Daroma (*see also* Lod), 110–11
Derrida, Jacques, 18–20, 89, 122, 191, 201, 205
dystopia, 25, 30–31, 200–201

Elijah (the prophet), 86, 113, 116, 188

fool, 42–43, 50, 57, 201
Fraenkel, Jonah, 10–11
Freud, Anna, 98
Friedman, Shamma, 56, 115, 147, 150–51

Gafni, Isaiah, 8, 119, 147, 169
Giddul, R., 93–94
Goldberg, Abraham, 82
gomel hisdaia, 85
gorna, 117
Greek-speaking diaspora, 9, 78
Gruen, Erich, 17, 40, 41, 206

Haggai, R., 117, 118
Hananiah (Ḥanina), the nephew of Rabbi Yehoshu'a R., 169–75, 176, 184
Ḥanina bar Ḥama, R., 33–34, 101, 106–11, 115, 165
Hasan-Rokem, Galit, 161–62, 165
ḥaye shaa, 50

General Index

Hayes, Christine, 13–14, 188, 191
Hengel, Martin, 72
Herman, Geoffrey, 181, 183, 186
Hezser, Catherine, 2, 4, 5, 39, 67, 72
Higger, Michael, 96
Hillel, 4, 84, 101–6, 112–14
honor/shame, 55, 74, 80–81, 88, 91–92
host/guest, 10, 18–20, 50–51, 78–79, 101–6, 119–20, 122, 155, 191, 196, 205
humor, 20, 26, 41, 51, 53–54, 76–77, 146, 157, 163–64, 173, 192, 200, 201, 206
Huna (*Resh Galuta*), 112–14, 116, 118–19
Huna, R., 5, 7, 47, 48, 49
Husserl, Edmund, 11, 90

identity markers, 39, 85, 188
identity shaping, 39, 89, 120, 140, 191, 200
Ilan, Tal, 40, 83, 197
impure land, 138–40, 198, 199
irony, 186, 206; self-irony, 10, 189
Isaac, Benjamin, 17
Ishmael ben Rabbi Yose, R., 9, 113–14

jokester, 67, 70–71, 74–75
Jordan, 129–30, 137, 144

Kahana, R., 34–35, 55–61, 67, 146–52, 167, 203–5
Kalmin, Richard, 2, 13, 121, 153
Krauss, Samuel, 28, 39, 97

Laodicea, 9
Lazar/Eleazar ben Pedat, R., 46, 92, 199, 203
Levi bar Sisi, R., 3
Levinson, Joshua, 12, 18, 89
lifeworld, 10–11, 89–90
liminality, 16, 69, 70, 161
lineage, 5, 39–40, 49–51, 114, 119, 124, 164, 165
litra, litreta (*libra*), 63–64
Lod, 133 (*see also* Daroma)
Lotman, Yuri, 8, 12

magic, 66, 152, 178, 179

mamzer, 40, 47, 48, 49, 50, 54
market, marketplace, 14, 62, 68, 69, 122, 123, 125
Martineau, William, 75–76
masculinity, 54, 75
Mehoza, 184
min (a heretic), 15, 144, 145, 153, 155–56, 176–77
minuy (rabbinic appointment), 101, 107
Mitchell, Alexandre G., 40–41
mockery, 42, 45, 54, 69, 70, 73, 74, 115, 119, 163, 165, 167, 193, 194

Na'eh, Shlomo, 57, 204
naḥotei, 6–7, 199
narrative as self-fashioning, 10–12, 16, 17, 56–57, 87–89, 90, 125–26, 140, 153, 162–63, 166–67, 172, 201, 205
Nazareth, 119, 177
Nehardea, 3, 132–33, 169, 181–84, 202
Nisbis, 171, 173
noble death, 74

olam sagin, 57
Other, otherness. *See* self\Other
otherness of a Babylonian, 21, 31, 49, 77–78, 89, 92, 94, 97, 106,122, 132, 145–46
otherness of a Palestinian, 163, 166–67, 169, 191–92, 206

Paqod river, 171, 172
Pas (or Apas), R., 110–11
permission (to leave the Land), 24, 32–35, 55–56, 59
Pshoi, 71
purqadal, 70

Rab, 2, 3, 5, 7
Redfield, James Adam, 7
Resh Galuta, 29, 114
resurrection, 39, 43–45, 47
return to Zion, 125, 126, 128, 129, 130
Roman judge, 70–71
Rubenstein, Jeffrey, 10–11, 45–46, 92, 109, 133

Safra, 153–55

Schwartz, Joshua, 12, 110, 111
Schwartz, Marcus Mordecai, 6–7
Schwartz, Seth, 11, 90–92, 97
self/Other, 17–21, 87–88, 122, 190–91, 201–6
Sepphoris, 107–8, 110–11
Shammai, 84, 161
Sheila, R., 3
Shemaiah and Abtalion, 102, 103, 105
Shenoute, 71
Sherira Gaon, 2, 3, 6
Shimeon ben Laqish (Resh Laqish), R., 18, 127–28, 129–30, 134–36, 148–52, 164, 167
Shinar, 28–30
Shmuel bar Rabbi Isaac, R., 32, 80–82, 85, 88–89, 127
Shmuel, R., 3, 7
Sperber, Daniel, 64, 147–48, 177, 192
Stein, Dinah, 20, 30, 157, 162
Sťock, Brian, 12, 15
Stroumsa, Guy, 18
Sura, 3
Sussman, Yaakov, 5, 90, 95, 111

terumah and tithes, 9, 29
textual community, 5, 10, 13, 15–16, 20, 37, 126

Tiberias, 7, 46, 66, 71, 92, 97, 98, 110–11, 129, 139
Tyre, 33, 42, 44–45

Ulla, 139, 191–99

Weiss, Haim, 88
winds and eddies 80, 86

xenophobia/philoxenia, 10, 13, 16, 54, 169, 206

Yalta, 195–97
Yasa, R., 32–33, 66–67, 71
Yehuda Ben Betera, R., 171, 173
Yehuda the Patriarch or Rabbi, 3, 119, 137, 172–73
Yoḥanan b. Zakai, Rabban, 23, 60
Yoḥanan, R., 7, 25, 27, 32–35, 36–37, 55–56, 59, 60–61, 90–91, 92, 94, 96, 98, 127–31, 133, 136–39, 148–52, 163–66, 185–86, 195–96, 203
Yose bar Zebid, R., 108

Zeira, R., 47–48, 61–66, 68, 80–82, 85–86, 88, 122–23, 125–27, 131, 143–46, 164–66

www.ingramcontent.com/pod-product-compliance
Lightning Source LLC
Chambersburg PA
CBHW031354230426
43670CB00006B/544